T0297467

Human–Computer Interaction Series

Editors-in-chief

Desney Tan
Microsoft Research, USA

Jean Vanderdonckt
Université catholique de Louvain, Belgium

HCI is a multidisciplinary field focused on human aspects of the development of computer technology. As computer-based technology becomes increasingly pervasive—not just in developed countries, but worldwide—the need to take a human-centered approach in the design and development of this technology becomes ever more important. For roughly 30 years now, researchers and practitioners in computational and behavioral sciences have worked to identify theory and practice that influences the direction of these technologies, and this diverse work makes up the field of human-computer interaction. Broadly speaking it includes the study of what technology might be able to do for people and how people might interact with the technology. The HCI series publishes books that advance the science and technology of developing systems which are both effective and satisfying for people in a wide variety of contexts. Titles focus on theoretical perspectives (such as formal approaches drawn from a variety of behavioral sciences), practical approaches (such as the techniques for effectively integrating user needs in system development), and social issues (such as the determinants of utility, usability and acceptability).

Titles published within the Human–Computer Interaction Series are included in Thomson Reuters' Book Citation Index, The DBLP Computer Science Bibliography and The HCI Bibliography.

More information about this series at http://www.springer.com/series/6033

Saskia Bakker · Doris Hausen
Ted Selker
Editors

Peripheral Interaction

Challenges and Opportunities for HCI
in the Periphery of Attention

 Springer

Editors
Saskia Bakker
Department of Industrial Design
Eindhoven University of Technology
Eindhoven
The Netherlands

Doris Hausen
Human–Computer Interaction Group
University of Munich (LMU)
Munich
Germany

Ted Selker
Center for Information Technology Research
  in the Interest of Society (CITRIS)
University of California Berkeley
Berkeley, CA
USA

and

Aarhus University
Aarhus
Denmark

ISSN 1571-5035
Human–Computer Interaction Series
ISBN 978-3-319-29521-3   ISBN 978-3-319-29523-7   (eBook)
DOI 10.1007/978-3-319-29523-7

Library of Congress Control Number: 2016932855

© Springer International Publishing Switzerland 2016
This work is subject to copyright. All rights are reserved by the Publisher, whether the whole or part of the material is concerned, specifically the rights of translation, reprinting, reuse of illustrations, recitation, broadcasting, reproduction on microfilms or in any other physical way, and transmission or information storage and retrieval, electronic adaptation, computer software, or by similar or dissimilar methodology now known or hereafter developed.
The use of general descriptive names, registered names, trademarks, service marks, etc. in this publication does not imply, even in the absence of a specific statement, that such names are exempt from the relevant protective laws and regulations and therefore free for general use.
The publisher, the authors and the editors are safe to assume that the advice and information in this book are believed to be true and accurate at the date of publication. Neither the publisher nor the authors or the editors give a warranty, express or implied, with respect to the material contained herein or for any errors or omissions that may have been made.

Printed on acid-free paper

This Springer imprint is published by Springer Nature
The registered company is Springer International Publishing AG Switzerland

Contents

1   Introduction: Framing Peripheral Interaction   1
    Saskia Bakker, Doris Hausen and Ted Selker

Part I   Theoretical Perspectives on Peripheral Interaction

2   "Unseen, Yet Crescive": The Unrecognized History
    of Peripheral Interaction   13
    John N.A. Brown

3   Theories of Focal and Peripheral Attention   39
    James F. Juola

Part II   Peripheral Interaction Styles

4   Peripheral Tangible Interaction   65
    Darren Edge and Alan F. Blackwell

5   Microgestures—Enabling Gesture Input with Busy Hands   95
    Katrin Wolf

6   Casual Interaction—Moving Between Peripheral
    and High Engagement Interactions   117
    Henning Pohl

7   Fluent Transitions Between Focused and Peripheral Interaction
    in Proxemic Interactions   137
    Jo Vermeulen, Steven Houben and Nicolai Marquardt

Part III   Peripheral Interaction in Context

8   Peripheral Displays to Support Human Cognition   167
    Tilman Dingler and Albrecht Schmidt

9   **Peripheral Interaction in Desktop Computing: Why It's Worth
    Stepping Beyond Traditional Mouse and Keyboard** 183
    Kathrin Probst

10 **Peripheral Interaction with Light** 207
    Dzmitry Aliakseyeu, Bernt Meerbeek, Jon Mason,
    Remco Magielse and Susanne Seitinger

Part IV   Visions on the Future of Peripheral Interaction

11 **Interactive Soundscapes of the Future Everyday Life** 239
    Berry Eggen

12 **Weaving Peripheral Interaction Within Habitable
    Architectures** 253
    Brygg Ullmer, Alexandre Siqueira, Chris Branton
    and Miriam K. Konkel

Editors and Contributors

About the Editors

Saskia Bakker is Assistant Professor at the Industrial Design department of the Eindhoven University of Technology, and held a visiting lectureship at the University College London Interaction Center in 2015. She obtained her Ph.D. in 2013 on her dissertation entitled "Design for Peripheral Interaction", from the Eindhoven University of Technology. With a background in industrial design, her expertise lies in research-through-design in the areas of tangible interaction, peripheral interaction and classroom technologies. Saskia is a co-organizer of international workshops on peripheral interaction and a member of the steering committee of the conference series on Tangible, Embedded and Embodied Interaction (TEI).

Doris Hausen is a user experience designer for mobile interaction. She is leading the UI/UX team in a Munich-based company working on mobile security. With a background in media informatics, she obtained her Ph.D. on the topic "Peripheral Interaction— Exploring the Design Space" at the Human–Computer Interaction Group at the University of Munich (LMU) in 2014. Although having left academia on a full-time basis, Doris stays in close contact with the research community. She is a co-organizer of international workshops on peripheral interaction and the editor of several publications around the topic of peripheral interaction.

Ted Selker has been creating and evaluating graphical, physical and cognitive interfaces throughout his career. He is director of Considerate Systems research at Carnegie Mellon Silicon Valley. He was Associate Professor at MIT Media Lab from 1998 to 2008. He was an IBM fellow before his work at MIT. Ted also taught at Stanford, and worked at Xerox PARC and Atari Research.

About the Contributors

Dzmitry Aliakseyeu is a Senior Scientist at Philips Research. Prior to this he has held the position of Assistant Professor at the Industrial Design department of the Eindhoven University of Technology. His research interests lie in the new forms of interaction and user interaction in the area of connected lighting.

Alan Blackwell is Professor of Interdisciplinary Design at the University of Cambridge Computer Laboratory, with qualifications in engineering, computing and psychology. He has designed industrial systems, electronic and software products, developed undergraduate design curricula, and supervised design research in fields including computing, architecture, psychology, languages, music and engineering.

Chris Branton holds appointments as research scientist at the LSU Center for Computation and Technology and Adjunct Professor in the Division of Computer Science and Engineering. His research interests include distributed system architectures, advanced human–computer interaction technologies, and interactive high performance computing.

John N.A. Brown is a dual citizen of Canada and the USA, currently working as Lecturer in the Institute of Informatics Systems at Alpen-Adria Universität Klagenfurt in Austria. His research focus includes Anthropology-Based Computing: the application of Human Factors to the design of tools and experiences for Human–Computer Interaction.

Tilman Dingler is a researcher at the Institute for Visualization and Interactive Systems at the University of Stuttgart. His research focuses on augmenting human memory by marrying concepts from the field of cognitive psychology with pervasive technologies. Tilman studied Media Computer Science, Technology Management, and Web Science in Germany and the USA.

Darren Edge is Lead Researcher in HCI at Microsoft Research Asia. He uses activity-based design to transform how people learn, create, and communicate across a variety of life roles. His Ph.D. at the University of Cambridge was the first work to develop and apply the concept of peripheral interaction.

Berry Eggen is Full Professor at the Industrial Design department of the Eindhoven University of Technology and Adjunct Professor at the Design, Architecture and Building faculty of the University of Technology, Sydney, Australia. As design researcher, his interests lie in ubiquitous computing, multimodal interaction (including intelligent lighting and sound design) and seamless interaction design for everyday life.

Steven Houben is a Research Associate at University College London. He works at the Intel Collaborative Research Institute on Sustainable and Connected Cities (ICRI-Cities) and UCL Interaction Centre on projects related to multi-device environments, physical computing and sensor-based systems.

James F. Juola (Ph.D. Stanford University), author of Chap. 3, is Emeritus Professor of Psychology at Kansas University, and of Human-Technology Interaction at Eindhoven University of Technology. He was also a Fulbright Fellow and Visiting Professor at the Autonomous University of Madrid and Gettysburg College. His research interests include human perception, robotics and HCI.

Miriam K. Konkel is Assistant Professor for Research within LSU's Department of Biological Sciences. Her research interests include genomic structural variation, mobile elements, evolution, primate genomics, personal genomics and tangible interfaces for large datasets (e.g. in the genomics domain).

Remco Magielse graduated as engineer in Industrial Design in 2009 at the Eindhoven University of Technology. In 2014 he completed his doctoral dissertation titled "Designing for Adaptive Lighting Environments—Embracing complexity in designing for systems". Currently he works as a system engineer in the pre-development team of Philips Hue.

Nicolai Marquardt is Lecturer (Assistant Professor) in Physical Computing at the University College London. At the UCL Interaction Centre he works on projects in the research areas of ubiquitous computing, interactive surfaces, sensor-based systems, prototyping toolkits, and physical user interfaces.

Jon Mason is Senior Scientist at Philips Research and since 2007 he has worked on concepts for new lighting applications and lighting UI. He has a background in Industrial Design and a Ph.D. in Design Methodology. He is interested in the application of scenario planning for design and ideation.

Bernt Meerbeek is Senior Scientist at Philips Research, applies his broad expertise in the field of user-system interaction and technology to develop innovative connected lighting solutions. He holds an M.Sc. degree in Information Systems and a

PDEng. in User–System Interaction. His main interest is to ensure that people feel in control while they interact with intelligent systems.

Henning Pohl is a Ph.D. candidate in Computer Science at the University of Hannover, Germany. His research focuses on casual interactions, i.e., enabling users to choose how much they want to engage with a system or device, in order to change how much control they have over an interaction.

Kathrin Probst is a Ph.D. student in the Media Interaction Lab, at the School of Informatics, Communications and Media (Hagenberg, Austria) of the University of Applied Sciences Upper Austria. Her research activities focus on human–computer interaction in the areas of smart office environments and novel interaction techniques.

Albrecht Schmidt is Professor of Human Computer Interaction and Cognitive Systems at the University of Stuttgart working on novel user interface and new interaction technique. He received a Ph.D. from Lancaster University. He is co-founder of the ACM conference on Tangible and Embedded Interaction (TEI) and is on the editorial board of the IEEE Pervasive Magazine.

Susanne Seitinger is Sub-segment Manager in Professional Systems at Philips Lighting. She leads the strategy on how connected LED lighting creates safe, inviting and responsive urban environments. Her interdisciplinary background spans architecture, urban planning and human–computer interaction. She holds a Ph.D. and an MCP from MIT and a BA from Princeton University.

Alexandre Siqueira is a doctoral student in LSU's School of Electrical Engineering and Computer Science (EECS) and Center for Computation and Technology (CCT). His research interests include tangible interfaces, augmented reality, and physical fabrication.

Brygg Ullmer is the Effie C. and Donald M. Hardy Associate Professor within LSU's School of Electrical Engineering and Computer Science (EECS) and Center for Computation and Technology (CCT). His research interests include tangible interfaces, computational genomics (and more broadly, interactive computational STEAM), visualization, fabrication and cultural computing.

Jo Vermeulen is a Postdoctoral Fellow in the InnoVis group at the Interactions Lab at the University of Calgary. Previously, he was a Research Fellow at the HCI Centre at the University of Birmingham. He is interested in addressing interaction challenges within ubicomp spaces, including designing for intelligibility, discoverability, feedback and feedforward for context-aware technologies.

Katrin Wolf is Professor of Media Informatics at the BTK, the University of Art and Design in Berlin. Earlier, she was a postdoctoral researcher in the Human–Computer Interaction Group at the University of Stuttgart. Katrin did her Ph.D. at T-Labs Berlin on "Grasp Interaction with Tablets".

Chapter 1
Introduction: Framing Peripheral Interaction

Saskia Bakker, Doris Hausen and Ted Selker

Abstract In everyday life, we perform several activities in our *periphery* of attention. For example, we are aware of what the weather is like and we can routinely wash our hands without actively thinking about it. However, we can also easily focus on these activities when desired. Contrarily, interactions with computing devices, such as smartphones and tablet computers, usually require focused attention, or even demand it through flashing displays, beeping sounds, and vibrations used to alert people. Hence, these interactions move more unpredictably between periphery and center of attention compared to non-computer-mediated activities. With the number of computers embedded in our everyday environment increasing, inevitably interaction with these computers will move to the periphery of attention. Inspired by the way we fluently divide our attentional resources over various activities in everyday life, we call this type of interaction "peripheral interaction." We believe that considering and enabling peripheral interaction with computing technology contributes to more seamlessly embedding of such technology in everyday routines. This chapter briefly explores the history of peripheral interaction as a field of research and lays out how peripheral interaction, in our view, fits into the larger domain of interactive systems and HCI.

S. Bakker (✉)
Department of Industrial Design, Eindhoven University of Technology,
Eindhoven, The Netherlands
e-mail: s.bakker@tue.nl

D. Hausen
Human-Computer-Interaction Group, University of Munich (LMU),
Munich, Germany
e-mail: doris.hausen@ifi.lmu.de

T. Selker
CITRIS, University of California Berkeley, Berkeley, USA
e-mail: ted.selker@gmail.com

T. Selker
Aarhus University, Aarhus, Denmark

© Springer International Publishing Switzerland 2016
S. Bakker et al. (eds.), *Peripheral Interaction*,
Human–Computer Interaction Series, DOI 10.1007/978-3-319-29523-7_1

1

Keywords Peripheral interaction · Human–computer interaction · Interaction design · Periphery of attention · Calm technology

1.1 Introduction

> It is a regular Thursday morning; Sandra and Patrick are about to have breakfast. The kitchen is filled with a pleasant smell of coffee and freshly baked bread. Sandra switches on the coffee-machine, while realizing she hears rain against the windows. She opens the curtains and contemplates which clothes to wear with this weather. A sound interrupts Sandra's thoughts: the breadmaker has finished. At the breakfast table, Sandra reads the news on her tablet computer and simultaneously sips from a hot cup of coffee. The cup is rather full; she briefly stops reading to concentrate on taking the first sip. Patrick takes a bite from his sandwich while browsing through his emails on his smartphone: he receives an urgent message from a business associate asking for a document. He puts down his sandwich, walks to his study-room, flicks on the lights, unlocks his computer, starts his email application and searches for the document by going through a number of folders. He finds it and sends the email. Patrick walks back to breakfast table while thinking about his meeting that will start in an hour. Just when he tells Sandra that he has to hurry to make it in time, his phone buzzes alarmingly. Patrick takes the phone from his pocket and unlocks the screen: a reminder for that meeting. "It must be busy on the road with the bad weather" Sandra says, and opens an application on her tablet to look up the traffic information. Patrick looks over her shoulder and sees that delays are expected. He kisses Sandra goodbye, grabs his coat and leaves for work.

The above story illustrates an everyday scenario in today's world. Lots of things are happening at the same time, and Patrick and Sandra almost continuously interact with their physical surroundings. They pick up, drink from and put down their cups of coffee, eat bread, open curtains, and switch on and off lights. No focused attention seems required to execute these activities; they can easily be conducted while at the same time reading the news, browsing through e-mails, or thinking about what clothes to wear. However, attention is also easily focused on these actions for brief moments of time, for example when Sandra realizes her cup is so full that she needs to attend to it, to avoid spilling. Similarly, Patrick and Sandra constantly perceive information from their surroundings without conscious thought, such as information about the weather or the bread being freshly baked. Such information may also quickly shift to the focus of attention when relevant, for example when realizing Sandra may need to change her choice of clothes because of unexpected bad weather.

Clearly, everyday activities and perceptions can take place in the background or *periphery* of attention, where they are performed on a routine basis and require minimum attention and effort. These activities, however, can also be consciously focused on in the *center* of attention when this is required. As evident from Patrick and Sandra's Thursday morning, activities can easily and frequently *shift* between periphery and center of attention. As a result, these perceptions and actions do not overwhelm or overburden, but instead form a fluent part of the everyday routine.

In the above story, Patrick and Sandra also frequently use computing devices: They receive messages and alerts, look for digital documents, send e-mails, and search for traffic information. Contrary to the above-discussed activities and perceptions that fluently shift between center and periphery of attention, their interactions with computing devices usually require focused attention. They consciously browse through folders to find a document, and alerting messages needlessly attract their attention away from their conversation or preparing to go to work. Clearly, computing devices are most often interacted with in the center rather than in the periphery of attention and move more unpredictably between periphery and center compared to non-computer-mediated activities.

The number of computing systems in our everyday environment is increasing. They are not only part of personal devices, but also integrated in everyday objects and environments such as water faucets, toilets, toothbrushes, irons, doors, thermometers, coffeemakers, and breadmakers. These developments bring along numerous opportunities, while they also raise challenges. In particular, we cannot simultaneously focus on all interactive devices that are available in our immediate surroundings. Inevitably, an increasing number of everyday computing devices have to be interacted with in the periphery of attention. Inspired by the way we fluently divide our attentional resources over various activities in everyday life, this type of interaction is called "peripheral interaction": interaction with everyday interactive systems that reside in our periphery of attention but can easily shift to the center of attention when relevant for or desired by the user. Considering and enabling peripheral interaction contributes to more fluently embedding of computing technology in everyday routines.

As computing systems and the physical world intermingle, studying peripheral interaction, as described above, has become increasingly relevant. This book aims to lay out the challenges and opportunities in the field and underpin these through research presented in various chapters. The goal is to help us contribute to a future where computing technology gracefully coexists with the physical world.

1.2 A Brief History

Integration of computing technology into our everyday lives is not a new advancement. For example, microprocessors began being integrated into bicycle computers and cars in the 1980s. Over two decades ago, Weiser (1991) described a vision for the twenty-first century in which computers of all sizes and functions are part of and integrated in the everyday environment. A vision he described as *ubiquitous computing*, which acknowledged that traditional human–computer interaction relies on the user's focused attention and therefore hinders the seamless integration of such interaction in everyday life. He argues not only that computational devices need to be physically hidden (e.g., in furniture), but moreover that people should be enabled to interact with such devices outside their attentional focus, i.e., in their periphery of attention. In his own words, people would thereby be "freed to use them without thinking and so to focus beyond them on new goals" (Weiser 1991, 94). Weiser and Brown (1997, 79) later introduced the term *calm technology*, which "engages both the center and the periphery of our attention, and in fact moves back and forth between the two". Making use of both the center and the periphery of attention, people are able to interact the same way with technology as they do with their everyday environment. They would be in control of their interactions with computing devices while at the same time not being overburden by them, leading to a seamless or unremarkable integration of technology in our everyday routines (Tolmie et al. 2002).

Inspired by visions on ubiquitous computing, several adjacent fields of research have emerged, which study the embedding of computers in the everyday environment. While some have used the term *pervasive computing* (Satyanarayanan 2001) as a synonym for ubiquitous computing, it was introduced as the infrastructure to support ubiquitous computing. The term *ambient intelligence* (Aarts and Marzano 2003) relates to using reasoning and learning in ubiquitous computing, to support people's actions in their everyday environments. Further exploring connected devices, the term *Internet of Things (IoT)* (Atzori et al. 2010) is used to present the powerful advantages of ubiquitous systems with sensors and actuators coalescing their value through address-based intercommunication. IoT celebrates interactions between sensed events and computational support for actions in the world. The term *context-aware computing* (Lieberman and Selker 2000; Abowd et al. 1999) was used to discuss not only ubiquitously present computing devices, but particularly to address the usage of various sensors to determine and take into account information from the environment in computer-initiated activity. This is, for example, applied in the domain of *considerate systems* (Selker 2011; Vastenburg et al. 2008), which adjust their notification behavior to the sensed context and thereby improve the appropriateness of notifications.

Among research inspired by the vision of ubiquitous computing, many endeavors have been inspired particularly by Weiser and Brown's (1997) notion of calm technology. Such work developed and studied computational devices that unobtrusively present relevant information to users, thereby exploring how digital information can be perceived in the visual or auditory periphery of attention (Hazlewood et al. 2011; Heiner et al. 1999; Ishii et al. 1998; Matthews et al. 2004; Mynatt et al. 1998; Pousman and Stasko 2006). From the scenario of Patrick and Sandra's morning routine, however, it is evident that not only *perceptions*, but also *physical activities* shift between center and periphery of attention in everyday life. Inspired by this observations, researchers have started to address a second facet of calm technology—*peripheral interaction* (Edge and Blackwell 2009; Hausen et al. 2012, 2013; Bakker et al. 2015a, b), which encompasses both perceptions of and physical interaction with computing technology shifting between people's center and periphery of attention.

Today, much of Weiser's vision has turned into reality. Digital technology is integrated in many devices ranging from water faucets to parking meters. Hence, the need to employ both the center and periphery of people's attention is unavoidable (also see Brown 2012) and will increase even more in the future. Although present-day interactions with digital devices are majorly different from such interactions 20 years ago, they are still carried out mainly in the user's focus of attention. Therefore, the challenge to embed technology into our everyday life and thereby to offer fluent shifts between the center and periphery of attention still prevails today.

1.3 Framing Peripheral Interaction

This book addresses challenges and opportunities for peripheral interaction: interaction with computing technology, which can take places in the periphery of attention and shifts to the center of attention when relevant. The goal of peripheral interaction is to fluently embed meaningful interactive systems into people's everyday lives. We now lay out how peripheral interaction fits into the larger domain of interactive systems and HCI. We will start by giving an example of possible (peripheral and non-peripheral) interactions with a very simple interactive system: a motion-detecting light switch.

Two years ago, Thomas and Mara installed a light in their front yard that automatically switches on when motion is detected after dark. When installing it, they walked around their yard a few times to check when and where exactly the light would be triggered. They are happy with the light; when someone approaches their front door at night, the light switches on which gives visitors an inviting feeling. Sometimes they sit in the yard to have a drink together. When they sit down for longer than ten minutes, the light automatically switches off. This has happened so often, that it has become a routine to quickly move the arms up to trigger the light: Thomas usually conducts this brief action while in a conversation with Mara.

Three types of interactions with the light switch are apparent from this scenario. First, Mara and Thomas intentionally walk around to actively search for the sensing area. This interaction is *conscious* and *intentional* and takes place in the *center of attention*: It is consciously performed with the intention to probe the system's function to understand how it switches on the light. Second, a visitor enters the yard, triggering the switch to turn on the light. This person's interaction with the system is *subconscious* and *unintentional*: He or she did not walk there with the

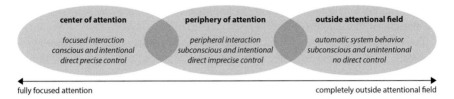

Fig. 1.1 Three types of interaction with computing devices, illustrated along a continuum ranging from "fully focused attention" to "completely outside attentional field"

intention to switch on the light, though the system interpreted this behavior as input (Schmidt 2000; Ju and Leifer 2011). The interaction was implicitly initiated and thus happened *outside the attentional field* of the visitor. Third, Thomas moves his arm as a routine activity in order to switch on the light, while in a conversation with Mara. Since another activity is performed simultaneously, this interaction takes place in the *periphery of attention*. Furthermore, the interaction is performed automatically and *subconsciously* as a result of a habit or routine, though clearly *intentional*, aimed at switching on the light.

These three types of interaction are illustrated in the basic model presented in Fig. 1.1 along a continuum ranging from "fully focused attention" to "completely outside attentional field." As evident from the example above, an interactive system may at one moment be interacted with in the center of attention, at another moment in the periphery, and in a third case outside a person's attentional field.

Though all three types of interactions are possible with the simple interactive light described in the above example, this light switch is clearly developed for interaction outside the attentional field of the people it affects. The other two types happen occasionally, or seem rather awkward. More and more modern interactive systems are developed for the very right end of the continuum in Fig. 1.1 (outside the attentional field), such as smart thermostats, ABS brakes, and automatic windshield wipers. Also, numerous interactive systems can be named that are designed to be interacted with in the center or attention and therefore are to be placed on the very left end of the continuum, for example, interactive games, traditional desktop computing including instant messaging, e-mailing, text processing, or image editing as well as the usage of many smartphone applications. Contrarily, not many interactive systems are developed for the middle of the continuum, where interactions may not be precise, but where users directly control these interactions, be it with minimal mental resources. While clearly many interactive systems benefit greatly from automatic system behavior or require the user's focused attention during interaction, there seems a gap in between these two extremes, a gap which peripheral interaction aims to help fill by providing an area of interactive systems that flexibly respect attention and support the embedding of computing technology in everyday life routines.

To illustrate this gap in more detail, we describe interaction scenarios with modern interactive lighting systems, designed for interaction in the center of attention and outside the attentional field, while interaction in the periphery of attention is not straightforward. Various interactive lighting systems are commercially available [e.g., ("Philips Hue" N.D.; "Belkin WeMo" N.D.; "Elgato Avea" N.D.; "LIFX" N.D.)] consisting of light bulbs of which the color and intensity can be controlled wirelessly. Users, who typically have multiple such light bulbs installed in their home, can directly control lights using a dedicated smartphone application which enables selecting a predefined configuration or dragging icons which represent each individual light bulb, to the desired color on a gradient map. Turning on the lights using such applications is clearly done consciously and intentionally in the center of attention: This interaction is located on the far left end of the continuum in Fig. 1.1. Alternatively, some of these interactive lighting systems can be programmed to perform automatic system behavior. For example, one may program the system to automatically switch on the lights when a user is near his house (measured through the GPS location of the user's smartphone). This type of interaction happens subconsciously and unintentionally (i.e., a user does not go near his house with the intention of switching on the lights, rather with the intention of going home) and is thus located on the far right end of the continuum in Fig. 1.1.

Imagine a house in which all light sources contain the above-described bulbs. If automatic behavior is preprogrammed, the lights switch on automatically when approaching this house. However, people may have different lighting needs at different moments. For example, when entering the house late at night, while other people in the house are already asleep, all lights switching on automatically would be highly inappropriate. Since automatic system behavior happens outside our attentional field, we have no direct control over it. Numerous scenarios may exist in which lighting needs differ, depending on the user's wishes, plans, intentions, and (social) context. Since interactive systems can unlikely be fully aware of and flawlessly adapt to all nuances of everyday life, its users must be given some form of direct control in addition to the automatic system behavior. This direct control is present in current systems by means of a smartphone application. If no automatic behavior is programmed, a person entering the house in the dark would need to get his smartphone out of his bag, unlock the screen, search for the application, and either select a setting or drag icons over the screen to turn on the lights. While such applications enable users to control their lighting down to every detail (selecting precisely the right color and intensity for each individual lamp), this seems like a needlessly long and complicated sequence of actions to simply switch on the light. This sequence of actions is more likely to interrupt one's everyday routine, than to seamlessly fit into it.

Interactive lighting systems enable direct and precise control in the center of attention, but also offer the possibility of automatic behavior without requiring any direct control from the user. However, a gap between these two extremes is apparent: A way of controlling the light quickly but imprecisely might support the system in seamlessly blending into people's everyday routines. In other words, a possibility to control the lights in the periphery of attention is lacking. While products have recently been launched to address this gap [e.g., "hue tap" ("Philips

Hue" N.D.) and "M!QBE" (N.D.)], these interactive lighting systems only stand exemplar for many modern interactive systems in which this gap is apparent.

As evident from Fig. 1.1, the periphery of attention on one side borders with the center of attention, while on the other side it borders with events that happens outside our attentional field. Depending on the user's current mind-set and his/her current context, interactions with modern systems may take place in any of these three fields. Therefore, the "borders" in this figure should be seen as overlapping grey areas. While peripheral interaction is intended to take place in the periphery of attention the majority of the time, shifts to the center of attention, and events happening outside the user's attentional field are certainly an important part of it. Different from interactions that are always in the center of attention, the aim of peripheral interaction is to enable interaction possibilities with minimal attentional resources. Different from autonomous system behavior, peripheral interaction aims to provide users a means to intentionally interact when needed and thus control their interaction, be it with a low amount of mental resources.

1.4 Challenges and Opportunities, Outlining This Book

While activities taking place in the periphery of attention are common in our everyday interactions with our physical environment, they are rare in our interactions with computing devices. This was already predicted over two decades ago (Weiser 1991), and with the increasing presence of computing devices in our everyday environment, seamlessly embedding computing technology in our everyday routines remains increasingly challenging. This book poses that peripheral interaction—enabling both perceptions of and interactions with computing technologies to reside in the periphery of attention—is a promising direction to overcome this challenge. The aim of this book is to capture the current state of the art with regard to peripheral interaction.

Part I presents **theoretical perspectives on peripheral interaction** and starts off with an analysis of everyday peripheral tasks, by **John N.A. Brown**, based on the principles of anthropology-based computing. This chapter covers people's preattentive use of tools in their everyday interactions with the physical world. The following chapter, by **James F. Juola**, digs deeper into human attention processes by presenting an overview of attention theories that underlie human abilities to effortlessly perform multiple tasks at the same time. These two chapters together cover important theoretical grounding for peripheral interactions and lay the basis for the following parts of the book.

Part II presents four chapters which each address a different perspective on **peripheral interaction styles**. First, **Darren Edge** and **Alan F. Blackwell** elaborate on tangible peripheral interaction. They consider how physical interaction styles afford rapid initiation and fluid execution of peripheral interactions with digital content. Second, **Katrin Wolf** discusses peripheral interaction through microgestures: an interaction style that relies on gestures that last only a few seconds. This chapter presents how microgestures can be suitable in contexts where the user's hands are busy and reviews design and technology for and requirements of microgestures. Third, **Henning Pohl** reviews casual interaction to support human–computer interaction in the periphery of attention. This chapter discusses the delicate relation between a user's engagement with an interface and the level of control offered. Fourth, **Jo Vermeulen**, **Steven Houben**, and **Nicolai Marquardt** explore how the proximity between users and interactive systems can be employed as implicit system input, by means of "proxemic interaction."

Part III presents three chapters discussing **peripheral interaction in context**. The first chapter, by **Tilman Dingler** and **Albrecht Schmidt**, explores how environments equipped with peripheral interaction technology could support human cognition and unintentional learning, by providing peripheral information relevant to the user's current activity. **Kathrin Probst**'s chapter then elaborates on the relevance of peripheral interaction for desktop computing, by reviewing a number of innovative interface designs for this context. Finally, **Dzmitry Aliakseyeu**, **Bernt Meerbeek**, **Jon Mason**, **Remco Magielse**, and **Susanne Seitinger** review interaction design in the field of lighting and consider how peripheral interaction can contribute to this ubiquitous medium.

Part IV collects **visions on the future of peripheral interaction**. These essays are aimed to provide the reader a taste of how the field may progress in the future. The first chapter, by **Berry Eggen**, elaborates on future directions involving the auditory modality as a means for peripheral interaction. Finally, **Brygg Ullmer**, **Alexandre Siqueira**, **Chris Branton**, and **Miriam K. Konkel** draw inspiration from historical demonstrations and fictional architecture to envision a future in which peripheral interaction may be operationalized.

Acknowledgments We would like to thank all collaborators and advisors who contributed to our research in the domain of peripheral interaction. Especially, we would like to thank Elise van den Hoven, Andreas Butz, and Berry Eggen for their invaluable support and advice.

References

Aarts, E. H. L., & Marzano, S. (2003). *The new everyday: Views on ambient intelligence.* Rotterdam: 010 Publishers.

Abowd, G. D., Dey, A. K., Brown, P. J., Davies, N., Smith, M., & Steggles, P. (1999). Towards a better understanding of context and context-awareness. In H. W. Gellersen (Ed.), *Handheld and ubiquitous computing* (Vol. 1707). Lecture Notes in Computer Science Berlin: Springer.

Atzori, L., Iera, A., & Morabito, G. (2010). The internet of things: A survey. *Computer Networks, 54*(15), 2787–2805.

Bakker, S., van den Hoven, E., & Eggen, B. (2015a). Peripheral interaction: Characteristics and considerations. *Personal and Ubiquitous Computing, 19*(1), 239–254.

Bakker, S., van den Hoven, E., & Eggen, B. (2015b). Evaluating peripheral interaction design. *Human–Computer Interaction, 30*(6), 473–506.

Belkin WeMo. (N.D.). *Belkin.* Accessed February 24, 2016. http://www.belkin.com/us/Products/home-automation/c/wemo-home-automation/.

Brown, J. N. A. (2012). Expert talk for time machine session: Designing calm technology "as refreshing as taking a walk in the woods". In *2012 IEEE International Conference on Multimedia and Expo* (p. 423).

Edge, D., & Blackwell, A. F. (2009). Peripheral tangible interaction by analytic design. In *Proceedings of the 3rd International Conference on Tangible and Embedded Interaction* (pp. 69–76).

Elgato Avea. (N.D.). *Elgato.com*. Accessed February 24, 2016. https://www.elgato.com/en/smart/avea.

Hausen, D., Boring, S., Lueling, C., Rodestock, S., & Butz, A. (2012). StaTube: Facilitating state management in instant messaging systems. In *Proceedings of the 6th International Conference on Tangible, Embedded and Embodied Interaction* (pp. 283–290).

Hausen, D., Richter, H., Hemme, A., & Butz, A. (2013). Comparing input modalities for peripheral interaction: A case study on peripheral music control. In P. Kotzé, et al. (Eds.), *Human-computer interaction—INTERACT 2013* (Vol. 8119)., Lecture Notes in Computer Science Berlin: Springer.

Hazlewood, W. R., Stolterman, E., & Connelly, K. (2011). Issues in evaluating ambient displays in the wild: Two case studies. In *Proceedings of the 2011 Annual Conference on Human Factors in Computing Systems* (pp. 877–886).

Heiner, J. M., Hudson, S. E., & Tanaka, K. (1999). The information percolator: Ambient information display in a decorative object. In *Proceedings of the 12th Annual ACM Symposium on User Interface Software and Technology* (pp. 141–148).

Ishii, H., Wisneski, G., Brave, S., Dahley, A., Gorbet, M., Ullmer, B., & Yarin, P. (1998). ambientROOM: Integrating ambient media with architectural space. In *CHI 98 Conference Summary on Human Factors in Computing Systems* (pp. 173–174).

Ju, W., & Leifer, L. (2011). The design of implicit interactions: Making interactive systems less obnoxious. *Design Issues, 24*(3), 72–84.

Lieberman, H., & Selker, T. (2000). Out of context: Computer systems that adapt to, and learn from, context. *IBM Systems Journal 39* (3.4), 617–632.

LIFX. (N.D.). Accessed February 24, 2016. http://www.lifx.com/.

Matthews, T., Dey A. K., Mankoff, J., Carter, S., & Rattenbury, T. (2004). A toolkit for managing user attention in peripheral displays. In *Proceedings of the 17th Annual ACM Symposium on User Interface Software and Technology* (pp. 247–256).

M!QBE. (N.D.). Accessed February 24, 2016. http://m-q.be/.

Mynatt, E. D., Back, M., Want, R., Baer, M., & Ellis, J. B. (1998). Designing audio aura. In *Proceedings of the SIGCHI Conference on Human Factors in Computing Systems* (pp. 566–573).

Philips Hue. (N.D.). Accessed February 24, 2016. http://meethue.com/.

Pousman, Z., & Stasko, J. (2006). A taxonomy of ambient information systems: Four patterns of design. In *Proceedings of the Working Conference on Advanced Visual Interfaces* (pp. 67–74).

Satyanarayanan, M. (2001). Pervasive computing: Vision and challenges. *IEEE Personal Communications, 8*(4), 10–17.

Schmidt, A. (2000). Implicit human computer interaction through context. *Personal Technologies, 4*(2–3), 191–199.

Selker, T. (2011). Understanding considerate systems—UCS (Pronounced: You See Us). In *Proceedings of the 2011 International Conference on Technologies and Applications of Artificial Intelligence* (pp. 1–12).

Tolmie, P., Pycock, J., Diggins, T., MacLean, A., & Karsenty, A. (2002). Unremarkable computing. In *Proceedings of the SIGCHI Conference on Human Factors in Computing Systems* (pp. 399–406).

Vastenburg, M. H., Keyson, D. V., & Ridder, H. (2008). Considerate home notification systems: A field study of acceptability of notifications in the home. *Personal Ubiquitous Computing, 12*(8), 555–566.

Weiser, M. (1991). The computer for the twenty-first century. *Scientific American, 265*(3), 94–104.

Weiser, M., & Brown, J. S. (1997). The coming age of calm technology. In P. J. Denning & R. M. Metcalfe (Eds.), *Beyond calculation: The next fifty years of computing* (pp. 75–85).

Part I
Theoretical Perspectives on Peripheral Interaction

Chapter 2
"Unseen, Yet Crescive": The Unrecognized History of Peripheral Interaction

John N.A. Brown

Abstract Peripheral interaction, the reflexive and reactive pre-attentive use of tools and techniques on the periphery of conscious attention, has always been a fundamental part of how humans interact with the world. In fact, it is very likely that our ancestors have been interacting peripherally since well before they were human. In the midst of searching for new paradigms for interaction with the ubiquitous networks of embedded systems that fill our homes and workplaces, it might be a good idea to look at the peripheral tasks we are already performing. Ironically, being on the periphery of our conscious attention, this complex assortment of internal and external interactions has gone largely unnoticed. In this chapter, we use the principles of anthropology-based computing to follow Mark Weiser's advice and drag these tasks to the center of our attentive focus for a closer examination before deciding whether or not to relegate them once more to the borders of our perception.

Keywords Peripheral interaction · Calm technology · Anthropology-based computing (ABC) · Triune brain · Brown's Representation of Anthropogenic Interaction in Natural Settings (BRAINS)

J.N.A. Brown (✉)
Interactive Systems Research Group, Alpen-Adria Universität-Klagenfurt,
Klagenfurt, Austria
e-mail: jna.brown@gmail.com

© Springer International Publishing Switzerland 2016
S. Bakker et al. (eds.), *Peripheral Interaction*,
Human–Computer Interaction Series, DOI 10.1007/978-3-319-29523-7_2

2.1 Introduction: An Anthropologist on Earth—*Observing Peripheral Interaction Among Humans, In re: Their Natural and Constructed Environments, Their Communities, and Their Cocktail Parties*

Can humans interact with information on the periphery of their senses? Yes, yes, of course peripheral interaction (PI) exists. Can you hear the sound of a car dopplering past you as you ride your bicycle? Does the changing noise inspire in you a change in either deliberate or unconscious behavior—or both? Any normal, healthy human is in a constant state of PI throughout their waking hours. In fact, I will argue that most of our interactions are so thoroughly peripheral that we execute them without even noticing. That is the reason for the title of this chapter.

> And so the Prince obscured his contemplation
> Under the veil of wildness, which, no doubt,
> Grew like the summer grass, fastest by night,
> Unseen yet crescive in his faculty."
>
> William Shakespeare,
Henry V, Act 1, scene i

Most of our interaction with the world around us is so unconscious and so fundamental that it is not only "obscured… under the veil" of our more obvious interactions, but it continues to happen while we are sleeping. Respiration and digestion take place on the periphery of our attention, until and unless some problem arises in their reflexive cycles. The problem pushes them to the center of our attention.

Let us move upwards through the layers of simple and complex reflexes processed in the peripheral nervous system, those controlled in the central nervous system, and even those managed in the cerebellum.[1] Consider typing or mousing, holding a book, or holding a stylus: any task in which you unconsciously coordinate multiple channels of neurological input in order to unconsciously coordinate complex neuromuscular interaction to serve your unthinking intent.

We learn these tasks reflectively and practice them until they move to the periphery of our attention. There, on the periphery, they grow and develop outside of our conscious awareness, becoming what Shakespeare described as "…unseen yet crescive.[2]" In fact, all computing tasks and every other task that we perform—not for the first time, but with the unconscious rituals of inattention that come with familiarity—are taking place on the periphery and stay there until an unexpected perception surprises us enough to be noticed.

In this chapter, I will reintroduce a simple model of the iterative feedback loops with which we perform these tasks at the most basic neurological level

---

[1]Cerebellum = the part of the brain in which complex reflex patterns are coordinated.

[2]Crescive = developing over time without conscious direction.

(Freides 2001) and tie them to the theory of anthropology-based computing (ABC) (Brown 2013b) through the concepts of dynamic environmental focus (DEF) and general human interaction (GHI) (Brown 2016). All of these support a three-tiered model of human interaction based on MacLean's triune brain (MacLean 1973). I call this new triune model Brown's Representation of Anthropogenic Interaction in Natural Settings (BRAINS) and propose that it provides a plausible explanation of the simple mechanics that enable and even force us to use PI. This model also allows for a possible explanation of two well-established psychological concepts: the cocktail party effect (CPE) (Cherry 1953; Moray 1959; Golumbic et al. 2013) and Csikszentmihalyi's "Flow" (Csikszentmihaiyi 1990). Before we get any further into this chapter, please allow me to offer a quick illustration of both CPE and "Flow."

Cherry described the natural human ability to focus on a single one of many audio streams in a noisy and crowded situation like a cocktail party (Cherry 1953). Moray took this further and showed that CPE is strengthened by emotional ties to the speaker or the words spoken (Moray 1959). Golumbic took that still further and showed that the brain recognizes all of the streams of conversation as noise, but recognizes only the attended voice and the affective factors as language (Golumbic et al. 2013). Let us take a quick look at this from an anthropological perspective. The cocktail party may actually be going on around you at a physical gathering, it may manifest as multiple streams of digital interaction—separate and shared overlapping strings of SMS and email, for example—or it may be a combination of the two, as when you exchange multimodal messages with many friends while in a crowded and noisy space. The human experience of filtering multiple streams of sensory information in real time predates both digital technology and cocktail parties.

With the exception of rare cases of brain injury or disease (Mirsky 1987), humans naturally process multiple streams of information, most of which are not at all central to their conscious and deliberate ratiocination[3] at any given time. There are situational exceptions, such as in cases of "Flow," that state in which we feel as though we are performing at peak ability—regardless of the specific setting—immersed in our performance and feeling as though our perception of the outside world has disappeared (MacLean 1973). In "Flow," we believe that nothing exists but the moment and the task, and we are certain that we are thinking and reacting faster than usual. We will return to this idea a little later in the chapter and offer an explanation for how and why we feel that way. For now, I hope that it is clear that the case of "Flow" as a recognized topic of study, and a commonly understood event, is a fine negative illustration of the common nature of PI. If PI were not the common state, then the disappearance of peripheral streams of input would not be at all remarkable, and it would never have proven necessary to coin the term "Flow."

---

[3]Ratiocination = rational thought, reflection.

2.2 Peripheral Interaction: As We DO Think—*Explaining the Mechanisms that Underlie "Peripheral Interaction," "Flow," "MultiTasking," "the Cocktail Party Effect," and "Cross-Generational Habit"*

In his 1945 monograph "As We May Think," Vannevar Bush predicted that technological innovations in the workplace would change the way that we use our brains and the way we value their use (Bush 1945). His predictions may, in time, prove not only to be visionary (Novak 2010), but even to be correct. Certainly, his thought experiment produced the mental model that underlies the GUI desktop on every one of our electronic devices (Smith et al. 1985). Unfortunately, the vast majority of papers referencing his seminal paper seem to ignore the most important part of his message, focusing on the technological aspect of his proposal, rather than the human (Reingold 1987).

Bardzell and Bardzell have proposed that this imbalanced perspective in computer science is precisely why Weiser's prediction of ubiquitous computing has come true, while his call for Calm Technology has largely been abandoned (Bardzell and Bardzell 2014). I propose that the answer lies in the fact there is a fundamental flaw in the way that most of us see ourselves in the world. We imagine that we are cognitive creatures—rational brains reasoning their way through life, while floating inside pools of life-giving nutrients that balance precariously on the top of our spines. We are the great thinking ape, Homo sapiens, deliberately shaping the world around us and consciously interacting with our environment and our fellows.

This is nonsense.

Well, the idea that we live inside a precariously balanced pool of nutrients is fairly accurate and can be taken further into the abstract and away from our ego-centric perspective, as illustrated so brilliantly in Dawkins' argument that the true function of humans is to serve as a nearly countless series of life pods for the primordial selfish genes that we carry around (Dawkins 1976). Be that as it may, our image of ourselves as rational creatures is a delusion. Rational thought is used sparingly by most humans and is quite literally counterintuitive. As scientists, we are supposed to apply the "scientific method," a series of deliberate techniques designed to force us to be rational and to make it easy for our peers to check and see whether we have succeeded—not in finding specific results, but in running our experiments rationally.

Outside of the laboratory, most of our interactions do not involve decisions at all, but are carried out reflexively. That is how we balance in our chairs and on our feet, and it is how we carry out all of the complex interactions that let us use our bodies to do what we want to do. Furthermore, most of the decisions we do make are not made rationally as evinced by the simple fact that we do not take the time to deliberate. Most of our decisions are made quickly and "intuitively," and we often do not consciously realize that we have made a decision until we find ourselves carrying out the resultant action—or failing to.

Consider what happens when you decide not to take another potato chip. Have you ever found yourself eating one anyway? Did you have to push the bowl away to force yourself to stop? Doesn't that very idea imply that there were at least two processors working in your head—and that one was being rational while another was not? This is where our myth of human multitasking takes root. Can you do more than one thing at once? Clearly. Are you willing to accept that you have conscious control of only one of them at a time? Why, that would mean that talking while driving is dangerous! Preposterous! We delude ourselves into believing that we are in control of what we are doing and of what we have done.

I believe that it is an observable fact that most of our non-reflexive interactions are not deliberate, but are based on pre-attentive decisions and patterns of behavior. Some of these learned and practiced patterns have been an unconsciously accepted part of our social and environmental lifestyle for much longer than we realize. I have spoken elsewhere about cross-generational habit and how it shapes our behavior (Brown 2013b, 2016). This is why, for example, lights have been glaring blindingly at us for as long as we have had internal lighting—even though we have long had the technology to make lighting soft and diffuse. The same unthinking pattern applies to the design of chairs and steering wheels and computer mouses. I believe that this is due to the fact that once we have learned to use these tools at the periphery of our attention, we do not deliberately examine them again—we do not even consider that they are changeable.

I believe that our ability to focus our thoughts is not the great gift that we like to consider it to be. Consider how often mis-focused attention leads to accidents, injuries, and death. That phones divert our attention, while we are driving is now considered the leading cause of death for young adults around the world (World Health Organization 2014). But I believe that it is not simply a question of being distracted by a sudden noise. Though the function of a message alert is to attract the conscious attention of the recipient, I believe that—because of prolonged experiences of Flow while texting—the message alert attracts the attention of the two "deeper" processing systems in our minds. As a result, the young driver reacts without thinking—with systems much faster than conscious thought—averting her eyes and her focus from the road to the phone.

To explain that reaction and other types of cognitive dissonance, I will propose a theoretical model of the human mind (Brown 2015a). We will look at how it offers explanations for PI (Bakker 2013) and Weiser's "Calm" (Weiser and Brown 1996), as well as a number of other popular concepts. Unlike many other models of the mind and the brain, this model is not intended to reflect the biochemical or electrical properties of the cellular structure (Freides 2001; Cooper et al. 2003), nor is it intended to associate specific realms of thought or behaviors with specific regions of the neocortex (Freides 2001; Broca 1861).

Fig. 2.1 An iterative
feedback loop

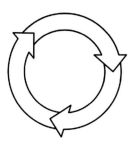

This model of the mind is purely conceptual, and it is intended to assist non-specialists in the visualization of the processes that are actually going on when humans receive, ratiocinate, and respond to stimuli from the outside world. The key to this model, though, is that it is not focused purely on rational thought, but that it illustrates the simultaneous (and much faster) processing that goes on in other more primitive parts of the neural and cerebral structure. Including these other structures allows for a simple understanding of the difference between "multitasking" and "task-switching"; of the difference between "reflex" and "reaction"; and of the difference between the emotionally overripe and intellectually fragile manner in which humans usually respond to stimuli and the actual process of rational thought. Before we tour the structure of this new idea, let us review a few of the foundations on which it has been built.

2.3 Iterative Feedback: As We May Learn—*Explaining the Mechanisms that Underlie Our Interactions with the World Around Us and How We Learn from that Interaction*

Human understanding of the world around us is built up from iterations of simple feedback loops, as shown in Fig. 2.1, which has been discussed in greater detail elsewhere (Brown 2013b). Taking the model of how feedback loops iterate at a neurological level, we perceive the world, process what we perceive, and act based on the results of that process. Then, we perceive the world again and see what has changed. Let us look at a simple exchange. We are constantly receiving proprioceptive data about the position and orientation of the different parts of our bodies and processing them unconsciously in order to maintain our balance or move precisely. Corollary discharge,[4] for example, signals the intent to initiate a movement. We perceive and react to these signals in unending, overlapping iterative

---

[4]Corollary discharge = this is a copy of the internal signal generated by our neuromotor system when we execute a movement. The copy seems to serve to let us know whether our body is moving under our own control, or under the influence of some other factor.

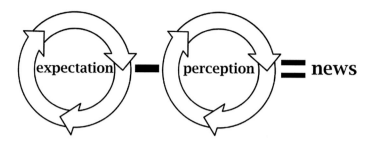

Fig. 2.2 As we may learn

feedback loops. A comparison that detects proprioceptive information regarding repositioning, but does not detect corollary discharge, informs us that we have been passively moved. Disorders in corollary discharge can cause us to attribute our actions, or even our thoughts, to others (Freides 2001; Frith and Done 1989).

Figure 2.2 shows how we might learn through these iterative cycles. This theory posits that it is the difference between what we expect and what we perceive that allows us to recognize new information and adjust our mental model (Staggers and Norcio 1993). The application of the same iterative cycle that allows us to maintain our posture, as a model for how we might learn to interact with the world, has recently received some evidentiary support in a publication from the Mayo Clinic (Stahl and Feigenson 2015).

One's understanding of the world grows and develops through the matching of experiences against expectations in the same kind of iterative feedback loop. The expectation that one holds about how to interpret environmental stimuli adapts to new information about the possibilities of stimuli, and more correct or mature (that is, more accurate or more useful) models are formed (Staggers and Norcio 1993).

This is more than a series of reactions, in that the comparison between the expected and the perceived allows us to modify our expectations, to build new models of the world around us and of our place in it. These models could include the models of self that allow us to navigate the physical spaces around us without bumping into other people and societal models that allow us to navigate the social spaces around us with the very same goal. It has even been shown that the use of well-understood mental models can facilitate interaction, with the possibility of making new devices seem intuitive (Brown 2015b).

Some of these iteratively developed models are private and reflexive, but others are shared and reflective.

2.4 Playing with Models: As We May Think We May Think—*Using Our BRAINS to Explain the Mechanisms that Underlie Simple Reflexes, Coordinated Reflexes, Pattern Recognition, Intuition, and Ratiocination*

In the brief history of HCI, several models of interaction have become popular. I have dealt with these in detail elsewhere (Brown 2014), but will refer to them here in passing so that the astute reader knows where to look for the original work. Norman proposed a cycle of interaction in which people incorporate their tools into their natural iterative behaviors (Norman 1988). Abowd and Beale created a *tennis court-style model* in which "user" and "system" communicate across an "interface" (Abowd and Beale 1991). MacKenzie added details to their model, in order to more closely reflect the processes taking place in virtual environments (MacKenzie et al. 1995). Coomans and Achten added multiple streams of input and output in their proposal of a "Design Information System" for VR (Coomans and Achten 1998). In all of these, two problems persisted: first, the fact that the *tennis court-style model* forced us to focus on the net, rather than the players (Brown 2016) and second, the deliberate ignorance of the possible importance of the fact that humans interact to different stimuli at different speeds (Hyman 1953).

Throughout history, those who have examined the workings of the human mind have proposed multitiered models based on reaction times and styles. Aristotle shared Plato's model of a three-tiered concept of the human mind—one based on the natural functions of the body, one centered on desires, and a final, deliberate one that was the realm of clear thought (Hammond 1902). Freud believed in a trifurcate mind ("ego," "superego," and "id") (Freud 1961), as did Jung ("collective unconscious," "self," and "personal") (Chang 2014).

MacLean proposed a triune model based on the evolution of the physical brain (MacLean 1973) that was popularized in Carl Sagan's book the Dragons of Eden (Sagan 1977). More recently, Kahneman's two-stage model of the brain has also attempted to explain the fact that some of our thinking is fast and emotional, while some is slower, more deliberate, and logical (Kahneman 2011).

The earlier model of interaction associated with anthropology-based computing was referred to as simply as the ABC model of HCI. BRAINS are a model of GHI, not limited to the use of machines or tools. This model explains that, according to the way that the brain has developed in different animals and in accordance with the way that the human brain can be seen to develop in utero, we have at least three separate processing systems, each of which is capable of separately perceiving, processing, and responding to external stimuli.

In Fig. 2.3, we represent those different evolutionary levels in two different ways, both of which come from the notebooks of the author and are used here as they have been used elsewhere (Brown 2013b). Figure 2.3a shows three iterative cycles. The largest represents our reflexive system, and as such, it overlaps between

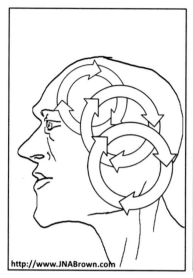 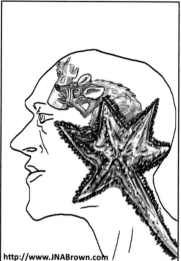

Fig. 2.3 Two renditions of the BRAINS model of general human interaction

the brain and the body. This is our primary level of interaction with our environs—from breathing the air to standing upright. The next cycle down (in z-depth and in control) is the reactive system, where we react quickly and emotionally to the world around us. Below that, and much smaller, is the reflective system in which we think logically and intellectually.

Figure 2.3b shows the same hierarchy, but uses cartoons to represent the different types of processing and the relationship between them. The foundation of the illustration is the echinoderm (starfish or seastar), chosen for this role because it has peripheral reflexes and seems to coordinate those reflexes through an unknown system that could be a precursor to the central nervous system. The echinoderm passes some sensory information on to wildly emotional protoprosimian.[5] This creature is really much too late in the evolution of life to represent fast, visceral pattern recognition, but has been chosen because it is a more pleasant and sympathetic ancestor than a bird or lizard. The protoprosimian is busy almost all of the time and is almost always emotionally charged. Occasionally, she either whispers or shouts into the ivory tower she carries in her hands. Inside this ivory tower, isolated and only capable of indirect interaction with the real world, is our reflective system.

Preliminary versions of this model have been presented before (Brown 2014, 2015b). Here, in the context of PI, we will present the model again in order to illustrate the anthropological basis of the human ability to interact with information

---

[5]Protoprosimian = ancient relatives who predate the division between our dry-nosed ancestors and their wet-nosed cousins.

at the center of our attention, while also keeping track of information that ranges from mildly to extremely peripheral. Let us take a look at the separate processors posited by this model.

2.4.1 Level One: Reflexive Interaction

What is a reflex? Well, it is some of the things that we commonly call by that name in spoken English, but the name is also often used incorrectly. Let us start our look at the model with a clear distinction between what is reflex and what is not.

When your foot snaps forward in response to a doctor stimulating your patellar ligament (with the edge of her hand or with a small rubber mallet), that movement is a reflex.

The patellar reflex is a commonly used example of a monosynaptic reflex arc, so-called because the stimulus sends an uninterrupted signal along a single synapse directly from the proprioceptor that detects the pressure to the motor neuron in the spinal cord that triggers the response.

In this type of reflex, detecting the input is the same as triggering the output. There are more complex reflexes, but this is one of many that you use almost constantly when walking, running, or trying to stand still. In fact, this reflex also triggers another, coordinated, and nearly simultaneous reflex that makes the opposing muscles in the hamstring relax. If you think about it for a moment, that coordination makes perfect sense, even though you may never have heard that additional information before. Most things are like that, aren't they: more complex than they might seem at first?

Well, it is the same with reflexes. They are triggered automatically, and you respond without any thought at all. All of the processing happens in the nerves. Multiple reflexive responses can be coordinated in the spinal cord, like in the example of the patellar reflex, where coordination happens in the spinal gray matter near the fourth lumbar vertebra.

It is also possible that reflexes can be coordinated at a "higher" level. The complex patterns of movement that turn repeatedly nearly falling forward into running are coordinated in the cerebellum. Here, one can develop physical skills as learned patterns of reflex coordination. These learned patterns are not to be confused with reflexes, in that they are not simple electrobiochemical responses to stimuli. Their coordination deteriorates with a lack of use. For the purposes of our model, all of these reflex areas (from the nerve endings just beneath the skin and deeply embedded in our organs to the gray matter of the pons and medulla oblongata[6]) are grouped with the cerebellum as a single processing system. This is

---

[6]Pons and medulla oblongata = parts of the brain stem linking the rest of the brain to the spinal cord.

the most primitive and the fastest of our natural systems for perceiving, processing, and responding to stimuli. For simplicity, we refer to it as "reflexive interaction."

2.4.2 Level Two: Reactive Interaction

When you respond angrily to a criticism of your favorite song, movie star, Web site, novel, religion, or scientist, you might say that the response is reflexive. You might say that, but you would be wrong.

If you really do not like snakes, or lizards, or puppies, and seeing one makes you feel icky, you might say that your response is just a reflex due to childhood trauma or a horrible accident in a psychology laboratory. You might say that, but you would be wrong.

Unless the response is actually rooted in a reflex arc of the sort described earlier, it is not a reflex. Now, you may feel that you had little or no conscious control of your response, and that may be right, but that does not make it a reflex, it just means that you were not consciously in control of your behavior. Let us take a closer look at what that means and how it can be.

When you are riding a bicycle, the coordination of your actions is the result of coordinated reflexes. The same kind of proprioceptive reflexes that allow you to stand upright also help you maintain your balance on two wheels. The same kind of learned patterns of coordination that allow you to establish and improve your skill as a runner also help you to establish and improve your skills as a cyclist.

On the other hand, at the same time that you are maintaining your balance and riding the bicycle on your chosen path, you are also perceiving the path itself and the still and moving obstacles to your intent. The patterns of relative movement of these obstacles tell you a lot about the conditions of the path and the speed at which you should proceed. These patterns are being compared with familiar patterns in a different part of your brain. This is where the familiar runs up against the unfamiliar. It is where you can quickly respond to the familiar and where you may try to fit new experiences into old categories. In fact, it is the same general region of the brain in which your emotional responses are processed. According to my model, this explains why so many of our fast pattern recognition thoughts become emotionally reinforced, even when there is nothing emotional about them, for instance, your irrational fear of other people's pets or your irrational love of Hedy Lamarr.

Of course, you can probably justify your fear, and Hedy Lamarr was both a great actress and a brilliant inventor... but you can't really trust rationalizations that you have invented to justify your emotional opinions. These justifications are not based on logic, but are facile and rapid emotional attempts to avoid the cognitive dissonance that would come with having to admit that we have done or believed something irrational (Festinger 1962).

This means that the rational part of our brain plays no role in our fastest decisions, but that we feel emotionally attached to the opinions we form in that manner.

It is understood in psychology that we all tend to create a perpetual fog of self-delusion in which our every past decision is justified, using new information and self-deception to convince ourselves that we have made wise decisions, even in the face of overwhelmingly contradictory evidence. This does not happen at a conscious level. It is like change blindness (Rayner 1978)—it is a pattern of accepting an overly simplified interpretation of the information we perceive and then defending the effects it has on our perception of the world. We apply our reason to justifying the reactive decisions we have made. This may be the root of our feelings of intuition and even of religious faith. As Steven Pinker explains:

> I will suggest that religion and philosophy are in part the application of mental tools to problems they were not designed to solve (Pinker 1997).

The rational resources of our brain can do more than compare and recognize, and they can also postulate, analyze, and form new ideas. This is the kind of processing we call "Reflective" or "Attentive." I have an informal postulate that we defend old patterns of knowledge emotionally, rather than rationally, in order to avoid having to reflect on them simply because reflection takes more energy. It might also explain why the surprises which should tell us we are about to have the chance to learn something new (Helson 1964) seem so often to trigger defensive emotional reactions rather than intellectual curiosity and eager anticipation (Jacobs et al. 2014).

2.4.3 Level Three: Reflective, Attentive, and Interaction

The highest and most evolutionarily modern level of our three-tiered hierarchy is the "Attentive" level of deliberate rational thought, or ratiocination, which we call "Reflective." This is the part of your brain that is reading these words and—I hope —considering their meaning.

Imagine two different ways of reading this chapter.

In the first case, you are feeling increasingly tired or bored. You are no longer giving the letters, words, and phrases your attention. Your eyes are still tracking along the lines and down the page according to learned reflex patterns, but your reflective thoughts have stopped following along. You lost "attentional focus" (Mesulam 1981). You catch yourself drifting off and realize that you have been reading without really *reading*.

In the second case, you are feeling interested and maybe even inspired, and the writing is leading you easily along a winding path from one idea to the next. In this second example, you are following the words and the ideas behind them; you are being "Reflective" and staying in what we call the "Attentive" level.

2.4.4 The Three Levels Cooperating... and Sometimes Conflicting

This hierarchy reflects the degree of to which we are consciously aware of what we are doing, but it also reflects (inversely) the degree to which we are consciously in control. Consider it like a lop-sided, non-cyclical version of rock–paper–scissors. Reflexive responses overpower reactive responses, even while reactive responses overpower reflective responses.

Not convinced? Make yourself blink. Now, stop yourself from blinking. Is it working? Keep trying while you turn your head quickly and stare at something far to the left of the room you are in. Did you blink? If not, you have successfully resisted an evolutionarily beneficial reflex and probably feel rather dizzy.

For another example, try to sneeze or hiccup through force of will. In most of us, these are reflexive actions, and it is not possible to directly control them. You can take snuff in order to trigger the sneeze reflex, but most of us have never even considered taking the time to learn to mentally trigger a sneeze.

But we do learn how to do things, and as we do, they move outward to different tiers. A toddler learning to walk must attentively coordinate the neuromuscular response to signals from the proprioceptors in feet, legs, hips, and spine in order to stand without falling. In fact, in early days, the more experienced shoulders, arms, and hands are also involved—waving in fast, asymmetric circles to help with balance. Soon, the recognition, processing, and response to these signals move from attentive control to pre-attentive, and you can see a toddler extend her left arm and leg simultaneously to try to keep from falling to the right. After a time, the process is fine-tuned and becomes purely a matter of coordinating reflexive responses.

With enough practice, we learn to add other deliberate tasks that we can perform simultaneously: balancing a full bowl of soup, for example, or carrying on a conversation. But the reflexive actions of walking supersede the reflective actions of walking while talking, or walking while balancing soup. If you stumble, the self-correcting reflexes that keep you on your feet prevent you from falling but interrupt your conversation and fling the soup across the room.

2.5 Peripheral Interaction: Unseen, and Crescive, and Ubiquitous—*A Brief Examination of the Fact that You Are Currently Interacting More Peripherally Than Deliberately, and an Argument for Why You Should Try to Stay that Way*

So, you are currently responding to countless reflexive stimuli that allow you to sit upright and breathe, etc, and you are currently responding to countless reactive stimuli that allow you to read and turn pages either electronically or on paper, all without any conscious recognition or disruption of the reflective attentional processes you are following in order to interpret these words as ideas. From an evolutionary perspective, this is exactly how your three parallel systems should work together—separate systems working at the same time. But there must be an additional mechanism—the ability to deliberately shift focused reflective processing away from one object and, at least temporarily, onto another. This natural ability was described by Weiser as a prerequisite of Calm, but he offered no mechanism to explain it (Weiser and Brown 1996).

In the ABC theory, this behavior is called DEF, and it is considered a key to our development of language and tools (Brown 2016). The interested reader should look to the references for a detailed explanation, but a simple one is offered here. The nesting habits of our protoprosimian ancestors might have allowed them the luxury of not having to always be on guard. Those on the inside of the pack could count on those on the outside to provide alarms when needed—either deliberately by screaming, or unintentionally by running off. Those on the inside, then, would have been free to be less vigilant and turn their senses to other activities. In the tight cluster, they could socialize by nattering and grooming. This could have led to additional social bonding and would have rewarded the ability to shift one's focus from that proximate and attentive task whenever peripheral sensory information gave hint of danger and to shift back again so as to maintain the relationship.

I have usually chosen to use examples from our ancestral line to illustrate the three tiers of processing described in my model (Brown 2013a). This is because I believe that their brain structure led them to perform daily routine activities in much the same way that we do now. That is to say that they divide their efforts between (a) what they want to do and (b) those things that they must do in order to be able to accomplish (a).

My use of anthropology-based examples has occasionally come under some criticism from computer scientists and psychologists who claim not to have any clear preconception of just how a protoprosimian would act in any situation whatsoever and, worse, who insist that I should not have any such preconceptions either. In response, we will now leave our protoprosimian ancestors to their grooming and turn to something (almost) completely different.

Imagine, if you will, a slimy, emaciated creature who might look a little like a skinny frog or a four-limbed spider, but with eyes like shining lamps. He is sitting in his cave and holding something very precious to him. He is concentrating both his stare and his attention on this precious thing clutched in his hands (Fig. 2.4a). Even if his attention is diverted to something else (along with his gaze), he remains at least partially attentive to his precious possession (Fig. 2.4b). This is in line with older theories of attentional focus which can be divided to some degree for some length of time.

Our model allows us to consider a more complex division of his attention, one that includes PI. Imagine the same character composing a reply to a new post on social media (Fig. 2.5). Here, we can see that, while his attention may be wandering in a way which belies the fixedness of his gaze, he is interacting unthinkingly with a keyboard, using it peripherally to serve his purpose, not as a purpose unto itself.

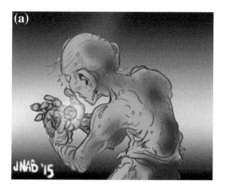 

Fig. 2.4 a Focused attention and **b** divided attention

Fig. 2.5 Peripheral interaction with the keyboard and more!

   This is, in fact, the very nature of a tool that we should be able to use it to accomplish something other than its use. Mark Weiser gave the example that once one puts on glasses, one should no longer have to pay attention to them (Weiser 1994). This is true of other well-designed or well-practiced tools and actions. A well-designed and well-maintained hammer should not require the conscious, reflective attention of the user under normal circumstances. One might use a hammer simply for the joy of using it, but the purpose of a hammer is usually the driving of nails or the performance of some other task, such as the breaking of rocks, the initiation of a patellar reflex in order to test nerve function between the L2 and L4 vertebrae, or the smiting of frost giants in order to protect Asgard.

This unthinking use of a tool is a fundamental example of PI. I believe that the same should be true of well-designed and well-maintained computerized technology. One reaches for one's mouse without looking and uses it to steer to and to select an icon, all without thinking of the mouse at all—unless something goes wrong. That would bring us back to the reverse-order imperative mentioned above, with the failure of the attempted PI would bring the tool to the center of our attention. Allow me to illustrate this.

Wanting to use the mouse, one reaches unthinkingly for where it should be, grasps it, and slides it in a manner that should move our cursor. We are not cognizant of the reaching and grasping and movement of the mouse, only of the attempt to move the cursor. The cursor is expected to behave as a natural extension of the human, so all of that is done at first-level attention—somewhere in the realm of learned patterns of reflexes (muscle memory) that we execute unthinkingly.

When the cursor fails to move, one's second-level attention is drawn to the failure and a pattern from early training is initiated. We repeat a smaller and faster version of the movement, or lift the mouse and put it back down again, or both of the above. Here, we are pre-attentively checking the mechanics of our attempt and unconsciously running through an iterative cycle that tries to answer the question: Is there a problem with how I am using this tool? When these simple tests still fail to make the cursor move, our full reflective attention is drawn away from the task and focused on the tool.

This is when we notice that we are trying to mouse with our smartphone.

Let us consider the smartphone a little more deeply in one final illustration of the application of our model to the understanding of PI.

2.6 Lost in the Flow: The Inherent Danger of Designing Ubiquitous Interactions to Be Immersive—*How We Might Use Our BRAINS to Avoid the Pitfalls of the Lack of Distraction*

According to a recent report from the World Health Organization, the leading cause of death among young adults worldwide is now the combined use of smartphones and automobiles (World Health Organization 2014). As has been remarked upon elsewhere, the shocking thing is not that there has been a worldwide response to this problem, but rather that the response is so obviously misdirected. In a total misunderstanding of the nature of human–machine interaction, manufacturers and lawmakers have focused almost universally not on prohibiting the use of smart-phones while driving, and not on transforming the interface so that the interaction becomes less distracting, but on forcing drivers to interact with their devices in a "hands-free" manner (Caird et al. 2014). We have not had the time to evolve in response to the feeling of "Flow" brought on by technologically enhanced interaction. The illusion that we are somehow fully aware of our environment while totally immersed in some task may be what is killing us.

The key to the problem is that studies persist in treating the smartphone as a distraction. Unfortunately, distraction is only one of the roles played by this device and its ubiquitous relatives, the tablet, the palmtop, the smart watch and smart glasses, and most especially, the navigational assistant. We will return to the idea of the smartphone as a distraction and a disruption in the next section. For now, let us look at a much more dangerous aspect of the device: the fact that it is designed to pull the user into a state of immersive "Flow."

Csikszentmihalyi's work in this area is inspiring (MacLean 1973), as is his devotion to the promotion of positive psychology (Csikszentmihalyi and Csikszentmihalyi 2006). But let us examine his concept of "Flow" from the perspective of human factors, and through the lens of our new model.

The BRAINS model can account for the perception during "Flow" that the ego has fallen away and that conscious decisions are replaced by jazz-like improvisation and an intuitive belief that you are performing at the highest level of your skills.

Could it be that these feelings come from the fact that the most peripheral iterative feedback loops, the ones that naturally serve the purpose of keeping us aware of our environment, have here turned instead to providing more unconscious resources to the focus on the task? Consider the following aspects of working or playing in flow:

- You have a feeling of being more skilled—you are using more processing power, processors that are vastly faster (Tovée 1994).
- You feel deeply engaged in the task at hand—the resources in your system that evolved for the purpose of keeping you alive are now being used to perform tasks that are much more restricted in their scope and in their possible negative outcomes (Klasen et al. 2011).
- Time seems to disappear—the rational part of your brain, the part that tracks time's passage, is not in use (Dennett and Kinsbourne 1992).
- You are no longer self-conscious—one might argue that you are not any sort of conscious. Your ego has disappeared—you are using resources that perform their tasks unconsciously—with your cognitive self literally left out of the loop (Carruthers 2014).

The beautiful fulfillment of being in "Flow" comes from the illusion that our peripheral sensors and processors are working smoothly and encountering only solvable problems. This is one of the ways that a game can feel just challenging enough to inspire the player to try harder. It fits into a natural feedback loop, one that rewards us for feeling that we are working well and safely.

But the feeling can be deceptive.

Exchanging a constant stream of shallow sms messages with one or more friends can give us the impression that we are successfully monitoring the world around us for danger. This feedback error will contribute to our learning the wrong reflexive and reactive patterns and create a self-deceptive illusion of attention and resultant safety. This may be why people are involved in accidents while texting. Not the distraction of having one's hands full, and not even the distraction of reflexive responses triggered by alerts and alarms, but rather the feeling of "Flow." The cause of all of these fatal accidents may be a side effect of the combination of unlimited communication and limited evolutionary pressures. As mentioned above, we have not had the time to evolve in response to the feeling of "Flow" brought on by technologically enhanced interaction. I propose that, rather than waiting for the violent resolution that natural selection will provide for this imbalance, we change the design of our interactive systems.

Incorporating the triune nature of the BRAINS model may enable HCI practitioners to deliberately infiltrate "Flow" without disrupting it during some situations and to interrupt it just as deliberately in others.

While deliberate human-to-device and device-to-human interaction during "Flow" has been clearly demonstrated, we are still trying to figure out how to provide important outside information to someone who is in "Flow." Traditionally, we attempt this through the use of blaring alarms, screaming ringtones, and other primitive concepts based on the observably false concept that if you scream at someone loudly enough, they will give you their full attention according to your schedule rather than their own.

2.7 ABC Ringtones: The Possibility of Alerts as Peripheral Information—*How We Might Apply Our BRAINS to a Practical Problem*

Traditional alerts and alarms are intended to draw our conscious attention, with the expectation that familiarization with our responsibilities and with the meaning of different alerts will allow us to make immediate rational decisions. In fact, as discussed above, such alerts stimulate a reflexive response and a reactive response that are much faster than any possible deliberate and reflective response. This means that our alarms and alerts should be designed with the expectation that they will trigger reflexes and reactions that supersede any reflective or deliberate response.

If this occurs at the wrong time, then the reflex and/or the reaction could interrupt an important rational process or preclude an important rational decision, or even a series of important decisions. For instance, let us take an example involving the limited-term, ongoing, and highly critical series of conscious decisions that allow someone to safely drive a car. You would not shout at a driver just as they are making a difficult turn, nor would you tickle the back of their neck. Coming at exactly the wrong moment, either of these distracting stimuli might result in an accident because the driver cannot consciously control their reflexive or reactive responses to those stimuli. The odds of there being an accident, and the odds of the accident being severe, increase in direct relation to speed and traffic density, and in inverse relation to familiarity with the route. Since navigational computers are designed specifically for use on unfamiliar routes, and since they are specifically designed to interrupt your ongoing thoughts and real-time decision-making processes, does it not seem as though they should be designed differently?

If so, then in what way(s) should the design be modified?

As mentioned above, the approach that is currently in favor is to move to hands-free interaction. Unfortunately, this does not address the issue of interruption at all. Let us look at it in the three different levels proposed by our model.

2.7.1 Interruption of Reflective Processing

The sudden arrival of an instruction to "turn left in 270 m" will still interrupt the driver's thought processes, and the nature of the instruction itself will still prove confusing, disrupting the driver's ability to navigate. What if there are three exits ahead, one after the other? Which one is 270 m away from where you were when the machine gave you your directions?

2.7.2 Interruption of Reactive Processing

The reactive system will also respond to the sudden announcement of directions, and it will do so faster than the reflective system. The triggered reaction will be based on well-established patterns of behavior. With the right deliberate preparation, the driver may have learned to ignore the sounds and wait for a reflective response, but how many drivers practice reacting to their navigational assistants before using them? It is more likely that an "intuitive" reaction will take place, based on the more established mental model of interacting with another human (Nass and Moon 2000). So, an experienced driver may hunch their shoulders or give some other unspoken sign that they do not want to be interrupted, while a less experienced driver might turn and glare at the machine, or tell it to be quiet—either one of which detracts from their performance by initiating a pattern recognition sequence that has nothing to do with driving.

2.7.3 Interruption of Reflexive Processing

The greatest danger lies in the interruption of reflexive processing, because this will happen so quickly that no other system can intervene. An unexpected noise may trigger a startled reaction in the driver, which can involve large muscle spasms—a dangerous thing when one is holding a steering wheel or gently applying pressure to an accelerator. That is for an unexpected noise. An expected noise may be even worse. What if the driver reacts to the noise according to a mental model of a more common irritating device, like an alarm clock? What if, in the "flow" of driving, the driver reflexively reaches for the device to turn it off? In a worst-case scenario, the driver becomes involved in this interaction for more than one cycle, moving it from the periphery to the center of their attention. They are now lost in the flow of interacting with the navigator, rather than with the car or the road or the rest of traffic.

Does that seem implausible to you? Consider the case of the pilots who got lost in their new vacation-scheduling software and flew 70 minutes past their target city while ignoring radio messages, fighter jets that had been sent to assess the possibility of a terrorist threat, and the flight attendants pounding on the door of the cabin (National Transportation Safety Board 2009; Brown 2012). This is just one extreme example of a very common event. As mentioned before, this kind of interactive problem is now seen as the primary cause of death among teens and young adults (World Health Organization 2014).

This issue reflects a well-documented, well-understood problem in tool design. Interaction suited to machine capabilities rather than human capabilities seems to persist wherever engineers are allowed to ignore human factors (Vicente 2003). Bardzell and Bardzell have proposed that this is due to the fact that it is easier to quantify machine factors (Bardzell and Bardzell 2014). In 2012, I posited that it should be possible to use the CPE to design alerts and alarms that inform us without interrupting us (Brown 2012). The idea is that

1. since the human brain is capable of filtering out "signal" from "noise," even when the noise is very loud, and
2. since the signal can then be understood without interrupting the ongoing actions or thoughts of the person for whom it is meaningful, then
3. it should be possible to build these features into deliberate computer output.

In 2014, a team working in Lisbon measured the effect of affective ringtones, that is, ringtones based on the ABC theory and the CPE. Though only preliminary data have been published so far (Brown 2016; Brown et al. 2015), the experiment clearly showed that it is possible to design alerts that will inform the intended recipient without disrupting their concentrated focus on another, deliberate task.

Figure 2.6 shows beta-wave activity[7] during the performance of a familiar but challenging task in a noisy environment, before and during the loud ringing of a

---

[7]Beta-wave activity = electrical activity between 12.5 and 30 Hz, a range of frequency commonly used in studies of the natural electrical activity in the brain.

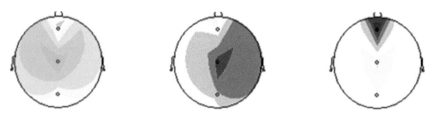

Fig. 2.6 Beta-wave density as measured with 5-point EEG—a loud unknown ringtone caused an increase in activity that persisted after the ringtone stopped

Fig. 2.7 Changes to beta-wave density when a loved one speaks your name too softly for you to consciously hear it

stranger's phone. Note the increase in activity in the prefrontal cortex[8] when the noise interrupts the participant's work.

Let us relate all of this brain activity back to our model. In a noisy environment, the reflective system is focused on a task. The reactive and reflexive systems are assisting in the performance of this task. Because you are focused on completing this task quickly and accurately, you ignore your own ringtone when you hear it, as you have learned to ignore other noises so that you can focus on your work. That said some noises are too soft to hear, while other noises catch your attention and interrupt your work. A stranger saying unimportant words is ignored at most volumes, as are most ringtones at most volumes. An unimportant word spoken by someone you love sometimes triggers a response, but sometimes does not.

ABC ringtones are different. When your name is spoken softly by the voice of someone you love—even if it is spoken too softly for you to consciously be able to react to it—some pre-attentive part of your brain reacts. As shown in in Fig. 2.7, there is a surge of activity in your reactive brain but no surge in your prefrontal cortex to interrupt focused work. Despite that, all participants reported hearing the ringtone. Without any interruption of your focus on the primary task, you are internally informed of the peripherally delivered information that your loved one has spoken your name.

---

[8]Prefrontal cortex = the front-most part of the neocortex—the crumpled up, six-layered brain hat we wear under our skulls.

The alert has not been delivered by a loud noise that demands attention; instead, it seems to have quietly triggered an internal information process. It seems as though the ABC ringtone can "…move easily from the periphery of our attention, to the center, and back" (Weiser and Brown 1996).

2.8 Conclusion: How Peripheral Interaction Has Remained Both Unseen and Crescive—*Gathering the Threads that Have Unfurled in Our Discussion and Attempting to Tie Their Fibers into a Knot upon Which the Reader Might Attempt to Climb to New Heights*

This chapter started with the simple statement that PI does exist. I have attempted to show that we all make use of it all of the time. I hope that the theory of ABC and the BRAINS model has helped to explain how PI happens. I also hope that the discussion of the ABC Ringtones Project in Lisbon has shown that it is possible to design human–computer interaction that makes good use of the natural qualities of PI.

Before concluding this chapter, let us have a quick review. To describe natural multitasking, task-switching, and the three very different speeds and qualities of human response to outside stimuli, I have proposed the BRAINS model, which has three hierarchical levels of processing. The first two happen unconsciously.

- The first fundamental level of processing deals with bodily functions. Aristotle called this the vegetative level, because even plants have some version of this. We include all of the simple, iterative reflex cycles—from the monosynaptic patellar reflex to the complex patterns of coordinated reflexes that let us breathe, shuffle playing cards, knit, or ride a bicycle—and we call it *reflexive*.
- At the second level, we do seem to think, but it is irrational and "intuitive" and often very emotional. This level addresses our desires with reactions that are too fast for conscious thought. The second is the level at which we respond to (internal or external) stimuli based on familiarity according to well-established patterns that are too complex for reflexive responses. Addressing primarily the desires and passions mediated at this level, Aristotle called this the appetitive level. Primarily addressing the speed and lack of consideration, we call it *reactive*.
- The third level is conscious. This is the level at which we use our intellect, our logic, and our ability to think formally. We call it *reflective*. Aristotle called this the rational or contemplative level and placed it at the top of Plato's hierarchy, saying it could take control of the other two. Many theorists continue to place it at the top of these interactive systems, in terms of both importance and control. From an ABC perspective, since this third processing system is the slowest and

the most expensive to the body's metabolism, it is the system that is used the least. In the BRAINS model, based on observations that reflexes supplant reactions, and reactions supplant reflection, we place this system at the bottom of the hierarchy.

It is important to consider that only the reflexive system can sense anything, and its limitations shape all of our understanding of the real, material world. The data that do get through must then pass through the filters and reconstructions of the reactive processing system and its emotional and self-serving distortions in order to reach our reflective processing system.

In other words, human perception is like an unending game of "broken telephone" in which the illogical players can process information at 10 or 100 or 1000 times the speed of the slow-thinking intellectual who is last in line. We best use those processors to interact with the vast field of peripheral information that surrounds us in the natural world. If they deal with that information, then we do not have to process it all slowly and deliberately.

On the other hand, those faster reflexive and reactive processors sometimes supplant our reflective process, taking actions that were not thought out and then, upon reflection, finding means to justify those actions, resulting in self-delusion and cognitive dissonance.

This tendency is precisely why we must design our interactions to suit specific processors. Fast answers will always be based on established patterns of reflexes or of reactions—they will only be logical if the logical decision was determined and ingrained ahead of time. I have tried to show the dangers involved in our misunderstanding of how very ubiquitous PI is in our daily lives and especially in our interactions with computerized technology. I have also tried to offer up some information for the reader on a recent advance in the application of PI to the design of HCI.

I believe that our ABC ringtones will make phones less annoying by allowing everyone to hear their phone ring even though the volume is too low to be noticed by anyone else. The same style of alert could inform a driver of navigational instructions or of an incoming text message in a way that does not disrupt their attentive focus.

I also believe that ABC ringtones could point the way to designing alarms that will always penetrate to the conscious and reflective mind—even in situations where that has not proven possible to date. For example, let us reconsider those pilots who got immersed in their software and lost track of time. When the air traffic controllers, the air force, and even the cabin crew were unable to get the attention of the pilots, maybe an ABC alert would have worked. What if they had each received customized messages—the voice of a loved one saying "why aren't you answering the radio?"

There could be other applications. Elsewhere, I have discussed the possibility of creating a formal system to help police who might otherwise get lost in a negative feedback loop of fear and preparedness that could lead to an unwarranted shooting

(Brown 2015c). The unconscious iterative feedback cycle could be interrupted by the voice of a loved one reminding them to slow down and consider their options.

Imagine a firefighter who must receive important new information about the structural integrity of the building they are in. Flashing lights and loud noises are of no use there, but what if the firefighter were to suddenly hear the voice of his daughter? In the same way, a soldier lost in the "fog of war" could be reminded of her role and responsibilities by hearing the voice of her distant lover.

To conclude, you are engaged in PI right now. Once, you had to focus on each letter in order to be able to read, and you had to work to improve. The improvements became crescive and the use of letters became peripheral, and in time, you were able to focus on the message rather than on its acquisition. What's more, every deliberate task that you learn to perform with fluency will also become peripheral in time. It is our responsibility to design tools that suit and even take advantage of the unseen and crescive processes of our ubiquitous PI.

References

Abowd, G., & Beale, R. (1991). Users, systems and interfaces: A unifying framework for interaction. *HCI*, 91, 73–87.

Bakker, S. (2013). Design for peripheral interaction (Doctoral dissertation, Technische Universiteit Eindhoven).

Bardzell, J., & Bardzell, S. (2014). A great and troubling beauty: Cognitive speculation and ubiquitous computing. *Personal and Ubiquitous Computing, 18*(4), 779–794.

Broca, P. (1861). Sur le principe des localisations cérébrales. *Bulletin de la Société d'Anthropologie, 2*, 190–204.

Brown, J. N. A. (2012). Expert talk for time machine session: Designing calm technology as refreshing as taking a walk in the woods. In *2012 IEEE International Conference on Multimedia and Expo* (pp. 423–423). IEEE.

Brown, J. N. A. (2013a). It's as easy as ABC: Introducing anthropology-based computing. In *Advances in Computational Intelligence. Proceedings of IWANN 2013: The International Work-Conference on Artificial Neural Networks*.

Brown, J. N. A. (2013b). It's as easy as ABC: Introducing anthropology-based computing. In *International Work-Conference on Artificial Neural Networks (IWANN2013)*. Hotel Beatriz Atlantis and Spa, Puerto de la Cruz, Tenerife, Spain. 14 June, 2013. Keynote Address.

Brown, J. N. A. (2015a). The expectation effect. In *The Bloomsbury Encyclopedia of Design* (In Press).

Brown, J. N. A. (2015b). Intuitive interaction with a smart environment. Fundamentals of Collective Adaptive Systems (FoCAS) Reading Room. January, 2015. http://www.focas-reading-room.eu/intuitive-interaction-with-a-smart-environment/. Last retrieved May, 2015.

Brown, J. N. A. (2015c). Making sense of the noise: An ABC approach to big data and security. In B. Akhgar, G. B. Saathoff, H. R. Arabnia, R. Hill, A. Staniforth, and S. Bayerl (Eds.), *Application of Big Data for National Security* (pp. 261–273). Oxford: Elsevier.

Brown, J. N. A. (2016). Anthropology-based computing: Putting the human in human-computer interaction. Springer human-computer interaction series. Springer.

Brown, J. N. A., Bakker, S., & Oliveira, J. (2015). I am calm—Towards a psychoneurological evaluation of ABC ringtones (Under Review).

Brown, J. N. A., Leitner, G., Hitz, M., & Català Mallofré, A. (2014). A model of calm HCI. In S. Bakker, D. Hausen, T. Selker, E. van den Hoven, A. Butz, B. Eggen (Eds.) Peripheral interaction: Shaping the research and design space. Workshop at CHI2014, Toronto, Canada. ISSN: 1862–5207.

Bush, V. (1945). As We May Think. *Atlantic Monthly, 176*(1), 101–108.

Caird, J. K., Johnston, K. A., Willness, C. R., Asbridge, M., & Steel, P. (2014). A meta-analysis of the effects of texting on driving. *Accident Analysis and Prevention, 71*, 311–318.

Carruthers, G. (2014). What makes us conscious of our own agency? And why the conscious versus unconscious representation distinction matters. *Frontiers in Human Neuroscience 8*, 434.

Chang, H. M. (2014). Emotions in archetypal media content (Doctoral dissertation, Technische Universiteit Eindhoven).

Cherry, E. C. (1953). Some experiments on the recognition of speech, with one and with two ears. *The Journal of the Acoustical Society of America, 25*(5), 975–979.

Coomans, M. K. D., & Achten, H. H. (1998). Mixed task domain representation in vr-dis. In *Proceedings of APCHI 1998: 3rd Asia Pacific Conference on Computer Human Interaction.*

Cooper, J. R., Bloom, F. E., & Roth, R. H. (2003). *The biochemical basis of neuropharmacology.* Chicago: Oxford University Press.

Csikszentmihaiyi, M. (1990). *Flow: The psychology of optimal experience.* New York: Harper and Row.

Csikszentmihalyi, M. E., & Csikszentmihalyi, I. S. E. (2006). A life worth living: Contributions to positive psychology. Oxford: Oxford University Press.

Dawkins, R. (1976). The Selfish Gene (Vol. 1, pp. 976). Oxford: Oxford University Press.

Dennett, D. C., & Kinsbourne, M. (1992). Time and the observer: The where and when of consciousness in the brain. *Behavioral and Brain Sciences, 15*(02), 183–201.

Festinger, L. (1962). A theory of cognitive dissonance (Vol. 2). Redwood: Stanford university press.

Freides, D. (2001). *Developmental disorders: A neuropsychological approach.* Oxford: Blackwell.

Freud, S. (1961). The ego and the id. In J. Strachey (Ed. and Trans.), The standard edition of the complete psychological works of Sigmund Freud (Vol. 19, pp. 3–66). London: Hogarth Press. (Original work published 1923).

Frith, C. D., & Done, D. J. (1989). Experiences of alien control in schizophrenia reflect a disorder in the central monitoring of action. *Psychological Medicine, 19*(02), 359–363.

Golumbic, E. M. Z., Ding, N., Bickel, S., Lakatos, P., Schevon, C. A., McKhann, G. M., & Schroeder, C. E. (2013). Mechanisms underlying selective neuronal tracking of attended speech at a "Cocktail Party". *Neuron, 77*, 980–991.

Hammond, W. A. (1902). *Aristotle's psychology: A treatise on the principle of life (De Anima and Parva Naturalia).* MacMillan, New York: S. Sonnenschein & Company, Limited.

Helson, H. (1964). *Adaptation-level theory: An experimental and systematic approach to behavior* (p. 732). Oxford: Harper and Row.

Hyman, R. (1953). Stimulus information as a determinant of reaction time. *Journal of Experimental Psychology, 45*(3), 188–196.

Jacobs, E., Broekens, J., & Jonker, C. (2014). Joy, distress, hope, and fear in reinforcement learning. In *Proceedings of the 2014 International Conference on Autonomous Agents and Multi-agent Systems* (pp. 1615–1616). International Foundation for Autonomous Agents and Multiagent Systems.

Kahneman, D. (2011). *Thinking, fast and slow.* New York: Farrar, Straus and Giroux.

Klasen, M., Weber, R., Kircher, T. T., Mathiak, K. A., & Mathiak, K. (2011). Neural contributions to flow experience during video game playing. Social cognitive and affective neuroscience, nsr021.

MacKenzie, I. S. (1995). Virtual environments and advanced interface design (Chap). In *Input devices and interaction techniques for advanced computing* (pp. 437–470). Oxford: Oxford University Press.

MacLean P. D. (1973). A triune concept of the brain and behavior. In. T. J. Boag, D. Campbell (Eds.) *The Hincks Memorial Lectures* (pp. 6–66), Toronto: University of Toronto Press.

Mesulam, M. (1981). A cortical network for directed attention and unilateral neglect. *Annals of Neurology, 10*(4), 309–325.

Mirsky, A. F. (1987). Behavioral and psychophysiological markers of disordered attention. *Environmental Health Perspectives, 74*, 191.

Moray, N. (1959). Attention in dichotic listening: Affective cues and the influence of instructions. *Quarterly Journal of Experimental Psychology, 11*(1), 56–60.

Nass, C., & Moon, Y. (2000). Machines and mindlessness: Social responses to computers. *Journal of social issues, 56*(1), 81–103.

National Transportation Safety Board. (2009). Operational Factors/Human Performance Group Chairman's Factual Report DCA10IA001 (Office of Aviation Safety Factual Report DCA1I0A001) Washington, D.C.: B. D. Tew and D. Lawrence. Retrieved from http://dms.ntsb.gov/pubdms/search/document.cfm?docID=322735&docketID=48456&mkey=74940

Norman, D. A. (1988). *The psychology of everyday things*. New York: Basic Books.

Novak, J. D. (2010). *Learning, creating, and using knowledge: Concept maps as facilitative tools in schools and corporations*. London: Routledge.

Pinker, S. (1997). *How the mind works* (p. 660). New York: W W Norton & Co.

Rayner, K. (1978). Eye movements in reading and information processing. *Psychological Bulletin, 85*(3), 618.

Reingold, N. (1987). Vannevar Bush's new deal for research: Or the triumph of the old order. *Historical Studies in the Physical and Biological Sciences, 17*(2), 299–344.

Sagan, C. (1977). Dragons of Eden: Speculations on the evolution of human intelligence. Ballantine Books.

Smith, D. C., Ludolph, F. E., Irby, C. H., & Chairman-Johnson, J. A. (1985). The desktop metaphor as an approach to user interface design (panel discussion). In *Proceedings of the 1985 ACM annual conference on The range of computing: mid-80's perspective* (pp. 548–549). ACM.

Staggers, N., & Norcio, A. F. (1993). Mental models: concepts for human-computer interaction research. *International Journal of Man-Machine Studies, 38*(4), 587–605.

Stahl, A. E., & Feigenson, L. (2015). Observing the unexpected enhances infants' learning and exploration. *Science, 348*(6230), 91–94.

Tovée, M. J. (1994). Neuronal processing: How fast is the speed of thought? *Current Biology, 4*(12), 1125–1127.

Vicente, K. J. (2003). The human factor. In *Frontiers of Engineering: Reports on leading-edge engineering from the 2002 NAE Symposium on Frontiers of Engineering* (pp. 31–38).

Weiser, M. (1994). The world is not a desktop. *Interactions, 1*(1), 7–8.

Weiser, M., & Brown, J. S. (1996). Designing calm technology. *PowerGrid Journal, 1*(1), 75–85.

World Health Organization. (2014). Health for the world's adolescents: a second chance in the second decade: summary.

Chapter 3
Theories of Focal and Peripheral Attention

James F. Juola

Abstract Attention has been regarded as the guardian of consciousness. This guardian has several modes of operation, e.g., attention that is guided by external sensory inputs (bottom-up activation) and that which is maintained by internal goals (top-down intention). Attention can be widely dispersed or focused on a single, narrow task. Attention can also be shared between two tasks to some extent, or switched from one focus to another, often more quickly than the eyes can move. One purpose of attention is undoubtedly to maintain a type of alertness for interesting or salient information, such as abrupt changes in the periphery, to which focal attention might be directed. Another purpose of attention is to satisfy one's need to maintain focus on the task at hand and prevent unwanted intrusions. Clearly, there are trade-offs between attention's dual roles of preventing interference yet enabling us to respond to important environmental or internal changes that might require a shift of focus. In this way, we should be capable of processing information free from interference when possible, yet also be able to respond appropriately to new information when necessary. The current review covers theories of attention that address its purpose, its limits, and the neurological processes that enable us to perform many tasks relatively effortlessly and successfully despite our individual limitations and the demands of a complicated and variable environment.

Keywords Attention theories · Visual search · Attention shifting · Attention sharing · Neuroscience of visual attention

J.F. Juola (✉)
Eindhoven University of Technology, Eindhoven, The Netherlands
e-mail: juola@ku.edu

J.F. Juola
The University of Kansas, Lawrence, USA

© Springer International Publishing Switzerland 2016   39
S. Bakker et al. (eds.), *Peripheral Interaction*,
Human–Computer Interaction Series, DOI 10.1007/978-3-319-29523-7_3

3.1 Introduction

Since the origin of introspective thought addressing the question of what it means to be human, attention has been viewed as a central psychological process, if not the single most important one. Leonardo da Vinci anticipated one modern view by stating that "Seeing is one of the most rapid operations possible: it embraces an infinity of forms, yet it fixes on but one object at a time" (Bramly 1991, p. 255). William James expressed a similar idea when he famously stated that "Every one knows what attention is. It is the taking possession of the mind, in clear and vivid form, of one out of what seem several simultaneously possible objects or trains of thought. Focalization, concentration, of consciousness are of its essence. It implies withdrawal from some things in order to deal effectively with others..." (James 1890, pp. 403–404). This definition is common to most modern theories of attention, including the idea that we have limited processing capacity to deal with the enormous amount of information available, both in the outside world and in our own recollections. Therefore, we must select from this mass a small subset for detailed processing. Attention, according to James and others, is the gateway to consciousness.

All contemporary theories of attention concentrate on the selection process as a means of maintaining focus on the task at hand while being able to accept interrupts if they are relevant to the task or potentially important for other reasons. These theories have dealt with both auditory and visual attention, but for most purposes the present review will concentrate on visual attention. The method of attentional selection has been described in numerous ways, such as a filter concentrated on a single information channel, a zoom lens that expands or contracts, a moving spotlight that illuminates small parts of the field, or a switch that engages or disengages from different information sources.

In the following sections, I will review some of these theories with emphasis on central versus peripheral attentional interactions. I will describe various theories and approaches to the study of human attention, placing it as a central process affecting selection of perceived information, deciding how to deal with it in terms of one's goals, and choosing appropriate responses. Although much of the following discussion emphasizes the role of attention in focusing on a central, main task, the way in which peripheral information can be monitored, selected, and added to or subtracted from main task performance will be discussed. Finally, I will review some of the neurological underpinnings of attention and how modern technology affects our attentional processing, for better or worse. It should be acknowledged, however, that attention is not a unitary concept, nor does it exist in limited neural substrates. Rather, it is a way for the brain to make the best possible use of its limited resources while enabling meaningful and successful interactions with the outside world.

3.2 Filter Theories of Attention

Broadbent (1958) is credited with developing the first information-processing model in psychology. In his theory, attention is viewed as a single-channel filter for selecting information from a multifaceted sensory register. Selected information is passed into a limited-capacity processor that acts on this information and stores some of it in a more permanent memory. Although the filter can be switched from one source to another, it does not allow for attention sharing between channels for information that is considered relatively demanding of cognitive resources. Broadbent's theory was based on the studies of dichotic listening, in which two different spoken messages were presented simultaneously, one to each ear. To insure that one of the messages was attended, the listener was instructed to repeat one of them, a procedure called shadowing. The typical result was that observers could follow and understand the shadowed message while they repeated it aloud, but they showed little awareness of, and no memory for, the non-shadowed message. From these and other results, Broadbent concluded that attention acts as a filter to channel only one physical information source through to central processes while eliminating all others that are essentially lost and gone forever.

Like any useful theory, Broadbent's filter theory was consistent with a large body of data, and it generated much research designed to test and improve it. It was not long before others showed that a non-shadowed message could get through to some level of consciousness if it were related in some way to the attended message (e.g., Treisman 1960, 1964). Similarly, Moray (1959) found that important information, such as the listener's own name, could attract conscious attention if it were presented in an unattended channel. It was as though relevant or important information could "leak through" an early sensory filter so that unattended information is only attenuated and not blocked out completely. Still others, such as Norman (1968) and Deutsch and Deutsch (1963), argued that at least some information such as familiar words and objects could directly impact conscious perception because they are encoded automatically to relatively deep levels of processing. They then must be filtered out, if at all, only after they have been perceived and understood at some level and not merely on the basis of their sensory properties alone.

The argument about whether attention filters unwanted information at early or late levels of processing has persisted for some time, but has been elegantly resolved, at least to some extent, by more contemporary theories of attention. For one example, a distinction has been made between processes that occur automatically, that is without awareness, effort, or attention, and those that occur willfully with controlled, deliberate attentional processing (e.g., Schneider and Shiffrin 1977; Shiffrin and Schneider 1977). It is clear that with practice, many skills including perception, recognition, decision processes, and their implementation through motor control of skilled behaviors are carried out with little or no attentional effort (think about how a professional hockey player scores on a penalty shot, or how an experienced driver avoids an unexpected obstacle in the road). For another example of how contemporary theories determine the level at which attentional selection affects behavior, a distinction has been made between the amount of attention that is engaged in some focal task and that which is "left over" to share with other tasks that are not within the current focus. Lavie (1995, 2001) has demonstrated this distinction by showing how the distribution of visual attention over the field of view is determined, at least in part, by the perceptual/cognitive demands of any given task. A demanding central task leaves little attention to be distributed over the periphery, whereas simple, or especially automatic, tasks leave attentional resources free to engage in other, more peripheral events.

Lavie's theory was based on research in which she varied the difficulty of a central processing task. She used a letter recognition task in which a letter presented at the center of the visual field was to be classified as either an "X" or an "N" by instructing the observers to press either of the two response keys, each assigned to one of the two letters. This is a very easy task, as there is much evidence that single letters can be identified more or less automatically (e.g., Posner 1976). Lavie's innovation was to use large letters presented in the periphery that were as identifiable as the smaller letters presented at the center, but the peripheral letters were supposed to be irrelevant to the task, and subjects were told to ignore them. One major manipulation was to include peripheral letters that were either irrelevant to the main task (e.g., "H"), identical to the central target (i.e., the peripheral and target letters were both "Xs" or both "Ns"), or critically, they were the other member of the target pair; e.g., the central target was an "X," whereas the peripheral distractor was an "N." Lavie found that responses to the central target were slowed when the peripheral distractor was assigned to the opposite response category. The other major manipulation was to make the task more difficult by embedding the central letter in a string of irrelevant letters in the center of the field while including peripheral distractors as in the initial study. When the central target was crowded among a string of adjoining letters, interference from the distractors disappeared. Lavie's conclusion was that if the central task demanded a high commitment of attentional resources, subjects behaved as if an early filter severely restricted processing of peripheral information. However, if the central task was non-demanding, as when only a single target letter was presented, some attentional resources were free to process peripheral information. Thus, interference was found only in the low-load condition, leading to longer response times when the central and peripheral letters were mapped to conflicting response tendencies.

Further evidence for the role of attentional demands of a central task on peripheral processing was provided by Rees et al. (1997). They measured brain activity in the medial–temporal lobe (area MT), a cortical area known to respond actively to moving stimuli. The background field in their task consisted of a number of moving dots which produced the expected MT activity. The central task was manipulated to be either easy (determine whether a word was in upper- or lower-case letters), or relatively difficult (count the number of syllables in the word). The important finding was that motion detection activity in area MT was reduced in the more difficult syllable-determination task, indicating that attentional demands can be quite general and lead to changes in activity in widely divergent brain areas. The important design implication is that as any focal task becomes more intensively demanding of perceptual/cognitive resources, the less likely it is that peripheral stimuli will result in awareness or control over behavior.

3.3 Spotlight Theories of Attention

One generally held belief about attention is that it has evolved to alert us to interesting and important aspects of the environment. Although we normally orient ourselves toward and fixate on things of interest with our eyes, attention is presumably more labile and capable of moving independently of eye fixations to recruit potential fixation locations. This idea was discussed in Neisser's (1967) seminal book, in which he envisioned a sensory world in which the overall scene of objects is registered automatically and in parallel in a preattentive processing stage. Attention then selects some subpart for focal processing, and the eyes are likely to move to the attended object. A similar distinction was made by Posner (1980) who distinguished between covert and overt orienting. Covert orienting includes the stages of disengaging from the current locus of focal attention, moving attention to a new object or point in space, and then engaging focal attention at the new location. All of this is done before the eyes have a chance to catch up, as has been demonstrated in a number of spatial cueing experiments.

In Posner's seminal research, a spatial cue was presented at a central fixation point indicating the peripheral location (left or right) of an upcoming target to which a fast response was required. The cue was an arrow pointing left or right, and the cue validly indicated the location of the following target on 80 % of the trials. On invalid trials, the target appeared on the side opposite that indicated by the cue. The time between the onset of the cue and the offset of the target was kept below 200 ms, so there was not enough time to move the eyes to the target position (overt orienting) before the target itself disappeared. Nevertheless, Posner demonstrated that response times were shorter on valid cue trials than on invalid cue trials, with times on uncued, control trials about in the middle. Posner argued that attention exists in a diffuse state when no cue is given, but when a potentially valid cue is presented, attention zooms in on the cued location (covert orienting). If the target is presented where attention is focused, it is processed more rapidly (processing benefit relative to the uncued condition), whereas if it occurs in another location, attention must be disengaged, moved, and reallocated, resulting in delayed response times (processing cost). He then defined the effectiveness of any cue as the difference between mean response times on invalid and valid cue trials, i.e., the cost plus benefits of the cue.

Questions were soon raised about how flexibly attention can be distributed over the field of view. Posner and others argued for diffuse versus focused modes, with the focus not necessarily overlapping the area of fixation. Juola et al. (1991) showed that observers could focus attention in areas defined by rings in foveal, near parafoveal, or peripheral areas, such that, for example, a cue to attend to the outer ring could result in a cost if the target were presented to the fovea. Others have suggested that attention is capable of quick movements from one focus to another or perhaps even of being divided among two or more focal areas.

Posner (1980) also distinguished between two types of control over spatial attention, a view anticipated by James (1890). The type that Posner originally investigated was covert orientation in response to the presentation of a central cue. In this case, the cue functions as an instruction to move attention to a particular location in the visual field. Posner called this type of attention endogenous (or voluntary, controlled) attention, to be contrasted with exogenous attention due to an involuntary, automatic orienting to a novel stimulus presented in the periphery. Jonides (1981) compared the two types of attentional controls directly in which a target letter's location was cued either by a central arrow indicating (with variable validity) the location of a target, or a peripheral arrow located near the peripheral target itself (on some proportion of the trials). Jonides found that peripheral cues attracted attention rapidly as well as independently of the cue's validity, whereas the less effective central cues resulted in slower allocations of attention that could be suppressed if the observers knew that the cues had low validity. He concluded along with Posner that the sudden onset of a peripheral stimulus is a powerful, automatic attractor of attention that is not easily ignored. Other properties of peripheral stimuli that increase their salience, such as flicker, motion, or contrasts in color and brightness can also attract attention in some cases, but not as powerfully as a sudden sound or an abrupt visual onset.

From these results of studies of attention, we can conclude that focal attention on a demanding task at hand is relatively immune to interruptions of mundane peripheral activities. However, if peripheral information is related to the focal task, it can result in positive results through a redundancy gain, or negative results through interference with the main task. Also, attention can almost always be directed toward peripheral stimuli if they are sufficiently salient in terms of their sudden onset or other unusual characteristics, or if they are related to the focal task.

3.4 Attention and Visual Search

One of attention's functions is undoubtedly to direct overt orientation, including movements of the eyes, to environmental points of interest. Such eye movements occur several times a second during most of our waking hours and are often involved in tasks such as reading, examining a scene, directing our movements while walking, cycling, or driving, and searching for an object. In visual search, we might be looking for some specific object, such as our car keys, on a desk littered with many other objects. How do we find what we are looking for, especially if the target of search is similar to many other objects in view? Treisman and colleagues (e.g., Treisman and Gelade 1980; Treisman and Gormican 1988) argued that object features are processed preattentively in parallel over the field of view, and attention serves to integrate these features into an object representation, usually one at a time. By this theory, targets that differ from the background by a single, salient feature can be found more or less automatically and will appear to "pop out" from the distractors. Alternatively, when the target shares features with some of the distractors, such that only a unique combination of features defines the target, focal attention must search through the display and integrate the features into object representations at each current focus to determine whether or not the desired target has been found. One of the defining sets of observations in support of the theory is that the search time required to find a target differing from the distractors by a single, salient feature is usually independent of the number of distractors (pop-out or parallel search), but a target differing by a unique conjunction of features that are present in other items results in a search that is linearly related to the number of distractor items (serial search).

Treisman's feature integration theory (FIT) successfully accounted for a large set of data in the visual search literature, but it failed in some cases. For instance, it was sometimes found that targets defined by unique feature conjunctions could be located very rapidly, whereas those defined by a single featural difference could take a long time to find, especially if the feature difference between targets and distractors was small. Treisman's feature integration theory has been contrasted with Duncan and Humphreys's (1989) attentional engagement theory (AET). FIT uses attention as a type of "glue" that solves the binding problem for integrating features into objects, whereas Duncan and Humphreys's AET maintained that an initial preattentive, parallel phase of perceptual segmentation could include descriptions of visual objects as structural units. Attention then serves to select some structured information for entry into visual short-term memory. Treisman's FIT assumes that spatial attention is a necessary condition for object recognition, whereas Humphreys and Duncan argue that visual elements can be bound together in an initial parallel phase without focal attention, and attention selects among the objects that result from the initial grouping.

Treisman's theory was improved upon by Wolfe and colleagues (Wolfe 1994; Wolfe et al. 1989) in what has been called guided search theory. The theory is similar to that of Treisman at the outset, in that individual features are detected and registered briefly in memory in terms of visual primitives, such as color, size, orientation, and motion. In guided search, however, the features receive extra activation to the extent that they are salient, e.g., that they differ from their immediate neighbors. In addition, besides the bottom-up activation from visual features that is proportional to their salience, top-down activation is added to them to the extent that they match the features in the object that is the target of search. Activation is then summed over bottom-up, salience-driven information and top-down, target-similarity information to produce an activation map over the visual field. Focal attention is directed to locations in order of their overall activation in the search for a target. This model reduces to special cases of Treisman's FIT for searches in which the target pops out and for those that require a detailed, serial search of all items until the target is found, i.e., if neither salience nor feature uniqueness homes in on the target. The design implications for these theories are clear: If something in the periphery must be attended to in order to perform a central task, it must be presented in a way that guarantees its contrast with other peripheral components of the scene, either by perceptual salience, by abrupt onset, or by similarity to focal information.

3.5 Attentional Distribution Over Time

Vigilance is the term used to describe prolonged attention to a single, specific task, such as watching a radar screen to follow air traffic patterns near a busy airport, or checking a series of road signs for an upcoming exit. Mackworth (1948) had observers monitor a clock-like display to look for small changes in the position of a marker that moved along its face like a second hand. He found that performance was very good at first, but after 20 or 30 min, performance fell off and cycled afterward between periods of alertness and distraction.

Subsequent research has shown that attention can be disrupted over much shorter periods of time due to changes in task demands. In an influential experiment, Raymond et al. (1992) designed a search task for target letters presented at a rapid rate to a single, central locus on a computer monitor, a procedure known as rapid, serial visual presentation (RSVP). For example, one target letter (T1) could be differentiated from the distractors by differing in color, and a second target (T2—defined as a specific letter, like "X," which is not always present) could follow T1 at various serial positions (lags). At rates of about 10 items per second (i.e., 100 ms per letter), T1 was almost always reported correctly, but T2 was often missed, especially at short lags after T1. Interestingly, both targets were often reported if the lag between them was 1 (i.e., if they occurred successively within 100 ms or so), a phenomenon known as lag 1 sparing. If the lag between T1 and T2 varied between about 2 and 5, T2 was often missed, although T2 report was more accurate at longer lags. The period lasting about 200–600 ms or so after T1 is presented, during which T2 processing is suppressed, has been called the attentional blink (AB).

Most theories of the AB assume that there are two stages of processing that occur during target search through the presentation of successive items (e.g., Chun and Potter 1995; Giesbrecht and Di Lollo 1998). In the initial stage, the RSVP stream is monitored for items that have the defining target feature (e.g., a white item among black ones or a letter among digits). When the target-defining feature is detected, an attentional gate is opened to pass the selected item to a more detailed processing stage in which the target is identified and consolidated into a reportable memory. During this second stage, attentional capacity for monitoring the stream for the second target is reduced, producing the AB. Lag 1 sparing sometimes occurs when the attentional gate is relatively sluggish with respect to the presentation rate, thereby allowing the target and a successive item both to receive detailed processing. The length of the AB effect is determined by many factors, such as the difficulty of processing T1, the similarity of defining features for T1 and T2, the item presentation rate, and whether the two targets are presented in the same RSVP stream, or if two or more RSVP streams are presented in close proximity (e.g., Peterson and Juola 2000).

Juola et al. (2004) found that target identification was worse if the two targets came from different categories (in their task, the targets were either white letters among black letters, or black digits among black letters, and all pairwise combinations were possible between T1 and T2). That is, a task-switching cost was incurred if T1 and T2 were different types of characters, and this performance decrement was largest at lag 1 and decreased asymptotically at later lags. Reconfiguration of the task set from detecting black digits to detecting white letters or vice versa entailed a cost of between 10 and 20 % at lag 1, which decreased to 5 % or less by lag 6 (see also Rogers and Monsell 1995). Chun and Potter (2001) asserted that the amount of lag 1 sparing is a sensitive index of task similarity between T1 and T2 (see also Enns et al. 2001; Potter et al. 1998; Visser et al. 1999).

There is evidence for significant costs if both category shifts and location shifts are required for the identification of two targets presented in the RSVP format. Furthermore, these two effects are apparently independent and influence the AB phenomenon in different ways. Switching the target category from digits to letters and vice versa entailed a significant cost on T2 report, at least at short lags, and this effect was as large whether T1 and T2 were presented in the same location or were horizontally displaced. The target category switch cost was also large when the participants knew that the switch would occur between T1 and T2 as when the switch occurred randomly on half the trials. Either the costs of preparing for different target categories outweigh the benefits of using such a strategy, or the time needed to reconfigure target selection criteria is too great to achieve a measurable benefit in the RSVP task (Nieuwenhuis and Monsell 2002). Since the task switch primarily involved encoding operations only (letters vs. digits), it apparently is due to difficulties in later visual processes involved in matching features to character representation in different categories, whereas target location shifts result in deficits at earlier visual processes primarily involved with signal-to-noise ratios in attended versus unattended areas of the display.

Design implications in the temporal domain are quite clear. Whenever the central task demands a high level of attention and/or cognitive resources, subsequent stimuli are likely to be missed. If the main task requires the identification of a well-known stimulus, attention can be reallocated in about 500 ms or less, but more resources-demanding tasks can result in significantly greater times in which important incoming information can be lost, e.g., when a text message is being read while driving.

3.6 Divided Attention and Attention Shifting

Trying to do two things at once, especially if they are complex tasks, can result in loss of efficiency relative to when they are performed alone. Walking and chewing gum at the same time is the classic example of multitasking that almost everyone can handle, but it is well known that talking on a mobile phone or texting while driving can have serious consequences (Redelmeier and Tibshirani 1997; Strayer and Drews 2007; Strayer et al. 2003). We seem to be designed primarily as single-channel processors for attention-demanding tasks, but attention can be switched from one task to another, often with its own task-switching costs. Alternatively, if the tasks are not completely demanding all of our attention, or if one or more of them can be performed automatically, multitasking is within the capability of most practiced people.

Multitasking involves tasks that are performed simultaneously (task sharing), or those that are performed sequentially with rapid changes from one task to the other (task switching). In principle, it is often difficult to determine whether people are truly sharing or switching between two tasks unless an experiment can be set up to force one or the other strategy. Response patterns can be observed when subjects are asked literally to do two things at once, such as to perform a visual discrimination task while at the same time listening for a tone that requires a different response. Posner et al. (1980) used two simultaneous tasks that were each performed quickly and accurately in isolation, namely deciding whether or not two successive letters had the same name (e.g., "A" and "a") and pressing a button whenever a tone was sounded. They found that tone detection times were just as rapid when they occurred between letter comparison trials as when they occurred during or shortly after the first letter was presented. However, when the second letter was presented, and subjects had to decide whether or not they matched in name, tone detection times were slowed.

Research has shown that when multitasking, people generally make more mistakes or perform their tasks more slowly, or both. Attention must be divided among all of the component tasks to perform each of them well, and even if performance appears to be normal on one or several of them, any increase in processing load can have disastrous consequences. For example, there has been little difference found between speaking on a hands-free cell phone and a handheld cell phone in so far as driving impairments are concerned (Strayer and Johnston 2001). Apparently, it is the strain on attentional systems that causes problems, rather than what the driver is doing with his or her hands. Telephone conversations are unlike personal conversations with a passenger in an automobile. Passengers are able to change the conversation based on the needs of the driver. If traffic congestion intensifies, a passenger might stop talking to allow the driver to navigate the increasingly difficult roadway; a conversation partner using a telephone would not be aware of the change in environment and might continue to engage in a stressful line of conversation unaware of any emergency. When the two simultaneous tasks use the same modality, such as listening to a radio station and writing a paper, it is much more difficult to concentrate on both because the tasks are likely to interfere with each other. The specific modality model was proposed by Navon and Gopher (1979), who theorized that interference would be greater if two simultaneous tasks demanded attention from the same processing resources, than if one were visual and the other auditory, for example. Resource theory also implies that as each complex task is automatized, performing that task requires less of the individual's limited-capacity attentional resources. In theory, performing an automatic task concurrently with some attention-demanding task could result in little or no multitasking costs.

Subsequent dual-task research has shown that attention-demanding tasks, especially those involving comparison and decision processes, seem to evoke a "psychological refractory period" (PRP) in which processing of one task is put off while another is being completed. Similarly, when two successive visual targets are briefly flashed, people may fail to detect the second target (attentional blink or AB). Although AB and PRP are typically studied in very different paradigms, research suggests that both might arise from the same serial stage during which stimuli gain access to consciousness and, as a result, can be arbitrarily routed to some other appropriate processor. In fact, peripheral perceptual and motor stages continue to operate in parallel, and only a central decision stage seems to impose a serial bottleneck (see Levy et al. 2006; Pashler 1994; Ruthruff and Pashler 2001; Sigman and Dehaene 2008). There are further problems with multitasking, since when the brain shifts attention from one activity to another, executive control processes in the prefrontal cortex, dorsal frontoparietal cortex, and striatum use oxygenated glucose, the same fuel they need to stay on task. Blood oxygen usage (BOLD) signals in left prefrontal and intraparietal sulcus regions have been observed to be higher in the early phase after the switch, while anterior cingulate, cuneus, precuneus, and temporal and more anterior frontal regions showed more activation later after the switch. These findings are compatible with the engagement of regions involved in the establishment and maintenance of attentional sets (Schultz and Lennert 2009). Repeated task switching can also result in increased anxiety, which raises levels of the stress hormone cortisol resulting in increased aggressive and impulsive behavior. The cognitive functions that are impaired after blockade of cortisol reabsorption in human subjects include selective attention, visuospatial memory, and mental flexibility (Otte et al. 2007). By contrast, once we engage the central executive mode to maintain task focus, the brain uses less energy than when multitasking (Levitin 2014).

3.7 Inattentional Blindness and Change Blindness

Inattentional blindness describes a common phenomenon in which a salient and apparently easily identifiable stimulus is neither detected nor remembered. For example, Mack and Rock (1998) described results from a difficult detection task, such as deciding which of two very similar lines crossing at the fixation point is longer. Unexpectedly, on one of the trials, a clearly visible stimulus was presented in one of the quadrants cut off by the lines. Not only was the object not identified in a later query, but subjects often did not report having seen it. In other cases, when it is impossible to attend to all the stimuli in a given scene, a temporary blindness effect can occur such that individuals fail to see objects or stimuli that are unexpected yet are quite salient.

The best-known studies of inattentional blindness (Neisser and Becklen 1975; Simons and Chabris 1999) involve situations in which subjects watch an engaging video with an unexpected event inserted. For example, a short video is shown in which two teams of people (wearing different colored T-shirts) pass a basketball around, and the subjects are told to count the number of successful passes made by one of the teams. In different versions of the video, someone walks through the scene carrying an umbrella, or wearing a gorilla suit. After watching the video, the subjects were asked if they had noticed anything out of the ordinary, and surprisingly, fully 50 % of the subjects failed to report seeing the gorilla (or the person with the umbrella). The failure to perceive the intrusive event is attributed to the failure to attend to it while engaged in the difficult task of counting the number of passes of the ball. If they are told to look for an anomaly, rather than count the passes, the unusual person is easily identified and the subjects are amazed that they could have missed it in the original task situation.

Mack and Rock (1998) concluded that no conscious perception can occur without attention, although it is possible that inattentional blindness reflects a problem with immediate memory rather than with perception. It is important to note that any memory failure is likely due to insufficient coding when the stimulus was present. The theory behind inattentional blindness suggests that attention is necessary for the conscious experience of objects and events, and the vast majority of information in our field of vision goes unnoticed. Mack and Rock note that most explanations for inattentional blindness reflect a basic failure of perceptual processes to be engaged by unattended stimuli.

A related phenomenon is called change blindness which is the failure to notice something different about two or more successive displays. Participants can be shown an image that is followed by another identical image but for a single change made in it. In a study by Rensink et al. (1997), a picture was presented followed by a blank screen or "masking" stimulus which was followed by the initial picture with a change. The masking stimulus mimicked a saccadic movement of the eyes which makes it more difficult to detect the change. Also, image changes without a blank interstimulus interval easily reveal the change due to apparent motion from one picture to the next where the change occurs. In the masking paradigm, an image and an altered image are switched back and forth with a blank screen in between them. Surprisingly, it usually takes subjects many seconds to identify the change, unless the change is a highly salient object that is likely to be fixated early in the sequence. Clearly, attention to a single feature or object is necessary for the change to be noticed. Minor changes that are not highly salient, even if they change the gist or important details of the scene, are unlikely to be noticed.

3.8 Attention and Vision in the Periphery

Attention has been shown to be labile in the sense that it can be directed away from the point of fixation. But what, if any, information can be processed from peripheral information without attention? Enns (2004) discusses the "grand illusion of complete perception" as one of the most common and pervasive of all visual illusions. Despite the fact that we can see fine detail only in the central two degrees or so of the visual field, we seem to form images of the world that encompass complete objects and events in rich detail. This illusion occurs because the mind is capable of extending visual details into three-dimensional objects that obey certain natural laws, as in the Gestalt principles of closure, symmetry, good continuation, figure–ground separation, and similarity. Further, outside of the laboratory, most of the world is unchanging between eye fixations, and it is easy to sample fine detail about anything in the visual scene simply by looking at it. Since the information is immediately available, it is as though we can see it all the time. Peripheral visual information serves as an "external memory" that can be accessed so easily, and it is as if it is in consciousness all the time (O'Regan 1994). Clark (2003) makes a similar analogy in the example of a response one might make to the question, "Do you know what time it is?" You could answer "yes" and make a quick turn of the wrist and glance at your watch to report the time. However, your answer is technically false, since you did not actually "know" the time when asked, but since the information is so quickly attainable, it is as good as known.

Still, the question remains what is actually seen and consciously processed in the periphery, particularly when there is some reason that it is not attended. Koch and Tsuchiya (2006) used the example of a dual-task paradigm in which a central task is computationally difficult (e.g., making a fine discrimination between line lengths or figure orientations) and another object is sometimes briefly flashed in the periphery. Although specific details of the peripheral stimulus are typically missed (e.g., Mack and Rock 1998), global information such as the gist of a scene or the gender of a face can often be processed and identified. Koch and Tsuchiya argued that consciousness sometimes can be achieved without top-down attention, as late-selection theorists have already claimed, but if the central task is highly attention-demanding, specific feature identification in the periphery is severely challenged. Other studies have shown that even unconsciously perceived stimuli can have long-lasting priming effects in neural responses, such that brain imaging and behavioral effects can be observed for some minutes after a non-perceived stimulus is presented (Gaillard et al. 2006).

Peripheral vision is worse than foveal vision and often much worse. Only about one million nerve fibers emerge from each eye, and rather than providing uniform vision, the eye trades off sparse sampling in the periphery for high-resolution foveal vision. This design continues into the cortex: The cortical magnification factor describes how resources are concentrated in central vision at the expense of the periphery. The representation in peripheral vision consists of summary statistics computed over local pooling regions (Balas et al. 2009; Levi 2008; Parkes et al. 2001; Pelli and Tillman 2008; Rosenholtz et al. 2012).

According to common wisdom in visual perception (e.g., Treisman and Gelade 1980), top-down selective attention is required in order to bind features into objects. In this view, even simple tasks, such as distinguishing a rotated T from a rotated L, require selective attention since they require feature binding. Selective attention, in turn, is conceived as involving volition, intention, and, at least implicitly, awareness. There is something non-intuitive about the notion that we might need so expensive a resource as conscious awareness in order to perform such a basic

52 J.F. Juola

(and frequently non-human) task as perception. In fact, all of us can carry out complex sensorimotor tasks, seemingly in the near absence of awareness or attention ("zombie behaviors," e.g., Blackmore 2004). More generally, the tight association between attention and awareness is problematic. Under normal viewing conditions, some processes of feature binding and perception might proceed largely independently of top-down selective attention, sufficient for gist recognition, pop-out target search, and navigation (Duncan and Humphreys 1989). Recent work suggests that there is a significant dissociation between some basic perceptual operations, such as feature binding, from both top-down attention and conscious awareness (Larson and Loschky 2009).

Some processes are presumably performed more acutely by peripheral than by foveal vision, such as general scene, or "gist" perception. Gist is defined as the overall sense or meaning of a scene, such as whether it is two- or three-dimensional, whether it is a structured or natural environment, and whether it is safe or threatening (e.g., van Montfort et al. 2005). Larson and Loschky (2009) compared accuracy of gist determination in an experiment in which only a central window or a peripheral view ("scotoma" condition) of a scene was briefly presented. They found that the peripheral view resulted in more accurate gist perception as the relative sizes of the central and peripheral portions were traded off until they were about equally effective for a window/scotoma of about 7.4° in diameter. That is, all of the fovea, near parafovea, and part of the peripheral field must be visible to generate the same amount of scene gist perception as the peripheral view alone, so that peripheral vision is all that is needed for recognizing the gist of a scene. Larson and Loschky concluded that the reason for a relative bias away from central vision in gist perception might be due to the fact that critical information for recognizing scene gist is processed at higher cortical areas, such as the parahippocampal place area, in which cortical magnification of central vision is largely absent. Design implications for these results include the generalization that certain meaningful and emotional states might be inferentially determined from peripheral stimuli, even if attention is dedicated to central processing.

3.9 Neurophysiological Studies of Attention

In the introduction, it was pointed out that attention is not a single process that can be identified with a specific brain mechanism. Rather, attention is distributed over a variety of sensory projection areas and deeper levels of analysis throughout the brain. Even when maintaining a single point of fixation, attention "…can affect perceptual performance and the activity of 'sensory' neurons throughout the visual cortex…[and]… attention actually affects tasks that were once considered pre-attentive, such as contrast discrimination, texture segmentation and acuity" (Carrasco 2011, p. 1485). It is likely that, rather than being modulated directly by attention, activity in the primary visual cortex (V1) is prepotentiated by feedback from higher-level, extrastriate areas (Hopf et al. 2009). Traditionally, early brain imaging studies identified different aspects of attention with widely divergent cortical processes. That is, alerting is presumably signaled by activity in the frontal and parietal lobes, primarily in the right hemisphere, orienting is associated with activity in the superior parietal lobes, the temporal–parietal junction, and the frontal eye fields, and executive control is maintained by the anterior cingulate and lateral prefrontal cortex. Certain automatic responses that influence attention, like orienting to a highly salient stimulus, are mediated subcortically, e.g., by the superior colliculi (Carrasco 2011; Knudsen 2007; Posner and Petersen 1990).

Attention also seems to have different cortical foci when it is directed to spatial locations and when it is directed to specific features or objects in the field of view, regardless of their location. Spatial attention has its effects earlier both in time and in levels of the visual system than feature-based attention, particularly when signaled by an external, peripheral cue. Exogenous cues can result in enhanced signal processing in the cued area and suppressed responses to noise in the areas surrounding the target that peak at about 100–120 ms after the cue. However, these responses are transient, in that without an endogenous reason to maintain attention (e.g., if the peripheral cue is known to have low validity), the attentional response dissipates and even results in a suppression of activity in the cued area, a phenomenon known as inhibition of return (Posner and Cohen 1984). Desimone and Duncan (1995) formulated the biased-competition hypothesis to describe attentional effects at many levels of the visual system. Within any level, neurons associated with the cued location are activated, whereas neurons with receptive fields in the adjacent areas are inhibited. Therefore, one of the primary roles of spatial attention is to increase the signal-to-noise ratio by enhancing signal processing while also excluding external noise in the target region and in effect, setting up spatial filters. Attention has also been shown to increase the amplitude of neural impulses and decrease their variability in the attended region, as well as to increase the synchronization of neural responses in successive layers of the visual system tuned to the target location (Fries et al. 2001). The result is that attended regions appear as if they are brighter and more salient than unattended areas.

Feature-based attention, on the other hand, is more likely to be based on endogenous cues related to basic visual primitives such as color, orientation, and direction of motion. Attending to the different feature dimensions can modulate activity in cortical areas specialized for processing those dimensions (Carrasco 2011). That is, attending to motion results in enhanced activity in the medial–temporal region (MT), color results in modulation in extrastriate areas V4 and V8, and orientation affects responses in V1 and V2. Bichot et al. (2005) showed that individual neurons in monkey cortex responded more strongly to an attended feature presented to their receptive fields than when the same feature was shown but not attended. Similarly, aftereffects resulting from prolonged exposure to specific colors, orientations, and motion directions are stronger when the relevant features are attended than when they are viewed but not attended. Furthermore, these changes in feature-based responses are simultaneously deployed throughout the visual field regardless of any specificity of location-based attention. Feature-based attention "…has the remarkable property that its effects are not constrained to the locations of the stimuli that are voluntarily attended; they spread across space" (Carrasco 2011, p. 1510). Neuronal modulations have even been observed in cells responding to spatial locations where no stimuli are present (McManis et al. 2007; Serences and Yantis 2007). Even when observers are directed to attend to one or the other visual hemifield, brain activity to items presented to the unattended field shows larger responses if they match the feature attended on the other side. Further, the motion aftereffect can be found in non-adapted areas of the visual field (Arman et al. 2006), indicating widespread selection for relevant visual features.

Regardless of whether attention is deployed in response to a salient visual object or event in the periphery, or whether it is directed to relevant visual features, there are at least two neural mechanisms hypothesized for attentional effects. One is gain modulation, or an increase in activity for neurons with receptive fields in the attended area or those that select for the relevant feature. The other is changes in the tuning curve, which can adjust either or both of the main aspects of the neuron's sensitivity function, i.e., its mean (or central tendency) or its variance (Carrasco 2011; Wolfe et al. 2012). It should be noted that these two hypotheses are not mutually exclusive, nor are they inextricably linked with a specific means of attentional control. However, the literature seems to converge on the idea that gain modulation is the major mechanism for spatial selection, in that target areas receive enhanced neural encoding activity, to the detriment of adjacent areas, whereas both gain and tuning modulations seem to occur for feature-based attention. Some studies have shown additive effects of spatial and feature-based cues, indicating that their effects might be independent (e.g., Hayden and Gallant 2009). These results affirm the main assertion held by modern theories of attention; i.e., it is not a unitary construct that can be identified with a simple underlying brain mechanism. Further, attentional effects can be found both far and wide in the visual field as well as in its various cortical representations.

The psychological refractory period refers to the fact that humans typically cannot perform two attention-demanding tasks at once. Behavioral experiments have led to the proposal that, in fact, peripheral perceptual and motor stages continue to operate in parallel and that only a central decision stage imposes a serial bottleneck. Sensory areas track the objective time of stimulus presentation, a bilateral parietal–prefrontal network correlates with the PRP delay, and an extended bilateral network that includes bilateral posterior–parietal cortex, premotor cortex, supplementary motor areas, the anterior part of the insula, and the cerebellum are shared by both tasks during dual-task performance. The results provide physiological evidence for the coexistence of serial and parallel processes within a cognitive task (Sigman and Dehaene 2008). The design implications for peripheral and dual-task processing imply that features relevant to the main task might alert observers to information in widely disparate parts of the visual field, whereas location-specific information, such as abrupt onsets, will attract attention to only a specific location. Either of these attractive elements of the periphery will be modulated by the amount of attention available during main task performance, as again, cognitively demanding processes such as decision-making and response selection will invariably put off or eliminate our abilities to attend to peripheral information.

3.10   Attention and Ubiquitous Computing

Weiser (1991) described the coming-of-age in which technology and computers will become integrated into all aspects of our everyday lives. Clark (2003) expanded this idea to include the possibility that wearable and implanted devices will become part of us, in a similar way that tools and technology have been used in the past to extend our abilities without much thought about their operation. In other words, technology should be transparent with use, such that a seamless interface exists between the user of some device and the task that the device accomplishes, without any attention being diverted to the device itself. A simple example would be the use of a pen to write a note, when the writer is focused solely on the content of the written message. However, if the pen produces some blobs of ink, attention must be diverted to how to hold the pen to avoid making a mess, and its transparency is lost.

The user's attention to technology should reside mainly in the periphery so that the technology and the information it provides can easily shift between the periphery and the center of attention when needed. The technology should be designed to increase the accessibility of useful peripheral information. This affords a pleasant user experience by not overburdening the user with information. Ideally, the technology relays a sense of familiarity to the user and allows awareness of the user's spatial and temporal context in the task environment.

Today, we are faced with the very real possibility that virtually everything we do will be expressed through electronic and digital media. Rather than necessarily improving our productivity, safety, efficiency, and satisfaction, technology can lead to problems to which our species has not yet adapted, such as information overload, disembodiment, uncontrollability, intrusion, and loss of privacy. In addition, new technology threatens to exacerbate existing social problems of inequality, deceit, degradation, alienation, and narrowing of experiences (Clark 2003). What do we make of a technological revolution that has given us a greater number of mobile phones than toilets worldwide?

Technology has opened a Pandora's box of information begging for our attention. We are confronted with facts, pseudo-facts, and rumor, all posing as information. Many "news" sources blend facts, commentary, and fiction in ways indiscernible even to expert viewers. Just as sorting out real information from chaff has become more difficult, there seem to be more demands on our time. Thirty years ago, travel agents made our reservations, and professional typists helped with correspondence. Now, we perform most of these activities ourselves. Our smartphones have become appliances that include a dictionary, calculator, Web browser, e-mail, Game Boy, appointment calendar, voice recorder, guitar tuner, photo gallery, video recorder, weather forecaster, GPS, texter, tweeter, Facebook updater, and flashlight. They can even start our cars and turn household appliances on and off. We use them everywhere, all the time, part of a twenty-first-century mania for cramming all we can do into every single spare moment of time (Levitin 2014).

Remember when people used to send written letters and cards to each other? The very act of writing each note or letter took many steps spread out over time, and we did not engage in these activities unless we had something important to say. Because such correspondence took several days to arrive, there was no expectation that we would get an immediate response, as the mail could sit on a desk until someone was ready to deal with it. Now, e-mail arrives continuously, and most e-mails demand some sort of action. The ease of sending e-mails has led to a change in manners, a tendency for people to be less polite about what is expected of others. Until recently, modes of communication signaled their relevance and importance. All of that has changed with e-mail, because it is used for everything, from the trivial, to the threatening, to items of serious consequence. We compulsively check our e-mail in part because we do not know what the purpose of the next message will be and whether it is something that has to be done now, later, or never.

Because it is limited in characters, texting discourages thoughtful discussion even more than e-mail, and its addictive problems are compounded by its hyper-immediacy. For many young people, texting has become the primary mode of communication, but it suffers from a new set of problems. Text messages magically appear on a phone and demand immediate attention since there is the social expectation that an unanswered text suggests an insult to the sender. This is a recipe for addiction: One receives a text, and that activates the attentional network. One responds and feels rewarded for having completed a task, yet nothing more than an empty "communication" might be the result (Levitin 2014).

The demands of the Internet and our mobile phones raise serious questions about whether they are ultimately work-savers or time-wasters. The new technology needs to be able to interact with people at multiple levels in order to gauge anyone's current level of attentional focus and task involvement. Just as environmental stimuli can interrupt focal attention due to their potential importance, salience, and relevance, external messages from ubiquitous technology should be sensitive to the user's attentional state, task goals, and even emotional status. Then, the appropriateness and means of peripheral information presentation can be determined, including the distinct possibility that interruptions should be suppressed for the time being. When an intelligent ubiquitous system senses that someone is in need of a break, or is in the act of beginning one, peripheral information systems could be modulated and their salience enhanced. At any time, relevant information could be channeled to the user when the system detects that now is the appropriate time to include it in the task at hand. In any case, ubiquitous computing will eventually enter a next-generation phase in which sensitivity to the user's level of task involvement, readiness for additional information, and even current emotional state trigger an appropriate and helpful response from the system.

3.11 Conclusions

Human visual and cognitive systems are remarkably adept at converting a series of neural impulses into a rich and largely veridical mental representation of the external world. Still, the infinite variety of physical information is greatly reduced by the capacities of our sensory systems, and the brain itself forces further information loss by its own limited bandwidth and processing power. Attention serves the crucial purpose of directing the brain's resources to that information most relevant to representing our environment, interpreting its meaning, and preparing for appropriate action. Attention is selective and guided both by spatial locations and by relevant featural information. It is controlled both by important and relevant external inputs and by our own goals and interpretations. Attention exists in a variety of forms and is represented in a myriad of cortical and subcortical processes. It has evolved to serve the dual purposes of allowing us to maintain focus on a central task while being ever ready to respond to relevant context, salient inputs, and important changes. The balance between its focus and its lability has evolved to make us capable masters of our environment.

In the future, designed environments will work best if they address as their starting points the human attentional and cognitive systems that have evolved for our survival in the natural world. We have the capability of using top-down control to focus on a task at hand, especially if it demands cognitive engagement. However, if the task is less demanding, or if we have practiced it sufficiently so that many of the subtasks are automatic, residual attention is free to engage in peripheral activities. Even when we are more or less fully engaged, attention is labile and can wander from the task often at our own peril. Further, peripheral thoughts and events can compete for attentional resources, especially if they are salient on their own or related to the main task. They can also result in physiological and behavioral changes in the absence of attention. Thus, peripheral inputs might either benefit or reduce performance on the main task, and technology needs to be designed to differentiate between these possibilities.

In human history, technology has had the means to shape our world to increase our safety, productivity, well-being, and entertainment. In the present day, rapid technological changes have the capability of shaping us in return to deal with unprecedented varieties of sensory stimulation. It is a valid question whether the traditional laboratory studies of human attention in controlled and artificial environments can produce the theories necessary to explain and predict human behavior in a technologically controlled world. Technology is able to imitate natural environments, as in virtual reality, as well as to create augmented and novel environments of unimaginable complexity. The designer has an entirely new set of challenges and opportunities in creating technology that extends human capabilities while at the same time respecting and compensating for human limitations.

References

Arman, A. C., Ciaramitaro, V. M., & Boynton, G. M. (2006). Effects of feature-based attention on the motion after effect at remote locations. *Vision Research, 46*, 2968–2976.

Balas, B., Nakano, L., & Rosenholtz, R. (2009). A summary-statistic representation in peripheral vision explains visual crowding. *Journal of Vision, 9*, 1–18.

Bichot, N. P., Rossi, A. F., & Desimone, R. (2005). Parallel and serial neural mechanisms for visual search in macaque area V4. *Science, 308*, 529–534.

Blackmore, S. (2004). *Consciousness: An introduction*. New York: Oxford University Press.

Bramly, S. (1991). *Discovering the life of Leonardo da Vinci*. New York: Harper Collins.

Broadbent, D. (1958). *Perception and communication*. London: Pergamon Press.

Carrasco, M. (2011). Visual attention: The past 25 years. *Vision Research, 51*, 1484–1525.

Chun, M. M., & Potter, M. C. (2001). The attentional blink and task-switching within and across modalities. In K. Shapiro (Ed.), *The limits of attention: Temporal constraints on human information processing*. Oxford: Oxford University Press.

Chun, M. M., & Potter, M. C. (1995). A two-stage model for multiple target detection in rapid serial visual presentation. *Journal of Experimental Psychology: Human Perception and Performance, 21*, 109–127.

Clark, A. (2003). *Natural-Born cyborgs*. Oxford, UK: Oxford University Press.

Desimone, R., & Duncan, J. (1995). Neural mechanisms of selective visual attention. *Annual Review of Neuroscience, 18*, 193–222.

Deutsch, J. A., & Deutsch, D. (1963). Attention: Some theoretical considerations. *Psychological Review, 70*, 80–90.

Duncan, J., & Humphreys, D. W. (1989). Visual search and stimulus similarity. *Psychological Review, 96*, 433–458.

Enns, J. T. (2004). *The thinking eye, the seeing brain*. New York: W.W. Norton.

Enns, J. T., Austen, E. L., Di Lollo, V., Rauschenberger, R., & Yantis, S. (2001). New objects dominate luminance transients in attentional priority setting. *Journal of Experimental Psychology: Human Perception and Performance, 27*, 1287–1302.

Fries, P., Reynolds, J. H., Rovie, A. E., & Desimone, R. (2001). Modulation of oscillatory neural synchronization by selective visual attention. *Science, 291*, 1560–1563.

Gaillard, R., Del Cul, A., Naccache, L., Vinvkier, F., Cohen, L., & Dehaene, S. (2006). Nonconscious semantic processing of emotional words modulates conscious access. *Proceedings of the National Academy of Sciences, USA*, April 2006.

Giesbrecht, B., & Di Lollo, V. (1998). Beyond the attentional blink: Visual masking by object substitution. *Journal of Experimental Psychology: Human Perception and Performance, 24*, 1454–1456.

Hayden, B. Y., & Gallant, J. L. (2009). Time course of attention reveals different mechanisms for spatial and feature-based attention in area V4. *Neuron, 47*, 637–643.

Hopf, J. M., Heinze, H. J., Schoenfeld, M. A., & Hillyard, S. A. (2009). Spatio-temporal analysis of visual attention. In M. S. Gazzaniga (Ed.), *The cognitive neurosciences* (Vol. 4). Cambridge, MA: MIT Press.

James, W. (1890). *The principles of psychology* (Vol. 1). New York: Henry Holt.

Jonides, J. (1981). Voluntary versus automatic control over the mind's eye movement. In J. B. Long & A. D. Baddely (Eds.), *Attention and performance IX*. Hillsdale, NJ: Erlbaum.

Juola, J. F., Botella, J., & Palacios, A. (2004). Task and location switching effects on visual attention. *Perception and Psychophysics, 66*, 1303–1317.

Juola, J. F., Bouwhuis, D. G., Cooper, E. E., & Warner, C. B. (1991). Control of attention around the fovea. *Journal of Experimental Psychology: Human Perception and Performance, 17*, 125–141.

Koch, C., & Tsuchiya, N. (2006). Attention and consciousness: Two distinct brain processes. *Trends in Cognitive Science, 11*, 17–22.

Knudsen, E. I. (2007). Fundamental components of attention. *Annual Review of Neuroscience, 30*, 57–78.

Larson, A. M., & Loschky, L. C. (2009). The contributions of central versus peripheral vision to scene gist recognition. *Journal of Vision, 2009*(9), 1–16.

Lavie, N. (1995). Perceptual load as a necessary condition for selective attention. *Journal of Experimental Psychology: Human Perception and Performance, 21*, 451–468.

Lavie, N. (2001). Capacity limits in selective attention: Behavioral evidence and implications for neural activity. In J. Braun, C. Koch, & J. Davis (Eds.), *Visual attention and cortical circuits.* Cambridge, MA: MIT Press.

Levi, D. M. (2008). Crowding—An essential bottleneck for object recognition: A mini-review. *Vision Research, 48,* 635–654.

Levitin, D. J. (2014). *The organized mind: Thinking straight in the age of information overload.* New York: Viking.

Levy, J., Pashler, H., & Boer, E. (2006). Central interference in driving: Is there any stopping the psychological refractory period? *Psychological Science, 17,* 228–235.

Mack, A., & Rock, I. (1998). *Inattentional blindness.* Cambridge, MA: MIT Press.

Mackworth, N. H. (1948). The breakdown of vigilance during prolonged visual search. *Quarterly Journal of Experimental Psychology, 1,* 6–21.

McManis, S. A., Fehd, H. M., Emmanouil, T.-A., & Kastner, S. (2007). Mechanisms of feature- and space-based attention: Response modulation and baseline increases. *Journal of Neurophysiology, 98,* 2110–2121.

van Montfort, X. A. N. D. R. A., de Greef, H. P., & Bouwhuis, D. G. (2005). Method to detect a gist change. *Journal of Vision, 8,* 555.

Moray, N. (1959). Attention in dichotic listening: Affective cues and the influence of instructions. *Quarterly Journal of Experimental Psychology, 11,* 56–60.

Navon, D., & Gopher, D. (1979). On the economy of the human-processing system. *Psychological Review, 86,* 214–255.

Neisser, U. (1967). *Cognitive psychology.* New York: Appleton-Century-Crofts.

Neisser, U., & Becklen, R. (1975). Selective looking: Attending to visually specified events. *Cognitive Psychology, 7,* 480–494.

Nieuwenhuis, S., & Monsell, S. (2002). Residual costs in task switching: Testing the "failure to engage" hypothesis. *Psychonomic Bulletin & Review, 9,* 86–92.

Norman, D. A. (1968). Toward a theory of memory and attention. *Psychological Review, 75,* 522–536.

O'Regan, J. K. (1994). The world as an outside memory: No strong internal metric means no problem of visual acuity. *Behavioral and Brain Sciences, 17,* 270–271.

Otte, C., Moritz, S., Yassouridis, A., Koop, M., Madrischewski, M., Wiedemann, K., & Kellner, M. (2007). Blockade of the mineralocorticoid receptor in healthy men: Effects on experimentally induced panic symptoms, stress hormones, and cognition. *Neuropsychopharmacology, 32,* 232–238.

Parkes, L., Lund, J., Angelucci, A., Solomon, J. A., & Morgan, M. (2001). Compulsory averaging of crowded orientation signals in human vision. *Nature Neuroscience, 4,* 739–744.

Pashler, H. (1994). Dual-task interference in simple tasks: Data and theory. *Psychological Bulletin, 116,* 220–244.

Pelli, D. G., & Tillman, K. A. (2008). The uncrowded window of object recognition. *Nature Neuroscience, 11,* 1129–1135.

Peterson, M. S., & Juola, J. F. (2000). Evidence for distinct attentional bottlenecks in attention switching and attentional blink tasks. *Journal of General Psychology, 127,* 6–26.

Posner, M. I. (1976). *Chronometric explorations of mind.* Hillsdale, N.J: Lawrence Erlbaum Associates.

Posner, M. I. (1980). Orienting of attention. *Quarterly Journal of Experimental Psychology, 32,* 3–25.

Posner, M. I., & Cohen, Y. P. C. (1984). Components of visual orienting. In H. Bouma & D. Bouwhuis (Eds.), *Attention and performance X.* London: Erlbaum.

Posner, M. I., & Petersen, S. E. (1990). The attention system of the human brain. *Annual Review of Neuroscience, 13,* 25–42.

Posner, M. I., Snyder, C. R., & Davidson, B. J. (1980). Attention and the detection of signals. *Journal of Experimental Psychology: General, 109,* 160–174.

Potter, M. C., Chun, M. M., Banks, B. S., & Muckenhoupt, M. (1998). Two attentional deficits in serial target search: The visual attentional blink and an amodal task-switch deficit. *Journal of Experimental Psychology. Learning, Memory, and Cognition, 24*, 979–992.

Raymond, J. E., Shapiro, K. L., & Arnell, K. M. (1992). Temporary suppression of visual processing in an RSVP task: An attentional blink? *Journal of Experimental Psychology. Human Perception and Performance, 18*, 849–860.

Redelmeier, D. A., & Tibshirani, R. J. (1997). Association between cellular-telephone calls and motor vehicle collisions. *New England Journal of Medicine, 336*, 453–458.

Rees, G., Frith, C. D., & Lavie, N. (1997). Modulating irrelevant motion perception by varying attentional load in an unrelated task. *Science, 278*, 1616–1619.

Rensink, R. A., O'Regan, J. K., & Clarke, J. J. (1997). To see or not to see: The need for attention to perceive changes in scenes. *Psychological Science, 8*, 368–373.

Rogers, R., & Monsell, S. (1995). The costs of a predictable switch between simple cognitive tasks. *Journal of Experimental Psychology: General, 124*, 207–231.

Rosenholtz, R., Huang, J., & Ehinger, K. A. (2012). Rethinking the role of top-down attention in vision: Effects attributable to a lossy representation in peripheral vision. *Frontiers in Psychology*, 06 February.

Ruthruff, E., & Pashler, H. E. (2001). Perceptual and central interference in dual-task performance. In K. Shapiro (Ed.), *Temporal constraints on human information processing*. Oxford, UK: Oxford University Press.

Schneider, W., & Shiffrin, R. M. (1977). Controlled and automatic human information processing: I. Detection, search, and attention. *Psychological Review, 84*, 1–66.

Schultz, J., & Lennert, T. (2009). BOLD signal in intraparietal sulcus covaries with magnitude of implicitly driven attention shifts. *Neuroimage, 45*, 1314–1328.

Serences, J. T., & Yantis, S. (2007). Spatially selective representations of voluntary and stimulus-driven attentional priority in human occipital, parietal, and frontal cortex. *Cerebral Cortex, 17*, 282–293.

Shiffrin, R. M., & Schneider, W. (1997). Controlled and automatic processing: II. Perceptual learning, automatic attending, and a general theory. *Psychological Review, 84*, 127–190.

Sigman, M., & Dehaene, S. (2008). Brain mechanisms of serial and parallel processing during dual-task performance. *The Journal of Neuroscience, 28*, 7595–7598.

Simons, D. J., & Chabris, C. F. (1999). Gorillas in our midst: Sustained inattentional blindness for dynamic events. *Perception, 28*, 1059–1074.

Strayer, D. L., & Drews, F. A. (2007). Multitasking in the automobile. In A. F. Kramer, D. A. Wiegmann, & A. Kirlik (Eds.), *Attention: From theory to practice*. New York: Oxford University Press.

Strayer, D. L., Drews, F. A., & Johnston, W. A. (2003). Cell phone-induced failures on visual attention during simulated driving. *Journal of Experimental Psychology: Applied, 9*, 23–32.

Strayer, D. L., & Johnston, W. A. (2001). Driven to distraction: Dual-task studies of simulated driving and conversing on a cellular telephone. *Psychological Science, 12*, 462–466.

Treisman, A. M. (1960). Contextual cues in selective listening. *Quarterly Journal of Experimental Psychology, 12*, 242–248.

Treisman, A. M. (1964). Monitoring and storage of irrelevant messages in selective attention. *Journal of Verbal Learning and Verbal Behavior, 3*, 449–459.

Treisman, A. M., & Gelade, G. (1980). A feature integration theory of attention. *Cognitive Psychology, 12*, 97–136.

Treisman, A. M., & Gormican, S. (1988). Feature analysis in early vision: Evidence from search asymmetries. *Psychological Review, 95*, 15–48.

Visser, T. A. W., Bischof, W. F., & Di Lollo, V. (1999). Attentional switching in spatial and non-spatial domains: Evidence from the attentional blink. *Psychological Bulletin, 125*, 458–469.

Weiser, M. (1991). The computer for the twenty-first century. *Scientific American*, pp. 94–10, September.

Wolfe, J. M. (1994). Guided search 2.0: A revised model of visual search. *Psychonomic Bulletin & Review, 1,* 202–238.

Wolfe, J. M., Cave, K., & Franzel, S. L. (1989). Guided search: An alternative to the feature integration model for visual search. *Journal of Experimental Psychology: Human Perception and Performance, 15,* 419–433.

Wolfe, J. M., Kluender, K. R., Levi, D. M., et al. (2012). *Sensation and perception* (3rd ed.). Sunderland, MA: Sinauer Associates.

Part II
Peripheral Interaction Styles

Chapter 4
Peripheral Tangible Interaction

Darren Edge and Alan F. Blackwell

Abstract Much of our everyday interaction in the physical world is peripheral—many of the objects that reside on the periphery of our *awareness* also require or allow actions in the periphery of our *attention*, as we briefly touch, handle, move, or avoid them. When these objects are digitally augmented, computational operations extend beyond dedicated display screens and leverage our capacity for occasional and low-attention interactions in the physical world. The research presented in this chapter analyzes this phenomenon of peripheral tangible interaction. Understanding the use qualities of the resulting tangible notations is critical to the design of interfaces aiming to facilitate peripheral interaction. We discuss when and how to design for peripheral tangible interaction based on systematic analyses of user activities and of system qualities. We illustrate both through a case study: the design of ShuffleBoard, a tangible interface for desk work in an office context, in which interactive surfaces and digitally augmented physical tokens support interaction with significant tasks, documents, and people, alongside and concurrently with focal workstation tasks.

Keywords Peripheral interaction · Tangible interaction · Analytic design · Cognitive dimensions · Office work

4.1 Introduction

Much of our everyday interaction in the physical world is peripheral—many of the objects that reside on the periphery of our *awareness* also require or allow actions in the periphery of our *attention*, as we briefly touch, handle, move, or avoid them.

D. Edge (✉)
Microsoft Research Asia, Beijing, People's Republic of China
e-mail: Darren.Edge@microsoft.com

A.F. Blackwell
University of Cambridge, Cambridge, UK
e-mail: Alan.Blackwell@cam.ac.uk

© Springer International Publishing Switzerland 2016
S. Bakker et al. (eds.), *Peripheral Interaction*,
Human–Computer Interaction Series, DOI 10.1007/978-3-319-29523-7_4

When these objects are augmented to represent digital information, computation extends beyond attention-grabbing display screens, supporting occasional, and low-attention interactions in the physical world. We call this *peripheral tangible interaction*.

In this chapter, we discuss when and how to design for peripheral tangible interaction based on systematic analysis of user activities and system qualities. We illustrate both forms of analysis through a case study: the design of ShuffleBoard, a tangible interface for desk work in an office context. ShuffleBoard is not intended to be the primary focus of the user's attention, but is designed to be used alongside a conventional workstation.

Tangible interfaces have more conventionally been categorized as either "graspable media" on the one hand—located in the foreground of activity and at the focus of users' attention—or "ambient media" on the other, existing in the background of activity and at the periphery of users' attention (Ishii and Ullmer 1997). Both types of system draw on the agenda of "calm technology" that "engages both the center and periphery of our attention, and in fact moves back and forth between the two" (Weiser and Brown 1995). However, these two categories also reified the center and periphery of attention in fundamentally distinct media forms. In the development of ShuffleBoard, we needed a hybrid concept to describe the periodic, tangible interaction with peripheral, ambient representations—interaction that neither fully nor continuously occupies the center of the user's attention, nor remains on the periphery. We termed this "peripheral interaction" (Edge 2008), or "peripheral tangible interaction" (Edge and Blackwell 2009) to distinguish it from other, non-tangible user experiences.

Unlike transient input modalities such as gesture and speech, the persistence of tangible objects allows them to provide a notation representing system state as well as enabling control of underlying information. Tangible notations leverage both the material form of objects and their configuration in space. In terms of Norman's action cycle (Norman 1988), this unification of representation and control can help to bridge both the gulf of execution (since physical affordances can indicate the availability of digital actions) and the gulf of evaluation (since physical state can be tightly coupled to digital state). In other words, the use of tangibles has the potential to lower cognitive demands to an extent that might not be possible through non-tangible visual or audio interaction. To help designers fully exploit this potential, our goal is to provide guidance on both the identification of opportunities for peripheral tangible interaction and the design of tangible notations that encourage peripheral interaction in use.

In the remainder of this chapter, we first introduce our case study by describing the design of ShuffleBoard. We then describe several other peripheral interaction systems that will be used in design comparisons. We characterize peripheral interaction through a model of how different *workload profiles* can help or hinder its emergence. We then present an analytic design process for the design of tangible interfaces that have the specific goal of facilitating peripheral interaction, using the design of ShuffleBoard as a running example. Finally, we conclude with an outlook for peripheral tangible interaction, connecting the contemporary concept to a broad range of theories, technologies, and trends.

4.2 Design of a Tangible Interface for Peripheral Desk Work

The design of ShuffleBoard arose from an investigation into the potential for tangible interfaces to support desktop work in an office environment. Interviews with staff at a multinational technology company had uncovered a number of problems with existing work practices that could benefit from dedicated interaction support (see Edge 2008 for more).

A perceived problem associated with default email communication was that people no longer talked to one another as much—not only about particular issues, but general status. With only weekly project meetings, this had resulted in a general lack of awareness about the work status of other team members. Other problems related to the inaccuracy of time sheets; the inability to share information from physical note books, whiteboards, and sticky notes; and the inappropriateness of planning work in calendars that failed to reflect the informal reality of how work was carried out. In all cases, the problems appeared to stem from the interactional and attentional costs of creating and updating digital information structures *about* work, in parallel with actually *doing* it.

4.2.1 Interface Design

The core of the ShuffleBoard interface is a collection of poker-chip-sized *tokens,* laser cut from acrylic sheet, that represent items of common interest wit detailshin a work group: tasks, documents, and people (Fig. 4.1). Each token has a rotationally unique, circular pattern of holes. Interaction with these tokens takes place on a personal *interactive surface* located to one side of the user's keyboard, on the side opposite their mouse (i.e., near the non-dominant hand). We implemented this interactive surface using a tablet PC augmented with a webcam pointing down at the surface. The identity of each token is determined from the pattern of light from the screen shining through its identifying holes. When a token is added to the surface, the attributes of the corresponding digital object are rendered as a dynamic "halo" that follows any movement of that token around the surface. This visual approach offered a reasonably low-cost sensing solution at the time it was developed, although many alternatives are now available, including the use of capacitive sensing (Chan et al. 2012), optical sensing through glass fiber (Baudish et al. 2010), and magnetic-field sensing (Liang et al. 2014).

Fig. 4.1 Physical token design: (*left*) red task token with edge texture corresponding to the task owner; (*center*) blue document tokens with material attachments for identification; (*right*) green contact tokens with edge texture corresponding to other people in workgroup

A typical physical arrangement of tokens is shown in Fig. 4.2. Specific token attributes are selected by nudging the token in the direction of that attribute, in the position where it appears within the surrounding halo. Tokens support up to four controllable attributes corresponding to the four principal directions of the interactive surface, thus striking a balance between information content and ease of selection. The selected attribute can then be manipulated by turning or pressing a

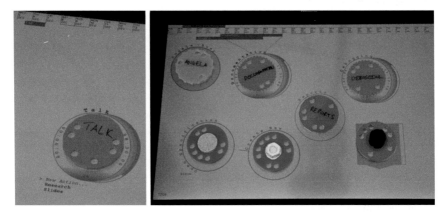

Fig. 4.2 Token halos on interactive surface. "Talk": a task token showing its name and connection to the time line above, estimated time remaining to the right, work time completed to the left, and action items below. "Documentation" and "Debugging": tasks overlapping in the time line. "Reports": a task token with its halo minimized. "Angela": a contact token showing a status of Busy and one task in the overlaid time line at the top of the screen. "Open Specification": a document token identified by a disk of sandpaper linking to a collaborative document called Specification. "Create New": an unbound document token. Unnamed red token with black Lego handle (*bottom right*): calendar tool

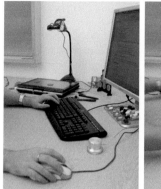

Fig. 4.3 Bimanual interaction design: (*left*) user working on the focal workstation PC, occasionally glancing at the interactive surface; (*center*) nudging a token in the direction of an attribute to change; (*right*) manipulating attribute with control knob

control knob (here, the Griffin Powermate) located on the other (dominant hand) side of the keyboard (Fig. 4.3).

The deliberate recruitment of both hands ensures that actions are intentional. Since we wanted to encourage casual touching without focused attention, it was important that unintentional actions should not require correction. An accidental knock to a token changes which attribute is selected, but does not change its value. This *bimanual safeguard* allows users to make rapid, intentional changes while also allowing tokens to be freely added, moved around, and removed from the interactive surface. Such use of bimanual interaction is supported by the prior experimental finding that given adequate visual feedback, the two hands can operate on distinct physical objects in disjoint physical spaces and still cooperate in the performance of a common task (Balakrishnan and Hinckley 1999).

All of the design elements introduced so far describe how we crafted each token as a *digital instrument*—a physical object that allows the creation, inspection, and modification of digital information (Edge 2008). Whereas conventional graphical interfaces require digital objects to either rest on the virtual desktop or be retrieved through transient menu and window structures, using tangible tokens as digital instruments allows such objects to be freely moved on, off, and around the surface. A screenshot of the ShuffleBoard surface displaying information "halos" around token positions is shown in Fig. 4.4.

The benefits of using tangible objects extend beyond their use as digital instruments. Our five-week field deployment of ShuffleBoard in a small technology company identified five further roles that tangible tokens can play in interface design. Tokens can act as a *knowledge handle*, helping users to remember, think about, and plan actions on its digital referent. Placing a token in a meaningful or memorable location, or arranging it with respect to other tokens, allows the token to act as a *spatial index* that leverages the structure of the physical environment. The physical form of a token allows it to act as a *material cue* for its visual detection and

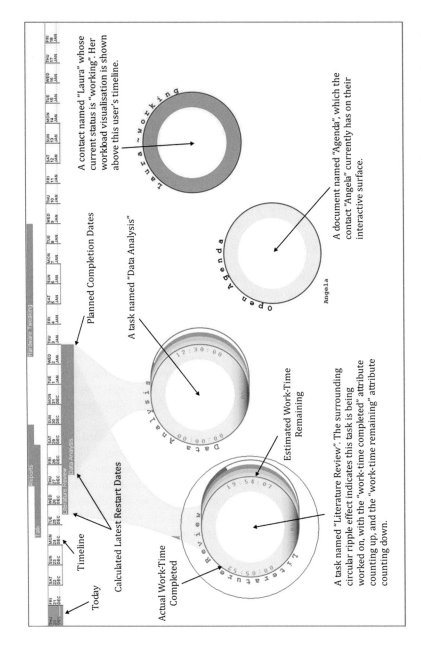

Fig. 4.4 Annotated screenshot of the tablet PC displaying information halos corresponding to tokens lying on its interactive surface. Specific visualisation elements are described in detail in the following sections

identification. In social settings, the persistence of a token allows it to act as a *conversation prop* supporting deictic references to digital objects. Tokens can also act as a *social currency*, signifying roles, rights, and responsibilities through possession and exchange. Each of these qualities brings potential advantages over graphical user interfaces. The following sections describe how we designed the ShuffleBoard token types to support such interactions.

4.2.2   Task Tokens

Task tokens are cut from red acrylic in sets of 20 per user, with each set having a distinctive edge texture associated with the owner. The number of task tokens belonging to each user is deliberately constrained such that they become a scarce resource; owners need to decide which tasks are most important, recycling tokens accordingly. The physical transfer of task tokens acts as a proxy for delegation of tasks. These interactions are facilitated by the ability to annotate the surface with dry-erase markers.

Task management and time management are closely interrelated, and the digital representation of tasks is coupled with the digital representation of time—a calendar "time line" that forms the uppermost border of the interactive surface (Fig. 4.4, top).

The conceptual model underlying the digital representation of tasks is based on three user-controllable attributes: *planned completion date, estimated work time remaining*, and *action items*. Each can be selected by nudging the token in that direction, allowing modification by the control knob. *Latest restart date* and *work time completed* are derived from these primary attributes. Each task attribute is now described in turn.

Planned completion date is represented by the rightmost arc extending from the top of the task halo to the corresponding date on the time line.

Estimated work time remaining is represented numerically on the *right* of the halo by a time value, and graphically by a series of five overlapping, semicircular scales, corresponding to durations up to 1, 4, 10, 40, and 100 h, respectively. Each scale is broken down into 12 increments, allowing time estimates to be specified at a granularity commensurate with their probable accuracy: to the closest 5, 15, 30, 90 min, and 5 h, respectively.

Latest restart date is represented by the leftmost arc extending from the top of the task halo to the corresponding date on the time line. It is derived from the planned completion date, the estimated work time remaining, the scheduled working hours per day over the course of the task, and the number of overlapping tasks (under the assumption of an equal division of labor among tasks overlapping in time).

Action items are represented as a list of actions below the task token, accompanied by a "New Action…" control. Rotating the knob moves a cursor through the list, while pressing the knob allows the user to enter a new item or edit the selected item on the focal PC.

Work time completed is represented on the left side of the task token halo, opposite the work time remaining. Nudging a task token then pressing the control knob toggles a timer that dynamically counts down from the estimated work time remaining. At most one token can be active at a time, and nudge-click on a different token will automatically transfer the timer to the new task. The currently active token is highlighted with an animated ring slowly pulsing around it.

4.2.3   Document Tokens

Document tokens are cut from blue acrylic and are plain disks, with no distinguishing edge textures. They are shared between all ShuffleBoard users, who can take them as desired from a single tray containing both document tokens and document-token materials. These materials are used for rapid recognition and identification of tokens in the physical environment and attach to tokens via circular recesses cut into the center of tokens' facing surfaces using Velcro.

Document tokens link to online collaborative editors, providing both identifiers and access control. Documents can be opened by placing the corresponding document token on an interactive surface and nudging it in any direction, followed by pressing the control knob. Placing an unlinked document token next to the token for an existing document activates a cloning mode in which clicking the control knob binds the new token to the existing document. There is no concept of document ownership, only of document-token possession. Anyone in possession of a document token may clone it and share access with anyone else.

Document tokens facilitate awareness among contacts by listing all users who are currently interacting with the document, or might do so. This lightweight form of social access control provides opportunities for ad hoc informal collaborations that are otherwise difficult to manage. It also creates opportunities for face-to-face interaction around the exchange of document tokens.

4.2.4   Contact Tokens

Contact tokens are cut from green acrylic and represent other members of the team or work group, existing primarily to support mutual awareness. Whereas document tokens provide a means of passively monitoring document interest, contact tokens allow the user to inspect and passively monitor the work status and work progress of other users. Each user has a contact token representing themselves, as well as tokens for each other ShuffleBoard user. The contact token representing a user has the same edge texture as the task tokens for that user.

When a contact token is placed on the interactive surface, the resulting digital "halo" displays the name and work status of the associated user. A user changes work status by nudging their own contact token upward and pressing the control knob.

When the contact token for another person is placed on the ShuffleBoard surface, the time line for that person is displayed above the user's own time line for comparison. This allows users to passively and peripherally monitor the work plans and progress of one another as they are updated in real time, which aims to address the reduced level of mutual awareness that can easily occur in the time between formal meetings.

4.2.5 Calendar Tool

Each user also has a special red token—a calendar tool—to interact with the time line. It can be used to adjust the expected number of available working hours, adjust the time line scale, and navigate the time line by scrolling with the control knob.

4.3 Related Work in Peripheral Interaction

In this section, we introduce systems and studies that have further demonstrated the potential for peripheral interaction since its initial conceptualization in the design and evaluation of the ShuffleBoard interface. In subsequent sections, we compare and contrast the associated system designs to the design of ShuffleBoard, focusing on their relative expression of use qualities that may help or hinder the emergence of peripheral interaction in practice. These comparisons also illustrate the generality of the presented use qualities themselves, through their application to systems targeting diverse user activities.

The CawClock (Bakker et al. 2012), NoteLet (Bakker et al. 2012), and FireFlies (Bakker et al. 2013) systems all aim to facilitate peripheral interaction in a primary school classroom context. The first system, CawClock, is an augmented analog clock visible to both teacher and children that allows partitioning of the clock face into discrete time sectors corresponding to the intended pacing of the current lesson. This partitioning is accomplished by arranging up to four tangible tokens, each with a different color and associated animal, around the perimeter of the clock face. As the minute hand passes through a particular sector, the system plays a soundscape based on the sound of the corresponding animal. The frequency of animal noises within a sector progressively increases until the minute hand leaves the sector. The tangible partitioning is sufficiently direct that the teacher can make adjustments through interaction on the periphery of her attention, while both teacher and children can benefit from peripheral aural awareness of lesson-time progression. The second system, NoteLet, combines a wearable wristband device and a camera located in the corner of the classroom. The teacher can make impromptu observations for later reference by either squeezing the wristband for a generic observation or by pressing a wristband button labeled with the name of a particular child being observed. The system responds by taking a time-stamped photograph that is also annotated with the child's name used to capture it (if any). The third system, FireFlies, is an open-ended tool for lightweight communication between teachers and children. It comprises a light object located on each child's desk, capable of illumination in each of four colors, a continuous animal-noise sound-scape based on the distribution of colors, and a wearable teacher tool that allows the teacher to assign colors to children's light objects (e.g., to indicate a general status like independent work time, specific feedback like "you are working well," or commands like "come to see me"). FireFlies adds the notion of a peripheral light display to the concepts of a peripheral soundscape (from CawClock) and a peripheral, wearable control tool (from NoteLet). It is similar to ShuffleBoard in the respect that multiple tangible representations distributed throughout environment are controlled through a single control tool located ready to hand.

Another desktop target for peripheral interaction is the control of background music with minimal interruption to the user's primary activity on a focal PC. In an 8-week in situ deployment study (Hausen et al. 2013), four different modalities for peripheral music control were evaluated: using dedicated media keys on a physical keyboard, using a graspable knob supporting turn and press actions, using tap and stroke gestures on a touchpad, and using hover and wave gestures in front of a freehand gesture sensor. Dominant-hand interaction with a graspable knob, as used in the ShuffleBoard interface, was found to offer the greatest support for interaction on the periphery. In another study on alternative forms of peripheral music control (Probset et al. 2014), an interactive chair that interprets directional tilt gestures was shown to offer a shorter transition time back to the primary task after executing the desired command, at the expense of greater execution time, than directional swipe gestures on a dedicated tablet or the use of arrow keys on the existing keyboard (both of which require a hand to leave the position established by the primary task). Participants also welcomed the "promotion" of music control through dedicated tangible means, which resulted in increased engagement with that activity. This aligns with one of the findings from the evaluation of ShuffleBoard that tangibility has symbolic value in terms of communicating what is most important to users in their spatial and social contexts (Edge 2008).

Finally, a similar pair of contrasting approaches has also been developed for peripheral interaction with social media status indicators. In Do Not Disturb (Olivera et al. 2011), the user orients a regular polyhedron (e.g., a 12-sided dodecahedron) such that the uppermost face depicts their current "mood" from a fixed set of alternatives. In StaTube (Hausen et al. 2012), the user rotates an illuminated cylindrical knob to set a color-coded presence status (online, away, or do not disturb). This knob sits on top of a stack of illuminated disks indicating the presence status of selected social media contacts, supporting peripheral awareness as well as peripheral control of presence in a similar manner to contact token status messages in ShuffleBoard.

4.4 Defining Peripheral Interaction

We have previously defined peripheral interaction from several perspectives. Our most general definition emphasized that peripheral interaction could arise through each of two possible channels: the digital objects of interaction (i.e., the information tasks achieved through action) being peripheral to the user's primary activity, and the physical objects of interaction (i.e., the tangible means of representation and control) being peripheral to the user's primary location and orientation in space.

> Peripheral interaction can be seen as any kind of interaction with objects – physical or digital – that do not occupy the typical center of the user's attention. (Edge 2008, p. 20)

Our more specific definition in the context of the ShuffleBoard case study built on both of these aspects and further highlighted the role of task switching over time:

> Peripheral interaction is about *episodic engagement* with tangibles, in which users perform *fast, frequent interactions* with physical objects on the periphery of their workspace, to create, inspect and update digital information which otherwise resides on the periphery of their attention. (Edge 2008, p. 20, emphasis added)

Expanding on these definitions, we observe that peripheral interaction can arise from related interactions that are sufficiently low-intensity or low-volume so as not to occupy the user's center of attention. To put it another way, interaction can remain peripheral as long as the *workload* imposed by the interaction does not consume so many resources that it becomes the de facto focus of attention.

An established method for the subjective assessment of workload is the NASA Task Load Index or NASA-TLX (Hart and Staveland 1988). Although developed for the analysis of task performance, the six factors it uses to differentiate different sources of workload—temporal demand, mental demand, physical demand, effort, performance, and frustration—all play a role in determining the extent to which interaction can be performed on the periphery of attention.

The most significant component of workload for peripheral interaction is *temporal demand*. The original definition refers to the perceived time pressure due to "the rate or pace at which the tasks or task elements occurred," which can also be quantified by "comparing the time required for a series of subtasks to the time available" (Hart and Staveland 1988). Translating this concept to the domain of peripheral interaction, we can say that the *peripheral work volume* with respect to the user's focus (which may vary, or be unoccupied) is the proportion of time spent preparing for, performing, and recovering from peripheral interactions. Beyond some threshold in that work volume, interaction will always cease to be peripheral, instead becoming the main focus. However, a sufficiently high *peripheral work intensity* of the peripheral interactions themselves, arising from the other five non-temporal components of workload, may also demand the user's attention to the extent that those interactions become focal. In the general case, however, it is the combined contributions of both these components—the *peripheral workload*—that determines the resources remaining for *focal work* and the potential for interaction

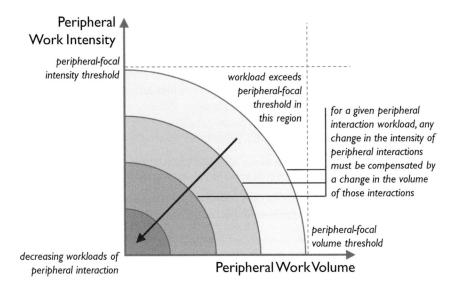

Fig. 4.5 How peripheral work intensity and peripheral work volume trade-off against one another for a given peripheral interaction workload. If interactions require too many resources or occupy too much time, they cease to be possible on the periphery of attention. *Curves* indicate that a balance between intensity and volume is more conducive to peripheral interaction than unbalanced combinations, since increases in either dimension have an additional, knock-on effect on the focus that can be achieve in the focal activity (Table 4.1)

on the periphery. These relationships are visualized in Fig. 4.5 and connected to the NASA-TLX components of workload in Table 4.1.

The value of this workload model is that it unifies the "attentional" and "temporal" definitions of peripheral interaction, in terms consistent with the attention investment framework for analysis of notation use (Blackwell 2002). During the design process, we can therefore describe how the abstract *use qualities* of an interface design combine to create a *workload profile* (expressed in terms of established NASA-TLX components) that determines the suitability of the interface for peripheral interaction. We give a detailed walkthrough of such a design process in the next section, using workload analysis to determine which use qualities best support peripheral interaction and illustrating each use quality with examples from the design of the ShuffleBoard interface and from other peripheral interaction systems.

4.5 Designing for Peripheral Tangible Interaction

We now present an analytic design process for the creation of interfaces aiming to facilitate peripheral tangible interaction. This process is a revised version of the process we have previously developed for the design of tangible interfaces in

Table 4.1 How NASA-TLX workload components affect peripheral interaction potential

Workload source	Workload component	Impact on peripheral interaction
Objective demands of the task	Temporal demand	Can increase *peripheral work volume* past the threshold at which interaction becomes focal and decrease the time available for *focal work*
	Mental demand	
	Physical demand	
Behavioral response to task	Effort	Can increase *peripheral work intensity* as well as induce and accumulate fatigue in ways that negatively impact *focal work* (equivalent to an increase in *peripheral work volume*)
	Performance (inverse scale)	
Psychological response to behavior	Frustration	Can increase *peripheral work intensity* and/or *peripheral work volume* if the user responds with greater attention and/or time in subsequent interactions, otherwise can negatively impact *focal work* by causing an ongoing distraction

general (Edge 2008; Edge and Blackwell 2009). It can be viewed as a rational, progressive refinement across three stages:

1. **Activity analysis** identifies user activities that could benefit from peripheral tangible interaction.
2. **Notation analysis** identifies the profile of use qualities that would facilitate or hinder peripheral tangible interaction with target activities.
3. **Interface design** generates candidate interface designs whose use qualities can be compared both to one another and to the target profile of use qualities.

The following sections elaborate on each of these stages, which together address the questions of *when* and *how* to design for peripheral tangible interaction.

4.5.1 Activity Analysis

Our design process begins with a consideration of which kinds of user activity might benefit from peripheral tangible interaction and the mechanisms by which it might help. We break this down by considering the potential for *Fluency* of peripheral interaction and how this might help lower the costs of activity switching, the different *Organizations* of activities and how they can create opportunities for peripheral interaction, the different *Rhythms* associated with episodes of peripheral interaction and how they might suit different purposes, and the different *Meanings* assigned to the objects of peripheral interaction and how they arise from different kinds of activity. We describe this as analyzing the potential *FORM* of peripheral interaction in support of a target activity. By answering a series of probing questions associated with each of these concerns, the designer can develop a deeper understanding of whether peripheral interaction could support a range of candidate activities in a given context or for a particular purpose, as well as how such interaction might be realized in the form of concrete interface designs.

4.5.1.1 The Fluency of Peripheral Interaction

Peripheral interaction can lead to a perception of economy compared with achieving the same goals through sequential actions that need complete attentional focus. In the neuroeconomic model of attention investment (Blackwell 2002), this corresponds to reduced *cost* of notational action. Three major contributing factors for fluent interaction are economy of orientation, economy of action, and economy of transition. Considering how each could support a target activity will provide an initial indication of the potential for peripheral interaction.

Economy of Orientation *How could peripheral tangible interaction help users to orient their attention toward potential activity goals that may otherwise become neglected or forgotten as a result of interruptions, distractions, and overload?* For example, the tokens in the ShuffleBoard interface provide persistent physical reminders (tasks to do, documents to work on, and people to follow) that can be freely distributed throughout the user's workspace for coarse, spatial orientation. A similar effect is achieved through the physical distribution of light objects in the FireFlies interface (Bakker et al. 2013). In general, increasing the economy of orientation can reduce the mental demand, temporal demand, and effort of recalling and comparing possible goals before taking actions toward the chosen goal.

Economy of Action *How could peripheral tangible interaction help users to achieve goals in fewer, simpler, or faster actions, in ways that leverage multiple physical objects, multiple degrees of freedom of physical objects, or multiple dimensions of the physical world?* For example, in the ShuffleBoard interface, coarsely nudging a token toward the location of an attribute in its digital information halo simultaneously selects both the corresponding digital object and attribute of that object. Accurate control of the selected attribute is then delegated to the single control knob, which is operated in parallel by the other hand.[1] A similar streamlining tactic is used in the NoteLet system (Bakker et al. 2012), in which pressing a button corresponding to a child's name simultaneously takes a photograph and annotates it with a time stamp and the name of the child. In general, increasing the economy of action can reduce the physical demand, temporal demand, and effort of executing related action sequences following an activity transition.

---

[1]The interactive surface and control knob are positioned such that the non-dominant hand leads with coarse "nudge" operations, setting a frame of reference for the dominant hand to follow with accurate "turn" operations. This *asymmetric bimanual division of labor* follows the kinematic chain model of human bimanual skill (Guard 1987) and allows interactions that are fast, accurate, and intentional.

Economy of Transition *How could peripheral tangible interaction help to minimize the costs of transitioning between the peripheral and focal activities, by digitally augmenting or reconfiguring the user, environment,[2] or activity?* For example, in the ShuffleBoard interface, the interaction elements can be acquired by pivoting slightly to one side.[3] Repeating this movement over time could help to develop the spatial and muscle memory that allows the transition to occur habitually and automatically, as occurs with mouse and keyboard. The interactive chair for peripheral music control (Probset et al. 2014) is motivated by a similar consideration of the user's relationship with the physical environment. In general, increasing the economy of transition can reduce the physical demand, temporal demand, and effort of repeatedly switching to and from the peripheral activity.

4.5.1.2 The Organization of Peripheral Interaction

Peripheral interaction can be configured in multiple ways with respect to the areas of separation and overlap between the focal and peripheral activities. Three prominent organizational forms are peripheral interaction with an embedded activity, a background activity, and a coupled activity. Considering how well a target activity could be supported by each of these forms will establish the focus against which interaction can be peripheral.

Embedded Activity *How could peripheral tangible interaction help the user to perform a neglected subactivity in parallel with its parent activity, in ways that allow timely processing of subactivity tasks resulting from the parent activity?* For example, the task tokens in the ShuffleBoard interface allow users to peripherally track the time spent on a task and update their estimate of the time remaining while actually working on that task on the focal workstation. Similarly, the FireFlies system (Bakker et al. 2013) is designed to support lightweight communication

---

[2]Reconfiguring the environment to create *entry points* for initiation and resumption of activities (Kirsh 2001) is known as *jigging* (Kirsh 1995). Strategies for arranging physical objects in the environment include arrangement by importance, function, frequency-of-use, and sequence-of-use (Sanders and McCormick 1987).

[3]Of the fundamental *kinematic pairs* (Reuleaux 1876) for the representation and control of 1D values—turning pairs (e.g., knob or joint), sliding pairs (e.g., slider or telescope), and twisting pairs (e.g., nut or bolt)—only the knob can be adapted as a stateless control of 1D values in an unlimited range (Edge and Blackwell 2006). Any other pair necessarily embodies a value (e.g., the angle of a joint or position of a slider). A knob is therefore superior for *temporal multiplexing* (Fitzmaurice 1996) in which the same control is bound to different representations over time. A mouse performs the same kind of control multiplexing in 2D, while the fixed key mappings of a keyboard and the fixed (until recycled) token mappings in the ShuffleBoard interface are examples of *spatial multiplexing* of control and representation, respectively.

about classwork while children are engaged in that work. In general, peripheral interaction with an embedded activity can reduce the mental demand of remembering to later switch to that activity and batch process the outstanding tasks, while also raising performance and lowering frustration compared with delayed serial processing.

Background Activity *How could peripheral tangible interaction help the user to perform a neglected activity in the background, independent of their current focus, in ways that encourage more frequent and habitual interactions?* For example, the contact tokens in the ShuffleBoard interface provide information about the status and activity of others. Developing the habit of adding contact tokens to the interactive surface and glancing at them periodically can help to increase mutual awareness within a team. StaTube (Hausen et al. 2012) operates on a similar principle. In general, prioritizing a background activity by creating the means for progress by peripheral interaction can reduce the mental demand of remembering to switch to that background activity (especially when there are no switching triggers in the user's focal activities) and increase the temporal demand of the background activity up to an acceptable level.

Coupled Activity *How could peripheral tangible interaction allow the coupling of activities as single hybrid activity, such that any time spent interacting for the purpose of one activity automatically makes progress in the other, coupled activity?* For example, in the ShuffleBoard interface, a side effect of using task tokens to manage the scheduling of individual tasks is that the user can immediately visualize the slack in their schedule after the overlap of tasks has been accounted for, i.e., time that can pass before the user must work full time on tasks in order to finish each task precisely on its deadline. Such "slack monitoring" is an important ongoing activity, but it no longer needs frequent user reflection after it has been offloaded to the "task management" interface. The CawClock (Bakker et al. 2012) similarly couples the activities of planning the pacing of a lesson and communicating that plan during the lesson itself. In general, coupling activities such that one or both may be performed on the periphery can reduce the temporal demand of scheduling independent activities and the mental demand of remembering to do so.

4.5.1.3   The Rhythm of Peripheral Interaction

The intervals between episodes of peripheral interaction can reflect the natural structure and flow of the target activity. Three significant rhythms are peripheral interactions at regular intervals, contracting intervals, and expanding intervals.

Regular Intervals *How could regular intervals between peripheral tangible interactions benefit user activities by helping to develop habits, maintain awareness, and support consistent progress?* For example, the interactive surface in the

ShuffleBoard interface provides a variety of information about tasks, documents, and people, with the goal of encouraging regular glances to maintain awareness of plans and progress even when the user is not in the process of actively updating token information. StaTube (Hausen et al. 2012) encourages similar regular glances to maintain awareness of contacts' presence status. In general, the more frequently the regular intervals occur, the greater the resulting temporal demand.

Contracting Intervals *How could contracting intervals between peripheral tangible interactions benefit user activities by helping users to track and manage their progress toward approaching times, dates, deadlines, or events?* For example, in the ShuffleBoard interface, interactions with task tokens are likely to increase in frequency as the task due date approaches. Our nonlinear scale for estimating the task work time remaining supports finer-grained estimates for shorter times remaining, encouraging more frequent interactions as tasks reach completion (e.g., to help others prepare for handover). Similarly, the density of animal noises in the CawClock soundscape (Bakker et al. 2012) increases as time runs out without a sector, encouraging more frequent time checks. In general, contracting intervals increase temporal demand for the target object, while across a collection of objects, the overall demand could remain relatively constant.

Expanding Intervals *How could expanding intervals between peripheral tangible interactions benefit user activities by following natural patterns of reinforcement, or reflecting a reduction in relevance over time?* For example, in the ShuffleBoard interface, a user may repeatedly interact with a document token as they author the document, but then interact with reduced frequency as the document stabilizes over time. On receiving a document token that links to an existing document, a user may also interact more frequently at the outset of the interaction when the content is unfamiliar, but then refer to it with reduced frequency over time as that content is reinforced through interaction. Similarly in FireFlies (Bakker et al. 2013), light–object interactions may follow expanding intervals with many early interactions as children encounter difficulties, followed by fewer and fewer interactions as children overcome those difficulties.

4.5.1.4 The Meaning of Peripheral Interaction

Peripheral interaction draws meaning from the activities it supports, and activities can demand support in a variety of areas. Three major sources of meaning are contributions to instrumental support, cognitive support, and communication support. Considering the extent to which each is required by the target activity will help to constrain the physical form and characteristics of the resulting notation.

Instrumental Support *How could tangibles facilitate peripheral interaction to create, inspect, or modify digital state in the context of the target activity?* For example, in ShuffleBoard, tokens provide privileged physical access to important digital tasks and documents, as well as dedicated physical control over their digital attributes. The tokens provide an instrumental advantage over conventional digital means of accessing and updating the same information. The interactive chair (Probset et al. 2014) provides a similar kind of privileged physical access to digital music control. In general, instrumental support is similar to economy of action in that it can reduce physical demand, temporal demand, and effort (although economy of action can apply to all interactions, not just instrumental ones).

Cognitive Support *How could tangibles facilitate peripheral interaction that creates and uses memory cues or other forms of external cognition*[4] *in the context of the target activity?* For example, in ShuffleBoard, tokens can be annotated, adorned with distinctive materials, and positioned in meaningful locations. Even though these physical actions have no direct effect on instrumental uses of tokens as ways of accessing and updating digital information, they make it easier for users to recall, think about, and make decisions about that information. The open-ended interpretation of light object colors in FireFlies (Bakker et al. 2013) provides a similar kind of support. In general, cognitive support is similar to economy of orientation in that it can reduce mental demand, temporal demand, and effort (although economy of orientation can also apply to instrumental actions).

Communication Support *How could tangibles facilitate peripheral interaction through their use as conversational props, communication channels, and representations of rights, responsibilities, and ownership?* For example, in ShuffleBoard, task tokens have edge textures representing the owner of that task. Provisionally assigning tasks to tokens in meetings allows people to take responsibility for completing different tasks. Receiving a task token from someone is a physical reminder to both complete the task and return the token, while receiving a document token represents the right to access the document. Finally, contact tokens provide a lightweight channel through which activity and status can be shared, like Do Not Disturb (Olivera et al. 2011). In general, communication support can improve the performance of teams meeting in the same space as well as the subsequent performance of individuals as a result of improved clarity and coordination.

4.5.2 Notation Analysis

The application of activity analysis results in a better understanding of how appropriate different forms of interface and interaction might be for supporting the activities of the target domain. The purpose of notation analysis—the next stage of

---

[4]The premise of *external cognition* is that cognition encompasses both internal representations "in the head" and external representations "in the world" (Scaife and Rogers 1996). It includes organizing physical objects to simplify choice, perception, or internal cognition, as well as using them to support epistemic actions that make mental computation easier, faster, or more reliable (Kirsh and Maglio 1994).

the analytic design process for peripheral interaction—is to describe the abstract use qualities of interfaces in a manner that allows them to be compared, both against one another and against the requirements of the context in which they would be deployed. By viewing interfaces as notations, or abstract structures of representation and control, we can analyze the usability and suitability of those interfaces independently of their surface appearance and application semantics.

The original and best-known form of such abstract analysis is the Cognitive Dimensions of Notations framework, originally created by Green (1989), and since revised and updated by Green and Petre (1996) and Blackwell and Green (2003). Cognitive Dimension analysis has four main premises:

1. Usability is not an absolute, but a function of the activities to be performed, the notation on or through which those activities are performed, and the environment in which the notation is manipulated.
2. Usability is not a unitary scale, but a multidimensional space. Each dimension can be given a distinctive label, as is the case with the Cognitive Dimensions, with the aim of providing a shared vocabulary for design discussion.
3. Dimensions of usability trade off against one another, so attempting to increase the usability of a notation along one set of dimensions is likely to have the side effect of decreasing the usability of the notation along a different set of dimensions.
4. Design is the process of selecting design maneuvers whose associated trade-offs move the notation toward the desired dimensional profile of the activities to be supported.

The core of the framework is a list of Cognitive Dimensions (CDs), which describe abstract usability properties of notations. They are around 15 in number, although new dimensions are frequently being proposed and the set of dimensions is essentially open. The dimensions are generally neither beneficial nor harmful properties in themselves: Their contribution to overall usability depends on the activities to be performed. We denote CDs with typesetting convention of Cognitive Dimension$_{<CD>}$. The application of CDs has been well documented in the CDs tutorial (Green and Blackwell 1998) and the CDs questionnaire (Blackwell and Green 2000). However, the analytic design of tangible interfaces is concerned not with purely digital notations, but with those that extend into the physical world. Rather than introducing new activities or dimensions to the CDs framework, we have previously identified particularly salient reinterpretations of the CDs that incorporated the characteristic features of physical media and the physical environment. We call these the Tangible Correlates of the Cognitive Dimensions (Edge and Blackwell 2006) and denote them as Tangible Correlate$_{<TC>}$.

Both the Cognitive Dimensions and Tangible Correlates describe use qualities of notations that affect their suitability for peripheral interaction. We now introduce each cognitive dimension and its tangible correlate or correlates (where they exist), along with typical trade-offs between dimensions and the anticipated effects of each dimension on the components of interaction workload. Note that the purpose of this section is simply to introduce and illustrate the use qualities in a general sense. In any particular application of this process, designers should re-evaluate the significance of each dimension according to the specific demands and characteristics of the target activity and its activity context.

Consistency$_{<CD>}$ Consistency describes the use quality that *similar semantics are expressed in similar syntactic forms.* For example, the digital tasks, documents, and contacts in ShuffleBoard share the same token form factor as they all represent objects of peripheral interaction, while the different colors of their respective tokens correspond to their different purposes. Higher levels of Consistency$_{<CD>}$ can accelerate learning by reducing the initial mental demand, but it has little long-term impact on peripheral interaction.

Provisionality$_{<CD>}$ Provisionality describes the use quality that *actions or marks can be reversed or removed.* For example, nudging tokens in ShuffleBoard makes provisional attribute selections with no lasting effects, unless they are followed by confirmatory manipulation actions with the independent control knob. Higher levels of Provisionality$_{<CD>}$ support more casual and informal interaction by reducing the effort associated with making changes, at the cost of increased Viscosity$_{<CD>}$ (since additional actions are required for confirmation or commitment). Lower levels have the potential to increase Premature Commitment$_{<CD>}$ and Error Proneness$_{<CD>}$.

Secondary Notation$_{<CD>}$ Secondary Notation describes the use quality that *information can be expressed outside the formal syntax.* For example, tokens in ShuffleBoard can be annotated with dry-erase ink or augmented with material attachments in ways that aid the user's identification of tokens beyond the sensing capabilities of the system. Tokens can also be placed in meaningful or opportune locations in the physical environment (e.g., on a paper document, or hanging on a pin-board), away from their formal use on the interactive surface. Higher levels of Secondary Notation support informal extensions of the primary notation that can provide cognitive support and reduce mental demand, at the cost of increased Viscosity$_{<CD>}$ (since additional actions are required to maintain the Secondary Notation when the primary notation is modified). Lower levels have the potential to exacerbate any problems with Role Expressiveness$_{<CD>}$.

Progressive Evaluation$_{<CD>}$ Progressive Evaluation describes the use quality that *progress-to-date can be checked at any time.* For example, the ShuffleBoard calendar shows the timings of scheduled tasks even when the associated task tokens are elsewhere. Higher levels of Progressive Evaluation$_{<CD>}$ can reduce the mental demand of estimating or calculating progress, at the cost of greater Diffuseness $_{<CD>}$ (since richer representations are necessary). Lower levels have the potential to increase Hard Mental Operations$_{<CD>}$ as a result of needing to mentally track progress-to-date.

Premature Commitment$_{<CD>}$ Premature Commitment describes the use quality that *the order of doing things is unnatural or overly constrained.* For example, the task tokens in ShuffleBoard support naming, time projection, due date setting, and action item setting in whichever order is most natural. Lower levels of Premature Commitment$_{<CD>}$ can reduce mental demand and frustration, at the cost of introducing Hidden Dependencies$_{<CD>}$ (since some attributes may depend on others in unanticipated ways). Higher levels have the potential to increase Viscosity$_{<CD>}$ and reduce Closeness of Mapping$_{<CD>}$.

Diffuseness$_{<CD>}$ $\rightarrow$ **Bulkiness$_{<TC>}$** Diffuseness describes the use quality that *many lower-level marks are required to express higher-level concepts.* Its tangible correlate, Bulkiness, denotes the quality that *physical objects or representations occupy space in three dimensions.* For example, the ShuffleBoard tokens and interactive surface have a small desktop footprint in two dimensions (low Bulkiness$_{<TC>}$) and the presence of one or two (in the case of document-token cloning) tokens on the surface is sufficient to enable all of the possible instrumental interactions with tokens (low Diffuseness$_{<CD>}$). In another example, the limited size of the lower forearm and the wrist-worn nature of the NoteLet device (Bakker et al. 2012) means that it suffers more from the increased Bulkiness$_{<TC>}$ of larger class sizes than the clip-on teacher tool of FireFlies (Bakker et al. 2013), which can freely grow with increasing child numbers. A minimum level of each dimension is required to reduce the effort associated with inspecting the current state. Higher levels have the potential to increase both Rigidity$_{<TC>}$ and Rootedness$_{<TC>}$.

Visibility$_{<CD>}$ $\rightarrow$ **Permanence$_{<TC>}$** Visibility describes the use quality that *components can be viewed easily.* Its tangible correlate, Permanence, denotes the quality that *physical representations and control mapping can be preserved for future use.* For example, the ShuffleBoard tokens can be freely arranged beyond the confines of the interactive surface (high Visibility$_{<CD>}$) and any one token can remain bound to its digital content for as long as desired (high representational Permanence$_{<TC>}$). However, the binding between control knob and token attribute is transient (low control Permanence$_{<TC>}$). A minimum level of each dimension is required to reduce the effort associated with recreating physical–digital mappings (if tangible objects are scarce) or physical representations of digital state (if physical space is scarce). Higher levels have the potential to increase the Bulkiness$_{<TC>}$ of the interface as a whole.

Error Proneness$_{<CD>}$ $\rightarrow$ **Shakiness$_{<TC>}$** Error Proneness describes the use quality that *the notation invites mistakes easily.* Its tangible correlate, Shakiness, denotes the quality that *physical representations are prone to accidental or irreversible damage.* For example, the physical size, texture, and weight of the ShuffleBoard tokens means that they are relatively stable on the interactive surface (low Shakiness$_{<TC>}$), while the lack of spatial syntax[5] for token positions or

---

[5]Ullmer and Ishii (2001) define a tangible interface as one in which the physical configuration of objects partially embodies the digital state of the system. Conventional structural forms are *interactive surfaces* (where objects move on planer surfaces), *constructive assemblies* (where objects connect to objects), and *token+constraint systems* (where objects move within the constraints of other objects or non-planar surfaces). Each structural form also supports one or more types of spatial syntax: *spatial* interpretation of absolute object positions, *relational* interpretation of relative object positions, and *constructive* interpretation of object connections. While the ShuffleBoard interface has the structural form of an interactive surface, it does not have a spatial syntax for reasons of Viscosity$_{<CD>}$ (explained later).

arrangements means that accidental movement of tokens has no effect other than to select token attributes (low Error Proneness$_{<CD>}$). In another example, the relative ease of accidentally rolling the status-setting polyhedra in Do Not Disturb (Olivera et al. 2011) results in greater Shakiness$_{<TC>}$ than the necessarily deliberate knob rotation in StaTube (Hausen et al. 2012). Lower levels of each dimension can reduce the frustration associated with dealing with errors and accidents at the potential cost of increased Viscosity$_{<CD>}$, increased Rigidity$_{<TC>}$, and reduced Structural Correspondence$_{<TC>}$.

Juxtaposition$_{<CD>}$ $\rightarrow$ Juxtamodality$_{<TC>}$ Juxtaposition describes the use quality that *components can be viewed and compared side by side*. Its tangible correlate, Juxtamodality, denotes the quality that *multiple interaction modalities are coordinated across different physical spaces, objects, or senses*. For example, in ShuffleBoard, the attribute halos of multiple tokens can be viewed side by side on the interactive surface (high Juxtaposition$_{<CD>}$), even while the value of the selected attribute is changing through eyes-free operation of the control knob in a separate physical space (high Juxtamodality$_{<TC>}$ of the visual–tactile kind). In another example, the correspondence between the distribution of light objects and the resulting soundscape in FireFlies (Bakker et al. 2013) results in high Juxtamodality$_{<TC>}$ of the audio–visual kind. The ideal level of Juxtaposition$_{<CD>}$ is dependent on the target activity, and higher levels could raise the Bulkiness$_{<TC>}$ of the interface (e.g., by requiring an increase in the size of the interactive surface). A minimum level of Juxtamodality$_{<TC>}$ can help to reduce Shakiness$_{<TC>}$ at the risk of increasing Hidden Augmentations$_{<TC>}$ and Unwieldy Operations$_{<TC>}$. The additional coordination required by higher levels has the potential to increase both mental and physical demand.

Viscosity$_{<CD>}$ $\rightarrow$ Rigidity$_{<TC>}$, Rootedness$_{<TC>}$ Viscosity describes the use quality that *many lower-level actions are required to satisfy higher-level goals*. It has two distinct tangible correlates for different scales of interaction. Rigidity denotes the quality that *manipulation of objects or their arrangement is resisted*. Rootedness denotes the quality that *movement of objects or their arrangement is resisted*. For example, in the ShuffleBoard interface, the bimanual nudge-turn control scheme supports rapid attribute selection and manipulation (low Viscosity$_{<CD>}$) with just the right amount of token sliding friction and knob rotational friction and inertia to ensure rapid yet accurate control (moderately low Rigidity$_{<TC>}$). Tokens can be independently and freely moved between the interactive surface and physical desktop, as well as between the interactive surfaces of different contacts, e.g., for task delegation and document sharing (low Rootedness$_{<TC>}$). In contrast, the interactive surfaces themselves are effectively confined to a single physical desktop location (high Rootedness$_{<TC>}$). A minimum level of each dimension can help to reduce Shakiness$_{<TC>}$, but higher levels are especially detrimental to peripheral interaction due to the additional physical demand, temporal demand, and effort required to modify information structures and manage their physical representations in space.[6]

Abstraction$_{<CD>}$ $\rightarrow$ Automation$_{<TC>}$, Adaptability$_{<TC>}$ Abstraction describes the use quality that *the notation offers different types and levels of abstraction mechanisms.* It has two distinct tangible correlates for different targets of abstraction. Automation denotes the quality that *new behavior can be programmed and redefined.* Adaptability denotes the quality that *new states can be specified and redefined.* The creation and management of all such kinds of abstraction has sufficient mental demand that it requires focused attention and cannot generally be performed through peripheral interaction, although once created, they can be used in much the same way as the primary notation. The ShuffleBoard interface does not employ any Abstraction$_{<CD>}$, either for the purpose of Automation$_{<TC>}$ or Adaptability$_{<TC>}$. Considering the abstraction potential of other interfaces, we can say that the use of a free-turning knob to set a user's status in StaTube (Hausen et al. 2012) has greater inherent Adaptability$_{<TC>}$ than the use of polyhedra with a fixed number of faces in Do Not Disturb (Olivera et al. 2011), since knob rotation can cycle through an arbitrary number of states.

Role Expressiveness$_{<CD>}$ $\rightarrow$ Purposeful Affordances$_{<TC>}$ Role Expressiveness describes the use quality that *the purpose of each component is readily inferred.* Its tangible correlate, Purposeful Affordances,[7] denotes the quality that *possible physical acions have a clear and meaningful purpose.* For example, ShuffleBoard tokens are symbolic[8] representations of tasks, documents, and people (low Role

---

[6]A fundamental trade-off between Rigidity$_{<TC>}$ and Rootedness$_{<TC>}$ exists when relations of association, dissociation, and order are expressed through the relative arrangement of physical objects in space. Engelhardt (2002) presents the six fundamental forms of spatial syntactic relation: spatial clustering; separation by a separator; lineup; linking by a connector; containment by a container; and superimposition (stacking). The relations of stacking, connection, and containment are based on physical bonding through gravity, linkage, and common enclosure, respectively, making them easier to move and relocate as a unit, but more difficult to reconfigure due to the requisite breaking and making of such bonds (high Rigidity$_{<TC>}$, low Rootedness$_{<TC>}$). In contrast, the relations of lineup, clustering, and separation are all based on perceptual arrangement, making them easier to reconfigure but more difficult to move and relocate as a unit (low Rigidity$_{<TC>}$, high Rootedness$_{<TC>}$). Since the auxiliary work activities in the case study would benefit from both low Rigidity$_{<TC>}$ and low Rootedness$_{<TC>}$, we developed an alternative, bimanual control mechanism based on Juxtamodality$_{<TC>}$ that avoided the need for a spatial syntax.

[7]The concept of *affordance* developed by Gibson (1979) refers to the opportunities for action arising from the relationship between an animal and its environment. In its introduction to the HCI community, Norman (1988) describes affordances as messages conveyed by objects "about their possible uses, actions, and functions." Purposeful Affordances$_{<TC>}$ are thus the use quality that messages conveyed by objects relate directly to their intended opportunities for interaction.

[8]The science of semiotics studies how something can stand for something else. In the semiotics of Peirce (1931–1958), *iconic* signs are those based on literal, analogical, or metaphorical similarity, while *symbolic* signs are those based on arbitrary or conventional rules or laws. Although iconic signs have greater Role Expressiveness$_{<CD>}$, they also have greater Bulkiness$_{<TC>}$ and lower Adaptability$_{<TC>}$.

Expressiveness$_{<CD>}$). Some initial instruction is required for users to learn these mappings, but once past this initial learning curve (as with low Consistency$_{<CD>}$), there is relatively little impact on the potential for peripheral interaction. While the physical form of the ShuffleBoard tokens is not a literal representation of the underlying information objects, the material affordances of the poker-chip-like form factor allow the tokens to be annotated with dry-erase ink, picked up, placed on, and slid across the interactive surface, and so on (high Purposeful Affordances$_{<TC>}$). In another example, the use of a free-turning knob to set the symbolic color of a user's status in StaTube (Hausen et al. 2012) has lower Role Expressiveness$_{<CD>}$ and lower Purposeful Affordances$_{<TC>}$ than the use of polyhedra with a fixed number of iconic "mood" faces in Do Not Disturb (Olivera et al. 2011). High levels of Purposeful Affordances$_{<TC>}$ provide an ongoing benefit in terms of physical demand, at the cost of a potential reduction in future Adaptability$_{<TC>}$.

Hidden Dependencies$_{<CD>}$ → **Hidden Augmentations$_{<TC>}$** Hidden Dependencies describes the use quality that *important links between components are not visible*. Its tangible correlate, Hidden Augmentations, denotes the quality that *physical objects are digitally augmented in a non-obvious manner*. For example, the calendar visualization in ShuffleBoard makes the dependencies between task time estimates, task due dates, and overlapping tasks explicit through the concept of "latest restart date" (low Hidden Dependencies$_{<CD>}$). While the position of the camera pointing at the interactive surface and the hole-based identification patterns cut into each token is a clear indication of the sensing mechanism, the bimanual control mechanism is not obvious (moderate Hidden Augmentations$_{<TC>}$) and must be learned. Although Hidden Dependencies$_{<CD>}$ could have a lasting effect on mental demand, Hidden Augmentations$_{<TC>}$ typically affects only the initial learning process.

Hard Mental Operations$_{<CD>}$ → **Unwieldy Operations$_{<TC>}$** Hard Mental Operations describes the use quality that *the notation places a high demand on cognitive resources*. Its tangible correlate, Unwieldy Operations, denotes the quality that *the notation places a high demand on physical resources because of the nature of objects (e.g., size, shape, structure, or weight) and the actions required on them*. For example, in the ShuffleBoard interface, the ability to visually scan the desktop environment for physical tokens reduces the mental demand of recalling and holding in mind a wide range of potential interaction targets (low Hard Mental Operations$_{<CD>}$). The coordination requirements of the bimanual nudge-turn control scheme exhibits the minimum level of difficulty (mild Unwieldy Operations$_{<TC>}$) to avoid Shakiness$_{<TC>}$, although in general higher levels of Unwieldy Operations$_{<TC>}$ have a direct and undesirable impact on physical demand. The use of an interactive chair for peripheral music control (Probset et al. 2014) could easily elevate Unwieldy Operations$_{<TC>}$ to a high level.

Closeness of Mapping$_{<CD>}$ → **Structural Correspondence$_{<TC>}$** Closeness of Mapping describes the use quality that *the representation closely resembles the* *domain.* Its tangible correlate, Structural Correspondence, denotes the quality that *the physical notation matches the structure of the underlying digital representation.*[9] For example, in the ShuffleBoard interface, the halo visualization of task token attributes is a direct representation of their values (high Closeness of Mapping$_{<CD>}$), while the single degree of freedom of the knob corresponds directly to the single dimension of those values and visually moves them in the same direction (high Structural Correspondence$_{<TC>}$). While low Closeness of Mapping$_{<CD>}$ might increase the mental demand of initial learning, low Structural Correspondence$_{<TC>}$ could have long-term effects on mental demand and frustration.

4.5.3 Interface Design

The third and final step of the analytic design process for peripheral tangible interaction is *interface design*. In this step, the designer generates interface design concepts inspired by the probing questions of the first step in the process, *activity analysis*. The prospective use qualities of these design concepts can then be analyzed and compared to the target profile of use qualities generated by the second step in the process, *notation analysis*. The purpose of these comparisons is to identify areas for improvement and to provide rationale for the design changes that aim to make such improvements. Since the use qualities of notations are holistic in nature, design changes have the potential to affect several use qualities simultaneously. Following a design change, all use qualities of the new notation should therefore be re-evaluated to check for unintended or unexpected side effects. When these side effects are negative, the designer must weigh up the resulting trade-off between the two design options. The abstract nature of use qualities means that the same analysis of trade-offs can be applied to the comparison of *any* competing designs, even if they embody fundamentally different notations.

In the design of ShuffleBoard, our application of activity analysis helped us to identify that in the desk-based, office context, the management of auxiliary work activities was a candidate for peripheral tangible interaction. It also suggested the basic idea of using physical tokens to represent items of shared interest within work groups: tasks, documents, and people. However, the final form of the interface, especially its separation of representation (tokens) and control (knob) as a way to facilitate bimanual interaction, was driven by notation analysis that highlighted problems with the use of spatial syntax for that particular activity context. Our

---

[9]In the instrumental interaction framework (Beaudouin-Lafon 2000), the match between physical degrees of freedom and digital dimensions of control is called *integration* and the similarity between physical actions and digital effects is called *compatibility*. Structural Correspondence$_{<TC>}$ combines these two properties and extends to the representational as well as control aspects of a notation. The third component of the instrumental interaction framework, *indirection*, refers to the spatial offsets between input and output that are created through Juxtamodality$_{<TC>}$.

analytic framework is sufficiently general that it has the potential to create similar insights into any form of interface that bridges the physical and the digital—not just tangible interfaces, but all kinds of mobile, wearable, and ubiquitous interfaces that aim to facilitate interaction on the periphery of the user's attention. We discuss this broader context of applicability in the following and final section.

4.6   Outlook for Peripheral Tangible Interaction

This chapter has described analytic and design considerations for peripheral interaction through detailed consideration of a specific case study, the ShuffleBoard system for peripheral task management. ShuffleBoard was an early example of a fully functional peripheral tangible interface, which at the time of development was nearly unique for being deployed for evaluation of usage in context ("in the wild") during routine professional activity.

Previous studies of tangible interaction in professional contexts at that time had mainly focused on existing tangible representations: These might subsequently have been augmented for interaction with digital systems, or even used alongside such systems without specific design interventions (e.g., MacKay 1999). The ShuffleBoard interface was a completely novel system design, featuring tangible interaction that was created in response to a specific set of contextual requirements. As a result, ShuffleBoard provided an opportunity to study explicit design rationale in far greater detail and to apply the resulting observations as a basis for future design of novel peripheral tangible interaction systems intended to be deployed in the wild.

Although the specific sensing and fabrication techniques used to implement ShuffleBoard employed the hardware capabilities of that time (laser cutting, pen-sensing tablets, rotary controllers, template-based machine vision), the analytic design process that we have presented in this chapter is wholly appropriate to more recent generations of interactive devices. The market drivers for these devices continue to reflect Weiser's manifesto for ubiquitous computing, and to support the "calm" interaction style that he hoped would replace intrusive digital technologies (Weiser and Brown 1995). However, it has become clear that Weiser's somewhat utopian vision has not yet been realized in user experiences of contemporary technology. While many would prefer that technology receded into the background as Weiser hoped, the reality of contemporary technology products is that they are even more foregrounded than when Weiser advocated calm computing. Personal mobile computing devices such as tablets and cell phones, rather than moving technology to the periphery of our attention, have placed it ever more constantly at the center, resulting in the familiar complaints that social structures and even physical infrastructure are being degraded by inappropriate focus on mobile devices rather than (say) spoken conversation or attending to vehicle control.

This current situation gives particular urgency to a more sophisticated understanding of the relationship between focus and periphery, just as Weiser himself hoped would be achieved. Our FORM framework for analysis of peripheral interaction in support of a target activity is a timely contribution to this understanding. When combined with notation analysis, it supports an analytic design process for the design of peripheral tangible interaction devices that fit within a wide range of task contexts.

The commercial opportunities associated with those contexts are now clear, especially in the growing markets for wearable devices, and for "Internet of Things" products. However, at the time of writing, many of the interaction design approaches developed for such products seem to have retained the old emphasis on capturing and holding the user's attention, whether through portable touch screens that can only be operated while looking at them, head-up displays that are superimposed on the user's visual field, gaze tracking that explicitly monitors the user's level of focus, or even immersive virtual reality headsets that prevent the user from employing peripheral attention.

This situation is not sustainable. It is clear that the number of CPUs in proportion to the number of people on Earth is a ratio growing so rapidly that it is inconceivable for us to continue giving focal attention to the user interface. If focal attention is not possible, peripheral interaction must be the central paradigm of the future.

Furthermore, computation is becoming embedded in the physical fabric of our material environment in increasingly diverse ways. Beyond the laser-cutting technique that we used to fabricate the ShuffleBoard tokens, other rapid fabrication methods such as 3D printing are combining with the popular culture of making and hackerspaces to result in a dramatic flowering of novel forms for digital devices. Before long, these will not simply imitate existing objects (such as phones, watches, or glasses), but will open up completely novel product categories. Similarly, the embedded computation of IoT products will mean that familiar household objects will become tangible interfaces, whether or not their shapes are explicitly modified.

Ultimately, humans are embodied beings who will interact with digital infrastructure through embodied actions and embedded physical forms. These forms will necessarily carry representational, control, and notational functions of the kinds that we have discussed in this chapter. It will become increasingly necessary to understand interactions of such products in relation to our own evolved physical capabilities (such as bimanual action and cross-modal sensing). The framework for peripheral tangible interaction that we have presented in this chapter is a comprehensive response to this urgent need.

Acknowledgments This chapter is based on research funded by The Boeing Company and conducted as part of a Ph.D. at the University of Cambridge Computer Laboratory, available as a Technical Report at http://www.cl.cam.ac.uk/techreports/UCAM-CL-TR-733.html.

References

Balakrishnan, R., & Hinckley, K. (1999). The role of kinesthetic reference frames in two-handed input performance. *UIST'99* (pp. 171–178).

Bakker, S., van den Hoven, E., Eggen, B., & Overbeeke, K. (2012). Exploring peripheral interaction design for primary school teachers. *TEI'12* (pp. 245–252).

Bakker, S., van den Hoven, E., & Eggen, B. (2013). FireFlies: Physical peripheral interaction design for the everyday routine of primary school teachers. *TEI'13* (pp. 57–64).

Baudisch, P., Becker, T., & Rudeck, F. (2010). Lumino: Tangible blocks for tabletop computers based on glass fiber bundles. *CHI'10* (pp. 1165–1174).

Beaudouin-Lafon, M. (2000). Instrumental interaction: An interaction model for designing post-WIMP user interfaces. *CHI'00* (pp. 446–453).

Blackwell, A. F. (2002). First steps in programming: A rationale for Attention Investment models. In *Proceedings of the IEEE Symposia on Human-Centric Computing Languages and Environments* (pp. 2–10).

Blackwell, A. F., & Green, T. R. G. (2000). *A cognitive dimensions questionnaire*. http://www.cl. cam.ac.uk/~afb21/CognitiveDimensions/CDquestionnaire.pdf. Accessed April 8, 2015.

Blackwell, A. F., & Green, T. R. G. (2003). Notational systems—the cognitive dimensions of notations framework. In J. M. Carroll (Ed.), *HCI models, theories and frameworks: Toward a multidisciplinary science* (pp. 103–134). San Francisco: Morgan Kaufmann.

Chan, L., Müller, S., Roudaut, A., & Baudisch, P. (2012). CapStones and ZebraWidgets: Sensing stacks of building blocks, dials and sliders on capacitive touch screens. *CHI'12* (pp. 2189–2192).

Edge, D. (2008). Tangible user interfaces for peripheral interaction. University of Cambridge Computer Laboratory Technical Report. http://www.cl.cam.ac.uk/techreports/UCAM-CL-TR-733.html

Edge, D., & Blackwell, A. F. (2006). Tangible correlates of the cognitive dimensions for tangible user interface. *JVLC, 17*(4), 366–394.

Edge, D., & Blackwell, A. F. (2009). Peripheral tangible interaction by analytic design. *TEI'09* (pp. 69–76).

Engelhardt, Y. (2002). *The language of graphics* (Ph.D. thesis). University of Amsterdam.

Fitzmaurice, G. W. (1996). *Graspable user interfaces* (Ph.D. thesis). University of Toronto.

Gibson, J. J. (1979). *The ecological approach to visual perception*. Lawrence Erlbaum Associates.

Green, T. R. G. (1989). *Cognitive dimensions of notations. People and computers* (pp. 443–460). Cambridge: Cambridge University Press.

Green, T. R. G., & Blackwell, A. F. (1998). *Cognitive dimensions of information artefacts: A tutorial*. http://www.cl.cam.ac.uk/»afb21/CognitiveDimensions/CDtutorial.pdf. Accessed April 8, 2015.

Green, T. R. G., & Petre, M. (1996). Usability analysis of visual programming environments: a cognitive dimensions approach. *Journal of Visual Languages and Computing, 7*, 131–174.

Guiard, Y. (1987). Asymmetric division of labor in human skilled bimanual action: The kinematic chain as a model. *Journal of Motor Behavior, 19*(4), 486–517.

Hart, S. G., & Staveland, L. E. (1988). Development of NASA-TLX (Task Load Index): Results of empirical and theoretical research. In P. A. Hancock & N. Meshkati (Eds.), *Human mental workload*. Amsterdam: North Holland Press.

Hausen, D., Boring, S., Lueling, C., Rodestock, S., & Butz, A. (2012). StaTube: Facilitating state management in instant messaging systems. *TEI'12* (pp. 283–290).

Hausen, D., Richter, H., Hemme, A., & Butz, A. (2013). Comparing input modalities for peripheral interaction: A case study on peripheral music control. *INTERACT 2013* (pp. 162–179).

Ishii, H., & Ullmer, B. (1997). Tangible bits: Towards seamless interfaces between people, bits and atoms. *CHI'97* (pp. 234–241).

Kirsh, D. (1995). The intelligent use of space. *Artificial Intelligence, 73*(1–2), 31–68.

Kirsh, D. (2001). The context of work. *Human Computer Interaction, 16*, 305–322.

Kirsh, D., & Maglio, P. P. (1994). On distinguishing epistemic from pragmatic action. *Cognitive Science, 18*(4), 513–549.

Liang, R.-H., Kuo, H. C., Chan, L., Yang, D. N., & Chen, B. Y. (2014). GaussStones: Shielded magnetic tangibles for multi-token interactions on portable displays. *UIST '14* (pp. 365–372).

MacKay, W. E. (1999). Is paper safer? The role of paper flight strips in air traffic control. *ACM Transactions on Computer-Human Interaction, 6*(4), 311–340.

Norman, D. A. (1988). *The psychology of everyday things.* New York: Basic Books.

Olivera, F., Garcia-Herranz, M., Haya, P. A., & Llinás, P. (2011). Do not disturb: Physical interfaces for parallel peripheral interactions. *INTERACT 2011* (pp. 479–486).

Peirce, C. (1931–1958). *Collected Papers of Charles Sanders Peirce* (8 Vols). Cambridge, MA: Harvard University Press.

Probset, K., Lindlbauer, D., Haller, M., Schwartz, B., & Schrempf, A. (2014). A chair as ubiquitous input device: Exploring semaphoric chair gestures for focused and peripheral interaction. *CHI'14* (pp. 4097–4106).

Reuleaux, F. (1876). The kinematics of machinery: Outline of a theory of machines. Reprinted by Dover Publications in 1963.

Sanders, M. S., & McCormick, J. (1987). *Human factors in engineering and design* (6th ed.). New York, NY: McGraw-Hill.

Scaife, M., & Rogers, Y. (1996). External cognition: How do graphical representations work? *International Journal of Human-Computer Studies, 45*(2), 185–213.

Ullmer, B., & Ishii, H. (2001). Emerging frameworks for tangible user interfaces. In J. M. Carroll (Ed.), *HCI in the New Millennium* (pp. 579–601). Reading, MA: Addison-Wesley.

Weiser, M., & Brown, J. S. (1995). Designing calm technology. Xerox PARC.

Chapter 5
Microgestures—Enabling Gesture Input with Busy Hands

Katrin Wolf

Abstract Microgestures, small movements of the digits that do not require moving the whole hand, are a promising input technique for peripheral interaction as they can be executed in parallel to many manual actions. Such interaction techniques can be used to augment or to extend everyday tasks, and therefore, have the great potential to enable interacting with busy hands as peripheral activity. For example, tipping a digit at a steering wheel while driving could be used for automotive control without requiring too much manual motor effort that might decrease the steering performance. Moreover, smart objects that are held in the hand can be controlled through tiny grasp modifications. This chapter describes relevant aspects of microinteractions. After explaining the motivation and value of microgestures in existing use cases, an overview on technology that allows for detecting microgestures is provided. Then the design of ergonomic microgestures that allow for being executed as peripheral action is explained. Finally, requirements that allow or permit the user to interrupt the primary task for interacting in the cognitive periphery through microgestures are presented and appropriate applications are discussed.

Keywords Microgestures · Microinteraction · Gesture · Multitasking · Interruption

5.1 Introduction

Microgestures have been used for a long time without being especially recognized as such. Switching on the turn signal in a car while steering is a microgesture executed to support the primary task of driving. Tapping the key of a clarinet while the music instrument is held shows that microgestures can also require the significant mental and motor resources, and holding the instrument is here a subtask.

K. Wolf (✉)
University of Stuttgart, Stuttgart, Germany
e-mail: katrin.wolf@vis.uni-stuttgart.de

© Springer International Publishing Switzerland 2016
S. Bakker et al. (eds.), *Peripheral Interaction*,
Human–Computer Interaction Series, DOI 10.1007/978-3-319-29523-7_5

95

While smoking a microgesture tap flicks the ash apart, ringing the bell of a bicycle or changing its gears is designed to ergonomically support riding by placing the bell and the gear switch where the hands are resting during the ride.

Microinteractions are interactions with a device that take a short time to complete (Ashbrook 2007). In contrast, keypresses (that are also short) usually belong to a longer sequence of interactions, e.g., while typewriting. Different interaction techniques, such as interaction through gaze, head, foot, hand, and foot motion, allow users to interact in such short time that is expected for microinteraction. Microgestures are one possibility to fast interact, which makes them also a good candidate for peripheral interaction.

Microgesture execution for interacting in the periphery of our focus is related to the concept of multitasking. Humans can divide their cognitive capacities, which allows them to multitask and therefore, to simultaneously interact with multiple persons and objects intentionally or in their attentional periphery (Bakker et al. 2010). Dividing the motor capacities, for example, microgesture execution while the hand is performing a non-precise action is an opportunity of interacting in the motor periphery. Examples of such non-precise primary task are carrying a bag and steering a car. Hence, microgestures are also possible if the hands are busy with rather coarse actions. And peripheral interaction themselves are typically often coarse interaction, for example when using TUIs (Edge and Blackwell 2009), when using hand gestures for switching between computer applications or for spatial memory (Hausen 2014), or when using different modalities, such as touch, gestures, or TUIS for peripheral music control (Hausen et al. 2013). In all these cases, the peripheral interaction is coarse and microgestures can be executed in parallel, e.g., for differentiating between a set of commands and interface functionalities. Microgestures then would extend the motor design space of peripheral hand gestures as well as provide possibilities for more interactions than coarse peripheral interaction allows for.

However, humans can often not divide their motor abilities, e.g., when executing high-precision motor tasks. Thus, multitask, if analyzed carefully, has been found to often not be executed as two or more tasks in parallel but sequentially by interrupting shortly the primary task and solving a secondary task in such task break, and then continuing the primary task (Czerwinski et al. 2004). However, in some cases, tasks can be done in parallel, e.g., steering a car and controlling the breaks at the same time and adequately, it is possible to execute microgestures with the digits while steering a car. Regarding interrupting the motor execution of a manual task or if done in parallel, microgestures can also support a secondary task that is dedicated to human–computer interaction.

Human–computer interaction has been focused on solitaire task using stationary desktop PCs. With the raise of mobile and ubiquitous computing, interacting with computers is central to users on the go, for instance in parallel to walking or while driving. During such multitasking situations, users are performing two competing tasks at the same time, which always requires splitting motor and attentional resources between a primary and a secondary task. A microinteraction—due to its short duration—is the secondary task, which makes it a peripheral interaction.

Reflecting on the existing use of small finger motions allows for separating different microgesture uses: (1) as part of the focused activity, (2) as an extra flourish, and (3) as a separate embellishment. Thinking about traditional microgesture-based tasks that are mentioned in the beginning of this chapter, tapping the keys of a clarinet, is truly part of the focused act of playing this instrument. Ringing the bell of a bicycle is an extra flourish but it is adding to the task of cycling. Executing a microgesture as a separate embellishment is rare in analog interaction with the world, but tapping the rhythm of the radio song at the steering wheel during a car ride can be seen as separate embellishment that in this case is often happening subconsciously and thus a peripheral action.

In the context of human–computer interaction, such microgestures have the potential to remotely control a system. Microgestures might make up focused interaction in the domain of gaming through a key press at gesture game controllers, as we know it from the button of the Wii controller. Buttons that are built in steering wheels already allow for controlling the car through microgestures as an extra flourish while controlling the steering wheel. For peripheral interaction, we can think of small gestural embellishments to enhance communication, for example while raising a cup to ones lips to drink coffee. In such situation, a playful toss of a finger might be used to subtly alert a waiter that you would like to get your bill. Such peripheral interaction would allow for communicating while being in a conversation without being impolite.

A modern and interactive bike would allow for an extra flourish. For example, having touch-sensitive handle bars would allow to change gears with touch gestures directly on the bars. The bicycle's navigation system could be controlled with microgestures, as shown in Fig. 5.1 using wearable sensors for microgesture

Fig. 5.1 Smart cycling through wearable sensors that detect microgestures allows for navigating through a map without releasing the handle bars

detection to control a navigation app. Swiping to the right/left handle might pan the map and tapping with the thumb or index finger at the handle bar can be used for zoom out of the map. A hand-held mobile keyboard, such as Twiddler (Lyons et al. 2004), is also an example for microgestures that are used for controlling the focused activity. Here, microgestures are used for typewriting on an ergonomically shaped keyboard that allows for one-handed typewriting on a device that is held with the typing hand.

Microgesture interaction is motivated by the unused resources of users' hands in many everyday situations, such as when driving, going by bus, or during a bike ride. Finger motions offer a much bigger input design space than is has been taken advantage of. We can slightly move our fingers when our hands are involved in a primary task, and we can do it quickly and unnoticeable. Of course, not every task will provide the cognitive and motor resources to interact through microgestures. Playing tennis, for example, does neither leave time nor cognitive and motor resources to do any tasks in the periphery. However, many situations do and this chapter aimed to describe the relevance microgestures can and will more frequently have in the future, particularly in peripheral interaction.

This chapter covers the most relevant aspects of microinteractions. First a review of the state of the art of current technology that supports interactive systems for peripheral microgesture interaction is provided. Afterwards, it is described how ergonomic microgestures that allow for being executed as peripheral action should be designed. Finally, a discussion on requirements that allow or permit the user to interrupt the primary task for interacting in the cognitive periphery through microgestures is presented and appropriate applications are discussed.

5.2 Microgesture Interaction Technology

Ubiquitous computing defines the environment as a "world of fully connected devices, with cheap wireless networks" (Weiser 1991), and one major research question in that area is how to seamlessly access ubiquitous computers. Weiser's vision of ubiquitous computing inspired many researchers to work on computing systems that are embedded in all kinds of devices, objects, and in the environment to enable the user to always and immediate interact with a highly personalized and always available computer system. To support Weiser's vision, Fukumoto and Suenaga (1994) suggest that input devices should allow immediate input to mobile devices, because the "Setup time" of activating a mobile device in order to use it takes too long. Brewster et al. (2003) also suggest separating input and output devices to improve the usability in the mobile context. Ashbrook (2007) introduced microinteraction to more easily interact with mobile devices when being on the go. Wolf et al. (2013) propose finger-mounted sensors as an input device for controlling mobile devices with microgestures.

Two main challenges are important for technology that considers finger movements for input: the *association of the user with the device or object* he/she aims to interact with and the *detection of the microgestures* using technology that fits the needs of being ubiquitous available and thus of wearing it constantly in everyday life.

5.2.1 Associating the User with Smart Objects or Devices

Recalling, for example, the interaction scenario of the microgestures done while drinking coffee to call the waiter makes clear that we need a system that can related to the cup that detected the gesture to its user as well as to his/her position in the café. If the user would wear a smart ring, the association of the user (through the ring) and the object or device he/she is addressing with his/her microgestures would be realized through *device pairing*. The immediate association of the user with the device or object intended to interact with (without the need of using switches or time to boot a system) is according to Weiser (1991) requiring *seamless interaction*.

If one input device is able to control more than one output device, then the transition between two output devices should be seamless for the user. Thus, the input and output device should not need an explicit connection and disconnection mechanism, instead they should know when they need to couple through the context. Ubiquitous devices should always be available (Fishkin et al. 1999), and the activation of these devices should be implicit (Schmidt et al. 2005) without requiring user's attention (e.g., no explicit connection through a settings menu). Implicit device pairing is a promising technique for enabling seamless interaction. Interaction is seamless when the user is not required to activate the device by an effort-costing trigger nor is required to change an input interface when changing a device. Also, the access to a device through an interface ought to be immediate (Fukumoto and Suenaga 1994). According to Ballagas et al. (2006), the connection between an input and an output device should be automatic, fast, and easy, because users want to concentrate on the interaction with a system rather than spending time on connecting input and output devices. The connection between input and output device is more comfortable when it is done wirelessly. Finally, in order to allow for seamless interaction, the process of switching from one device to another should also be implicit, thereby saving time and effort, which allows for continuous and non-interrupted task-solving, as recommended by Suh et al. (2008).

Therefore, no matter what technology is tracking the microgestures, the ubiquitous input device has to fulfill three requirements: (1) recognizing all potential smart objects and devices the user may want to interact with, (2) seamlessly pairing the input device with the object/device the user wants to interact with, and (3) disconnecting the paired devices if the interaction is over to avoid unintended control action.

Here work is discussed that fulfills one or more of the requirements needed to enable seamless microgesture control in everyday life. Researchers followed different approaches to detect the moment when a user intends to interact with a device as well as to detect the device the user aims to interact with. Some approaches are aiming to detect the moment an object is taken into hand by grasp recognition, detecting when the user's hand is close to a device or comparing the motion of the user's hand and the device to interpret a similar motion as pickup action.

For grasp recognition, devices that enable grasp recognition using capacitive sensors (Wimmer and Boring 2009) and RFID reader in combination with accelerometer (Berlin et al. 2010) have been explored. *Ubi-Finger* (Tsukada and Yasumura 2001) makes it possible to almost seamlessly connect the user with devices. This is done when a user is pointing with an infrared sensor that is attached to a user's finger to a unique infrared light source of the devices it can control. The system then knows which device is selected and the user can control the device remotely with mid-air gestures. *Ubi-Finger* uses an indirect 1:1 connection of the input and the output devices. To seamlessly control every device or object taken into hand, pairing with several devices has to be taken into account.

Work has been carried out using finger-attached and device/object embedded actuators and sensors for associate an object with its user (Fukumoto and Suenaga 1994; Fukomoto and Tonomura 1997). A number of projects allowed for a 1:1 connection between devices. Tsukada and Yasumura (2001) used infrared sensors. An IP-based Bluetooth connection was used by Wolf et al. (2013). Nanayakkara et al. (2013) detected objects through processing the image of a camera that is built in the wearable device. For device-to-device authentication, similar movement patterns of both devices indicate whether they were shaken together (Mayrhofer and Gellersen 2007). This concept has been adapted by Wolf and Willaredt (2015) in the *PickRing* project for pairing a ubiquitous ring device with a device when it is taken into hand. Wolf and Willaredt compared the motion data of the hand and of any nearby device and paired them if the motion was similar.

PickRing was the first of its kind fulfilling all three requirements for seamlessly pairing a ubiquitous input device with generic devices (which are placeholders for everyday smart objects). It allows the user to interact with grasped devices. It also separates the input and output interfaces. The natural movement that occurs when a device is grasped is detected and interpreted as intention to interact with the device. This allows for automatically activating a device when taken into the hand. Thus, *PickRing* enables control of multiple devices seamlessly. The immediate pairing between the ubiquitous controller and a ubiquitous device could be realized seamlessly through providing an ad hoc Bluetooth Piconet connection and through comparing the motion of the user's hand and all devices in the piconet (see Fig. 5.2). The paring is disabled in the moment the device is not held in the hand anymore.

Technologies allow for associating a user with a device or objects, and sensors do not necessarily have to be attached to the fingers. The advantage of using a ring interface for ubiquitous computing is that a ring is a transparent device (Dey et al. 2001) as people are using wearing rings on their fingers as jewelry (Drossos et al. 2007). For detecting closeness between smart objects and the user's hand, RFID/NFC tags have been mounted on fingers (Bainbridge and Paradiso 2011) or embedded in jewelry (Vega and Fuks 2014).

Fig. 5.2 After PickRing is connected to nearby devices via Bluetooth. The devices are automatically paired through interpreting a pickup action as activation gesture. The gesture is recognized if the device's and hand's motions are similar by applying cross-correlation

The drawback of embedded RFID/NFC tags for grasp or intention of use detection is that RFID/NFC only allows for detecting closeness. The benefit of these tags is that they are passive and cheap.

Detecting motion allows for detecting the object that is picked up by a user wearing a ubiquitous input device, but here the technical limitation is that batteries still are quite large and do not last for several days. Some technical challenges, for example power supply or device size, are remaining. However, smart rings are addressed a lot in recent research, and thus, it is very likely that a consumer product that fulfills the requirement of seamless everyday object interaction using microgestures will be available soon. Another benefit of using motion detection sensors by a smart ring for device pairing is that the microgestures that follow the step of pairing could be detected by the same technology as it will be explained in the following paragraph.

5.2.2 Detection of Microgestures

The detection of microgestures requires detecting tiny movements of digits, preferably using wearable technology that is, by default, already associated with the identity of the user. There is a huge body of research on tracking finger and hand motions with wearable sensors for gesture-based interaction, mainly using motion detecting sensors such as accelerometers, gyroscopes, magnetometers, and optical sensors. Passive RFID/NFC tags [attached to nails (Vega and Fuks 2014) or mounted on fingers (Bainbridge and Paradiso 2011)] were used to capture gestures. These gestures have been described as useful, when interacting with a wearable display or other mobile computers where a keyboard is not appropriate.

As mentioned earlier, others detect finger and hand gestures using optical sensors, sensing muscle activities or magnetometers. *Digits* (Kim et al. 2012) is a wrist-worn device containing an inertial measurement unit (IMU) sensor to detect the hand direction and an infrared depth camera to detect the hand pose. However, although wearable optical systems allow detecting finger gestures, hand-held

objects can easily occlude the camera view on the fingers. That matters when the
hands are used as they are in many mobile scenarios, e.g., when carrying bags or
riding a bicycle. Furthermore, variation in lightning may add too much noise to the
optical signals.

In contrast to optical gesture detection, other sensors can sense finger motions
under any light conditions and do not require "free" hands. For instance, finger
gestures have been detected by measuring capacitance on a wristband. *GestureWrist*
(Rekimoto 2001) recognizes hand gestures by measuring wrist deformation through
capacitive sensors that are embedded in a wristband. Others used acoustic signals
generated by tapping on the forearm or by forming a fist for hand gesture detection
(Harisson et al. 2010). Saponas (2009) used an armband that measures the
Electromyography (EMG) signal in a user's arm to extract movements and gestures
of a user's finger. More magnetometers were used (Ashbrook et al. 2011; Harrison
and Hudson 2009) that track the position of a magnetic ring worn on the user's
finger, while *FingerPad* (Chan et al. 2013) detected gestures drawn on the fingertips using magnets.

Ubi-Finger (Tsukada and Yasumura 2001) and *Tickle* (Wolf et al. 2013) detect
finger motions of accelerometer and gyroscope sensor data for gesture classification. Scroll gestures have been recognized in *Ubi-Finger* using bend sensors and
accelerometers for measuring finger movements. *Tickle* proposed a ring interface
with an embedded IMU. Tap, release, swipe, and pinch gestures could be detected
on uneven surfaces to interact with generic smart objects and devices. The design of
Tickle was driven by the desire to have a situation-independent as well as
device-independent interface that can be controlled through microgestures. The
vision of the design was to develop an interface for interacting with generic smart
objects that are held in the hand. Aiming for ergonomic microgestures, finger taps
and slide movements performed with the index and middle finger were chosen as
gesture set, and the commands tap, release, swipe, and pitch had been implemented
(see Fig. 5.3).

The gesture detection in Tickle was realized through threshold-based classification of the accelerometer and gyroscope data. A user study showed that the
microgestures could be performed and detected not only on commonly used smooth

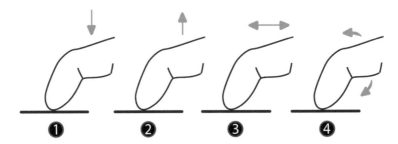

Fig. 5.3 *Tickle* used *1* tap *2* release *3* swipe *4* pitch as microgesture performed on any generic
surface that are measured through finger worn sensors

Fig. 5.4 Microgestures performed on smooth, convex, and concave surface shapes

surfaces but also on concave and convex shapes. Users were able to perform pitch and swipe gestures independent of the surface shape. This microgesture execution and detection evaluation shows that such gestures can be used in different situations. Moreover, the interface allows the user to interact through microgestures while grasping devices with a large variety of shapes including smooth, convex, and concave surfaces (Fig. 5.4).

The technologies discussed here focus on detecting finger motions in situations in which users are mobile. Moreover, the split between input device and output device is considered. However, surfaces may have embedded touch sensors. Using another technology, such as RFID/NFC, could add information about the user's identity. Thus, combinations of the technologies discussed here enable further microgesture-detecting possibilities. Machine learning approaches rather than thresholds for classifying gestures out of sensor data are recommended for a stable gesture classification that also enables to distinguish between an intended gesture and natural hand movements. In the following paragraph, works on gesture and microgesture classification and sensor data segmentation using machine learning approaches are introduced.

5.2.3 Gesture Segmentation and Classification Using Machine Learning

Approaches that have been successfully used for speech recognition have been shown to gain similar good results in gesture detection.

Before a gesture can be classified, the relevant segment, which contains the gesture, has to be separated from noise data that do not represent gestures. Ward et al. (2006) present a procedure using an IMU sensor and 2 microphones near the hand to detect a certain movement of the arm during an activity through detecting the activity-corresponding characteristic noise. Arm movements and audio signals provide information whether the activity was performed and when. Such information was used to distinguish arm movements from parts where the activity was performed. Junker et al. (2008) presented an approach using a two-stage segmentation system. First, a general pattern of the motion was detected in the data stream. Second, if the data fitted to a motion pattern this segment was classified again using a hidden Markov model (HMM) to reduce the false positive rate.

After motion data are cropped into segments or if clutch events (e.g., a button pressed to identify and activate a gesture) are used to label the gesture data, several approaches are used for gesture classification. Li, for example, introduced the *Protractor* algorithm that recognizes gestures on touch screens. This classifier seeks similarity between gestures in the angular space. Thus, this algorithm is by default scaling invariant, which makes it useful for gesture recognition. Furthermore, *Protractor* classifies with a closed-form analytic approach resulting in a fast and efficient algorithm. This algorithm can handle two-dimensional gestures. The *Protractor* algorithm was expanded by Kratz and Rohs (2011), who added a third dimensional input and introduced the *Protractor3D* algorithm.

Kratz et al. (2013) showed that the gesture recognition using 3D accelerometer data can be improved for the regularized Logistic Regression (LR) algorithm using an additional 3D gyroscope. They compared *Protractor3D*, Dynamic Time Warping (DTW), and LR and showed that *Protractor3D* and DTW have better gesture recognition rates than LR. For segmenting the gesture data, they had used a push-to-gesture clutch button, which was pressed by the participants to indicate the start and the end of a gesture. This trick prevents accidental activation, but it also reduces the usability of the approach as a push-to-gesture action interrupts the interaction flow and reduces the impression of a seamless interaction. The motions of the user that are misunderstood as an intended gesture cause the Midas touch problem that describes accidentally release computer commands through natural movements, such as gaze or gestures. In gesture classification, these classification errors are called false positives—gestures that are falsely positively classified.

Ruiz and Li (2011) also addressed the problem of false positive gestures using a clutch event, the *DoubleFlip* gesture, to reduce the false positive rate in a data stream of natural movements. An essential property of clutch events, such as the *DoubleFlip*, is that it is easy to learn and execute, but its motion trajectory has still to be different from our everyday movements to not being executed unintentionally.

Although microgestures are promising for remote mobile interaction, micro-gesture detection is still not used in products. They do not work with either current mobile devices or the gesture classification requires clutch events. Then, the interaction does not match with requirements of natural mobile situations. Thus, there are still some open research questions to be answered before seamless microgesture control in a ubiquitous computing is a commonly available interaction technology.

5.3   Ergonomics in Microgesture Design

The human hand is highly specialized for performing fine-motor movements which, for example, are needed to perform microgestures. The motor skills of the human hand become obvious when thinking how humans can play piano, use tools with specialized shapes, such as scissors, or tie shoe laces. Of course, these objects are designed to be used by the human hand. Thus, microgestures should be designed according to the hand's freedom of movement, especially when constrained by grasps. Only if both the digit's movability and the hand's configuration during a grasp are considered for microgesture design, microinteraction can be easily performed, which is crucial for using them for peripheral interaction.

5.3.1 Biomechanics of the Human Hand

The biomechanics of the human hand is the basis of the motor design space for microgestures, which is limited by the degree of freedom of the hand.

The hand has 26 degrees of freedom (DOF) as shown in Fig. 5.5(1). The two upper joints of each digit have one degree of freedom, while the lowest finger joints have two and that of the thumb has three DOFs. Additionally, two DOFs for the wrist and three DOFs for the entire hand allow for moving the whole hand. Each digit joint allows for being flexed up to 110° as shown in Fig. 5.5(2). Hence, in theory the possibilities for designing gestures are extremely high, but, in praxis, many aspects, such as the biomechanical constraints, limit the design space for hand gestures.

It is impossible to bend all joints separately to a desired degree within the possible ranges per digit presented in Fig. 5.5(2). Furthermore due to tendon connections between the ring and the middle finger, it is difficult to bend the metacarpophalangeal joints (MCP) of these fingers separately at the same time. Bending the ring finger will tend to bend other joints, e.g., those of the middle and little finger. Motion dependencies are known for joints of the same finger (*intra-finger dependencies*) as well as for joints of different fingers (*inter-finger*

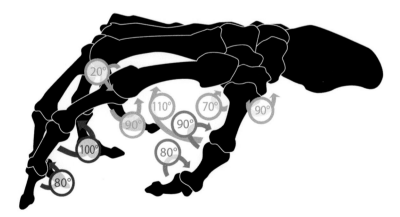

Fig. 5.5 Hand from side with finger flexibility. The thumb has three joints: the thumb basal joint (TBJ), the thumb metacarpophalangeal joint (TMCP), and the thumb distal interphalangeal joint (TDIP). The joints of the fingers are metacarpophalangeal joint (MCP), the proximal interphalangeal joint (PIP), and the distal interphalangeal joint (DIP)

dependencies). Those who learn to play piano especially train their hands to overcome inter-finger dependencies by training to move their neighbor fingers separately to avoid coupling movements of fingers.

5.3.2 Ergonomic Microgestures During Everyday Device Control

Grasping is a motor task that requires muscle contraction for bending fingers and for applying pressure toward the grasped objects. If two motor tasks are performed at the same time with one hand, such as grasping and moving fingers for micro-gesture execution, the physical load of the hand increases as both tasks, grasping and gesture execution, require manual work. However, the idea of microinteraction through microgestures is motivated by the position that both tasks' users are engaged in parallel; one microgesture may be easily performable while grasping an object while another may not. For example, intra-finger dependencies can affect the grasp stability during microgesture performance. While the ring finger cannot easily be moved independently from the middle finger, the thumb and the index finger allow for microgesture execution during most grasp configurations, especially those relying on the middle, ring, and little finger.

The microgestures in Fig. 5.6 can be executed in parallel with everyday task, especially those that require grasping objects. They have been defined in a participatory design process by HCI researchers and experts on physio-ergonomics and evaluated according their ease of execution (Wolf et al. 2011). The gesture set can be used for designing microinteractions using a wide range of everyday objects in parallel or during a primary task as the three main grasp types (palm, pad, and side) are supported.

The microgesture set contains 21 expert-evaluated finger gestures that are performable while grasping objects with all three main grasp types. Most gestures have several subtypes by performing them with different digits (index, middle, ring, and little finger, such as gesture (1) in Fig. 5.6). Moreover, some gestures allow for

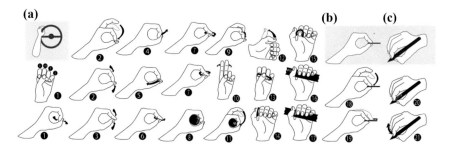

Fig. 5.6 Ergonomic microgesture repertoire for microinteraction during everyday tasks: (**a**) car driving (**b**) dealing with smart cards (**c**) using pens for writing or drawing

gesture design variations. For example, the gesture (1) of the repertoire can be performed as a tap and as a press gesture depending on how much force is applied and how long the fingers are held in the final gesture. Furthermore, the gesture (6) could be performed as drag gesture and as a swipe gesture, which would depend on the digit acceleration and motion duration.

Comparing the collected gestures with the established touch gestures for mobile devices shows a clear overlap. Almost all gestures [except (4), (10), and (12)] are the combinations of tap, press, and drag gestures that are commonly used as touch gestures in mobile device control, while the gestures (4), (10), and (12) rather rely on motions or static hand gestures, such as "flip" (4), "scissor" (10), or "okay" (12).

For designing interaction considering microgestures, the gesture set presented here can serve as starting point to choose actions that are performable in parallel to a daily task in which the hands are busy. However, some challenging aspects have to be kept in mind when using microgestures while holding objects and devices in everyday settings.

For example, the movability of the digits that are meant to perform microgestures may be limited depending on the physical objects that are grasped, for example, the diameter of a steering wheel. On the other hand, movability can be limited by biomechanics, e.g., inter-finger dependencies. Three parameters, the *form factor*, the *digit-dependent limitations*, and the *grasp stiffness,* are explained here in more detail:

Form factor-dependent limitations. Particularly when the hand is holding rather thick objects, the ability to bring together the thumb and a finger depends on the finger length as well as on the object's diameter. This, for example, matters when driving and the execution of a microgesture is done while surrounding the wheel with the hand and to reach the fingers with the thumb. As shown in Fig. 5.7, the thumb can tap easily at the middle finger (2) and the ring finger (3) while holding the steering wheel, but depending on the wheel diameter tapping the thumb with the little finger (4) or sometimes also with the index finger (1) can be difficult, especially for people with small hands.

Digit-dependent limitation. The movability of the individual fingers varies a lot because the middle and the ring finger are more strongly connected through joint tendons, and thus, these fingers are harder to flex independently. The majority of users will be able to perform a separated index finger tap without any problems. Also, moving the little finger separately from the others was rated by experts as not

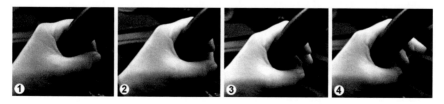

Fig. 5.7 Pinch or tap gesture performance without releasing the steering wheel depends on the thumb and finger length as well as on the diameter of the steering wheel

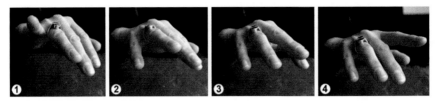

Fig. 5.8 Ability to stretch the little (*1*), ring (*2*), middle (*3*), and index finger (*4*) separately differs a lot and the ring finger can cause comovements of the middle and that of the ring finger

being a problem. The separate flexibility of the middle finger is much worse than that of the index finger. It is still feasible, but it requires more effort from the user. The range of finger inflexibility varies individually, but the ring finger is considered to be the least flexible for all users, followed by the middle finger while the index finger can usually be moved much easier [Fig. 5.8(4) vs. Fig. 5.8(2, 3)]. While the little finger is also very flexible, it may not be very useful for grasp-based gestures as described above. The abandoned thumb works best in comparison with all other fingers, even for sideways movements.

This good performance is due to the previously mentioned larger degree of freedom of the thumb as shown in Fig. 5.5.

Grasp stiffness. A grasp can be rather loose or stiff. Holding a steering wheel, for example, allows the user to execute a large number of gestures while steering a car. This is because the steering wheel is attached to the car, which allows to loose the grasp while executing a gesture. Other scenarios, such as using a pen or a cash card, require "carrying" the object. Here, loosing the grasp for gesture execution is not possible. Thus, if an object is grasped, only few gestures, such as tap, drag, press, and swipe, can be executed without dropping the object.

Cognitive ergonomics and learnability. The microgestures shown in Fig. 5.6 are designed to be easy to perform with a focus on motor ergonomics. Cognitive ergonomics means here that users can easily learn the gestures—ensured through their little complexity—but also that the commands released by gestures can easily be remembered. Different approaches have been shown to increase the learnability of commands. Wagner et al. (2014) introduces categorical chord–command mapping that is the logical posture–language structure for learning the meaning of multitouch gestures. Using this mapping approach, people adapted to logical memorization strategies, such as "exclusion," "order," and "category," to minimize the amount of information to retain. Another approach for decreasing the cognitive effort in learning is the use of image schemas when defining the command–gesture mapping. For example, users intuitively relate load with an upward movements and quiet with a motion down if the context of volume control is known (Hurtienne 2011). Utilizing intuitive mappings and learning methods is essential for gestural interaction as here mostly no GUI is supporting the user in telling him/her the available commands or the gestures that have to be done to release these commands.

Midas touch problem. The error happening when human movements are accidental interpreted as input command for computers is called Midas touch problem. Here, a natural motion of a user that was not performed with the intention to interact would wrongly be considered as input. That would cause interaction errors and frustration. From the gesture repertoire shown in Fig. 5.6, the most simple and thus best feasible gestures, tap and drag, also often contain the risk to be executed without intention. For instance, a tap can be a natural movement, and people often tap the steering wheel while driving a car in the rhythm of music or when waiting on a junction. Other gestures, for instance, sliding the thumb against the index finger may not unconsciously be executed. The risk that such a gesture would be randomly executed is lower than for a tap.

Beside the ergonomics of the gesture design, another important issue is using them for an appropriate application. Thus, the next section will explain applications that experts could image in the mentioned participatory design session in the future (Wolf et al. 2011).

5.4 Microgesture Applications

Microgestural interfaces can be seen as opportunity toward letting I/O devices disappear. That consequently allows for having more calm technology, described as technology embedded in our environment and fitting to our lives (Weiser and Brown 1997). Interacting through free movements (and not through modifying input devices) supports the illusion of disappearing interfaces. The input device, for example a phone, could become invisible with novel technologies, which opens up new design opportunities. Holding a phone can easily be replaced with on-body worn sensors, (pico-) projectors, speakers, and microphones. Attaching sensors to fingers allows not just free spatial gestures but also (because of the incredible motor and sensory abilities of our hand) performing tiny finger movements while grasping daily objects. As less static, the computers we interact with are designed as more flexible and diverse application can be designed. For interacting with everyday objects, these concepts have to be reunderstood, rethought, and redesigned. An important characteristic is that the interaction is established when grasping an object. Sensors are attached to the fingers, but the semantics of the finger gestures are established only in the moment of grasping the object. This is similar to Beaudouin-Lafon's (2000) notion of "instrumental interaction," in which the mouse is generic and its concrete semantics only gets established temporarily, while "grasping" a virtual object, such as an icon on the screen. The approach of microinteraction design, including microgesture design, detection technology, and applications, while grasping can push the vision of ubiquitous computing to a next level (Wolf 2012). Possible applications will be discussed in the following paragraphs.

5.4.1 Appropriate Conditions for Peripheral Microgesture Interaction

The appropriateness of microgesture interactions depends on the following aspects: the *object* possibly held in hand and the characteristics of the primary *task* (Wolf et al. 2011).

Object. The object influences the way to grasp it by its form as well as through the intended use (Wimmer 2011). Furthermore, the grip affects the possibility to perform gestures while grasping as the grip requires a certain hand pose and applied force per digit. The required force is influenced by the object's weight. An object with a certain form and weight requires to be held in a certain way. The grasp changes completely as a function of the force applied per digit if the object is installed in the environment, e.g., a steering wheel in a car. As less manual resources are involved in grasping, more resources are available to perform gestures. Thus, performing microgestures while grasping a steering wheel is a very appropriate context for grasp-based interaction. On the other hand, holding the object with one hand (like a stylus or a cash card) limits the ability to execute gestures (Fig. 5.9). Objects that are held with two hands, such as tablet devices, are also promising to allow the user to execute gestures while grasping. That would allow one hand to loose the grasp for gesture execution, while the other is still holding the device stable.

Task. Parameters that are given by the primary task can decrease the possibility to execute gestures while grasping. Tasks may be too short and not allow the user to execute a gesture. Moreover, the task may require too much cognitive load for allowing interacting in parallel (e.g., target acquisition when inserting an ATM card). That decreases the ability to perform gestures at the same time. On the other hand, a task that lasts long and requires (occasionally) less precision, such as steering a car, is most appropriate for performing gestures in parallel. Again, the

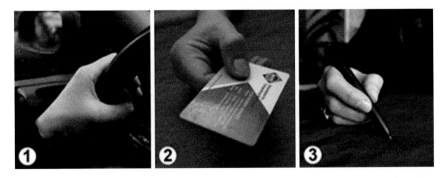

Fig. 5.9 While performing microgestures are easily performable at a steering wheel (*1*), the gesture performance decreases if an object has to be held without support and even more if it has to be kept in a precise position or moved with high accuracy (*2, 3*)

usage of tablet devices or similar form factors fits to that need as holding such shaped object with two hands requires almost no precision and takes as long as desired. If the device is held with two hands, one can easily occasionally release a digit and execute a gesture while the other is mainly holding the device.

5.4.2 Appropriate Applications

In the literature, a variety of microgesture applications have been proposed to interact with a device or smart object when it (or another) is held in the hand.

Saponas (2009), who detected microgestures with an EMG arm band, proposed to open a car remotely when approaching it through bending the fingers, which is even possible when the user is carrying a bag. Saponas proposed a hands-free application of controlling a music player while running. In that scenario, hands shake a lot through the run activity, which makes button acquisition difficult.

Addressing interaction while hands are busy is problematic for traditional input techniques, such as mouse, keyboard, and gestures on a touch screen device, but may be possible using microgestures. From an ergonomic perspective, two setups were mentioned to fit the requirements of microgesture execution best: holding an object or device with two hands or holding something that needs not to be carried as it is attached in the environment, such as the steering wheel in a car.

In cars, many automotive functions can easily be controlled with microgestures without releasing a hand from the steering wheel (see Fig. 5.10), but also a mobile phone or any other mobile or wearable device could be controlled using micro-gestures if the pairing with the microgesture controller is done. Alternative sce-narios that would also not require a grasp applied with force are riding a bicycle. Similar to the car scenario, functions related to cycling could be supported through microgestures, such as navigating through a map or changing gears.

Fig. 5.10 The steering wheel setup (*left*) allows for easily perform microgestures (*center, right*), which could turn any automotive, mobile device, or wearable device control into a microinter-action that is done as secondary or peripheral task during driving

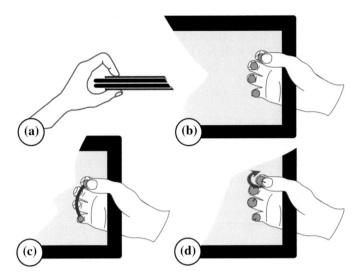

Fig. 5.11 A two-handed grip allows for microinteraction while holding a device (**a**), while browsing the Internet, and while watching a film on a tablet. The grip configuration allows for item selection (**b**), slider control (**c**), and for controlling a rotary knob, which is possible using see-through devices but also due to the human's sense of proprioception (Wolf et al. 2012b)

Almost similarly easy is executing microgestures when a lightweight object is held especially if that is done with two hands. Hence, microgestures could be used for extending the interaction design space of tablets (Wolf 2015), but also digital paper or e-readers could be controlled as microinteraction while reading, browsing, or watching media content (as proposed in Wolf et al. (2012a) and as shown in Fig. 5.11).

Another advantage of microinteraction during holding devices is that if micro-gestures are detected through wearable sensors, there is no need to limit the device control to the physical representation of buttons. A button-less camera control has been demonstrated in the *Tickle* project (Wolf et al. 2013). Here a mobile phone was attached to a traditional camera body to simulate an authentic ergonomic device shape that would not allow for embedding touch pads into the concave camera body. A camera application for an Android phone was developed and the Android device was attached as display on the user-facing side of a SLR camera, just at the place where usually the camera display is (see Fig. 5.12). The sensors for finger movements were worn on the index and on the middle finger. That allowed controlling two parameters of the Android camera application. Thus, the picture brightness could be controlled with the index finger for lights and with the middle finger for shadows. That allows fast and seamless picture configuration under difficult light conditions. As currently many devices, not only cameras, run the Android operating system, microinteraction with all kinds of devices becomes already possible.

Fig. 5.12 An Android-running camera application is controlled through microgestures that are performed wherever the fingers are best placed to hold the device, without any restriction of the position of physical or digital buttons

5.5 Summary

Microgestures performed in the periphery of attention used by a primary task open a broad spectrum of novel ways to interact with computers. The unused resources of users' hands in many everyday situations are providing the space for interacting through microgestures. Microgestures allow for seamlessly interacting with ubiquitous devices and smart objects, which enables microinteraction as part of the focused activity, as an extra flourish, and as a separate embellishment. Microgesture interaction using wearable devices to detect the gestures can add an interface to any graspable thing and to everyday objects. Hence, Weiser's vision of ubiquitous computing is becoming more realistic, and users can in almost situations and everywhere interact with computers. Even if not every task provides the cognitive and motor resources to interact through microgestures, many situations do. This chapter explained how microgesture interaction should be designed and how it should not be, driven by the belief that this interaction technique has great potential for future ways to interact with computers for both focused and peripheral interaction. However, even though the benefit of microgestures has been explored for some UIs, task types, and applications, the design space of peripheral interaction still contains many underexplored but promising interaction scenarios. Questions worth raising in future work may be how microgestures can extend the design space of coarse peripheral interactions or what modalities other than finger gestures are useful to support microinteractions in the cognitive and/or motor periphery of the user.

References

Ashbrook, D. (2007). *Supporting Mobile Microinteractions*. Georgia Institute of Technology.: Diss.

Ashbrook, D., Baudisch, P., & White, S. Nenya. (2011). Subtle and eyes-free mobile input with a magnetically-tracked finger ring. In *Proceedings of the SIGCHI Conference on Human Factors in Computing Systems (CHI'11)* (pp. 2043–2046). New York, NY, USA: ACM.

Bainbridge, R., & Paradiso, J. (2011). Wireless hand gesture capture through wearable passive tag sensing. In *Proceedings of IEEE International Conference on Body Sensor Networks (BSN'11)* (pp. 200–204).

Bakker, S., Hoven, E. van den, & Eggen, B. (2010). Design for the periphery. In *Proceedings of the Eurohaptics 2010 Symposium on Haptic and Audio-Visual Stimuli: Enhancing Experiences and Interaction* (pp. 71–80).

Ballagas, R., Borchers, J., Rohs, M., & Sheridan, J. G. (2006). The smart phone: A ubiquitous input device. In *Proceedings IEEE Pervasive Computing 2006* (pp. 70–77).

Beaudouin-Lafon, M. (2000). Instrumental interaction: An interaction model for designing post-WIMP user interfaces. In *Proceedings of the SIGCHI conference on Human Factors in Computing Systems (CHI'00)* (pp. 446–453). New York, NY, USA: ACM.

Berlin, E., Liu, J., van Laerhoven, K., & Schiele, B. (2010). Coming to grips with the objects we grasp: detecting interactions with efficient wrist-worn sensors. In *Proceedings of the fourth international conference on Tangible, embedded, and embodied interaction (TEI'10)* (pp. 57–64). New York, NY, USA: ACM.

Brewster, S., Lumsden, J., Bell, M., Hall, M., & Tasker, S. (2003). Multimodal 'eyes-free' interaction techniques for wearable devices. In *Proceedings of the SIGCHI Conference on Human Factors in Computing Systems (CHI'03)* (pp. 473–480). New York, NY, USA: ACM.

Chan, L., Liang, R., Tsai, M., Cheng, K., Su, C., Chen, M., Cheng, W., & Chen, B. (2013). FingerPad: private and subtle interaction using fingertips. In *Proceedings of the 26th annual ACM symposium on User interface software and technology (UIST'13)* (pp. 255–260) New York, NY, USA: ACM.

Czerwinski, M., Horvitz, E., & Wilhite, S. (2004). A diary study of task switching and interruptions. In *Proceedings of the SIGCHI Conference on Human Factors in Computing Systems (CHI'04)* (pp. 175–182) New York, NY, USA: ACM.

Dey, A. K., Ljungstrand, P., & Schmidt, A. (2001). Distributed and disappearing user interfaces in ubiquitous computing. In *CHI'01 Extended Abstracts on Human Factors in Computing Systems (CHI EA'01)* (pp. 487–488) New York, NY, USA: ACM.

Drossos, N., Mavrommati, I., & Kameas, A. (2007). Towards ubiquitous computing applications composed from functionally autonomous hybrid artifacts. In *The Disappearing Computer* (pp. 161–181). Berlin: Springer.

Edge, D. and Blackwell, A. F. (2009). Peripheral tangible interaction by analytic design. In *Proceedings of the 3rd International Conference on Tangible and Embedded Interaction (TEI'09)* (pp. 69–76) New York, NY, USA: ACM.

Fishkin, K. P., Moran, T. P., & Harisson, B. L. (1999). Embodied user interfaces: Towards invisible user interfaces. In *Engineering for Human-Computer Interaction* (pp. 1–18) US: Springe.

Fukumoto, M. & Suenaga, Y. (1994). "FingeRing": A full-time wearable interface. In Catherine Plaisant (Ed.), *Conference Companion on Human Factors in Computing Systems (CHI'94)* (pp. 81–82) New York, NY, USA: ACM.

Fukumoto, M., & Tonomura, Y. (1997). "Body coupled FingerRing": Wireless wearable keyboard. In *Proceedings of the ACM SIGCHI Conference on Human factors in computing systems (CHI'97)* (pp. 147–154) New York, NY, USA: ACM.

Harrison, C., & Hudson, S. E. (2009). Abracadabra: Wireless, high-precision, and unpowered finger input for very small mobile devices. In *Proceedings of the 22nd annual ACM symposium* on *User interface software and technology (UIST'09)* (pp. 121–124) New York, NY, USA: ACM.

Harrison, C., Tan, D., & Morris, D. (2010). Skinput: Appropriating the body as an input surface. *Proceedings of the SIGCHI Conference on Human Factors in Computing Systems (CHI'10)* (pp. 453–462). New York, NY, USA: ACM.

Hausen, D. (2014). Peripheral interaction: exploring the design space (Doctoral dissertation, München, Ludwig-Maximilians-Universität, Diss., 2014).

Hausen, D., Richter, H., Hemme, A., & Butz, A. Comparing input modalities for peripheral interaction: A case study on peripheral music control. In *Human-Computer Interaction–INTERACT 2013* (pp. 162–179).

Hurtienne, J. (2011). Image schemas and design for intuitive use. Exploring new guidance for user interface design (Doctoral dissertation, Technische Universität Berlin).

Junker, H., Amft, O., Lukowicz, P., & Tröster, G. (2008). Gesture spotting with body-worn inertial sensors to detect user activities. *Pattern Recognition, 41*(6), 2010–2024.

Kim, D., Hilliges, O., Izadi, S., Butler, A. D., Chen, J., Oikonomidis, I., & Olivier, P. (2012). Digits: freehand 3d interactions anywhere using a wrist-worn gloveless sensor. In *Proceedings of the 25th annual ACM symposium on User interface software and technology (UIST'12)* (pp. 167–176) New York, NY, USA: ACM.

Kratz, S. & Rohs, M. Protractor3D: A closed-form solution to rotation-invariant 3D Gestures. (2011). In *Proceedings of the 16th international conference on intelligent user interfaces (IUI'11)* (pp. 371–374) New York, NY, USA: ACM.

Kratz, S., Rohs, M., & Essl, G. Combining acceleration and gyroscope data for motion gesture recognition using classifiers with dimensionality constraints. In *Proceedings of the 2013 International Conference on Intelligent User Interfaces (IUI'13)* (pp. 173–178) New York, NY, USA: ACM.

Lyons, K., Starner, T., Plaisted, D., Fusia, J., Lyons, A., Drew, A., & Looney, E. W. (2004). Twiddler typing: One-handed chording text entry for mobile phones. *Proceedings of the SIGCHI Conference on Human Factors in Computing Systems (CHI'04)* (pp. 671–678). New York, NY, USA: ACM.

Mayrhofer, R. & Gellersen, H. (2007). Shake well before use: Authentication based on accelerometer data. *Pervasive computing* (pp. 144–161). Berlin: Springer.

Nanayakkara, S., Shilkrot, R., Yeo, K. P., & Maes, P. (2013). Eyering: A finger-worn input device for seamless interactions with our surroundings. In *Proceedings of the 4th Augmented Human International Conference (AH'13)* (pp. 13–20). New York, NY, USA: ACM.

Rekimoto, J. (2001). Gesturewrist and gesturepad: Unobtrusive wearable interaction devices. In *Proceedings IEEE Fifth International Symposium on Wearable Computers 2001* (pp. 21–27).

Ruiz, J. & Li, Y. (2011). DoubleFlip: a motion gesture delimiter for mobile interaction. In *Proceedings of the SIGCHI Conference on Human Factors in Computing Systems (CHI'11)* (pp. 2717–2720) New York, NY, USA: ACM.

Saponas, T. S. (2009). Enabling always-available input: through on-body interfaces. In *CHI'09 Extended Abstracts on Human Factors in Computing Systems (CHI EA'09)* (pp. 3117–3120). New York, NY, USA: ACM.

Schmidt, A., Kranz, M., & Holleis, P. (2005) Interacting with the ubiquitous computer: Towards embedding interaction. In *Proceedings of the 2005 joint conference on Smart objects and ambient intelligence: Innovative context-aware services: usages and technologies* (pp. 147–152).

Suh, S.-B., Hwang, J.-Y., Shim, J.-Y., Ryu, J., Heo, S., Park, C., et al. (2008). Computing state migration between mobile platforms for seamless computing environments. In *5th IEEE Consumer Communications and Networking Conference (CCNC 2008)* (pp. 1216–1217).

Tsukada, A., & Yasumura, M. (2001). Ubi-finger: Gesture input device for mobile use. In *Proceedings Ubicomp 2001 Informal Companion* (p. 11).

Vega, K., & Fuks, H. (2014). Beauty Tech Nails: Interactive Technology at your Fingertips. In *Proceedings of the 8th International Conference on Tangible, Embedded and Embodied Interaction* (TEI'14). New York, NY, USA: ACM, 61–64.

Wagner, J., Lecolinet, E., & Selker, T. (2014). Multi-finger chords for hand-held tablets: recognizable and memorable. *Proceedings of the 32nd annual ACM conference on Human factors in computing systems (CHI'14)* (pp. 2883–2892). New York, NY, USA: ACM.

Ward, J. A., Lukowicz, P., Tröster, G., & Starner, T. (2006). Activity recognition of assembly tasks using body-worn microphones and accelerometers. *IEEE Transactions on Pattern Analysis and Machine Intelligence, 28*(10), 1553–1567.

Weiser, M. (1991). The computer for the 21st century. *Scientific American*, 94–104.

Weiser, M. & Brown, J. S. (1997). The coming age of calm technology. *Beyond calculation* (pp. 75–85). (Springer, New York).

Wimmer, R. (2011). Grasp sensing for human-computer interaction. In *Proceedings of the fifth international conference on Tangible, embedded, and embodied interaction (TEI'11)* (pp. 221–228). New York, NY, USA: ACM.

Wimmer, R., & Boring. S. (2009). HandSense: discriminating different ways of grasping and holding a tangible user interface. In *Proceedings of the 3rd International Conference on Tangible and Embedded Interaction (TEI'09)* (pp. 359–362). New York, NY, USA: ACM.

Wolf, K. (2012). When hand and device melt into a unit: microgestures on grasped objects. In *CHI Extended Abstracts on Human Factors in Computing Systems (CHI EA 2012)* (pp. 959–962).

Wolf, K. (2015). Grasp interaction with tablets (Springer, Berlin). ISBN: 978–3-319-13980-7 (Print) 978-3-319-13981-4 (Online).

Wolf, K., Müller-Tomfelde, D., Cheng, K., & Wechsung, I. (2012a). PinchPad: Performance of touch-based gestures while grasping devices. In: Stephen, N.S. (Ed.), *Proceedings of the Sixth International Conference on Tangible, Embedded and Embodied Interaction* (TEI'12) (pp. 103–110) New York, NY, USA: ACM.

Wolf, K., Müller-Tomfelde, D., Cheng, K., & Wechsung, I. (2012b). Does proprioception guide back-of-device pointing as well as vision? In *Proceedings of the ACM annual conference extended abstracts on Human Factors in Computing Systems Extended Abstracts (CHI EA 2012)* (pp. 1739–1744).

Wolf, K., Naumann, A., Rohs, M., & Müller, J. (2011). Taxonomy of microinteractions: defining microgestures based on ergonomic and scenario-dependent requirements. In *Proceedings of IFIP TC international conference on human-computer interaction—Volume Part I (INTERACT 2011)* (pp. 559–575).

Wolf, K., Schleicher, R., Kratz, S., & Rohs, M. (2013). Tickle: A Surface-independent interaction technique for grasp interfaces. In *Proceedings of the International Conference on Tangible, Embedded and Embodied Interaction (TEI 2013)* (pp. 185–192).

Wolf, K. & Willaredt, J. (2015). PickRing: Seamless interaction through pick-up detection. In *Proceedings of the Augmented Human International Conference (AH 2015)* (pp. 13–20).

Chapter 6
Casual Interaction—Moving Between Peripheral and High Engagement Interactions

Henning Pohl

Abstract In what we call the focused-casual continuum, users pick how much control they want to have when interacting. Through offering several different ways for interaction, such interfaces can then be more appropriate for, e.g., use in some social situations, or use when exhausted. In a very basic example, an alarm clock could offer one interaction mode where an alarm can only be turned off, while in another, users can choose between different snooze responses. The first mode is more restrictive but could be controlled with one coarse gesture. Only when the user wishes to pick between several responses, more controlled and fine interaction is needed. Low control, more casual interactions can take place in the background or the periphery of the user, while focused interactions move into the foreground. Along the focused-casual continuum, a plethora of interaction techniques have their place. Currently, focused interaction techniques are often the default ones. In this chapter, we thus focus more closely on techniques for casual interaction, which offer ways to interact with lower levels of control. Presented use cases cover scenarios such as text entry, user recognition, tangibles, or steering tasks. Furthermore, in addition to potential benefits from applying casual interaction techniques during input, there is also a need for feedback which does not immediately grab our attention, but can scale from the periphery to the focus of our attention. Thus, we also cover several such feedback methods and show how the focused-casual continuum can encompass the whole interaction.

Keywords Casual interaction · Engagement · Control–change

H. Pohl (✉)
University of Hannover, Hannover, Germany
e-mail: henning.pohl@hci.uni-hannover.de

© Springer International Publishing Switzerland 2016
S. Bakker et al. (eds.), *Peripheral Interaction*,
Human–Computer Interaction Series, DOI 10.1007/978-3-319-29523-7_6

117

6.1 Introduction

Most systems around us are only designed for focused interactions (interaction with full attention and full control of the process), limiting us in how to interact with them. Consider something very basic such as going on a day trip. You decide to head to the sea and go to the station to catch some train going in that direction. However, once you stop to buy a ticket you encounter an obstacle. The ticket machine requires you to select a specific destination and a specific departure time. You might very well not care which destination to go to; after all you just wanted to go to any place next to the sea. But the machine forces you to make a selection, while it could easily access additional information to help you in your task. Which town is least crowded? Which train has the shortest wait time? Which beach has the best weather forecast for the day? Yet, the input from the user has to be exact, and such a ticket machine does not allow for more relaxed selections. If this machine offered what we call casual interactions, you could, e.g., just pick *"I'd like to go to the sea"* and have the system assist you with the details. This requires yielding some control over the task, which is the defining characteristic in casual interactions.

Casual interaction touches on similar topics as peripheral interaction, but offers a different perspective on what characterizes the shift from foreground to background, from focused to casual. In peripheral interaction, *"interactions with technology could be designed to shift between center and periphery of the attention"* to *"enable digital technologies to better blend into our everyday lives"* (Bakker et al. 2012). This, e.g., results in *"objects that could drift between the focus and periphery of a user's attention according to the momentary demands of their activity"* (Edge and Blackwell 2009). Where peripheral interaction focuses on the aspects of physical placement and attention, casual interaction builds on a user's desired level of control (also see Fig. 6.1). An interaction is *casual* when control is yielded to the system, whereas it is *peripheral* if low attention is given to the interaction. Those two aspects can overlap, e.g., when yielding control means using coarser interactions at the side, but at other times those two views diverge. Users can, e.g., have an

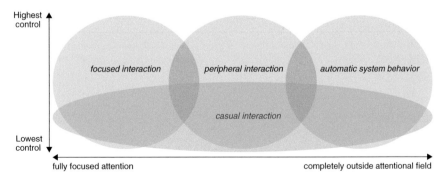

Fig. 6.1 Interactions become casual when users yield control to a system. Instead of requiring precise or focused input, they can then interact with more ambiguous or imprecise inputs

interaction in the center of their attention, yet choose to give up control (e.g., by providing ambiguous input and expecting the system to partly take over). The ticket machine mentioned above is such a system, where users are focused on the inter-action, yet might wish to yield some control over the precise outcome to the machine in order to lower their interaction load.

The concept of casual interaction thus revolves around the notion of control—as an aspect of user engagement. Engagement, as defined by O'Brien and Toms (O'Brien and Toms 2008), encompasses multiple attributes of an interaction, such as *attention, novelty,* or *challenge.* When focusing on engagement through *control* —a user is said to be more engaged in an interaction when she is asserting more control (e.g., by being precise) and vice versa. A central point in casual interaction then is that these are not just two choices to pick from. Instead, interaction with a system or device can happen at any point between those extremes. Users pick the interaction they find most appropriate for their chosen level of control. Thus, users can pick between having tight control of a system (focused interactions) and giving up some control over the outcome (casual interactions).

One might assume that users always would desire high control. However, control comes at a cost: To provide very precise and accurate input to a system (and thus exert high control), users need to do the same: give precise and accurate input. However, this is not always possible or desirable. For example, users might be tired or have their hands full, precluding them from fully controlling a device. Thus, there is a trade-off between how much they engage with a device (the level of control of their input) and the resulting control they thus receive over the device. In casual interactions, we closely investigate this tension. One might wonder why a user would choose one or the other. And what are the trade-offs to be considered here then? We will explore this further in this chapter and will also have a look at several examples of casual interaction systems.

In the following sections, we will first take a look back at a scenario similar to this book's introduction and examine *light control* from a casual interaction per-spective. After a brief overview of related previous concepts, we will then inves-tigate individual aspects of casual interaction more in depth. This covers basic aspects of why casual interaction is desirable, a closer look at the design space (how to yield control and how to design for multiple levels of control). Over the span of the chapter, we will look at concrete examples of systems that were designed for casual interactions, allowing users to scale back and assert less control during their interaction.

6.2 Light Control from a Casual Interaction Perspective

As in the introductory example from this book, we can envision a scenario where casual interaction supports controlling the lights in a smart home environment. To support casual interactions, multiple ways to affect the lighting are available, each with varying levels of control. This is in line with Offermans et al. (2014), who report that for users "*depending on the particular situation context, both a high degree of control and low effort can be considered important.*" In this example, those different interaction options are all integrated into one device–a bracelet controller. The user in our scenario then picks the one option she deems most fitting for her currently desired level of control.

Catherine comes home from work. Once she enters her house, the lights turn on and provide a neutral ambience. However, Catherine is tired after a long day at work and would like to change the lighting to a more calm and relaxing setting. She wears a bracelet that allows for multiple different ways to control the lighting. To switch to a different lighting preset, she quickly rotates her wrist outwards and back and then performs a waving gesture in the air. This is detected by the bracelet, and the lighting changes to the desired mood. After a short nap, she sits down on her sofa and decides to read. For reading, Catherine would like to increase the ambient light slightly. She grasps around the bracelet to activate the brightness mode. While holding the bracelet, she now turns her arm to increase the brightness to the desired level. She does not care much about the light color at this point and just desires an overall brightness increase. Now, a game of her favorite hockey team is about to be shown in TV. For the game, Catherine would like to change her living room lighting to her team's color. She is an avid fan and thus is much pickier in the exact lighting color. Thus, she uses the exact color control mode of the bracelet. She uses the embedded capacitive slider to pick just the right values for hue, saturation, and lightness that she wants. She can toggle between the different slider modes with light taps on the bracelet.

In this scenario, we encountered multiple ways to control the lighting. In their effect, they are all the same: The lights change to a different setting. However, they differ in the amount of control the user has and how much precision and focus they require. They also each make use of a different combination of sensing in the bracelet (as illustrated in Fig. 6.2). Catherine used three different interaction modes:

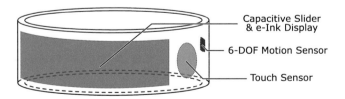

Fig. 6.2 In our envisioned mood lighting scenario, Catherine uses a bracelet that supports a range of interactions. She can directly control the color values with a capacitive slider or perform arm gestures which are picked up by the built-in motion sensor

Casual interaction By gesturing, she switched to some preset lighting pattern. This allows for large changes in lighting mood, but restricts user freedom to the available presets. The gestural interaction for this change can vary in complexity. Conventionally, users would pick simpler gestures for common presets and only move to more complex gestures for more rarely used mood settings. Catherine does not need to observe the bracelet while making preset changes, potentially allowing her to perform such interaction peripherally.

Semi-casual interaction When using the whole bracelet as a brightness slider, freedom of lighting choice is rather restricted. Instead of switching to a precise color setting, users in this mode can only enact a more general mood shift. However, the interaction needed for this is minimal and can be performed in the periphery of attention. The complexity is lower than in gesturing as no memorization of presets is required. While the user here does give away some control (after all, not all colors are reachable with just brightness changes), there is only minimal required inter-action with the device. This also makes this kind of interaction more appropriate when guests are present. While they might not appreciate Catherine to fiddle with color sliders, a quick dimming action on the bracelet is less disruptive.

Focused interaction Toggling between different slider modes and then using the precise built-in sliders allows Catherine to pick any color in the available space. However, this freedom comes at a significant interaction cost. Switching between and manipulating three different sliders is a complex task that required precision and thus cannot easily be relegated to the periphery. Thus, a user will likely only resort to this mode when other input modes are too restrictive.

We can see that each mode sits at a different point of the control space. Catherine in each situation picked the mode that provided her the needed level of control (i.e., precision when specifying the lighting change) while minimizing the put in effort. Note that this choice is not made by some system, but she retained control in picking the desired level of control.

In the given example, three different modes were available. However, this dis-cretization is a design choice, and for each system complexity and freedom have to be carefully weighted. With an increasing number of modes, users gain flexibility, but the risk of a mode error increases as well. Catherine could have instead chosen a bracelet with only one casual interaction mode (e.g., only using it for dimming). Here, she would use her phone for more precise interaction and switch between those two devices depending on how much control she desires. We will revisit this choice between integration and separation of interactions later in the chapter.

6.3 Related Work

There has been interest in concepts of interaction where users are less engaged or give up control for a long time. Buxton in 1995 already described the space between foreground and background interaction (Buxton 1995) using the example of a video chat system. He notes that foreground interaction uses higher bandwidth than background interaction but also happens intermittently, while background interaction allows for longer running, persistent interactions. While he specifically relates this to video chatting and relaying presence, this relation holds true for a more general interaction channel as well. In Buxton's model, though, these modes are discrete and, while users can move between foreground and background, he does not address how gradual change in ground would be addressed.

Interaction in the background has been taken a step further toward incidental (Dix 2002) or implicit (Ju et al. 2008) interactions. In Dix's incidental interaction, users might not even be aware of the interaction itself (they retain no conscious control in this instance). Once users become aware of the interaction, however, interactions become expected or even intended (users regain control through awareness). Here, a user's experience with a system drives how much control they can have. Ju et al.'s implicit interaction extends the foreground background model with an additional *initiative* dimension. Hence, a system, during foreground interaction, could be *reactive* and have the user in control, or act *proactively* on its own. They specifically explore proximity as a way to transition between these different modes.

A larger range of work has investigated concrete scenarios for foreground and background interactions. Hinckley et al. (2005), e.g., build on Buxton's work and explore how sensors in mobile devices can support both grounds. Along the same line, Hudson et al. (2010) detect *"whack gestures"* to enable interaction with mobiles without taking them out of a pocket. Olivera et al. (2011) instead look at tangibles and find that those can support background interactions by being less distracting and more fitting for concurrent interaction. In peripheral interaction, the background is described as the *periphery of attention* and designs hence focus on the aspects such as awareness [e.g., in the *CawClock* (Bakker et al. 2012)], or input in the periphery (e.g., using tangibles without looking at them).

In the presented concepts, the choice of ground is commonly based on attention and the grounds themselves are discrete or even binary. In contrast, casual interaction is concerned with users' level of control in an interaction. Casual interaction systems also can offer continuous change in ground, dependent on a user's changing level of control. The concept of yielding control builds upon the H-Metaphor by Flemish et al., who proposed a varying control system for automated vehicles where drivers can yield and take control as they choose.

> You can let your vehicle go without being completely out-of-the-loop, or you can reassert a more direct command, for example, by taking a tighter grip on your haptic interface (Flemish et al. 2003).

One example they use to describe this change is riding a horse. A rider can *"loosen or tighten the reins"* to change how much control to exert on the horse. Tightening the reins can, e.g., mean making more deliberate and decisive movements or interacting with the horse more frequently. When the reins are loose, the horse is given more freedom to decide where to go. By tightening the reins, a rider can take back control and steer the horse more closely. The horse itself contributes to the task. It can, e.g., see a path ahead and follow it even under loose reins. External cues thus inform the behavior of the horse. However, the rider retains the option to tighten the reins and steer off the path if so desired. Similarly, casual interaction systems are designed to allow looser reins when using a device— yielding some control to it as desired to offload some of the effort of the interaction.

6.4 Why Would We Want to Have Less Control?

As described earlier, there can be many reasons users might choose to yield control to a system. Here, we further explore why this might be the case. We group reasons for asserting low control into three categories: (1) mental reasons, (2) physical reasons, and (3) social reasons. These three categories, respectively, cover (1) internal, cognitive aspects; (2) those regarding a user's presence in the world; and (3) those arising from interactions with other people.

Mental reasons often relate to notions of distraction, exhaustion, or focus. This is often the case when a user is engaged in a different task primarily. In such situations, a secondary task in the periphery might only receive a small amount of attention. Focus in such a scenario can move back and forth numerous times (Bakker et al. 2012). If we design interactions to work at lower levels of focus, we might reduce the cost of such switching. Avoiding effort, however, is not necessarily bound to restriction by another task. In fact, just being exhausted after a long day can lead to active-choice avoiding behavior due to ego depletion (Baumeister et al. 1998)—a concept that postulates that willpower is finite and self-control decreases over time, leading us to avoid making active choices.

Physical reasons for choosing low control include scenarios such as wearing gloves, carrying bags, or the hands being busy with another task (e.g., driving). A user encumbered in such a way is not able to engage as much with her devices as an unimpaired user (Oulasvirta and Bergstrom-Lehtovirta 2011). For example, consider carrying home several grocery bags—the hand holding them cannot hold the phone as well. While having our hands full might mean that we cannot closely control our devices, in casual interaction there should be ways of interaction left for us to give commands even when thusly encumbered. An example of such interactions—performed while the hands are already busy—is microgestures (Wolf et al. 2011). As described in Chap. 5, such gestures make use of remaining degrees of freedom, not yet involved in the primary task (e.g., fingertip movements).

Social reasons for low control are often related to how we would like to be perceived when interacting (Goffman 1959), but also include questions of acceptable behavior. In situations such as meetings or dates, it is seen as rude to take out a phone and interact with it. We use attention to signal to others that we value our time with them. Engaged use of our devices can then negatively influence our relationships. Low-engagement interactions (possible without shifting focus a lot) can still be ok though. Imagine the mood lighting device from earlier: Sitting on a couch next to your date, taking out the phone to dim the lights could be seen as disruptive while the proposed dimming interaction is much more subtle and can be performed less visibly. Interacting casually not only allows signaling attention to others, but also gives users a general way to signal to observers how little engaged they are. A public image of being in control, yet not putting in too much effort for this, can be quite desirable (Warrington et al. 2000). Appearing to others as if one is trying too hard can have negative connotations.

6.5 Are Users Willing to Exert Less Control?

One key question in casual interaction is whether giving users a way to trade control for comfort is something they actually appreciate. It might well be that users want to have full control all the time and shy away from relinquishing some of it. However, we found that, when given a choice, users are willing to do just that if they felt they could retain an appropriate level of control to achieve their task. We tested this with a very simple setup: a steering task, where users had to control the movement of a ball and maneuver it to a goal area (Pohl and Murray-Smith 2013).

To complete this simple steering task, we gave them three different means of control, each at a different point in the focused-casual range. They could use (1) touch interaction to directly control the ball, (2) hover interaction to rate-control the ball (similar to a joystick), or (3) in-air swipe gestures to move the ball in a general direction. From (1) to (3) control degrades, while less and less focused interaction with the device is needed. When interacting in the most casual way, users could lean back, wave their hand over the device once, and be done. Compare this to touch interaction, where users had to move their finger over the screen multiple times to move the ball around. While this gives very precise control of the trajectory, it also requires much more work from the users. Note that the "*level of control*" for those three modes is not defined on an interval, but on an ordinal scale.

Participants completed multiple levels, where the difficulty of each level is determined by Accot and Zhai's (1997) steering law. We found that users indeed scale back their interaction if the task is sufficiently easy and they do not require full control—control correlates with task difficulty. In fact, users were very attracted to the more casual control modes and would try those first before resorting to more controlled interactions. Imagine we had built a system only allowing for focused and precise interaction. Those users would have had no way to scale back their control. So even when they would not have required a high level of control, they would have been forced to provide this input anyway. We feel forcing users to do more when they could get away with doing less is somewhat cruel. If we can design our devices in a way that allows users to lower their control when appropriate and push the interaction to the periphery, we should do so.

6.6 Integrated and Separated Casual Interaction Systems

When designing for casual interactions, there are two approaches: (1) try to design one device so it offers multiple ways to interact across the range of control, or (2) design for multiple devices where each device covers just a subset of the control range. Both options can be good choices, but offer distinct advantages and disadvantages.

Earlier, we already looked at one example of a device that incorporates different interaction modes: the light-control bracelet. With more casual interactions often using around-device space or coarser movements, such coexistence of different modes is feasible. However, this approach does make devices more complex. Instead of learning one way to use them, users now have to learn multiple techniques. Users might get confused when accidentally activating the wrong mode or might be overwhelmed when functionality is overloaded (e.g., when slider movements are interpreted differently depending on the active device mode). There is a fine line between a device that empowers users to do less and a device that frustrates users because they cannot figure out how to use it in a given moment. It will be up to system designers to pick the right number and kind of modes to combine for every specific instance.

In current systems, an incremental learning approach is often used to lessen the impact of required initial effort complexity somewhat. Instead of learning all different modes at once, users take up the general mode first. Over time, as they use the system, they then discover additional commands or modes (e.g., the keyboard shortcuts for often used menu items) slowly increasing their skills and capabilities. Similarly, users of integrated casual interaction systems could start with the focused mode first and then add more casual interactions as they see fit. This process can be supported by casual interaction systems pointing out more casual ways to achieve the same effect after a user interaction.

Instead of integrating several interaction techniques into one device, users could be given different devices for different levels of control. Most people already carry one device for focused interactions: their phone. Thus, there is little need to introduce additional focused interaction devices. Instead, wearables (such as watches or bracelets) are an example of a device class that supplements phones and could be utilized to support casual interactions complementary to the focused interactions of the phone. This could be a simplified form of the light-control bracelet, e.g., only allowing dimming of the lights. Similarly, we can envision such modes being integrated into clothing, furniture, or tools. For example, some lamps, such as the *TaoTronics TT-DL05*,[1] already come with integrated touch sliders for dimming. Such integrated dimmers allow for a way to change the lighting with less effort than taking out a phone, opening the lighting app, selecting the specific light,

---

[1]http://www.taotronics.com/taotronics-tt-dl05-led-portable-eye-care-lamp.html.

Fig. 6.3 This button enables a low-effort way of user recognition by observing button pressing behavior. For small groups of users, establishing who, e.g., entered a room can then be as easy as pressing a button. In addition to conflating the action with the recognition, this allows for recognition in the periphery as the button can, e.g., be pressed while entering the room

and then using the on-screen sliders to do the same. Instead, users can just touch and hold the lamp or drag along the base or stand.

One scenario where we specifically explored custom low-control devices is user recognition. For this, we modified a light switch and embedded a distance sensor (see Fig. 6.3). By observing how users press the button, small groups of users can be reliably distinguished (Pohl et al. 2015). While this does not offer the same level of security as, e.g., keycards, this setup allows performing user recognition in the periphery. Users are recognized as they enter the room and switch on the lights. Should they require a higher level of authorization, they can still switch to a traditional authentication method. The button, however, enables them to put less effort in and devote less attention to the task should they not require such a high level.

Instead of having objects in the environment imbued with interaction capabilities, we have also explored the concept of making use of any object for casual interactions (Pohl and Rohs 2014). Imagine your whole living room being tracked (e.g., by your phone or a stationary setup), and thus, any touch or other interaction with objects in the room being available as a means for input (as illustrated in Fig. 6.4). Instead of, e.g., having a dimmer control embedded into a device, you could repurpose any nearby object to temporarily fulfill the same role. Objects repurposed in this way can offer good affordances for many tasks (e.g., round

Fig. 6.4 Instead of embedding input capabilities into objects around us, we can leave them as is and track them externally. Manipulations of such objects or touches on them can then be used as a means of input. We can, for example, temporarily make a nearby coffee mug a volume slider or press down on a hacky sack to use it as a transient button. Such appropriation of objects can be limited to a given interaction window (e.g., the hacky sack is only a button when a call is coming in), or persist over longer durations (when objects are explicitly set aside for specific interactions)

objects invite turning and squishy objects invite pressing). While this makes them well suited as interactors, this also means less attention has to be paid when interacting with them. Turning a mug around can be done in the periphery, while modifying an on-screen dial requires at least visual focus on the interface.

Which one of those options is more appropriate when designing a casual interaction system is not a clear-cut decision. Integrating everything into one device increases portability but comes at the price of added complexity. On the other hand, one would not want a large number of specialized objects lying around everywhere. This would lead to clutter, making it hard to find a currently required one. A balance could be struck via a mixture of both models: having one centralized device for all focused and some casual interactions, in combination with a small number of casual interaction wearables and any number of casual interfaces integrated into objects. A lamp with an integrated dimmer (as described earlier) provides an additional casual interaction path that is fixed to one specific location. When next to the lamp, users then have the option of interacting with it casually. When away, they can use their phone to select and then dim the lamp. Should this level of control (remote) be required, having to resort to focused interaction is acceptable.

6.7   How to Design for Low Control

While we have already seen some examples of low-control systems, here we will take a closer look at what can be done when building low-control interfaces. Examples of casual interactions are interactions that (1) happen further away from a device, (2) use low-fidelity proxies, (3) are performed less accurately, (4) use a more restricted input repertoire, or (5) require less concentration or thought. By definition, an interaction is casual when control is given up. What that entails specifically then is dependent on the actual device and how one can interact with it.

As shown in Fig. 6.5, distance to the device can be one way to delineate casual interactions (Marquardt and Greenberg 2015; Marquardt et al. 2011). If we imagine a phone lying on a table, then picking it up and using touch interactions requires more effort and precision than waving in the general direction of the device. With increased distance feedback from the device becomes harder to receive, and often sensing fidelity will decrease as well. Thus, the bandwidth in the interaction goes down accordingly. Touch interaction allows users to provide more complex and rapid command sequences compared to gestures away from the device. This natural regression of input in around-device interactions can be used to either separate the around-device space into distinct zones of casualness or continuously change the control level.

As shown previously, repurposing nearby objects for interaction allows creating temporary control proxies. For example, when your phone rings, you can dismiss that call using any nearby object with some marker property (e.g., anything colored red and *pressable*). Not having to take out your phone for this results in an interaction where less attention is diverted. By using physical objects as proxies, we enable eyes-free interaction and allow users to move this interaction to their periphery.

Fig. 6.5 When designing for different input options in one device, distance from the device can be used to switch between them. Here, focused interaction happens on the device when using touch. In the above-device space, users can perform rough or precise gestures. In this example, close space is used for more complex gesturing, while the space far away from the device is used for more casual waving gestures. With increased distance the level of control decreases, but interactions become more casual

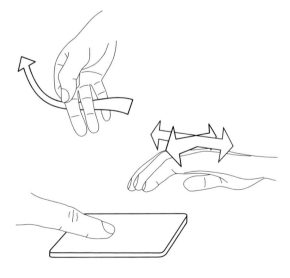

While distance to a sensing device naturally results in input regression, the coarseness of input can also be adapted independently. For example, in interaction with a touch screen, users can do both: precisely select small targets or use swipe gestures over the whole screen. One example of this is available in many current phones as *swipe to delete*. In the inbox view of their email app, users can either delete messages by touching them and then selecting a delete action from a menu bar or they can swipe over the message to directly delete it. The first action allows for more elaborate actions (selecting multiple messages, archiving instead of deleting, moving messages, ...), but also requires more precise input and thus more attention from the user. Another example are on-screen gestures, which can scale from very simple and easy to perform (e.g., horizontal swipes) to much more complex and harder to perform (e.g., drawing Chinese characters). In the framework of casual interactions, we can regard coarse input as more casual and precise input as more focused.

Similar to making input coarser, we can also just restrict the number of available inputs. Instead of showing twenty buttons on a screen, we might reduce this to three more general buttons. Here, the interaction stays the same (touch on a screen), but as the number of choices goes down, we decrease the mental load for selection and, by increasing target size, can also make acquiring targets easier. One example of this approach can be found in some smartwatches. Displaying a full keyboard on a smartwatch necessitates very small key sizes. Instead, messaging apps such as the one in the *Apple Watch* only display a smaller number of predefined replies (e.g., "*I'll call you back*"). The small number of available messages severely limits control of the user in what she can reply, but does enable replying fast and without much effort. By making shown information glanceable, users can take it in with less effort (and presumably better maintain focus elsewhere). This can tie in closely with a reduced number of input choices (showing less overall), but can also mean keeping the same number of controls but restricting the information shown per control (e.g., only displaying emoji abbreviations on message template buttons instead of full message texts). Reduced visual complexity and increased size of visual features already allow users to interact with their device at a distance by allowing them to perceive feedback without requiring them to pick up the device.

Overall, the more casual an interaction is, the more constrained, coarser, and distanced from the device the input can be. This is counter to the kind of interaction we are used to: focused on our devices and in a tight control loop where we quickly alternate perceiving output and providing new input. Note that none of the markers of casualness presented here are absolutes. For example, reducing the number of choices does not mean reducing them down to one (such as in *Amazon's Dash Button*[2]—an attachable physical button one can press to, e.g., order new detergent) or even zero (as in agent systems). Instead, there is a continuum where we can make

[2]https://www.amazon.com/oc/dash-button.

things more casual in several degrees. We can also combine two or more aspects. Further away from the device, we might use coarse and large gestures for input but at the same time also reduce the number of available options.

6.8   What Does Yielding Control to a System Require?

So far, we have described the general approach of yielding control and examined one scenario where this occurs when changing lighting mood. However, we should dive deeper into what it means from a system's perspective when we yield control to it. After all, while we have seen that users are willing to have less control and give some power to the system (see Sect. 5), this requires systems to actually do something sensible with this power. Asking your lighting system to change the mood to something a bit cozier and that system then playing back a wild light show would not match up with our intentions. Thus, yielding control usually requires a conceptual model of the space a system operates in. This often requires system designers to think about the problem space on a higher than usual level. For example, designing a lighting system that only exposes one color slider to users (leaving the choice of color completely up to them) can be done without much understanding of color theory. On the other hand, allowing users to manipulate mood requires dedicating design resources to that aspect as well.

Models used in casual interaction systems can come in many different forms. They can, for example, be based on some notion of *error* (e.g., in text entry), *likelihood* [e.g., in music retrieval such as in (Boland and Murray-Smith 2013)], or on a *designer's intuition* of important feature points (e.g., when limiting selection of lighting color to a list of known "*good*" colors). One difference in such models is thus whether they are more strongly based on a describable algorithmic principle or whether they encode a more human understanding of importance. The very extreme example of a model-based system is agents—here users completely delegate tasks. Based on a model, the agent system then makes all choices on behalf of the user. The model is typically informed by a set of sensor inputs (say, time of day and door status) and infers some action (e.g., sounding an alarm). As such, agents provide system behavior to the user with no required effort, but also take away all control. In casual interactions, we similarly make use of models to inform what to do once some control is ceased, but have the user stay in the loop. System behavior is not fully automated but instead steered to varying degrees by the user. As users are kept in the loop, they receive feedback and can correct or adapt system behavior as they choose.

One example of casual interaction using an error-centric model is adaptive autocorrection (Weir et al. 2014). As text entry on touch screen phones is more error-prone than on a physical keyboard, autocorrection algorithms are used to change an entered sequence with typos to the one most likely intended. There are actually two models at play here: (1) a touch model and (2) a language model. The touch model describes how we might not hit the center of a key on a touch screen

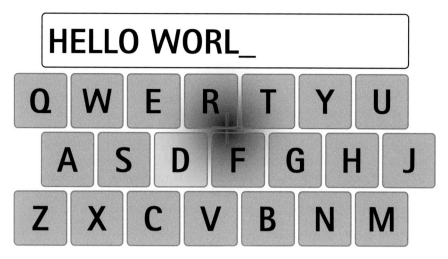

Fig. 6.6 In a touch screen keyboard, a language model provides a probability for the next letter (shown here as key color) and a touch model gives a measure of certainty for a user's touch (here shown as a gradient around the touch position indicated by a cross). The combination of both models determines the most likely next letter. We vary how much influence the language model has by changing the size of the touch area. When users press harder, it shrinks and keys closer to the touch are much more likely to be chosen. As users relax and only press lightly, the area increases and many more keys are potentially chosen—increasing the influence of the language model

keyboard but instead deviate to some degree. The language model on the other hand knows about likely character sequences and thus can, e.g., determine that a user probably did not want to enter "*hellp,*" but instead might have meant to enter "*hello.*" Together, these models help correcting for off-target touches and typos in the resulting text.

While this system behavior is generally very useful, it can get in the way the moment one tries to enter a word not known to the system. Then, autocorrection corrects something we did not want to have corrected at all. This is commonly problematic when mixing languages, using slang, or entering abbreviations. However, currently there is no way to take back some degree of control from the autocorrection system to override the behavior. If we think back to the horse riding example, this would be similar to a horse that always stays on the path. If you would like to ride out into the open field, you would be out of luck. Instead, we have explored using typing pressure to allow users to override autocorrection (as illustrated in Fig. 6.6). When they want to enter a word and have it not changed, they can do so by pressing down a bit harder. Note that this is a gradual shift between high and low control. There are no distinct control levels. When typing softly, users allow autocorrect to jump in and "*fix*" what they entered. Only for parts where autocorrection is not desired, control is taken. This combines both casual interaction when assistive behavior is welcomed and focused interaction when tight control over the system behavior is needed.

We already encountered one example of a designed model earlier: predefined answers in a smartwatch messaging app. Because typing on a smartwatch is cumbersome, the Apple Watch allows users to reply using a number of predefined messages. Thus, one can send back a quick "*ok*" without typing. The watch also generates contextual reply options to choose from (e.g., enabling "*sushi*" and "*pizza*" as replies when the previous message was "*should we get sushi or pizza?*"). In this way, the watch actually combines both algorithmic and designed models. With the Apple Watch, users also retain the option to dictate a reply. So while the default reply interface is more casual, a focused interaction is available if more control is needed. Another example of a designed model can be seen when looking back at the lighting change system described in the beginning. Programming the system to make sense of what it means to change the mood of the lighting (e.g., to make it more calm or cozy) comes down to hand-tuning mood-color mappings.

6.9 How to Adapt Output in Casual Interaction Systems?

So far we have mostly focused on casual interaction as a way to scale back control of a system. However, to allow for true casual interaction, there also need to be corresponding feedback techniques. Such casual feedback is designed for low attention capture and for use in the periphery. If we look at feedback used in current phones, then this is currently not considered. Vibration feedback, for example, is very disruptive and not suitable for casual feedback at all (Haller et al. 2011). Current fidelity of screen design also does not work well for peripheral and casual interaction. One approach is to have different visualization modes for levels of focused or casual interaction. *Stock Lamp* is one example of such a system specifically designed to adapt differently to focused (actively and passively) or peripheral use (Tanahashi and Ma 2015).

We have begun to investigate pressure as a feedback modality that can support the kind of peripheral feedback unsupported by vibration feedback (Pohl et al. 2015) (see also Fig. 6.7). In such compression feedback devices, pneumatic

Fig. 6.7 We are experimenting with pneumatics in cuffs around the wrist to apply compression feedback as a modality for low-disruption background notifications

actuation is used to tighten a strap around, e.g., a user's wrist. We found that at low pressures, feedback can be sustained over long periods, while not disrupting the user yet being perceivable. Such background feedback can help alleviate some of the disruption of notifications. Instead of sounding an alarm with every new incoming message (independent of urgency), casual feedback systems can notify users in the background that something is available for them to look at. By increasing the pressure in the strap, attention capture of the feedback can be increased to levels exceeding those of vibration feedback. Thus, this kind of feedback supports the whole range from casual to focused interaction. We can have it persist in the background (barely perceivable but readily noticeable when concentrating on it), but move it to the foreground when necessary.

Some current devices already try to incorporate their own version of more casual feedback. Some *Microsoft Lumia* phones come with *Glance screen* functionality and show basic notifications, while the main screen's backlight is off. Phones can be configured to only display this low-fidelity feedback for a short while after a hover interaction. Such glance screens try to provide some feedback at lower levels of interaction than unlocking the phone or activating a notification center. The Samsung Galaxy Note Edge takes another route and extends the screen over one of the outer edges. This allows displaying notifications at the side, allowing easier viewing when the phone is lying, e.g., more than arm's length away on a table. Ideally, this would be combined with a way for the phone to sense hands in the space in front of the phone. Users could then use casual interactions to, e.g., check active notifications and send quick replies, without even picking up the phone.

6.10 Conclusion

In this chapter, we have outlined the concept of casual interactions. Casual interactions try to provide options for lower control interaction to users. We feel that there is already a pressing need to be able to interact with less effort, which will only increase in the next couple of years. Our phones are focused interaction devices, which are with us at all times. It currently looks like, in addition, we might be carrying around several wearables as well (which will all want some of our attention). At the end of the day, we come back to our smart home full of internet-of-things devices (again wanting us to engage with them). Casual interaction is one approach to keep the assault of attention grabbing at bay. Casual interaction allows us to relegate some control back to a system, while keeping us in the loop and enabling us to take back control as we see fit. This is different from agent-based systems that try to automate things and move the user out of the loop.

Fundamentally, casual interactions built onto the assumption that completely modeling user state is unfeasible. Instead of trying to predict when a user is tired, encumbered, or in a demanding social situation, we relegate that to the users themselves. They are the ones able to pick how much control to give away, not a system on their behalf. With current system design ingrained with the assumption of focused interaction, we should try to investigate more how to do things with less. This will require specific models for each use case, but once we find underlying concepts, we can reduce complexity where appropriate, yet retain a way back to interaction with said complexity where users demand so.

References

Accot, J., & Zhai, S. (1997). Beyond Fitts' law: Models for trajectory-based HCI tasks. In *Proceedings of the SIGCHI conference on Human factors in computing systems—CHI '97* (pp. 295–302). New York, USA: ACM Press.

Bakker, Saskia, van den Hoven, Elise, & Eggen, Berry. (2012a). Acting by hand: Informing interaction design for the periphery of people's attention. *Interacting with Computers, 24*(3), 119–130.

Bakker, S., van den Hoven, E., Eggen, B., & Overbeeke, K. (2012b). Exploring peripheral interaction design for primary school teachers. In *Proceedings of the Sixth International Conference on Tangible, Embedded and Embodied Interaction—TEI '12* (Vol. 1, pp. 245–252). New York, USA: ACM Press.

Baumeister, Roy F., Bratslavsky, Ellen, Muraven, Mark, & Tice, Dianne M. (1998). Ego depletion: Is the active self a limited resource? *Journal of Personality and Social Psychology, 74*(5), 1252–1265.

Boland, D., & Murray-Smith, R. (2013). Finding my beat: Personalised rhythmic filtering for mobile music interaction. In *Proceedings of the 15th International Conference on Human-computer Interaction with Mobile Devices and Services—MobileHCI '13* (pp. 21–30). New York, USA: ACM Press.

Buxton, B. (1995) Integrating the periphery and context: A new taxonomy of telematics. In *Proceedings of Graphics Interface—GI '95* (pp. 239–246).

Dix, A. (2002). Beyond intention—Pushing boundaries with incidental interaction. In *Proceedings of Building Bridges: Interdisciplinary Context-Sensitive Computing* (pp. 1–6). UK: Glasgow University.

Edge, D. & Blackwell, A. F. (2009). Peripheral tangible interaction by analytic design. In *Proceedings of the 3rd International Conference on Tangible and Embedded Interaction—TEI '09* (pp. 69–76). New York, USA: ACM Press.

Flemish, F. O., Adams, C. A., Conway, S. R., Goodrich, K. H., Palmer, M. T., & Schutte, P. C. (2003). The H-metaphor as a guideline for vehicle automation and interaction. Technical report TM-2003-212672. NASA.

Goffman, Erving. (1959). *The presentation of self in everyday life.* New York, NY: Anchor.

Haller, M., Richter, C., Brandl, P., Gross, S., Schossleitner, G., Schrempf, A., et al. (2011). Finding the right way for interrupting people improving their sitting posture. In *Proceedings of the 13th International Conference on Human-Computer Interaction—INTERACT '11* (pp. 1–17).

Hinckley, K., Pierce, J., Horvitz, E., & Sinclair, M. (2005). Foreground and background interaction with sensor-enhanced mobile devices. *ACM Transactions on Computer-Human Interaction, 12*(1), 31–52.

Hudson, S. E., Harrison, C., Harrison, B. L., & LaMarca, A. (2010). Whack gestures: Inexact and inattentive interaction with mobile devices. In *Proceedings of the fourth international conference on Tangible, embedded, and embodied interaction—TEI '10* (pp. 109–112). New York, USA: ACM Press.

Ju, W., Lee, B. A., & Klemmer, S. R. (2008). Range: Exploring implicit interaction through electronic whiteboard design. In *Proceedings of the ACM 2008 conference on Computer supported cooperative work—CSCW '08* (pp. 17–26). New York, USA: ACM Press.

Marquardt, N., & Greenberg, S. (2015). *Proxemic interactions: From theory to practice*. USA: Morgan & Claypool.

Marquardt, N., Jota, R., Greenberg, S., & Jorge, J. A. (2011). The continuous interaction space: Interaction techniques unifying touch and gesture on and above a digital surface. In *Proceedings of the 13th IFIP TCI3 Conference on Human Computer Interaction—INTERACT'11* (pp. 461–476).

O'Brien, H. L., & Toms, E. G. (2008). What is user engagement? A conceptual framework for defining user engagement with technology. *Journal of the American Society for Information Science and Technology, 59*(6), 938–955.

Offermans, S. A. M., van Essen, H. A., & Eggen, J. H. (2014). User interaction with everyday lighting systems. *Personal and Ubiquitous Computing, 18*(8):2035–2055.

Olivera, F., García-Herranz, M., Haya, P. A., & Llinás, P. (2011). Do not disturb: Physical interfaces for parallel peripheral interactions. In *Proceedings of the 13th IFIP TC 13 International Conference on Human-Computer Interaction—INTERACT'11* (pp. 479–486). Berlin: Springer.

Oulasvirta, A., & Bergstrom-Lehtovirta, J. (2011). Ease of juggling: Studying the effects of manual multitasking. In *Proceedings of the 2011 annual conference on Human factors in computing systems—CHI'11* (pp. 3103–3112), New York, USA: ACM Press.

Pohl, H., Becke, D., Wagner, E., Schrapel, M., & Rohs, M. (2015a). Wrist compression feedback by pneumatic actuation. In *CHI'15 Extended Abstracts on Human Factors in Computing Systems on—CHI EA'15*.

Pohl, H., Krause, M., & Rohs, M. (2015b). One-button recognizer: exploiting button pressing behavior for user differentiation. In *Proceedings of the 2015 ACM International Joint Conference on Pervasive and Ubiquitous Computing—UbiComp'15*.

Pohl, H., & Murray-Smith, R. (2013). Focused and casual interactions: Allowing users to vary their level of engagement. In *Proceedings of the SIGCHI Conference on Human Factors in Computing Systems—CHI'13* (pp. 2223–2232), New York, USA: ACM Press.

Pohl, H., & Rohs, M. (2014). Around-device devices: My coffee mug is a volume dial. In *Proceedings of the 16th international conference on Human-computer interaction with mobile devices & services—MobileHCI'14*.

Tanahashi, Y., & Ma, K. L. (2015). Stock lamp: An engagement-versatile visualization design. In *Proceedings of the 33rd Annual ACM Conference on Human Factors in Computing Systems—CHI'15* (pp. 595–604).

Warrington, M., Younger, M., & Williams, J. (2000). Student attitudes, image and the gender gap. *British Educational Research Journal, 26*(3), 393–407.

Weir, D., Pohl, H., Rogers, S., Vertanen, K., & Kristensson, P. O. (2014). Uncertain text entry on mobile devices. In *Proceedings of the 32nd Annual ACM Conference on Human factors in Computing Systems—CHI'14* (pp. 2307–2316), New York, USA: ACM Press.

Wolf, K., Naumann, A., Rohs, M., & Müller, J. (2011). A taxonomy of microinteractions: Defining microgestures based on ergonomic and scenario-dependent requirements. In *Proceedings of the 13th IFIP TC 13 International Conference on Human-Computer Interaction—INTERACT'11* (pp 559–575).

Chapter 7
Fluent Transitions Between Focused and Peripheral Interaction in Proxemic Interactions

Jo Vermeulen, Steven Houben and Nicolai Marquardt

Abstract Proxemic interaction is a vision of computing that employs proxemic relationships to mediate interaction between people and ensembles of various digital devices. In this chapter, we focus on aspects of peripheral interaction in proxemic interactions. We illustrate how to facilitate transitions between interaction outside the attentional field, the periphery, and the center of attention by means of the Proxemic Flow peripheral floor display. We summarize and generalize our findings into two design patterns: slow-motion feedback and gradual engagement. We propose slow-motion feedback as a way to draw attention to actions happening in the background and provide opportunities for intervention, while gradual engagement provides peripheral awareness of action possibilities and discoverability and reveals possible future interactions.

Keywords Proxemic interactions · Cross-device interaction · Slow-motion feedback · Gradual engagement · Interactive floors

7.1 Introduction

The field of human–computer interaction has traditionally focused on designing user interfaces and interactions that rely on the user's undivided attention. This changed with the introduction of visions of *ubiquitous computing* (Weiser 1991)

J. Vermeulen (✉)
Department of Computer Science, University of Calgary, Calgary, Canada
e-mail: jo@jovermeulen.com

J. Vermeulen
HCI Centre, University of Birmingham, Birmingham, UK

S. Houben · N. Marquardt
UCL Interaction Centre/ICRI Cities, University College London, London, UK
e-mail: s.houben@ucl.ac.uk

N. Marquardt
e-mail: n.marquardt@ucl.ac.uk

© Springer International Publishing Switzerland 2016   137
S. Bakker et al. (eds.), *Peripheral Interaction*,
Human–Computer Interaction Series, DOI 10.1007/978-3-319-29523-7_7

and *context-aware computing* (Schilit et al. 1994), Buxton's background–foreground model (1995) and the notion of *calm technology* (Weiser and Brown 1996). Calm technology is a vision of digital interactions that—just as many of our interactions in the physical world—take place in the background or *periphery* of attention. While calm technology mostly focused on perceiving information in the periphery—as with ambient displays such as Jeremijenko's Live Wire (Weiser and Brown 1996)—Hausen (2014) and Bakker et al. (2015) extended this idea by introducing the notion of *peripheral interaction*, which also included interacting in the periphery of attention. As described by Bakker et al. (2015), interactions that occur in the periphery can also dynamically *transition* between being peripheral to being the center of attention when relevant or desired.

This chapter focuses on aspects of peripheral interaction within *proxemic interactions*. The idea of proxemic interactions in computing extends the classic vision of context awareness and uses proxemic relationships (e.g., distance and orientation between entities) to mediate interaction between people and *ensembles* of various digital devices (Ballendat et al. 2010; Greenberg et al. 2011). In particular, this chapter discusses how to *facilitate transitions* between outside the attentional field, the periphery, and the center of attention in proxemic interactions.

We start with a brief overview of proxemic interactions and highlight potential problems. We then explain solutions to address these problems with the use of a peripheral floor display called Proxemic Flow. Next, we analyze the different techniques used in Proxemic Flow and explain how these facilitate transitions between outside the attentional field, the periphery, and the center of attention, grounded in Norman's Stages of Action model. Finally, we generalize our experiences with designing such interactions into two general design patterns: slow-motion feedback and gradual engagement.

7.2 Proxemic Interactions

In this section, we introduce proxemic interactions and provide an overview of potential interaction challenges with proxemics-aware devices.

7.2.1 Background

Proxemic interactions (Greenberg et al. 2011; Marquardt and Greenberg 2015) feature devices that have fine-grained knowledge of nearby people and other devices—such as their precise *distance*, *orientation*, how they *move* into range, and their *identity* or *location*, depicted in Fig. 7.1.

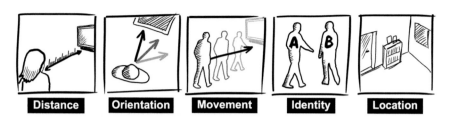

Fig. 7.1 Proxemic interactions imagine a world of devices that have fine-grained knowledge of nearby people and other devices. When designing proxemic interactions, five key proxemic measures (or dimensions) between people, digital devices, and non-digital objects can be considered: *distance, orientation, movement, identity*, and *location* (*image source* Greenberg et al. 2011)

Proxemic interaction is based on anthropologist Edward T. Hall's *theory of proxemics* (1966), which investigated the use of interpersonal space in nonverbal communication. In particular, proxemics theory identified the culturally specific ways in which people use interpersonal distance and orientation to understand and mediate their interactions with others. The idea of proxemics is not limited to interpersonal communication; it also extends to '*the organization of space in [our] houses and buildings, and ultimately the layout of [our] towns*' (Hall 1963). As put forward by Marquardt, Greenberg, and colleagues (Ballendat et al. 2010; Greenberg et al. 2011; Marquardt et al. 2012), proxemic relationships are used to mediate interaction between people and *ensembles* of different digital devices, such as mobile devices or large interactive surfaces, as shown in Fig. 7.2. Additionally, they envision devices to take into account the non-digital, semi-fixed, or fixed objects in the user's physical environment (Greenberg et al. 2011).

One of the most commonly featured aspects of Hall's theory applied in HCI is the use of four *proxemic zones* that correspond to interpretations of interpersonal distance: the *intimate, personal, social*, and *public* zone (Greenberg et al. 2011). In earlier research, these different interaction zones have been used to mediate interaction with large interactive surfaces (Prante et al. 2003; Vogel and Balakrishnan 2004; Ju et al. 2008). Inter-entity distance in the context of proxemics has also been used to facilitate cross-device interaction (Hinckley 2003; Hinckley et al. 2004; Kray et al. 2008; Gellersen et al. 2009).

In recent years, large interactive surfaces such as vertical displays or tabletops are appearing increasingly in semi-public settings (Brignull and Rogers 2003; Ojala et al. 2012). With the availability of low-cost sensing technologies (e.g., IR range finders, depth cameras) and toolkits such as the Proximity Toolkit (Marquardt et al. 2011) or the Microsoft Kinect SDK, it is fairly straightforward to make these large displays react to the presence and proximity of people. This has been picked up both by researchers, e.g., (Ju et al. 2008; Müller et al. 2009a, 2012; Jurmu et al. 2013), and by commercial parties—see (Greenberg et al. 2014) for several examples. Although

Fig. 7.2 An example of proxemic interactions with the Proxemic Media Player (Ballendat et al. 2010). **a** The system is activated when the person enters the room, **b** continuously reveals more content when approaching the display, **c** allows explicit interaction through direct touch in close proximity, and **d** switches implicitly to full-screen mode when the person is taking a seat (*image source* Ballendat et al. 2010)

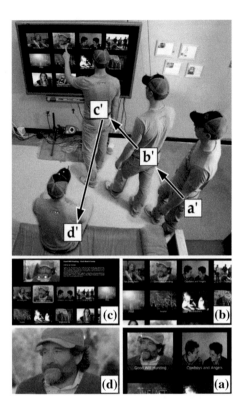

these low-cost sensing solutions tend to apply fairly crude measures of proxemics and only take into account a few proxemic dimensions (Fig. 7.1), proxemic interactions are becoming more commonplace in our everyday environments.

People have natural expectations regarding increasing engagement and interactivity when approaching others. In proxemic interactions, these expectations are applied to interactions with devices. Given that this is learned and often implicit behavior, the fact that people expect increasing interactivity and engagement when approaching digital devices (Greenberg et al. 2011) can be characterized as occurring in the *periphery* of attention.

7.2.2 Interaction Challenges with Proxemic Interactions

We provide a brief summary of potential interaction challenges within proxemic interactions. These motivate the *peripheral floor visualizations* that we will introduce in Sect. 7.3.

7.2.2.1 Interaction Challenges with Implicit Interaction: The Need for Fluent Transitions Between the Center and the Periphery of Attention

One of the core issues causing interaction challenges with proxemics-aware interactive surfaces is their reliance on implicit interaction. The Proxemic Media Player (Fig. 7.2) automatically pauses videos when two people are both oriented away from the display (e.g., when starting a conversation), which might be surprising and disturbing for users when they first encounter this. Ballendat et al. (2010) argue that defining the rules of behavior that indicate how systems using proxemic interactions interpret and react to users' movements is critical. It is important to indicate how users are being tracked by the system and also to indicate how the system is taking action based on people's movements. When the system is doing something that could potentially be surprising or disturbing to the user, peripheral interactions could subsequently transition to the center of attention to make the user aware of what is happening.

Transitions between interaction outside the user's attentional field, or the periphery of attention and the center of attention are necessary to avoid unintended actions, undesirable results and difficulties in detecting or correcting mistakes (Bellotti et al. 2002; Ju et al. 2008). When designing proxemic interactions, it should be possible for systems to fluently moving between the periphery and the center of attention. Proxemics-aware systems should partially reside in the periphery, where they inform people about what is happening without overwhelming them, while still allowing people to move to focused interaction at the center of attention when they want to take control and intervene.

Ju et al. (2008) introduced a framework for implicit interaction and proposed interaction techniques along two axes: *initiative* (which party is driving the interaction: user or system) and *attentional demand* (the degree of cognitive/perceptual load: background or foreground interactions), building on Buxton's background/foreground model (1995). Their implicit interaction framework can be used to design systems that can easily transition between outside the attentional field, the periphery, and the center of attention, providing the right amount of balance between proactive behavior and user control. Transitions between different combinations of the degree of attentional demand—i.e., background or foreground interaction—and the degree of initiative—e.g., whether the system acts, indicates that it can act or waits for the user to act—allow systems to transition between outside the attentional field, the periphery, and the center of attention and back to prevent, mitigate, and correct errors in proactive behaviors. A system could for example transition from a proactive/background state to a proactive/foreground state to make the user aware of what it is doing. This is illustrated in Ju et al.'s (2008) proximity-aware interactive whiteboard by its use of the *user reflection, system demonstration,* and *override* interaction techniques.

7.2.2.2 Invisibility of Action Possibilities and Lack of Guidance

Users can have difficulty knowing how they can interact with proxemics-aware large displays. As stated by Müller et al. (2010), the commonly used interaction modalities for public displays (e.g., proximity, body posture, mid-air gestures) can be hard to understand at first glance. For example, when the display reacts to the user's location in different interaction zones (Vogel and Balakrishnan 2004), the invisibility of these zones causes problems with identifying the exact zone where the display reacts to their input. This is particularly difficult when the display is also reacting to the input of other people (Jurmu et al. 2013). Next to showing the possible actions that users can perform, people may want to know what will happen, for example, when approaching the display.

7.2.2.3 Lack of Support for Opt-in and Opt-out Mechanisms

Another problem is the lack of explicit opt-in or opt-out mechanisms, which is especially important in (semi-)public spaces. Jurmu et al. (2013) and Brignull and Rogers (2003) found that users sometimes wish to avoid triggering the display and rather just passively observe it. Greenberg et al. (2014) further discuss how interactive surfaces in semi-public settings typically lack opt-in and opt-out choices (either deliberately or unintentionally). They state that at the very least, a way to opt-out should be provided when people have no desire to interact with the surface. Furthermore, users could want to know what would happen if they leave or opt-out. Will the surface be reset to its original state? What will happen to their personal information still shown on the surface?

In the next section, we explore how we addressed interaction challenges with proxemic interactions in the Proxemic Flow system using a peripheral floor display.

7.3 Proxemic Flow: Dynamic Peripheral Floor Visualizations for Revealing and Mediating Proxemic Interactions

As mentioned earlier, devices that react to the presence and proximity of people and devices can bring about interaction challenges, due to the implicit nature of interaction with these devices. Proximity and presence are typically sensed in the background, outside people's attention. People may not notice that the device is interactive, commonly referred to as *display blindness* or *interaction blindness* (Huang et al. 2008; Müller et al. 2009b; Ojala et al. 2012) in the domain of large public displays. This can lead to people being uncertain about possibilities for interaction, or unaware of how to recover from mistakes such as accidental interactions.

Fig. 7.3 Proxemic Flow
providing awareness of
tracking and fidelity, zones of
interaction, and invitations for
interactions (*image source*
Vermeulen et al. 2015)

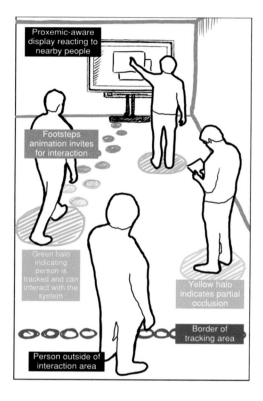

Proxemic Flow (Vermeulen et al. 2015) is designed to address these challenges
using a secondary, *peripheral floor display* that provides a set of dynamic visualization strategies to help people interact with a primary proxemics-aware display
(Fig. 7.3). The floor reveals the interaction area through borders and zones, shows
halos around people's feet when they are recognized by the display, and invites
spatial movement and next interaction steps through waves and steps animations.
Information shown in the periphery—on the floor display—can seamlessly become
the center of the attention and move back to the periphery in *fluent transitions*
(Weiser and Brown 1996).

Due to their low visual complexity, a quick glance at the floor visualizations is
often sufficient, for example, when users are unsure about action possibilities, or
whether or not they are correctly tracked. Since the visualizations do not coincide
with the content on the primary display, users can focus their attention on the
primary display. The floor visualizations nevertheless provide continuous peripheral awareness of tracking, interaction zones, and possibilities for future interactions. Similar to Bakker et al. (2015), we imagine that these floor visualizations
could move further into the periphery after users get more acquainted with them.
During informal observations of people interacting with the floor, we noticed that
essential concepts such as halos and zones were easy to understand.

Next, we provide an overview of the different floor visualizations supported by
Proxemic Flow, and explain how the combination of two interactive surfaces, one
targeting interaction at the center of attention (the primary vertical display) and
another aimed at interaction at the periphery of attention (the secondary floor display), allows for seamless transitions between both types of interaction across the
user's attentional field. The peripheral floor visualizations provide awareness of
tracking status and quality (Sect. 7.3.1); awareness of entry and exit points for
interaction (Sect. 7.3.2); and invite approach, encourage movements, and suggest
possible next interactions (Sect. 7.3.3).

7.3.1   Tracking Feedback with Halos

A fundamental challenge for designing interaction with proxemics-aware displays
is providing a person with immediate feedback about how the system is currently
recognizing and interpreting spatial movements, gestures, or other input from the
user.

7.3.1.1   Personal Halos

The personal halo provides immediate feedback on the floor display about the
tracking of a person in space. When the person enters the area in front of the public
display, a green halo (an area of approximately 1 m diameter) appears underneath
the person's feet (Fig. 7.4a). The halo moves with them when moving in the
tracking area and therefore gives continuous, peripheral feedback about the fact that
the person is being recognized and tracked by the system.

In addition to information about the fact that a person *is* tracked, the floor
provides information about the *quality* of tracking. Most computer vision-based
tracking systems (RGB, depth, or other tracking) have situations in which tracking
works well, does not work well, or does not work at all (e.g., due to lighting
conditions, occlusion, limited field of view). Therefore, the personal halo visualization encodes the quality of tracking in the color of the halo. To indicate tracking
quality, we use three colors (Fig. 7.4b). A green halo indicates optimal tracking of
the person in space. Its color changes to yellow when the quality of tracking
decreases, for example, when the person moves to the limits of the field of view or
when partially occluded by another person or piece of furniture. Finally, a red halo
color is shown when the tracking of the person is lost, such as when moving too far
away from the camera, or if occlusion is hiding the person completely. For this last
case, since the person is no longer tracked, the red halo visualization remains static
at the last known location of the person, fades in and out twice, and then disappears
(the duration of this animation is approximately 4 s). If the person moves back into
the field of view of the camera and the tracked region, the halo color changes back
to green or yellow accordingly.

Fig. 7.4 Halos: **a** providing feedback about active tracking and **b** the tracking quality (*image source* Vermeulen et al. 2015)

7.3.1.2   Multi-user Halos

Interactions around interactive surfaces are often not limited to a single person. With multiple people, information about active tracking and its fidelity becomes even more important due to the likelihood of occlusions causing increased tracking problems.

If multiple people are present in front of the screen, each person's individual position that the system currently tracks is shown with a colored halo (Fig. 7.5a). Color changes indicate a change in how well the user is tracked. For example, in case another person walking into the space interrupts the tracking camera's view of

Fig. 7.5 Halos for multi-user interaction: **a** both people are visible to the system; **b** one person is occluding the camera's view of the other person, indicated by the red halo (*image source* Vermeulen et al. 2015)

a person, the changing color of the halo from yellow to red tells the person that they are no longer being tracked (Fig. 7.5b). Similarly, if two people stand very close to each other, making it difficult for the computer vision algorithm to separate the two, the halo color changes to yellow.

7.3.1.3   Trails: Revealing Interaction History

As a variation of the halo technique, the *spatial trail* feedback visualizes the past spatial movements of a person in the interaction area. The trails are shown as illuminated lines on the floor that light up when a person passes that particular area (Fig. 7.6). The illumination fades out after a given time (after 5 s in our application), thus giving the impression of a comet-like trail. The colors that are used to light up the floor are identical to those of the person's halo (i.e., green, yellow, red) and therefore still provide information about the tracking quality. As the trail visualization remains visible for a longer time, it provides information about past movements of people interacting with the system. The trails can potentially help to amplify the *honeypot effect* (Brignull and Rogers 2003)—the effect that people are attracted to a device that they see others interacting with—by showing the past trails of other people moving toward the interactive display, thereby inviting other bystanders and passersby to approach the display as well.

7.3.2   Zones and Borders as Entries and Exits for Interaction

The next set of floor visualization strategies aimed to reveal interaction possibilities and facilitated opt-in and opt-out. Zones reveal spatial regions around the primary display, while borders make the boundaries of the interaction area explicit.

Fig. 7.6 Trails, visualizing the history of spatial movements of a person (*image source* Vermeulen et al. 2015)

7.3.2.1   Opting-in: Proxemic Interaction Zones

Many designs of large interactive displays make use of spatial zones around the display for different kinds of interaction (Vogel and Balakrishnan 2004) or to change the displayed content dependent on the zone, a person is currently in. These zones, however, are not always immediately understandable or perceivable by a person interacting with the display. Our floor visualizations explicitly reveal zones of interaction, enabling a person to see where interaction is possible and make deliberate decisions about opting-in for an interaction with the display by entering any of the zones.

We demonstrate the use of zone visualizations with the Proxemic Flow system and an example photograph gallery application. Similar to earlier examples of proxemics-aware displays (Vogel and Balakrishnan 2004; Ballendat et al. 2010), our photograph gallery application uses discrete spatial zones around the display that are mapped to the interactive behavior of the application on the large display. When no users are interacting with the system, a large red rectangular zone indicates the area furthest away from the display that triggers the initial interaction with the display (Fig. 7.7a). This serves as an entry zone for interaction, i.e., an area to opt-in for interaction with the system. In our current implementation, we use a 3 s pulsating luminosity animation, fading the color in and out. Once a person enters this zone, the large display recognizes the presence of the person, tracks the person's movement, and their halo is shown. The first zone then disappears and a second zone appears— an area to interact with the display when in front of it (visible as the blue rectangle in Fig. 7.7b). When the person begins approaching the display, the content gradually reveals more of the photograph collection on the display. As the person draws closer, more images are revealed. This is a behavior identical to the Proxemic Media Player (Ballendat et al. 2010). Once entering the second zone, the person can use hand gestures in front of the display to more precisely navigate the temporally ordered photograph gallery (e.g., grabbing photographs, sliding left or right to move forward or back in time). Again, once the person enters the close-interaction zone in front of the display, the floor visualization of that zone disappears.

7.3.2.2   Opting-out and Exit Interaction: Borders

While we envision zone visualizations primarily as explicit cues to convey the zones for interacting, and for allowing a person to deliberately engage and opt into interact with the system, we can also consider visualizations that help a person leave the interaction area (i.e., opting-out). We illustrate this concept with borders shown in the Proxemic Flow application. In continuation of the application example from before, once the person entered the interaction zone (blue) directly in front of the display and interacts with the display content through explicit gestures, a red border around the actively tracked interaction area surrounding the display is shown to make the boundaries of that interaction space explicit and visible (Fig. 7.7c). We chose to dynamically show the border only in situations when a person engaged

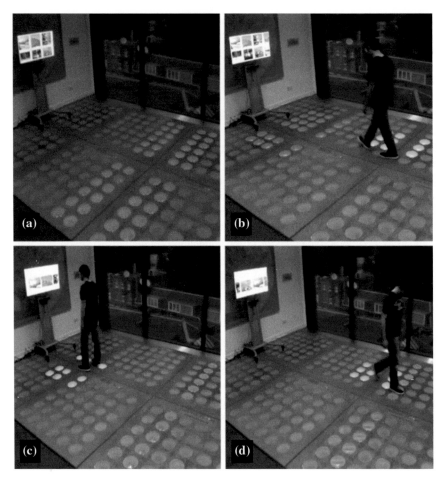

Fig. 7.7 The interaction areas in front of the display represented as **a** *red* and **b** *blue rectangular zones*; **c** borders indicate thresholds to cross for **d** leaving the interaction space in front of the display (*image source* Vermeulen et al. 2015)

with the system, but this could alternatively remain a fixed feature of the visualizations shown on the floor. A reason for showing a fixed visualization of the interaction boundaries with borders could be always to clearly indicate where a person can both enter and leave the interaction area (Fig. 7.7d).

7.3.3 Footsteps and Waves to Invite Interaction

Finally, we introduce floor visualization strategies to invite approach, encourage a person to move to a new location, and suggest possible next interaction steps. In particular, in this category of visualizations, we introduce two strategies: waves and footsteps.

7.3.3.1   Waves: Encouraging Approach

Our first strategy is intended to invite people to move closer to the large display for interaction. With our waves technique, we make use of the output capabilities of the illuminated floor for showing looped animations of lights fading in and out, with the effect of a wave of light going toward the large screen (Fig. 7.8a). Different visual designs of the wave effect are possible, for example, a circular wave effect with the large display at the center, starting with larger circles and continuously decreasing the radius.

7.3.3.2   Footsteps: Suggesting Next Action Possibilities

The footstep visualization is designed to offer a person clues about possible next interaction steps, in particular for encouraging spatial movements in the environment. The visualization shows animated footsteps (in our case, these are represented through glowing circles) beginning at one location on the floor and leading to another location. This technique is inspired by the earlier work of the *Follow-the-light* (Rogers et al. 2010) design that uses animated patterns of lights embedded in a carpet to encourage different movement behaviors by luring people away from an elevator toward the stairs.

To illustrate this technique, we revisit our Proxemic Flow example application with the large-display photograph gallery viewer. When a person enters the interactive (i.e., tracked) space in front of the display and stands still for over 5 s, the floor begins the footstep animation (Fig. 7.8b) to invite the person to move closer to

Fig. 7.8   a Waves inviting for interaction and **b** footsteps suggesting action possibilities (*image source* Vermeulen et al. 2015)

the display, in particular, to move to the interaction zone in front of the display, enabling the person to use mid-air gestures to further explore the image collection. The footstep animation begins directly in front of the person and leads toward the blue rectangular area highlighted in front of the display (Fig. 7.8b). The footsteps visualization strategy can be used to reveal interaction possibilities, particularly those involving spatial movements of the person. This strategy can be used in many other contexts for guiding or directing a user in the environment and for encouraging certain movements in a space.

7.3.4 Proxemic Flow in Norman's Stages of Action Model

Next, we position the Proxemic Flow floor visualizations in Norman's *Stages of Action model* (Norman 2013). We illustrate how they assist users in interacting with the primary display by providing essential information during the stages of execution and the stages of evaluation.

7.3.4.1 Norman's Stages of Action Model

Norman introduced the *Action Cycle* as a way to analyze how we interact with 'everyday things,' including doors, light switches, kitchen stoves, and also computers and information appliances. Norman (2013) suggests there are two main parts to any action in an interface: executing the action and evaluating the results, or 'doing and interpreting.' Furthermore, actions are related to our goals; we formulate a goal, execute certain actions to achieve that goal, then evaluate the state of 'the world' to see whether our goal has been met, and if not, execute more actions to achieve our goal or otherwise formulate new goals that again result in more action (Fig. 7.9).

Norman introduces the *Stages of Execution* and the *Stages of Evaluation* as a breakdown of these two parts, which together with goal formulation form the *Seven*

Fig. 7.9 Norman's Stages of Action: formulating goals, executing actions that impact the 'state of the world,' and evaluating these changes to see whether the goals have been met. The Seven Stages of Action consist of one stage for goals, three stages for execution, and three for evaluation (*image* based on Norman 2013)

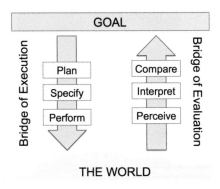

Stages of Action. Starting from our goal (the first stage), we go through three stages of action: plan (the action), specify (an action sequence), and perform (the action sequence). To evaluate the state of the world, there are three more steps: perceive (what happened), interpret (make sense of it), and compare (was what happened what I wanted?), as illustrated in Fig. 7.9.

With respect to peripheral interaction, Norman notes that not all activity in these stages is conscious—he states that even goals may be subconscious: '*we can do many actions, repeatedly cycling through the stages of while being blissfully unaware that we are doing so. It is only when we come across something new or reach some impasse, some problem that disrupts the normal flow of activity, that conscious attention is required.*' (Norman 2013, p. 42).

7.3.4.2 Peripheral Floor Visualizations in Norman's Stages of Action Model

The peripheral floor visualizations in the Proxemic Flow system act as cues that enable people to more easily navigate between implicit and explicit interaction. In other words, they enable interaction in the periphery of attention and focused interaction. Figure 7.10 shows how the different floor visualizations are situated within Norman's Stages of Action model.

Personal halos (Figs. 7.4 and 7.5) improve peripheral awareness of how the system is tracking people's spatial movements (*tracking feedback*), and help people

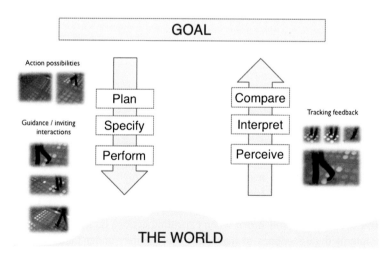

Fig. 7.10 The floor visualizations in the Proxemic Flow System, situated in Norman's Stages of Action model. Tracking feedback helps users know-how their input is being interpreted by the system during the stages of evaluation (*right*). Borders and zones reveal action possibilities and help users in the stages of execution (*left*). Finally, waves and steps animations invite and guide interactions, again helping users in the execution phase (*left*)

evaluate the 'state of the world.' The landing area (Fig. 7.7a) reveals an *entry zone* for interaction to help users know where they should go to engage with the system, and thus assists users in executing actions. When a user is engaging with the primary display, borders appear around the actively tracked interaction area to make the boundaries of the interaction space explicit and visible, and reveal *exit zones* for opting-out or disengaging with the system. Again, these visualizations help people discover action possibilities and thus can be situated within the stages of execution. Finally, Proxemic Flow uses the waves and steps visualizations (Fig. 7.8) to *invite* interaction, *guide* people's interactions, and *suggest next interactions* (e.g., direct people to a certain location using the footsteps visualization). This category of visualizations helps people to execute and perform actions. All the floor visualizations are shown in the user's periphery and do not require constant attention.

7.4 Design Patterns

Based on our experiences in designing proxemic interactions that transition between outside the attentional field, the periphery, and center of attention, we generalize and summarize our insights into two design patterns: *slow-motion feedback* and *gradual engagement*. The strengths of design patterns (Borchers 2001; Tidwell 2005) lie in unifying prior work, synthesizing essential and generalizable interaction strategies, and providing a common vocabulary for discussing design solutions. Most importantly, patterns can inform and inspire future designs and also allow for variations of the pattern applied to different domains.

7.4.1 The Slow-motion Feedback Pattern

One of the core design patterns we employ to enable fluent transitions across a person's attentional field is *slow-motion feedback* (Vermeulen et al. 2014). We start by illustrating how slow-motion feedback can enable interactions that transition from outside the user's attentional field toward their periphery of attention, to the center of attention, and then back. Next, we provide a definition of slow-motion feedback and illustrate how it is used in Proxemic Flow.

The idea of slow-motion feedback is simple: Just as we speak slowly when we explain something to someone who has difficulty understanding what is being said, interactive systems can *slow down* when executing actions on the user's behalf and provide intermediate feedback to make sure that the user understands and is aware of what is happening. Slow-motion feedback is a way to provide users with sufficient time to (i) *notice* what is going on, and provide them with the opportunity to (ii) *intervene* if necessary.

7.4.1.1   Applications of Slow-motion Feedback

Slow-motion feedback allows people to control devices in the periphery of attention, when they are made aware of what is happening outside their attentional field. We illustrate how this might work by referring back to the example in Chap. 1, in which the lights automatically turn on in the home when inhabitants enter late at night, even though others are already asleep.

In this case, the lighting control system could use slow-motion feedback to provide users with control over this automatic action. It could first increase the brightness of the lights slowly and provide a simple means to cancel or control this action (e.g., by flicking one of the light switches). After noticing what the system is doing (or about to do), and deciding that it is an unwanted action, the user can then override the system action so that the lights do not turn on. In this example, we have effectively moved from an automatic action occurring *outside the user's attentional field* with the motion-sensitive lighting control, over the *periphery of attention* when using slow-motion feedback to make the user aware of what is going on, to the user's *center of attention* when they decide to control the lighting and turn the lights off (see Fig. 7.11). Finally, the lighting control system moves back into the periphery and outside the user's attentional field.

A similar example is illustrated by Vermeulen et al. (2009): A system action that automatically turns off the lights is slowed down. In this technique, animated lines are projected on the walls of the room to visualize what is happening (Fig. 7.12). These animated lines represent connections between sensors and output devices and they progress toward the target output device. In this case, line animations are drawn toward each of the lights in the room. The lights will only turn off when the animated lines reach the lights, providing people with the opportunity (and time) to intervene if necessary.

Another example of an action by the system being 'slowed down' to allow users to intervene is Gmail's 'undo send' feature (Fig. 7.13). This feature provides users with a configurable 5 to 30 s window to undo sending an e-mail. While Gmail shows feedback to the user informing them about the sent e-mail, the actual sending

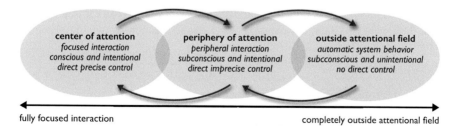

Fig. 7.11 The three types of interaction with computing devices, as explained earlier in Chap. 1, along a continuum ranging from fully focused attention to interaction occurring completely outside the attentional field. Slow-motion feedback (Sect. 7.4.1) and gradual engagement (Sect. 7.4.2) allow us to transition between these different types of interaction (*image* reproduced from Chap. 1)

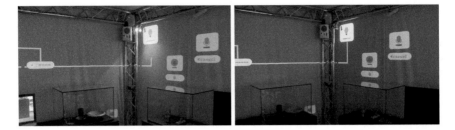

Fig. 7.12 An application of slow-motion feedback. Animations show that the system is about to dim the lights (*left*). The system's action is *slowed down* to allow users to notice what is happening, and provide sufficient time to intervene, if necessary. The lights are only dimmed when the animated line reaches them (*right*) (*image source* Vermeulen et al. 2009)

Fig. 7.13 Another example of slowing down the system action: providing a specific time window during which sent e-mails can be 'undone' (*source* Gmail)

of the e-mail is delayed so that users have a chance to undo this action in progress. The e-mail is sent after the specified time-out unless the user clicks the 'Undo' button. In the meantime, the user can go about other activities in the e-mail interface, while the 'Undo Send' label essentially provides them with a control mechanism in the periphery of attention.

A final example of slow-motion feedback can be found in the Range proximity-aware whiteboard (Ju et al. 2008). The whiteboard transitions between an ambient display mode and a whiteboard mode based on the user's distance to the display. It does so by showing an animation where all content is moved from the center of the board to the borders when a user steps closer. This happens slowly enough so that users both notice it and have sufficient time to react if this was not what they wanted. Users can override this automatic action of making space by grabbing content and pulling it back to the center.

7.4.1.2 Defining Slow-motion Feedback

Slow-motion feedback essentially manipulates the time frame, in which the system executes actions to realign it with the time frame of the user (Bellotti et al. 2002). With slow-motion feedback, the system's actions are deliberately *slowed down* to increase awareness of what is going on outside the user's attentional field and provide opportunities for user intervention. Slow-motion feedback is less relevant for long running tasks or tasks that are being performed at the center of attention, where users have no difficulty noticing that something is happening and have sufficient time to intervene.

We now define slow-motion feedback using a two-dimensional design space that allows us to articulate the different possibilities for how and when information about the result of an action can be provided. The two dimensions in this design space are the *time* at which information is provided about the result of an action and the *level of detail* of that information (Fig. 7.14). We define two key moments: At time t_0, the action is started (either by the user or the system), and at time t_1 the action has been completed by the system. Likewise, we define two important values for the level of detail dimension: The level d_0 represents the situation, in which the user does not receive any information about the result of their action, while at level d_1, the user receives fully detailed information about the result of the action.

Slow-motion feedback amplifies the time difference between t_1 and t_0 ($t_1 - t_0$) or the duration of an action in the user's time frame. Execution of the action is postponed by delaying t_1 to t_2 (with $t_2 > t_1$). The available time to notice that the action is happening thus increases to ($t_2 - t_0$), as shown in Fig. 7.14. Designers can rely on animations (Chang and Ungar 1993) to transition between t_0 and t_2, such as *slow-in/slow-out*, in which the animation's speed is decreased at the beginning and at the end of the motion trajectory to improve tracking and motion predictability (Dragicevic et al. 2011).

7.4.1.3 Slow-motion Feedback in Proxemic Flow

To draw people's attention and thus move from the periphery to the center of attention, the floor visualizations rely on animations. For example, when tracking is lost, Proxemic Flow uses slow-motion feedback to make the user aware of this: A pulsating *red halo* visualization is shown at the person's last known location, which disappears after approximately 4 s (Fig. 7.4). When something goes wrong with tracking, users are given cues to alert them to this, and they can intervene if necessary (e.g., when occluding another user, or stepping outside of the tracked area).

Fig. 7.14 Slow-motion feedback amplifies the time to intervene by showing feedback until t_2 (*orange line*) instead of t_1 (*gray line*) (*image source* Vermeulen et al. 2014)

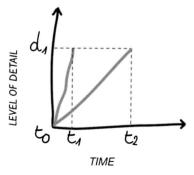

Similarly, the *trails* strategy effectively uses a slowed down version of the tracking halos to display traces of previous movements on the floor to make bystanders aware of people's movements (which occur outside the attentional field or in the periphery), and amplify the honeypot effect (Brignull and Rogers 2003).

7.4.2 The Gradual Engagement Pattern

Gradual engagement (Marquardt et al. 2012) is the second design pattern facilitating the transitions from peripheral to focused interaction and one of our core design principles. Essentially, this pattern describes how interfaces can be designed to gradually engage users by progressively revealing connectivity and interaction possibilities as a function of inter-device proximity. The capabilities of a system follow this pattern flow across three distinct stages: (1) *awareness* of device presence/connectivity, (2) *reveal* of exchangeable content, and (3) interaction methods for *transferring* content between devices tuned to particular distances and device capabilities. We first explain the gradual engagement pattern and then apply it to the peripheral-to-focused interaction transitions in Proxemic Flow.

7.4.2.1 The Gradual Engagement Design Pattern

The gradual engagement pattern recognizes that a person may not be directly attending to a system (i.e., the system is *outside the person's attentional field*). The system can still try to be helpful by presenting an interface that selectively and progressively informs the user of information of interest. The pattern synthesizes and generalizes strategies from earlier work, in which designed systems interpret decreasing distance and increasing mutual orientation between a person and a device within a bounded space as an indication of a person's gradually increasing interest in interacting with that device (Vogel and Balakrishnan 2004; Ju et al. 2008). As mentioned earlier, Vogel and Balakrishnan (2004) directly applied Hall's theory (1966) to a person's interaction with a public display. They defined four discrete zones around the display that affect a person's interaction when moving closer: from far to close, interactions range from ambient display of information, to implicit, subtle, and finally personal interaction. The interaction moves from the periphery of attention to focused interactions. Similarly, Ju et al.'s (2008) interaction techniques with the digital whiteboard remain public and peripheral or implicit from a distance, and become increasingly more private and explicit when the person moves closer to that display.

We generalize the sequence inherent in these (and other) systems as a design pattern called gradual engagement. There are three basic stages, which we will further elaborate later:

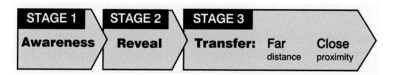

Fig. 7.15 Stages of the gradual engagement design pattern: from awareness, to reveal, to information transfers (*image source* Marquardt et al. 2012)

Stage 1. Background information supplied by the system provides awareness to the person about opportunities of potential interest when viewed at a distance;
Stage 2. The person can gradually act on particular opportunities by viewing and/or exploring its information in more detail simply by approaching it; and
Stage 3. The person can ultimately engage in action if desired.

The pattern can be further refined and applied to different contexts. For example, to mitigate challenges when creating cross-device interactions, we can refine the general gradual engagement design pattern by considering fine-grained proxemic relationships between multiple devices allowing seamless transitions from awareness to information transfer. Specifically, engagement increases continuously across three stages as people move and orient their personal device toward other surrounding devices (Fig. 7.15). The refined three stages are given below:

Stage 1 Awareness of device presence and connectivity is provided, so that a person can understand which other devices are present and whether they can connect with one's own personal device. We leverage knowledge about proxemic relationships between devices to determine when devices connect and how they notify a person about their presence and established connections.
Stage 2 Reveal of exchangeable content is provided, so that people know which content of theirs can be accessed on other devices for information transfer. At this stage, a fundamental technique is progressively revealing a device's available digital content as a function of proximity.
Stage 3 Transferring digital content between devices, tuned to particular proxemic relationships and device capabilities, is provided via various strategies. Each is tailored to fit naturally within particular situations and contexts: from a distance versus from close proximity; and transfer to a personal device versus a semi-public device.

An interesting feature in the gradual engagement pattern is that users control the speed at which information is revealed. The faster the users approach a device, the faster the information is shown, which realigns the system's time frame with their own. In this case, the natural hesitation of novices and the rapid approach of experts can have the intended consequences.

7.4.2.2   Applications of the Gradual Engagement Design Pattern

To illustrate how the gradual engagement pattern can be applied, consider the following use of a proximity-dependent progressive reveal for mitigating cross-device interactions. A brainstorming application, shown in Fig. 7.16, provides awareness (Stage 1) of nearby recognized tablet computers by showing proxy icons on the screen. These indicators on screen are representations supporting the transition from peripheral to focused interaction. The application continuously reveals content during Stage 2—in this case, multiple sticky notes located on people's tablets—as they move closer to the large display. The wall display shows thumbnails of all sticky notes located on the tablets above the awareness icons (Fig. 7.16). For the person sitting at a distance, the actual text on these notes is not yet readable (Fig. 7.16a), but the number of available notes is already visible. For the second person moving closer to the wall display, the thumbnails increase in size continuously (Fig. 7.16b). For the third person standing directly in front of the display, the

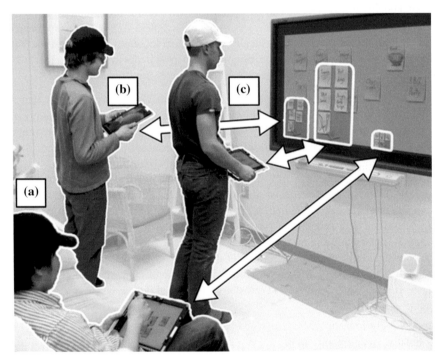

Fig. 7.16 Proximity-dependent progressive reveal of personal device data of multiple users at different distances to the display: **a** minimal awareness of a person sitting further away, **b** larger, visible content of a person moving closer, and **c** large awareness icons of person standing in front of the display (*image source* Marquardt et al. 2012)

sticky notes are shown at full size (Fig. 7.16c), allowing the person to read the text of all notes stored on the tablet and to pursue Stage 3 interactions. While in Stage 3, digital content can be exchanged through various interaction techniques, such as direct touch drag-and-drop of content or device gestures initiating transfer of information.

Next, we consider the characteristics of the gradual engagement pattern in the context of the Proxemic Flow visualizations, and how this pattern can support transitions from peripheral to focused interactions.

7.4.2.3   Gradual Engagement in Proxemic Flow

As mentioned in Sect. 7.3, the different visualizations in Proxemic Flow can be categorized into different phases. Similar to the gradual engagement design pattern, the floor visualizations gradually reveal possible interactions as a function of proximity to, and increasing engagement with, the primary display.

As people move around the space in front of the primary display, the secondary peripheral floor display progressively moves through three phases that afford gradual engagement: (1) awareness of tracking status and quality through *personal halos*, (2) awareness of entry and exit points for interaction through *borders and zones*, and (3) inviting approach, encouraging movements, and suggesting possible next interactions with *waves and footsteps*.

Borders and personal halos correspond to *Stage 1* of the gradual engagement design pattern, providing awareness of tracking and entry and exit points for interaction. Note that phases (1) and (2) of Proxemic Flow can be interchanged, depending on whether borders are always shown around the interaction area, or only after initially engaging with the system (as discussed in Sect. 3.2.2). When the floor initially does not show borders or zones, people can still become aware of the floor display as they enter the tracking zone and notice their personal tracking halos.

As people increasingly engage with the primary display by approaching it, the floor reveals more detailed information in the user's periphery through *zones* that reveal where interaction is possible, for example to interact with the display using gestural interaction, as shown in Fig. 7.7b. Zones can be revealed continuously as users approach the primary display or may be shown in discrete steps (e.g., as in Fig. 7.7 where a possible next zone is shown after the user entered an initial landing zone). This corresponds to *Stage 2* in the gradual engagement design pattern: progressively revealing action possibilities.

Finally, once people are directly engaging with the primary display, the floor provides additional inviting and guiding visualizations to suggest future interaction steps and encourage movements around the display. These visualizations serve the purpose of assisting users in their interactions and correspond to *Stage 3* in the gradual engagement design pattern.

7.5 Discussion

In this chapter, we discussed how designers can enable interactions that transition between outside the attentional field, the periphery, and the center of attention while interacting with proxemics-aware devices.

First, we demonstrated the use of dynamic, in situ visualizations on a peripheral floor display with the Proxemic Flow system to mediate proxemics-aware interactions with large interactive surfaces. Our floor display (1) provides peripheral information about current tracking and tracking fidelity; (2) reveals action possibilities for easy opt-in and opt-out; and (3) provides cues that invite users for movement across the space and possible next interaction steps. These proposed techniques target several important interaction problems with large interactive surfaces that were identified in earlier work. The fluent transitions between the periphery and the center of attention made possible by these floor visualization strategies have the potential to improve walk-up-and-use interaction with future large surface applications in different contexts, such as gaming, or for entertainment or advertisement purposes. During initial observations, we noticed that users only need to pay attention to the floor occasionally, which allows them to stay focused on the main application running on the primary large interactive display.

Secondly, we generalized our experiences with designing proxemics-aware systems that can transition between interactions outside the attentional field, peripheral interactions, and focused interactions using two design patterns: slow-motion feedback and gradual engagement. We propose slow-motion feedback as a way to draw attention to actions happening in the background and provide opportunities for intervention, while gradual engagement provides peripheral awareness of action possibilities and discoverability and reveals possible future interactions. These design patterns are not limited to the specific form factor of a multi-display setup with a floor display and large vertical display. They can also be applied to smaller-scale proxemic interactions and other ubicomp spaces.

There are some limitations to our proposed techniques and design patterns. Proxemic Flow is targeted at walk-up-and-use interaction with proxemics-aware large displays in sparsely populated semi-public spaces. In very crowded spaces, the floor visualizations can be less effective due to people obstructing the floor. Moreover, there are limitations to what the low-resolution floor visualizations can convey. Nevertheless, the visualizations were intentionally designed to be minimalistic and act as effective peripheral cues that minimize the required visual bandwidth for attending to them. Furthermore, slow-motion feedback could be a problem for time-critical tasks, as it could have a negative effect on the overall task completion time. Ideally, users should also be able to control the extent to which interactions are slowed down and the speed at which increasing feedback is provided (e.g., as in gradual engagement), as the optimal speed will be different for each user.

During informal observations of people interacting with the floor display, we noticed that essential floor visualizations such as zones and halos were easy to understand. In the future, we plan further studies to confirm these early findings and further explore the use of peripheral floor displays to mediate proxemic interactions with large interactive surfaces.

Acknowledgments We thank our collaborators and co-authors of joint publications which formed the basis of the content covered in this chapter: Till Ballendat, Jon Bird, Sebastian Boring, Karin Coninx, Rob Diaz-Morino, Saul Greenberg, Ken Hinckley, Kris Luyten. We also thank Lindsay MacDonald for editing drafts of this book chapter.

References

Bakker, S., van den Hoven, E., & Eggen, B. (2015). Peripheral interaction: Characteristics and considerations. *Personal and Ubiquitous Computing, 19*, 239–254. doi:10.1007/s00779-014-0775-2

Ballendat, T., Marquardt, N., & Greenberg, S. (2010). Proxemic interaction: Designing for a proximity and orientation-aware environment. In *Proceedings of ITS '10* (pp. 121–130). New York, NY, USA: ACM.

Bellotti, V., Back, M., Edwards, W. K., et al. (2002). Making sense of sensing systems: Five questions for designers and researchers. In *Proceedings of CHI '02* (pp. 415–422). ACM.

Borchers, J. (2001). *A pattern approach to interaction design* (1st ed.). London: Wiley.

Brignull, H., Rogers, Y. (2003). Enticing people to interact with large public displays in public spaces. In *Proceedings of INTERACT '03*.

Buxton, W. (1995). Integrating the periphery and context: A new taxonomy of telematics. In *Proceedings of Graphics Interface '95* (pp. 239–246). Citeseer.

Chang, B.-W., & Ungar, D. (1993). Animation: From cartoons to the user interface. In *Proceedings of the 6th Annual ACM Symposium on User Interface Software and Technology* (pp. 45–55). New York, NY, USA: ACM.

Dragicevic, P., Bezerianos, A., Javed, W., et al. (2011). Temporal distortion for animated transitions. In *Proceedings of CHI '11* (pp. 2009–2018). New York, NY, USA: ACM.

Gellersen, H., Fischer, C., Guinard, D., et al. (2009). Supporting device discovery and spontaneous interaction with spatial references. *Personal and Ubiquitous Computing, 13*, 255–264. doi:10.1007/s00779-008-0206-3

Greenberg, S., Boring, S., Vermeulen, J., & Dostal, J. (2014). Dark patterns in proxemic interactions: a critical perspective. In *Proceedings of DIS '14*. New York, NY, USA: ACM.

Greenberg, S., Marquardt, N., Ballendat, T., et al. (2011). Proxemic interactions: The new ubicomp? *Interactions, 18*, 42–50. doi:10.1145/1897239.1897250

Hall, E. T. (1963). A system for the notation of proxemic behavior. *American Anthropologist, 65*, 1003–1026.

Hall, E. T. (1966). *The hidden dimension* (1st ed.). Garden City, NY: Doubleday.

Hausen, D. (2014). Peripheral interaction—exploring the design space. PhD Thesis, University of Munich.

Hinckley, K. (2003). Synchronous gestures for multiple persons and computers. In *Proceedings of the 16th Annual ACM Symposium on User Interface Software and Technology* (pp 149–158). New York, NY, USA: ACM.

Hinckley, K., Ramos, G., Guimbretiere, F., et al. (2004). Stitching: Pen gestures that span multiple displays. In *Proceedings of the Working Conference on Advanced Visual Interfaces* (pp. 23–31). New York, NY, USA: ACM.

Huang, E. M., Koster, A., & Borchers, J. (2008). Overcoming assumptions and uncovering practices: When does the public really look at public displays? In *Proceedings of the 6th International Conference on Pervasive Computing* (pp. 228–243). Berlin, Heidelberg: Springer.

Ju, W., Lee, B. A., & Klemmer, S. R. (2008). Range: Exploring implicit interaction through electronic whiteboard design. In *Proceedings of CSCW '08* (pp. 17–26). ACM.

Jurmu, M., Ogawa, M., Boring, S., et al. (2013). Waving to a touch interface: Descriptive field study of a multipurpose multimodal public display. In *Proceedings of PerDis '13* (pp. 7–12). New York, NY, USA: ACM.

Kray, C., Rohs, M., Hook, J., & Kratz, S. (2008). Group coordination and negotiation through spatial proximity regions around mobile devices on augmented tabletops. In *3rd IEEE International Workshop on Horizontal Interactive Human Computer Systems, 2008. TABLETOP 2008* (pp. 1–8).

Marquardt, N., Ballendat, T., Boring, S., et al. (2012). Gradual engagement: Facilitating information exchange between digital devices as a function of proximity. In *Proceedings of ITS '12* (pp. 31–40). New York, NY, USA: ACM.

Marquardt, N., Diaz-Marino, R., Boring, S., & Greenberg, S. (2011). The proximity toolkit: prototyping proxemic interactions in ubiquitous computing ecologies. In *Proceedings of UIST '11* (pp. 315–326). New York, NY, USA: ACM.

Marquardt, N., & Greenberg, S. (2015). Proxemic interactions: From theory to practice. San Rafael: Morgan & Claypool Publishers.

Müller, J., Alt, F., Michelis, D., & Schmidt, A. (2010). Requirements and design space for interactive public displays. In *Proceedings of MM '10* (pp. 1285–1294). New York, NY, USA: ACM.

Müller, J., Exeler, J., Buzeck, M., & Krüger, A. (2009a). Reflective signs: Digital signs that adapt to audience attention. *Proceedings of the 7th International Conference on Pervasive Computing* (pp. 17–24). Berlin, Heidelberg: Springer.

Müller, J., Walter, R., Bailly, G., et al. (2012). Looking glass: A field study on noticing interactivity of a shop window. In *Proceedings of CHI '12* (pp. 297–306). New York, NY, USA: ACM.

Müller, J., Wilmsmann, D., Exeler, J., et al. (2009b). Display blindness: The effect of expectations on attention towards digital signage. In *Proceedings of Pervasive '09* (pp. 1–8). Berlin, Heidelberg: Springer.

Norman, D. A. (2013). *The design of everyday things*. New York, NY: Basic Books.

Ojala, T., Kostakos, V., Kukka, H., et al. (2012). Multipurpose interactive public displays in the wild: Three years later. *Computer, 45*, 42–49. doi:10.1109/MC.2012.115

Prante, T., Röcker, C., Streitz, N., et al. (2003). Hello. Wall–beyond ambient displays. In *Adjunct Proceedings of Ubicomp* (pp. 277–278). Citeseer.

Rogers, Y., Hazlewood, W. R., Marshall, P., et al. (2010). Ambient influence: Can twinkly lights lure and abstract representations trigger behavioral change? In *Proceedings of Ubicomp '10* (pp. 261–270). New York, NY, USA: ACM.

Schilit, B., Adams, N., & Want, R. (1994). Context-aware computing applications. In *Proceedings of WMCSA '94* (pp. 85–90). Washington, DC, USA: IEEE Computer Society.

Tidwell, J. (2005). Designing interfaces: Patterns for effective interaction design (1st ed.) Sebastopol: O'Reilly Media.

Vermeulen, J., Luyten, K., Coninx, K., et al. (2015). Proxemic flow: Dynamic peripheral floor visualizations for revealing and mediating large surface interactions. In *Proceedings of INTERACT 2015*.

Vermeulen, J., Luyten, K., Coninx, K., & Marquardt, N. (2014). The design of slow-motion feedback. In *Proceedings of DIS '14* (pp. 267–270). New York, NY, USA: ACM.

Vermeulen, J., Slenders, J., Luyten, K., & Coninx, K. (2009). I bet you look good on the wall: Making the invisible computer visible. In *Proceedings of the European Conference on Ambient Intelligence* (pp. 196–205). Berlin, Heidelberg: Springer.

Vogel, D., & Balakrishnan, R. (2004). Interactive public ambient displays: Transitioning from implicit to explicit, public to personal, interaction with multiple users. In *Proceedings of the 17th Annual ACM Symposium on User Interface Software and Technology* (pp. 137–146). New York, NY, USA: ACM.

Weiser, M. (1991). The computer for the 21st century. *Scientific American, 265*, 66–75.

Weiser, M., & Brown, J. S. (1996). Designing calm technology. *PowerGrid Journal, 1*, 75–85.

Part III
Peripheral Interaction in Context

Chapter 8
Peripheral Displays to Support Human Cognition

Tilman Dingler and Albrecht Schmidt

Abstract The availability of tools greatly determines the effectiveness of people. While some of us may be genuinely good at maths, calculators can extend our capabilities significantly. Tools in general empower people: both physically and mentally. In this chapter, we explore the feasibility and design space of using displays in the periphery of people's attention as a tool to augment the human intellect. By embedding displays into home and office environments, these peripheral displays create stimulating environments and display personal content with the goal of supporting people's cognition and memory. In this chapter, we describe how we envision such displays to strengthen episodic memory, boost people's productivity, and support learning tasks based on concepts from the field of cognitive psychology. By using context awareness through sensors, such systems can be designed to look for opportune moments for content delivery in order to keep attention switches at minimum costs and therefore live up to the promise of 'calm computing.'

Keywords Memory display · Peripheral learning · Microlearning · Priming · Retrospection

8.1 Introduction

Human effectiveness is closely linked to the tools at disposal. Asking how much sand a person can move in 1 h is meaningless without specifying the tools the person can use: Using the bare hands, a shovel, or a digger will make much more difference than the (physiological) fitness of the person. Looking at things humans build—ranging from towns and buildings to microcontrollers—it is obvious that tools are essential to what we can achieve. Over the last 5000 years, we have seen a

T. Dingler (✉) · A. Schmidt
University of Stuttgart, Stuttgart, Germany
e-mail: tilman.dingler@vis.uni-stuttgart.de

A. Schmidt
e-mail: albrecht.schmidt@vis.uni-stuttgart.de

© Springer International Publishing Switzerland 2016
S. Bakker et al. (eds.), *Peripheral Interaction*,
Human–Computer Interaction Series, DOI 10.1007/978-3-319-29523-7_8

massive progress in the tools humans built and used. Since the beginning of interactive computing, the vision of augmenting the human intellect (Engelbart 2001) has been a strong driver. The last 2 decades have shown stunning progress in what people can do, once they have access to computing technology. Ubiquitous access to information is transformational to society, but it comes at the price of technologies requiring human attention, which has become one of the most scarce resources.

In this chapter, we focus on how peripheral displays can be used to support human cognition. The basic idea is to use display space in the periphery, on screens in the environment or using mobile and wearable devices, to provide information for peripheral consumption, and to cue recall. We believe that by using peripheral displays, we can create environments that are more pleasant, provide more stimulation and information, and make us more effective in our actions. We expect that adding information to our periphery can be done in a way that is not adding to the information overload, which we experience on traditional computing devices if we add more functionality and information.

This chapter first revisits concepts related to ambient media (Ishii and Ullmer 1997) and calm computing (Weiser and Brown 1997), which build the foundations for work in this area. Then, we argue why peripheral information spaces are useful and interesting to explore. We show that there is a long history of how technology shapes the way we live and that this becomes, once implemented, quite normal. We then give an overview of technology types that facilitate peripheral interaction and invite for reflection and retrospection. In the final part of the chapter, we introduce the *Deja vu* concept, where peripheral displays are used to make upcoming events more familiar. By combining such concepts from cognitive psychology with current technologies, we explore in this chapter the use of displays in the periphery of people's attention to support memory and learning.

8.2   Calm Computing and Ambient Media Revisited

Weiser and Brown foresaw the coming age of calm technology, which they defined as the inevitable consequence of the ubiquitous computing era: Since we would soon be constantly surrounded by technology—in walls, chairs, clothing, light switches, and cars—it will be futile to get them out of the way (Weiser and Brown 1997). This calmness then allows people to focus on being human. Further, calm technologies can be used to make the invisible perceivable. In her *Dangling String* installation, Natalie Jeremijenko visualizes the flow of bits through the wires of a computer network by using the motion, sound, and also touch of a string hanging from the ceiling (Weiser and Brown 1996). Light and heavy network traffic is thereby communicated to a bystander without the need to directly look at it. This additional conveyance of information of ambient media does not seem to fulfill the encalming claim of such technologies, especially in a world with frequent complaints about information overload. Hence, the premise of calm computing is to find ways to communicate information without heavy strain on the users' cognitive capacities.

When speaking of *calm computing* we refer to the definition that Weiser and Brown (1997) have given: 'Calm technology engages both the center and the periphery of our attention, and in fact moves back and forth between the two (Weiser and Brown 1997).' Ishii elaborated on this concept and coined the term *ambient media* for using sound, light, airflow, or water movement for background interfaces at the periphery of human perception (Ishii and Ullmer 1997). We see peripheral displays as a piece of technology that is generally located at the periphery of people's perception providing cues that invite users to switch their attention back and forth. Hence, people's *peripheral perception* is utilized to temporarily bring these displays into focus, explicitly interact with them as the case may be, and turn attention back to their primary task. Content and display behavior can be triggered by implicit user characteristics, such as proximity. In this case, we speak of *peripheral interaction*.

Hence, we believe that peripheral displays can be used to communicate information without drastically demanding people's attention, but rather offering information in a subtle way until a temporary attention switch or 'glance' is feasible. Interactions should be designed in a way where information overload is minimized. Apart from taking into consideration cognitive capacities, it is essential to make use of users' mental models. In previous work, we introduced the concept of *ambient counterparts* (Gellersen et al. 1999; Schmidt et al. 1999) where information that is traditionally being handled in people's virtual worlds relates to a natural counterpart in their physical environment. The idea is that similar chunks of information relate to collections of similar ambient media, thereby supporting an awareness of, for instance, comparative information. Much of the information people handle in their digital world has a natural counterpart in their physical environment to which it can be related intuitively. For example, people often deal with physical versions of digital information, such as printouts of documents or pen-written calendar entries. More abstract matches include digital product information that relates to products in a showroom or incoming e-mail from family relating to photographs kept on the physical desktop. Identifying such counterparts helps ambient media design to support smooth transition between the digital and real world. By using such ambient links, users can create and control these relationships. We explored the augmentative use of non-computer artifacts in people's surroundings for peripheral display of digital information and concluded their utility as extensions to our digital information spaces. Not only are we surrounded by physical artifacts, but also by our digital companions: Due to their ubiquity, we further explored the applicability of mobile phones as ambient displays (Schmidt et al. 2006). Thereby, we explored, for example, possibilities to use phone screens to convey information of interest to users in an ambient way. In a special design task, we focused on ambient visualizations of communication behavior and showed its feasibility.

In our more recent work, we explore the use of ambient media, and more specifically peripheral displays, in order to support memory tasks. Therefore, content displayed in people's periphery aims to provide cues to strengthen memory, to act as inspiration, or to help transition chunks of information to long-term memory by showing these cues spaced over time. When designing peripheral displays for memory support, it is essential to understand the discrepancy between the desire for a 'calm' design and the necessity to pay attention to content in order to process it. Schacter (1999) identified absent mindedness as one of the key reasons why information when consumed is not encoded correctly and therefore later memory retrieval is being compromised. So calm technologies for memory enhancements need to find a way to switch the focus of attention in a subtle and non-disruptive way. This can be done by embedding information in the environment in a context-sensitive way and detecting opportune moments for content delivery. For example, Pielot et al. (2015) harvested usage patterns of mobile phones in order to derive different states of attention. Based on their models, they were able to recommend content to users during moments of boredom. Another example for harvesting opportune moments has been investigated by Cai et al. (2015): They integrated a second language learning application into an online messenger. By using idle moments, when users waited for their conversation partners to respond, they pushed foreign language vocabulary to the focus of users' attention where a temporary attention switch was non-critical. Ashbrook (2010) defined microinteractions in a mobile context as instances where the user performs input, and once the computer has responded, the interaction is effectively finished in under 4 s. Peripheral displays should seek out moments where attention can be easily shifted to the periphery for such microinteractions in order to consume the information displayed. Such opportune moments usually present themselves in a context where the main task is conceptually not far from the peripheral task.

Calm technologies can move between center and periphery of our attention and back. Weiser speaks of enhancing the peripheral reach by bringing more details into the periphery. The question is how far this reach can be extended. Peripheral displays give potential access to a lot of detail. Information granularity, however, can be dynamically adapted. Using sensors, the user's context can be taken into account when deciding how much information is to be displayed. Context factors could be of physical (e.g., stress levels through galvanic skin response (GSR) or electroencephalography (EEG) data) or of cognitive nature [e.g., attention levels as measured by mobile devices (Pielot et al. 2015)].

So the idea of peripheral displays is to use information displays in the periphery of users' attention in order to convey rich information to the user. When placed at locations where users pass by occasionally, opportunities for microinteractions present themselves. These rather brief periods where the user's mind is not focused on a particular task can be used as opportune moments for learning: With the goal of acquiring new or reviewing known information, peripheral displays can be used in that way to commit such information to long-term memory. In the remains of this chapter, we will go deeper into the concept of fostering memories and learning. Thereby, we combine the concepts of *priming* and *retrospection* with peripheral displays.

Priming describes an implicit memory effect where the exposure to a current stimulus triggers a response to another stimulus in the future (Baddeley et al. 2009). Hence, context awareness and anticipation of user states can be used to feed information to people that will become useful at a certain point in the future.

Retrospection on the other hand is an activity that invites people to reflect on episodes and memories from the past. Retrospection can be triggered by feeding relevant memory cues, for example, through peripheral displays. As a tool for retrospection, they provide users with means to four of what Sellen calls the five R's (Sellen and Whittaker 2010): (1) recollecting: thinking back to past experiences (episodic memory), (2) reminiscing: reliving past experience for sentimental reasons, (3) retrieving: accessing specific information encountered in the past, and (4) reflecting: reviewing past experiences with the goal to recognize. The fifth R (remembering) describes the ability to remember prospective events as opposed to things that happened in the past and falls therefore under what we categorized as a function of *priming*.

In the remains of this chapter, we will explain how we relate these concepts to peripheral displays and adjust content for the purpose of memory augmentation, thereby coining the term 'memory displays.'

8.3   Why Is the Peripheral Information Space Interesting?

We perceive and process information from our environment through our five senses of sight, hearing, smell, taste, and touch. When perceived information makes it to our attentional focus, we speak of conscious processing. The stages from sensual perception all the way to focused attention are tightly coupled with the three types of memory or memory functions: sensory buffers, short-term memory or working memory, and long-term memory. Each function is discussed in detail by Baddeley et al. (2009), but for the design of peripheral information displays, it is worth taking a look at the first two stages: Our sensory buffers throw away most of the incoming information before the remaining sensations are passed on to the short-term memory through attention, thereby filtering the stimuli to only those which are of interest at a given time. Attention is the concentration of the mind on one of the currently competing stimuli or thoughts. Selective attention allows us to choose to attend one thing over another. Peripheral displays should be designed in a way where they allow brief attention switches—or 'glances'—in situations where the costs of such switches are minimal. Hence, such displays do not constantly try to grab people's attention, which should also account for the content shown. As one use case focuses on memory augmentation by showing episodes from the past, content needs to be compiled from previously captured data.

With the rise of the quantified self-movement, there is an increased amount of personal data available: fitness trackers, such as *Fitbit* or *Jawbone* log steps taken and sleep phases. Lifelog cameras, such as the *Narrative Clip* or *Autographer,* automatically take pictures from a first person perspective in regular intervals throughout the day. Most of these systems focus on statistically feeding that information back to the user with the goal of behavior change. Ajzen (1985) found that people were more likely to achieve intended behavior if they were reminded of their (positive) attitudes toward this same behavior. Instead of having to actively review each dataset, peripheral displays show summaries, goals, and activity recommendations embedded in people's homes. Pervasive awareness interfaces, such as calm and ambient displays, can be used for influencing people to make such behavior changes by bringing previously inaccessible information to users' attention. Consolvo et al. (2009) proposed design strategies for persuasive technologies for behavior change. They came up with a set of eight strategies: (1) abstract and reflective, (2) unobtrusive, (3) public, (4) aesthetic, (5) positive, (6) controllable, (7) trending/historical, and (8) comprehensive. These strategies are not meant to be mutually exclusive and are able to overlap. Besides the purpose of behavior change, making activity data retrospectively accessible to users can also be used to foster their memory. By bringing current goals as well as memories of positive experiences to the front of users' attention, we may be able to help people overcome initial motivational obstacles. Therefore, peripheral displays could be used to show information relevant to prospective events throughout the user's day. The idea behind this is based on the previously mentioned *priming* effect: Users can be mentally prepared for pending meetings and the people they will meet, thereby showing, for example, the notes taken during the last meeting of that kind or faces of the people signed up for it.

Classic ambient information displays, such as the information percolator (Heiner et al. 1999) or the ambientroom (Ishii et al. 1998), have a limited information bandwidth, so the question arises just how much information can be conveyed through peripheral displays. We think that such displays can provide richer information by taking advantage of opportune moments where user attention can be attracted 'on the go' and interactions are kept brief, but focused. In order to occasionally grab the user's attention, the location of such displays is crucial. To avoid interruption and distractions, places are preferred where users are rather unoccupied. Hence, locations, such as hallways or the living room (see Fig. 8.1), are preferred over, for example, office desks. Taking a more futuristic look at office and home spaces and the use of displays therein, research suggests the prevalence of large screen displays as well as interactive display floors (Augsten et al. 2010). As entire walls become interactive displays, the possibilities for peripheral information consumption increase. In opportune moments, such displays can provide a personalized selection of information and allow users to take a brief glance at information when they are, for example, passing through the hallway. By making content accessible in the periphery, we can design systems for both: strengthening existing memory and preparing the user for future experiences.

Fig. 8.1 Examples for display locations throughout the home: in the hallway (*left*), living room (*middle*), and as a fridge display (*right*)

8.4   Concept: Technologies Are Shaping Our Environment

People adapt and shape their environments to better suit their needs. Creating effective shelters and storage, easing transport and paving paths, supporting communication, and enabling preservation of memories are central examples that are as old as human civilizations. Looking at these traditional examples, it becomes clear that there is an inherent relationship between the technologies available, the way we use them to shape the environment, and the impact of the created (artificial) environment on humans.

Motivating Example: A Mountain Path is Manipulating me

Assume there are three villages A, B, and C with a mountain range in between. Without a path between these villages, exchange or trade is rare since climbing the mountains is time-consuming and dangerous. Once a donkey path is built over the mountain area connecting A and B, exchange between these villages will increase. Later, when village B is connected to village C with a railway link through a mountain tunnel, exchange between B and C will flourish. This simple example shows that technologies put in place will impact or manipulate human actions. This hypothetical example is not far from our everyday experience—did you walk this morning on the paved path from the car park to the office or did you go through the bushes?

This example is to highlight that influencing and shaping behavior through technologies is not a novel phenomenon. It is as old as technological interventions, and it helps to reduce complexity. Walking along the mountain path reduces physical and cognitive effort. You do not constantly need to decide which way is the best to go. In the physical world, we are very much used to being influenced.

In the digital world, this is still often controversial and considered manipulation. Examples of search results are one example. The big difference in our view is the visibility of the technologies and the understandability of how it influences our behavior for things in the physical world. It does not require much knowledge to understand how a paved path changes your behavior, but in contrast, most people would not understand how the sorting algorithm in a search engine impacts what they will look at.

As more and more things around us become computer controlled and more information we consume become digital, we have to face the issue that our experiences are strongly determined by software.

For peripheral interaction, it is important to be aware of this fact and to understand that information presentation will always have an impact on users. In order for users to accept these systems, it is essential not to trick the user or manipulate them into actions they would not want to do. The following basic rules give guidance on designing such systems:

- Empower the user to explore why certain information is presented and why other information is not presented;
- Make it apparent to what contextual factors the information is adapting and enable the user to personalize the adaptation.

It is apparent that any information presented (or not presented) may impact the user. At the same time, providing information that is contextualized will ease many cognitive tasks. There is no silver bullet here, but it is central for developers to consciously make these decisions when creating the system and to make them explicit in their system design.

Putting information in the periphery makes things easier. Let us consider the following examples:

- A person is writing software for an interactive Web page. The peripheral displays in the office examples of similar Web pages are shown together with the information which frameworks and libraries they use. How this information is selected and presented can have an influence of how the person will implement the Web page.
- When entering the kitchen for cooking, the peripheral display in the kitchen shows pictures of foods and dishes that are related to the things in the fridge. These pictures with associated recipes can inspire the person, but clearly may change their behavior.
- When facing the task of designing and creating a wooden chair, peripheral displays support each step of the task by showing a variety of design styles, different processes of manufacture, and design patterns. Such inspirational visualizations can trigger creativity and eventually shape the outcome.
- During a chat with a friend, content about trending topics or common interests can be displayed in order to trigger or enhance conversations. Pictures of common activities can be displayed to invite bystanders to reminisce about good times spent together. How will this affect the depth of the friendship?

As discussed, enhancing cognition in these ways can offer a range of opportunities from changing behavioral patterns to enhancing creativity. However, there are potential risks to it, too, such as the risk of exposing sensitive content in the wrong context. Most peripheral displays are placed in a semipublic environment and therefore accessible by more than a single person. Ambient media should be able to sense sensitive contexts and pick the content accordingly. However, sophisticated context sensing is a challenge and the risk of guessing that context wrong can render the technology annoying or useless to the user. Here, we need not only reliable sensing and algorithms, but also a way for users to provide feedback to the system in order to avoid repetitive mistakes. Such challenges will need to be addressed by a careful system design which allows users to be in full control of the content and its sources of aggregation. Another issue of proactively displaying content arises whenever that content is used to support the user without risking to patronize creativity. By suggesting content the system seems fit, the user is put into the jeopardy of receiving a filtered selection imposed by the system. This selection may differ from what the user really needs in order to fulfill a task or to trigger new forms of ideas. Last, but not least, the pure presence of peripheral displays seems to disrupt the current 'calm' of the environment. Hence, we propose a context switch in opportune moments when there is a minimum cost to the user's current cognitive capabilities.

8.5   Technologies for Peripheral Interaction

There are two general approaches to place technologies for peripheral interactions: infrastructure-based and user-worn. Technologies that are fixed in the user's environment provide an infrastructure to display information at a certain location. User-worn devices, on the other hand, are considered to be mobile and in the immediate proximity of the user. Typical devices in a home environment include besides computer screens, the TV, tablets, and electronic picture frames. Mobile technologies comprise the devices carried by a user, such as mobile phones, watches, glasses, and other wearables. Further, we can distinguish between semipublic and private displays: Semipublic displays are typically found as part of environments such as people's home or office. As opposed to public displays, which are accessible to the general public, e.g., on public spaces like train station or market squares, semipublic displays can only be accessed by a limited amount of people; they can be focused on a specific person or group of people and hence may contain rather personal context streams. As opposed to private displays, which are typically accessible to a single user, such as the mobile phone or a smart watch, semipublic displays are rather deployed in the environment serving as peripheral displays.

Equipped with sensing capabilities, information displays can become context aware. For example, proximity sensors can detect the pure presence of a user, whereas cameras can identify individual users. Context awareness can enrich a peripheral display environment by providing flexible screen real estate: Depending on the user's position and activity, specific displays can be used to display information in the environment or rather on the person. For example, the user's proximity could be used as a context variable to determine where to display certain information, e.g., in the hallway rather than in the living room in order to not interrupt a conversation. Marquardt and Greenberg (2012) coined the term *Proxemic Interaction* for describing systems that take people's and devices' spatial relationship into account in order to provide seamless interactions. In previous work, we explored different interaction zones in front of displays to map functionality across space (Dingler et al. 2015). By using proximity sensors, such as depth cameras, for example, different interaction zones can span the space in front of peripheral displays, thereby allowing users to interact with them by their pure presence or increase interaction granularity by stepping closer to the display (e.g., allowing gesture interaction or touch input). However, context awareness can go beyond solely detecting user proximity. Depending on the current user activity detected (e.g., in a conversation) and the urgency of the information, a network of peripheral displays can route information in real time from peripheral locations to spaces that may more directly grab the user's attention. Retrospective memory aids are less time-sensitive than prospective cues. Hence, many systems use notifications to alert the user about timely issues or required interventions. Notifications can be delivered to all devices connected to a particular user account. However, often this does not take into account the user's current activity, location, or openness to interruptions, which is why delivery strategies, such as bounded deferral (Horvitz et al. 2005), have been proposed: If a user is predicted to be busy, alerts are held back until a more suitable moment is detected. In previous work, we showed that generally there were enough of such opportune moments sufficiently stacked together, since people tend to return to an attentive state within only a few minutes (Dingler and Pielot 2015).

Peripheral displays are not limited to devices with monitors; reminders can be triggered through various modalities. A classic example is the alarm clock which uses sound cues to wake up the user, or an egg timer which notifies the user about the state of the cooking progress. Sound is convenient although rather intrusive. Brewster et al. looked into smell-based interactions (Brewster et al. 2006) and showed how scents could be used to evoke connotations. Haptic alarms, on the other hand, can be designed in more subtle ways when a particular user should be notified through a smartphone vibration or an actuator in the user's clothes, for example.

More recently, large screen displays, projected walls, and floor space are being explored as ubiquitous and interactive displays throughout home and office environments (Augsten et al. 2010). When any space can be used as a display, memory cues can be placed in locations where they can dynamically move in and out of the user's focus of attention.

8.6 Use Cases and Scenarios

Peripheral displays can be applied in various ways. In Sect. 8.2, we introduced *priming* and *retrospection* as two psychological concepts and described the connection between information, its presentation, and human processing. While *retrospection* can be used to activate past experiences, *priming* is used to infer insights for future experiences. For our peripheral displays, we combine *priming* with the notion of *Deja vu*, which is defined as a feeling of having already experienced the present situation (Oxford Dictionary) to build proactive systems that prepare people's memory for what is to come. The goal of this technology concept is to make new situations, and encounters appear more familiar and help building out multiple association points for people to link new information to.

8.6.1 Deja Vu—Utilizing Peripheral Interaction Technologies

The basic idea of this concept is to facilitate the coping with new situations: Visiting new places, getting to know new people, or engaging new tasks is part of everyday life. Naturally, such situations create a sense of excitement or anxiety when people face the unknown. The goal of our approach is to utilize peripheral displays in the home to present small information chunks that potentially have future relevance for a person and lower the barrier to the unknown. We investigate whether people are able to learn incidentally and without conscious effort about new environments and people. By providing visual information on peripheral displays, we can create a sense of *Deja vu* when people are actually facing new situations. Such a system should be designed in a way that people firstly value the aesthetic qualities and only afterward consider the images presented to be general pointer to future events. Eventually, users would realize that some of the information pieces will appear in the real world and thus will create a positive sense of *Deja vu*.

For example, one application scenario includes overcoming culture shock. When migrating for work or spending extended periods of time studying abroad, such change is potentially challenging. People often experience frustration and difficulty when adjusting to new cultural situations. Even the most basic daily tasks may require an unanticipated degree of adaptation and new learning (Geeraert et al. 2014). Making use of a peripheral display showing a *Deja vu* board, a user can be warned about potential challenges and solutions offered by fellow travelers or expatriates who have made similar experiences. Local customs, rules, and regulations can be pointed out in advance by displaying text, images, or even short videos. Such rich multimedia examples can be used to illustrate what to expect and how to overcome those challenges.

So while the scenario of creating *Deja vu* effects is fueled by the *priming* effect, the effects of *retrospection* can be utilized to strengthen episodic memory. As described in Sect. 8.5, we can use lifelogging data to create mashups of personal data inviting people to reflect on their activities: For example, a dashboard view could show summaries of activities throughout the day (see Fig. display dashboard); how many steps taken, miles walked, calories burned, places been, and people met. By showing pictures of recent encounters alongside with people's names and context-relevant information, peripheral displays could help strengthen face recognition memory and help committing details of an encounter to long-term memory. Further, peripheral displays can support learning tasks by presenting information relevant to a certain topic: For example, by displaying vocabulary, language skills could be strengthened.

8.6.2   Learning Environments

As pointed out, peripheral displays can collect activity data from wearables, mobile devices, and online sources to feed a processed summary of this information back to the user. This can include places visited, people encountered, or passages read: By showing pictures of recent encounters alongside with people's names and context-relevant information, such displays could help strengthening face recognition memory and help committing details of an encounter to long-term memory. By repeatedly exposing users in this way to their past activities, our displays aim to support people's episodic memory, i.e., the capacity to remember specific events. They can be further used to enhance semantic memory, which is assumed to store accumulative knowledge of the world: Displays deployed throughout the user's home can support learning tasks by presenting information relevant to a certain topic. For example, by showing vocabulary, language skills can be strengthened. Findings in language learning show how spaced exposure (Dempster 1987) and continued exposure (Webb 2007) to stimuli result in greater learning gains. The objective is to use memory displays in order to help foster memory by moving content from people's short-term to long-term memory. In the case of utilizing the priming effect to create *Deja vu* experiences, peripheral displays are used to convey information about an event in the future. Similarly, the displayed content could focus on learning goals, e.g., language learning, accumulating facts about a certain topic, or for preparing students for a specific exam. Each day a specific lesson can be scheduled to be displayed in easily digestible chunks. Individual learning units can be spaced out over time and repeatedly tested. Memory benefits have been found to arise from using distributed study and testing by spacing multiple tests of information within learning sessions and by distributing tests across multiple review

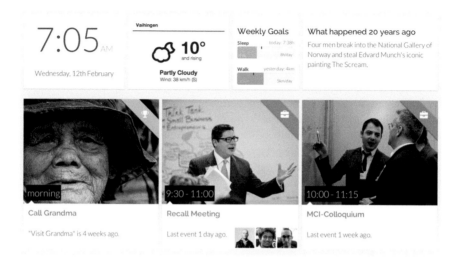

Fig. 8.2 Dashboard view of a peripheral display showing upcoming events, related pictures, and context information

sessions (Cull et al. 2000). Such retrieval practices can easily supported by using peripheral displays. From a conceptional and technological point of view, it may be worthwhile to consider adaptions of textbooks to a specific format fit for presentation in the periphery (see Fig. 8.2).

Whether being used for strengthening episodic memory or preparing users for future events, content displayed on peripheral displays needs to be highly personalized. Personal data mainly originate from devices and sources collecting information and activity data of a specific person. This information can include locations visited, steps taken, sleep patterns, pictures taken, calendar entries, or communication data. Further, this data can be enriched by external context information, such as location-specific weather reports or relevant news articles. The resulting personal content stream is subject to a number of privacy implications whose in-depth discussion would go beyond this chapter. Since such displays are deployed in the privacy of users' homes, we speak of semipublic displays. Convenient display locations are those which users pass frequently, such as hallways, living room, or kitchen walls (see Fig. 8.1). However, placement can also depend on the purpose of and content on the display. The type of information displayed depends on the memory concept the display implements, of which we described the two application scenarios above. We think there is great potential for future work looking at these scenarios and their effects on users in depth: from a psychological perspective, but also from an interaction, attention, and user experience point of view.

8.7 Summary

In this chapter, we argued that people's capabilities and effectiveness are linked to the tools they have at their disposal. For physical enhancements, such as tool kits, this is straightforward. For enhancing cognitive capabilities, we discussed the feasibility and design space of using peripheral displays to augment the human intellect. Where the notion of 'calm' comes in is where technologies compete for people's attention. By embedding displays into home and office environments, task-related content can be displayed at the periphery of people's attention. By using context awareness through sensors, we can design such systems to look for opportune moments for content delivery in order to keep context switches at minimum costs. We discussed a number of usage scenarios where peripheral displays can be used to facilitate a task at hand, enhance creativity, and support human relations. We based our concepts on human memory effects, such as *priming* and *retrospection*, and introduced the utilization of a controlled *Deja vu*. With the ubiquity of wearables, mobile devices, and the emergence of large screen display, we see a manifold of opportunities for using this growing screen real estate for ambient media and peripheral interaction.

References

Ajzen, I. (1985). *From intentions to actions: A theory of planned behavior*. Berlin: Springer.

Ashbrook, D. L. (2010). Enabling mobile microinteractions.

Augsten, T., Kaefer, K., Meusel, R., Fetzer, C., Kanitz, D., Stoff, T., et al. (2010). Multitoe: High-precision interaction with back-projected floors based on high-resolution multi-touch input. In *Proceedings of the 23nd Annual ACM Symposium on User Interface Software and Technology* (pp. 209–218). ACM.

Baddeley, A., Eysenck, A., & Anderson, M., (2009). Memory.

Brewster, S., McGookin, D., & Miller, C. (2006). Olfoto: Designing a smell-based interaction. In *Proceedings of the SIGCHI Conference on Human Factors in Computing Systems* (pp. 653–662). ACM.

Cai, C. J., Guo, P. J., Glass, J. R., & Miller, R. C. (2015). Wait-learning: Leveraging wait time for second language education. In *Proceedings of the 33rd Annual ACM Conference on Human Factors in Computing Systems* (pp. 3701–3710). ACM.

Consolvo, S., McDonald, D. W., & Landay, J. A. (2009). Theory-driven design strategies for technologies that support behavior change in everyday life. In *Proceedings of the SIGCHI Conference on Human Factors in Computing Systems* (pp. 405–414). ACM.

Cull, W. L., et al. (2000). Untangling the benefits of multiple study opportunities and repeated testing for cued recall. *Applied Cognitive Psychology, 14*(3), 215–235.

Dempster, F. N. (1987). Effects of variable encoding and spaced presentations on vocabulary learning. *Journal of Educational Psychology, 79*(2), 162.

Dingler, T., Funk, M., & Alt, F. (2015). Interaction proxemics: Combining physical spaces for seamless gesture interaction. In *Proceedings of the 4th International Symposium on Pervasive Displays* (pp. 107–114). New York, NY, USA: ACM, PerDis '15. doi:10.1145/2757710.2757722, url http://doi.acm.org/10.1145/2757710.2757722

Dingler, T., & Pielot, M. (2015). I'll be there for you: Quantifying attentiveness towards mobile messaging. In *Proceedings of the 17th International Conference on Human-Computer Interaction with Mobile Devices and Services* (pp. 1–5). New York, NY, USA: ACM, MobileHCI '15. doi:10.1145/2785830.2785840, url http://doi.acm.org/10.1145/2785830.2785840

Engelbart, D. C. (2001). Augmenting human intellect: A conceptual framework (1962). *PACKER, Randall and JORDAN, Ken Multimedia From Wagner to Virtual Reality New York: WW Norton & Company* (pp. 64–90).

Geeraert, N., Demoulin, S., & Demes, K. A. (2014). Choose your (international) contacts wisely: A multilevel analysis on the impact of intergroup contact while living abroad. *International Journal of Intercultural Relations, 38*, 86–96.

Gellersen, H. W., Schmidt, A., & Beigl, M. (1999). Ambient media for peripheral information display. *Personal Technologies, 3*(4), 199–208.

Heiner, J. M., Hudson, S. E., & Tanaka, K. (1999). The information percolator: Ambient information display in a decorative object. In *Proceedings of the 12th Annual ACM Symposium on User Interface Software and Technology* (pp. 141–148). ACM.

Horvitz, E., Apacible, J., & Subramani, M. (2005). Balancing awareness and interruption: Investigation of notification deferral policies. In *User Modeling 2005* (pp. 433–437). Berlin: Springer.

Ishii, H., & Ullmer, B. (1997). Tangible bits: Towards seamless interfaces between people, bits and atoms. In *Proceedings of the ACM SIGCHI Conference on Human Factors in Computing Systems* (pp. 234–241). ACM.

Ishii, H., Wisneski, C., Brave, S., Dahley, A., Gorbet, M., Ullmer, B., et al. (1998). Ambientroom: Integrating ambient media with architectural space. In *CHI 98 Cconference Summary on Human Factors in Computing Systems* (pp. 173–174). ACM.

Marquardt, N., & Greenberg, S. (2012). Informing the design of proxemic interactions. *IEEE Pervasive Computing, 2*, 14–23.

Pielot, M., Dingler, T., San Pedro, J., & Oliver, N. (2015). When attention is not scarce—detecting boredom from mobile phone usage. In *Proceedings of the 2015 ACM International Joint Conference on Pervasive and Ubiquitous Computing*. New York, NY, USA: ACM, UbiComp '15.

Schacter, D. L. (1999). The seven sins of memory: Insights from psychology and cognitive neuroscience. *American Psychologist, 54*(3), 182.

Schmidt, A., Gellersen, H. W., & Beigl, M. (1999). Matching information and ambient media. In *Cooperative Buildings. Integrating Information, Organizations, and Architecture* (pp. 140–149). Berlin: Springer.

Schmidt, A., Häkkilä, J., Atterer, R., Rukzio, E., & Holleis, P. (2006). Utilizing mobile phones as ambient information displays. In *CHI'06 Extended Abstracts on Human Factors in Computing Systems* (pp. 1295–1300). ACM.

Sellen, A. J., & Whittaker, S. (2010). Beyond total capture: a constructive critique of lifelogging. *Communications of the ACM, 53*(5), 70–77.

Webb, S. (2007). The effects of repetition on vocabulary knowledge. *Applied Linguistics, 28*(1), 46–65.

Weiser, M., & Brown, J. S. (1996). Designing calm technology. *PowerGrid Journal, 1*(1), 75–85.

Weiser, M., & Brown, J. S. (1997). The coming age of calm technology. In *Beyond calculation* (pp. 75–85). Berlin: Springer.

Chapter 9
Peripheral Interaction in Desktop Computing: Why It's Worth Stepping Beyond Traditional Mouse and Keyboard

Kathrin Probst

Abstract When computers entered our workplaces and other areas of our everyday life, many of the opportunities to use our physical abilities diminished. The macromonotony of large movements in, e.g., line production has become the micromonotony of small movements in computer-based office work. At the same time, looking at our everyday activities that do not involve technology, we naturally make use of our perception and motor abilities and continually interact with our surroundings. Our research has thus focused on achieving similar fluidness in our interactions with the digital world. While traditional desktop work usually involves controlling computers by pressing buttons, dropping menus, and sliding bars, we invite users to act with their physical surroundings, i.e., furniture embodied as handles to actions in the digital world. Based on our research on peripheral embodied interaction through smart furniture and insights from related research, we provide a conceptual overview of the seemingly minor, yet accumulatively powerful, benefits that this interaction style can provide as additional input dimension in desktop settings.

Keywords Desktop computing · Physical computing · Embodied interaction · Gestures · Metaphors

9.1 Motivation

Today, many people find themselves spending a majority of their working day in front of a computer screen. Computer technology has become an integral part of our work activities: We use Web browsers to gather information on the Internet, e-mail

K. Probst (✉)
Media Interaction Lab, University of Applied Sciences Upper Austria,
Hagenberg, Upper Austria, Austria
e-mail: kathrin.probst@fh-hagenberg.at

© Springer International Publishing Switzerland 2016
S. Bakker et al. (eds.), *Peripheral Interaction*,
Human–Computer Interaction Series, DOI 10.1007/978-3-319-29523-7_9

clients, and instant messengers (IMs) for electronic communication, word processors for writing and reading documents, etc. We deal with multiple applications in parallel, constantly switching between multiple windows on the screen, reacting to digital notifications, or communicating with our coworkers. Multitasking and the parallel management of multiple activities, tasks, and working spheres have become everyday practice for most of us (González and Mark 2004).

9.1.1 The Reality of Everyday Desktop Computing

While doing so, we are surrounded by omnipresent graphical user interfaces, which have been introduced decades ago with the development of mouse and keyboard, and the rise of the personal computer (Shneiderman 1998). In fact, aside from a slightly improved mechanical construction and visual polish, the input and output devices connected to average desktop computers today are virtually identical to first-generation computers (see Fig. 9.1). Although there have certainly been several developments along the way, such as improved graphics, trackpads, flat-panel displays, and touch screens, we still fundamentally operate our computers with a single pointing device and a keyboard. In light of other domains such as mobile computing, wearable computing, or digital entertainment systems increasingly making use of novel input technologies, many have predicted death of the mouse and keyboard (Lee 2010). However, the reality of everyday desktop computing seems to persistently stick with the same "point-and-click" interaction.

Reflecting upon the evolutionary development of this "traditional" computer interface, we can identify some of the critical factors for the mouse and keyboard's endurance: Typing technology has come a long way over the past centuries, starting

Fig. 9.1 Today's desktop interface is virtually identical to first-generation personal computers (*images via* DigiBarn Computer Museum)

with the invention of early mechanical typewriters, changing shape over the years, and finally resulting in the birth of the keyboard as we moved into the age of computers. Typing speed with minimum effort (two-handed typing allowing visual focus to stay on the screen, without paying much attention to actual finger movements) was one of the main reasons why it became so successful. The invention of the computer mouse then brought a major shift toward direct interaction on a graphical user interface (Smith et al. 1982). Precision with minimum effort (moving quickly to a specific point on the screen, without needing to move one's hand very far) was the main advantage that it added to the desktop interface. Even today, these features make up for mouse and keyboard as our number-one input devices in desktop computing—which remains to be the habitat of most *productivity tasks*, where it is all about getting things done in a fast and accurate way.

More recently, many innovations for interacting with computers have followed the invention of the keyboard and mouse. New generations of input technologies have opened up a whole new space of interactions via gesture control (e.g., Apple Magic Trackpad, LeapMotion), vision control (e.g., Tobii Eye Tracking), or voice control (e.g., Siri, Cortana). To date, such solutions have not succeeded in replacing mouse and keyboard as primary input devices due to various practical limitations (e.g., speed, recognition reliability, pointing accuracy, physical effort). However, we believe they provide great potential for peripheral interaction in desktop computing to complement high-precision mouse and keyboard with an additional input domain that naturally blends into our existing digital workflows. In particular, our research interest lies in *peripheral gestural interaction* to extend the traditional desktop interface with inattentive, bodily actions in the physical world.

9.1.2 Taking the Step Beyond

Comparing our everyday activities on the screen with our activities that do not involve technology, the physical world often seems so much easier to handle: We naturally make use of our perception and motor abilities, continually interact with our surroundings, and deal with numerous parallel activities in the periphery of attention (e.g., relying on our spatial memory when grabbing a mug from a kitchen board, coordinating our hands when pouring coffee into the mug, reading a newspaper while drinking the coffee). In contrast, interactions with computing technologies usually involve deliberate actions in the focus of attention.

Based on this argument, we identify two main properties of mouse and keyboard, which on the one hand make up for their versatility and on the other hand come with inherent interaction gaps that are discussed in the remainder of this section. Addressing these gaps, Sect. 9.2 points out the potential of peripheral interaction to bridge these gaps by providing a powerful add-on to traditional desktop settings.

9.1.2.1 Digital Versus Physical

First, traditional desktop interfaces provide a generic interaction style that is consistent across a wide variety of applications and actions in the digital world. On the one hand, this allows interactions to be achieved with minimum effort by employing the same bodily actions, i.e., clicking, scrolling, and typing. Mouse and keyboard can thus function as general-purpose input devices providing access to a wide range of functions with a small set of basic operations. On the other hand, this means that the richness of human skills is exploited only to a limited extent, as the underlying actions are the same across applications.

From an evolutionary perspective, we have traded the variety of skilled movements that we once used to perform in crafting and agricultural domains against the macromonotony of large movements in industrial production and later against the micromonotony of small movements in desktop work. When computers entered our workplaces and other areas of our everyday life, many of the opportunities to use our physical abilities diminished. Having an office job today, all too often involves sitting all day at a computer, making the same small repetitive movements with our fingers, hands, and eyes over and over again (see Fig. 9.2), while the rest of our body remains largely unchallenged (O'Sullivan and Igoe 2004). As a result, work-related disorders have become one of the most common chronic diseases, often resulting from years of poor posture and sedentariness at the workplace (Owen et al. 2009; McCrady and Levine 2009).

Fig. 9.2 A limited number of senses are challenged with present-day desktop interfaces: Fingers are engaged in clicking, scrolling, or typing on mouse and keyboard. Eyes continuously watch the visual results on the screen. Ears come in from time to time when audio feedback is provided

From an interaction perspective, we have traded the direct mapping between form and function that we once found in artisan tools against reduced numbers of mechanical controls on machines and early computers and later against the basic operations of point-and-click interaction in desktop computing. The shape, size, and form of computing technology have reduced the physical actions that are possible to perform as human–machine interfaces moved from a one-function-per-control toward a many-functions-per-control approach. In traditional desktop interfaces, there is no longer a perceptually meaningful link between actions, form, and feedback. Very different functions are triggered by the same actions, which result in similar output. As a result, they increasingly challenge users' cognitive skills to learn and remember various digital functions and input sequences, while largely neglecting their perceptual motor skills (Djajadiningrat et al. 2007).

Our five senses are naturally designed for different types of interaction, and much potential of the parallel architecture of our brains is lost when human–computer interfaces exploit only few of them. Desktop computing thus faces the challenge of more effectively matching interfaces to the richness of human capabilities. Novel interaction styles hold great potential to move us toward this goal by engaging various parts of our body and taking advantage of our perceptual and motor skills. Moving actions into the physical world, it has been shown that the bodily, tangible nature of such embodied interaction styles (Dourish 2001) opens up a parallel interaction channel for parallel processing of multiple resources (Wickens and McCarley 2007; Olivera et al. 2011). Increased movement diversity can furthermore decrease the monotony of computing tasks (Silva and Bowman 2009), or improve overall physical activity and mental well-being (Levine 2002).

Thus, similar to our everyday activities that do not involve technology, where we make use of our perception and motor abilities and continually interact with our surroundings, peripheral interaction around the desktop holds the potential for extending interaction from the screen toward the physical world around us.

9.1.2.2 Focused Versus Peripheral

Second, traditional desktop interfaces provide a structured environment, where the majority of interaction happens visually, on a computer screen. The interface is usually separated into different workspaces, i.e., a primary workspace that holds the currently active application, a secondary workspace that holds artifacts related to the primary space (e.g., tool palettes), and an offscreen workspace that holds the remaining artifacts (e.g., menus) to be made visible through direct user interaction (Hausen et al. 2013a). On the one hand, this allows interface designers to make efficient use of the available screen space by distributing UI elements across all available workspaces. On the other hand, this causes users to spend too much time manipulating the interface, all too often ending up frustrated by too many layers of point-and-click or cluttered screens due to overlapping windows, hierarchical menus, widely dispersed icons, nested toolbars, etc.

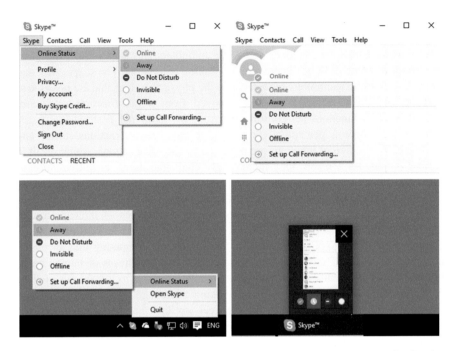

Fig. 9.3 Possible ways of updating a user's online status in an instant messenger application: by **a** navigating through the menu hierarchy in the messenger window, **b** accessing a drop-down menu from the current status icon in the messenger window, **c** accessing the context menu from the messenger icon in the system tray, **d** revealing the hover preview of the messenger window's representation in the taskbar, and or **e** executing a custom-defined hot key combination

Since the actions that we can perform on the on-screen elements are very simple, they oftentimes need to be repeated or combined to complete a specific operation, which leads to long sequences of simple actions that require users' focused attention to achieve an intended goal. Even very simple tasks often require a context switch, precise pointing, or exact knowledge about certain key presses. If we consider the simple task of adjusting one's status in an IM application for example (see Fig. 9.3), this can usually be achieved in several ways, which all include multiple steps of shifting application windows between foreground and background modes, navigating through menu hierarchies, or revealing hidden controls. Alternatively, keyboard shortcuts can provide direct access to application functions, but require users to remember a number of different key combinations. Either way, people are required to divert attention away from their primary task, which comes at the cost of increasingly interrupted work.

In the reality of everyday desktop computing, this is especially relevant for secondary or background tasks, which can take place concurrently with a primary task (Chewar et al. 2002). When the demands of the secondary task cause it to become the user's primary focus, negative performance effects on the primary task can occur (Czerwinski et al. 2004).

Fig. 9.4 Seven Stages of Action: *The Stages of Execution* start at the top with the goal, the state that is to be achieved. The goal is translated into an intention to do some action. The intention must be translated into a set of internal commands, an action sequence that can be performed to satisfy the intention. The action sequence is still a mental event: Nothing happens until it is executed, performed upon the world. The *Stages of Evaluation* start with our perception of the world. This perception must be interpreted according to our expectations and then evaluated with respect to both our intentions and our goals (reproduced from Norman 2002)

   Research has consistently documented the negative consequences of interruptions to ongoing work tasks including context-switching costs such as distraction, errors, work delay, stress, and frustration (e.g., Finstad et al. 2006; Iqbal and Horvitz 2007; Jin and Dabbish 2009). Considering this problem in light of Norman's action cycle (see Fig. 9.4), we can identify that this is especially relevant for the execution stage, where long sequences of point-and-click interaction lead to a bottleneck in the action cycle.

   Desktop computing thus faces the challenge to bridge this gulf of execution by removing roadblocks that cause extra thinking and actions that distract the user's attention from the task intended, thereby preventing the flow of his or her work and decreasing the chance of successful completion of the task. Novel interaction styles hold the potential to move us toward this goal by involving multiple of our senses and naturally taking advantage of our ability for subconscious perception and control of bodily actions. Engaging both the center and periphery of attention, it has been shown (Weiser 1996) that such activity-based approaches (MacIntyre et al. 2001; Bardram 2009) can support common multitasking practices through smooth transitions between primary and secondary workspaces, or off-loading of information into the physical environment.

   Thus, similar to our everyday activities that do not involve technology, where we deal with numerous activities at the same time, peripheral interaction through bodily actions in the physical world holds the potential for supporting increasingly subconscious control of secondary tasks in parallel with an ongoing primary task.

9.2   Peripheral Interaction Around the Desktop

Research in the areas of embodied interaction (Dourish 2001) and tangible user interfaces (Ullmer and Ishii 2000) has revealed potential benefits of extending the traditional desktop interface with an additional bodily input domain to for peripheral interaction in desktop settings (e.g., see Fig. 9.5). *Peripheral tangible interaction* has shown as "particularly suitable for the office context, complementing the existing monitor, mouse, and keyboard, and supporting the performance of auxiliary work activities in parallel with primary workstation-intensive tasks" (Edge 2008). Extending this concept, *peripheral embodied interaction* has shown to "improve multiple task situations by moving secondary tasks from the classical computer interface into the physical world around us" (Hausen and Butz 2011). We believe that such physical manipulators are a natural step toward making

Fig. 9.5 Examples of peripheral interaction in desktop scenarios: office-based peripheral TUI (Edge 2008), *StaTube* tangible presence indicator (Hausen et al. 2012), peripheral music controller (Hausen et al. 2013b), and *Unadorned Desk* extended input canvas on a physical desk (Hausen et al. 2013a)

the next UI metaphor the real world itself by providing an interaction modality that can be controlled in the periphery of attention.

Karam and Schraefel (2005a) were one of the first to consider gestures for the support of secondary task interactions in multitasking environments, by investigating the use of semaphoric hand gestures for control of an ambient music system. Edge and Blackwell (2009) offered an alternative perspective on tangibility in interaction by presenting an office-based TUI that allowed users to manage auxiliary work activities (e.g., e-mail management, time sheet completion, information sharing) by freely arranging digitally augmented physical tokens around the periphery of their workspace. Cheng et al. (2010) presented the *iCon* prototyping platform that employs a novel approach to utilizing everyday objects in the physical desk environment (e.g., bottles, mugs) as instant tabletop controllers. Hausen et al. designed an ambient appointment projection that supports peripheral interaction with upcoming events through freehand gestures (Hausen and Butz 2011), the *StaTube* tangible presence indicator that allows users to change their IM state in a peripheral fashion (Hausen et al. 2012), a peripheral music controller and e-mail notification system that compared different input modalities for peripheral interaction (Hausen et al. 2013b, c), and the *Unadorned Desk* that demonstrates the use of coarse hand gestures to arrange and retrieve virtual offscreen artifacts on a physical desk (Hausen et al. 2013a).

Overall, this body of research demonstrates that extending traditional desktop interfaces with a supplementary input dimension that smoothly shifts interactions between the focus and periphery of attention is particularly suitable for interaction with background (secondary) tasks in multitasking scenarios. This can help us to overcome some of the problems with traditional interfaces, complement our current interaction vocabulary, and enhance user experience.

In our research, we have extended this concept toward the physical workspace environment, investigating the potential of body movements on a flexible chair (Probst et al. 2014a), and other of smart furniture prototypes (Probst et al. 2014b) to enable quasi-parallel control of primary and secondary tasks. Based on this research on peripheral interaction through smart furniture, we provide a conceptual overview of the seemingly minor, yet accumulatively powerful, benefits that this interaction style can provide as additional input dimension in desktop settings. In the remainder of this section, we present two themes that we believe are particularly relevant for taking the mundane reality of everyday desktop computing to the next level. The first theme, *from the screen to the world*, describes how our knowledge of our lived body can allow for subconscious control of bodily actions in the world, in parallel with an ongoing primary task. The second theme, *from the world to the mind*, describes how applying basic concepts from our real-world and bodily experience can provide meaningful, understandable shortcuts to application commands. Throughout these themes, we discuss relevant theoretical backgrounds and how these are put into practice in the related work on peripheral interaction in the desktop domain and provide concrete examples from our research on peripheral interaction through smart furniture.

9.2.1   From the Screen to the World

The richness of human knowledge and understanding is far deeper than we can explain. To illustrate this assertion, consider the example of riding a bicycle: We are simultaneously navigating, balancing, steering, and pedaling to smoothly make our way along the road. We are able to sense, store, and recall our own muscular effort, body position, and movement to build this skill. Yet, it is not possible for us to articulate all of the nuances of this activity when we try to teach somebody how to ride a bicycle (Klemmer et al. 2006).

This kind of **procedural (tacit) knowledge** is involved in knowing how to ride a bicycle, how to steer a car, how to swim, and how to perform music. It is largely subconscious, but reliable and robust. It is best taught by demonstration and best learned through practice. Even the best teachers usually cannot describe what they are doing.

The basis of this knowledge is our *sensorimotor control*, which is the combination of body movements into intended actions (Weiss and Jeannerod 1998). This involves the integration of proprioceptive information (detailing the position and movement of the musculoskeletal system) with the neural processes in the brain and spinal cord (planning, transmitting, and controlling motor commands). To produce coordinate movements, our brain holds an internal prediction of the sensory consequences of a movement and compares it with the actual feedback from the joints and muscles. As a result of this continuous comparison, corrective commands are issued, and the prediction is adapted accordingly (see Fig. 9.6).

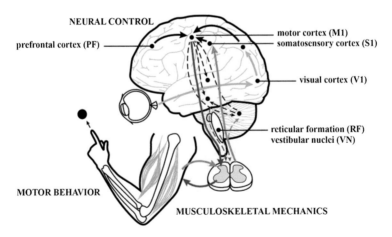

Fig. 9.6 The basic brain circuit for sensorimotor control: At the lowest level, the spinal cord integrates motor output and sensory input from skin, muscles, and joints to basic movements and reflexes. At the second level, brain stem regions (RF, VN) improve these patterns with postural control and locomotion patterns. At the highest level, the cerebral cortex supports a large and adaptable motor repertoire. The diagram illustrates some of the key regions that are involved in goal-directed reaching movements: PF for action goals and planning, M1 for motor planning, V1 for visual feedback, and S1 for somatosensory feedback (reproduced after Scott 2004)

Essential for this sensorimotor control is our *kinesthetic sense (proprioception)*, which allows our body to keep track of the joint position in the body and their location in space and regulate the muscular effort that we use to move our bodies. As a key component for hand–eye coordination and kinesthetic memory, it is how we can position our hand to catch a ball, or touch our nose with our eyes closed. Humans are remarkably fast and accurate at using tactile and kinesthetic cues to locate and recognize objects without vision (Lederman 1987; Huynh et al. 2010). On keyboard and mouse, users can thus rely on their proprioception to develop a rough idea of the physical location of keys and buttons (e.g., bumps on the F and J keys support correct positioning of the hands).

The appropriate integration of proprioceptive input enables us to walk without watching where we put our feet, or drive a car without watching the pedals and gearstick. The kinesthetic sense is essential whenever learning a new motor skill and forms the basis for various forms of procedural knowledge:

- *Two-handed (bimanual) coordination* and *hand–foot coordination* allow us to interact with both hands at the same time (e.g., when tying our shoelaces, or eating with knife and fork), or move our hands and feet in a coordinated manner (e.g., when playing football, or swimming). Using keyboard and mouse, this allows us to interact with both hands in parallel (Buxton and Myers 1986).
- *Kinesthetic memory (muscle memory, motor memory)* involves consolidating a specific motor task into memory through repetition. When a movement is repeated over time, a long-term muscle memory is created for that task. Once an activity is encoded in muscle memory, it requires little conscious effort to perform, which allows it to become automated and performed unconsciously in parallel with other activities (Newell and Rosenbloom 1981; Wickens and McCarley 2007). Examples can be found in many everyday activities that require rapid bodily responses for which planning by explicit cognition is simply too slow, e.g., driving a car, riding a bike, or playing an instrument.
- *Spatial memory* involves the recording of information about one's environment and its spatial orientation. It is a cognitive process that enables a person to remember different locations as well as spatial relations between objects. This allows us to remember where an object is in relation to another object, e.g., when navigating through a familiar city, or recalling the location of items in a room. In computer interfaces, users can thus rely on spatial memory to recall the locations of keys on a keyboard, or on-screen controls in a GUI (Scarr et al. 2012).

Put together, this kind of procedural knowledge is the reason that we can perform multiple actions simultaneously, when they are done automatically, with little or no need for conscious attention:

> Doing several things at once is essential even in carrying out a single task. To play the piano, we must move the fingers properly over the keyboard while reading the music, manipulating the pedals, and listening to the resulting sounds. But to play the piano well, we should do these things automatically. Our conscious attention should be focused on the

higher levels of the music, on style, and on phrasing. So it is with every skill. The low-level, physical movements should be controlled subconsciously (Norman 2002).

In the context of peripheral interaction around the desktop, the richness of human skills has been successfully applied for secondary tasks to be controlled in parallel with an ongoing primary task. Table 9.1 provides an overview of such actions and their coverage in the related work (e.g., see Fig. 9.5).

For example, *StaTube* (Hausen et al. 2012) builds on people's ability to sense ambient information in the periphery to let them observe the status of their favorite IM contacts with a tangible presence indicator. Simply turning the topmost layer of the tangible device, they can also change their own IM state in a peripheral fashion. Similarly, *iCon* (Cheng et al. 2010) builds on people's real-world experience with everyday objects that can be sensed with our peripheral awareness and provide inherent affordances due to their tangible, movable, and graspable properties. The office-based TUI by Edge and Blackwell (2009) leverages users' kinesthetic sense to allow for distinction of tangible tokens based on their characteristic engravings on the edges. Building on people's bimanual coordination abilities, the system supports two-handed interaction with coarse-grained manipulation of physical tokens under the non-dominant hand and fine-grained manipulation of a control knob under the dominant hand. The *Unadorned Desk* (Hausen et al. 2013a) extends this concept toward utilizing the physical desk space around a computer as input canvas for peripheral interaction with virtual items. Taking advantage of people's proprioception and spatial memory, it demonstrates that users have a good under-standing of where items are located and can easily—even with closed eyes— retrieve such objects.

Table 9.1 Examples of secondary tasks and their coverage in peripheral interaction

Applications	Commands
Application management	Launch/exit (Edge and Blackwell 2009; Cheng et al. 2010; Hausen et al. 2013a), switch (Cheng et al. 2010; Hausen et al. 2013a)
File management	Create (Edge and Blackwell 2009), open/close (Edge and Blackwell 2009)
Data manipulation	Copy/paste (Cheng et al. 2010), undo/redo (Cheng et al. 2010), save (Cheng et al. 2010)
Navigation	Previous/next (Karam and Schraefel 2005a; Cheng et al. 2010; Hausen et al. 2013b), zoom, scroll, rotate (Cheng et al. 2010), bookmark (Cheng et al. 2010)
Task management	Schedule (Edge and Blackwell 2009), track progress (Edge and Blackwell 2009), delegate (Edge and Blackwell 2009)
Music playback	Play/pause (Karam and Schraefel 2005a; Cheng et al. 2010; Hausen et al. 2013b), increase/decrease volume (Cheng et al. 2010; Hausen et al. 2013b), mute/unmute (Cheng et al. 2010)
Messaging	Set status (Edge and Blackwell 2009; Hausen et al. 2012), view status (Edge and Blackwell 2009; Hausen et al. 2012), show, tag, delete message (Hausen et al. 2013c)

Fig. 9.7 Prototype for peripheral interaction through smart furniture: interactive office chair

Similarly, in our research, we constructed several prototypes that leverage human's bodily skills and real-world knowledge for peripheral interaction through smart furniture (Probst et al. 2014b). In a first prototype (Fig. 9.7), we explored the potential of gestural chair interaction during desktop computing. By tracking the movements of a seated person, different chair gestures are identified and directly translated into input commands to a desktop computer (e.g., tilting to play the next track in a playlist, bouncing to launch an application, rotating to attend to a notification on a distant screen). This way, the chair becomes a ubiquitous input device (Probst et al. 2013, 2014a). In an iterative design process, we elicited user input on suitable gestures, collected early feedback on the user experience, and evaluated the performance of our chair-based application control. From the analysis of the collected data and user interviews, we learned several lessons about how users interact with such an augmented chair interface.

Overall, they agreed that the chair gestures provided a useful add-on to their daily desktop work, which they would preferably use in an *opportunistic, casual* manner whenever they wanted to gain direct access to application functions, or just break up the monotony of traditional point-and-click routines. In a study comparing the performance of the chair interface to traditional keyboard and touch input, task recovery time was significantly shorter with the chair gestures. In line with the related work, this can be largely contributed to the reduced requirements on the visual and motor channels (Karam and Schraefel 2005a), i.e., *eyes-free* interaction as visual focus remains on the primary task and *hands-free* interaction as people's hands can remain on mouse and keyboard. Based on these unique features, the chair gestures allowed users to effortlessly interact with an application and rapidly refocus on other ongoing activities. To support this kind of fluid transitions between primary and secondary tasks, we thus learned that bodily gestures for peripheral

Fig. 9.8 Prototypes for peripheral interaction through smart furniture: smart furniture modules for under-the-desk kicking, rolling, and touching

interaction should be of rather *imprecise and inattentive* nature, i.e., concise, quick to issue, avoiding movements over extended periods of time.

In a second prototype (Fig. 9.8), we designed three types of smart furniture modules for under-the-desk interaction, which include a kick interface on the underpart of the desk, a roll interface on the floor beneath the desk, and a touch interface on the underside of the desk surface. Interaction with the modules builds on people's preexisting real-world skills and knowledge, such as their understanding of naïve physics (e.g., friction, velocity), their bodies (e.g., proprioception), and the environment (e.g., spatial memory). The kick and roll modules leverage motor capabilities to perform basic gestures with the foot (e.g., tapping, nudging). The touch module transfers experience with multitouch devices toward simple touch gestures on the underside of a desk (e.g., swiping).

In a preliminary study, where users were invited to test our prototypes within their regular work environments, we found that participants assigned the basic hand and foot gestures to a variety of secondary tasks that we identified as particularly suitable for peripheral interaction through smart furniture to smoothly blend into traditional desktop configurations (i.e., music control, status updates, notification handling, task switching, window handling). In line with the related work, this was found to "*reduce barriers to interaction by facilitating the performance of periodic, low-attention activities in parallel with workstation-intensive tasks*" (Edge 2008). Over time, participants were increasingly able to perform coordinate hand and foot movements, and recall the spatial location of the individual modules. Previous studies on peripheral interaction confirmed that such interaction styles need to be trained and learned to be effective (e.g., Hausen et al. 2014). This may continually develop with routinely execution and further practice. Thus, besides being imprecise and inattentive in nature, we recommend bodily gestures for peripheral interaction to be assigned to *frequently used input commands* that people would make use of on a regular basis during their daily routine.

9.2.2   From the World to the Mind

At the very core of meaning—the way we categorize, remember, talk about, and act in the world—are our experiences as physical beings in the physical world. To illustrate this assertion, consider the metaphorical concept of time as used in contemporary English in expressions like spending time, saving time, wasting time, losing time, or running out of time. Time is money, time is a limited resource, and time is a valuable commodity are all metaphorical concepts, since we are using our everyday experiences with money, limited resources, and valuable commodities to conceptualize time (Lakoff and Johnson 1980).

This human ability to project the structure of physical and cultural experiences onto a conceptual domain is what is meant by **metaphor**. The basis for this kind of metaphor is the assumption that basic physical concepts acquired in early infancy and childhood (e.g., time, space, distance, temperature) provide meaningful guides for the development of more abstract, newer concepts (Williams et al. 2009). For example, the understanding that some objects are able to move themselves through space (e.g., people, animals) provides the foundation for understanding the concept of agency. This allows us to understand or experience one concept in terms of another, which helps us understand complex concepts in a way that appears more real and tangible to us. When cognitive structures of higher-order thinking emerge from recurrent patterns of bodily or sensorimotor experience, they are called *embodied schemata* and *embodied metaphors* (see Fig. 9.9).

According to (Lakoff and Johnson 1980), metaphor involves four basic categories:

- An **orientational (spatial) metaphor** involves explaining a concept in terms of spatial orientations, which arise from how our bodies function in our physical environment (e.g., up–down, in–out, near–far, front–back). This allows us to associate abstract concepts with spatial orientations of up and down (e.g., good is up, bad is down; more is up, less is down), right and left (e.g., progress is right, regression is left), or ahead and behind (e.g., future is ahead, past is behind).[1]
- An **ontological metaphor** involves explaining a concept in terms of basic categories of our physical existence (e.g., entity, substance, container). This allows us to view abstract concepts as entities (e.g., ideas are entities, "*I can't put my ideas into words*"), substances (e.g., vitality is a substance, "*I'm

---

[1]As metaphor is largely dependent on culture, their underlying meaning may largely vary across cultures (e.g., progress is right and future is ahead are primarily true for Western countries).

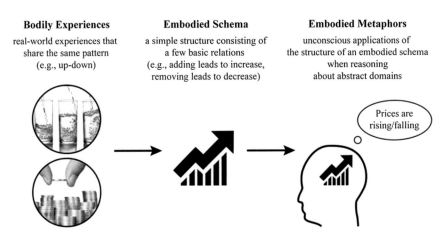

Bodily Experiences	**Embodied Schema**	**Embodied Metaphors**
real-world experiences that share the same pattern (e.g., up-down)	a simple structure consisting of a few basic relations (e.g., adding leads to increase, removing leads to decrease)	unconscious applications of the structure of an embodied schema when reasoning about abstract domains

Fig. 9.9 An example of an embodied schema is the *up–down* schema. The corresponding *more is up* and *less is down* metaphors are grounded in the common experiences of pouring more fluid into a container and seeing the level go up or down, or seeing a pile grow higher or lower as we add or remove things to/from it. These are thoroughly pervasive experiences that we encounter throughout our daily lives. Such embodied schema are used to reason about abstract domains: e.g., when we say "The price is rising" or "Stocks are plummeting," we (unconsciously) apply the embodied schema *up–down* to structure our understanding of the abstract concept of monetary values (in analogy to Bakker et al. 2011)

overflowing with energy"), or containers (e.g., love is a container, "*I've fallen in love.*").

- A **structural metaphor** involves characterizing the structure of one concept in terms of another (e.g., eating, moving, transferring objects from place to place). This allows us to structure one kind of experience or activity by comparing it to another experience or activity (e.g., understanding is seeing, "*I see what you are saying*"; life is a gambling game, "*I'll take my chances*").
- A **metonymy** involves the use of one entity to refer to another that is related to it. For example, this allows us to structure abstract concepts in terms of "the part for the whole" (e.g., the face for the person), or "the producer for the product" (e.g., talking about a Picasso when referring to a painting).

Just as metaphors are omnipresent in our everyday life, so do they occur on digital systems where they provide meaning by representing computer systems with objects and events from a non-computer domain (Wozny 1989). User interface metaphors, for example, incorporate spatial metaphors for quantification and navigation (e.g., vertical sliders increasing toward the top, next buttons pointing to the right), ontological metaphors for illustrating system elements (e.g., a file is an object), structural metaphors for explaining system functions (e.g., storage is filing), or metonymy for iconic representations in menus and toolbars (Barr et al. 2002).

Besides that, novel interaction styles have increasingly made use of metaphors to simplify human–computer interaction. Tangible user interfaces have, for example, used the affordances of physical objects (e.g., shape, size, color) to invoke metaphorical links (Fishkin 2004). Similarly, different styles of gestures are implicitly based on underlying metaphorical structures, such as *deictic gestures* that involve pointing to establish the identity or spatial location of an object (e.g., pointing to interact on a large-scale display), *manipulating gestures* that apply a tight relationship of the movement of a gesturing hand/arm with an entity being manipulated (e.g., mimicking manipulations of physical objects in VR interfaces), or *semaphoric gestures* that employ a stylized dictionary of static or dynamic hand or arm gestures (e.g., joining the thumb and forefinger to represent the OK symbol) (Karam and Schraefel 2005b).

In the context of peripheral interaction around the desktop, our natural understanding for basic metaphors has been successfully leveraged for simple bodily actions that facilitate learning and recall through meaningful mapping to frequently used application commands. Table 9.2 provides an overview of such simple interactions and their coverage in the related work (e.g., see Fig. 9.5).

For example, the semaphoric hand gestures in the ambient music player control by Karam and Schraefel (2005a) use basic spatial metaphors (e.g., *progress is right*; left-to-right-hand wave for the next song) and structural metaphors (e.g., vertical hand in midair signaling a halt gesture to stop playback). In a study comparing the gestures against function keys on a keyboard, results showed that the simple hand gestures were easier to recall than the abstract key assignments. Similarly, Hausen et al. (2013b) use spatial metaphors to provide the same shared meaning to peripheral music player commands across different input modalities (e.g., *more is up*; upward tilting of a graspable device, upward swiping on a touch surface, or upward flicking of the hand in midair to increase volume). In a second use case of peripheral e-mail notifications (Hausen et al. 2013c), they use a combination of spatial and structural metaphors to provide a consistent mapping of possible actions along the four canonical directions (e.g., *important is up*, upward movement to flag a message; *unimportant is down*, downward movement to delete a message; *pulling*

Table 9.2 Examples of simple bodily gestures and their coverage in peripheral interaction

Gestures	Commands
Left-to-right/right-to-left move, swipe, tilt	Next/previous (Karam and Schraefel 2005a; Hausen et al. 2013b), decline/show (Hausen et al. 2013c)
Upward/downward move, swipe, tilt	Increase/decrease (Hausen et al. 2013b), bookmark/delete (Hausen et al. 2013c)
Circular hand motion	Play (Karam and Schraefel 2005a)
Vertical hand in midair	Stop (Karam and Schraefel 2005a), pause/continue (Hausen et al. 2013b)
Hover above	Preview (Hausen et al. 2013a)
Touch down/tap	Select (Cheng et al. 2010; Hausen et al. 2013a), toggle state (Cheng et al. 2010; Hausen et al. 2013b)
Clockwise/counterclockwise object rotation	Increase/decrease (Cheng et al. 2010; Hausen et al. 2013b), next/previous (Cheng et al. 2010; Hausen et al. 2012), redo/undo (Cheng et al. 2010)

is bringing closer, movement toward the user to show a message; *pushing is moving away*, movement away from the user to mark message as read). *iCon* (Cheng et al. 2010) extends this concept for metaphors to provide meaningful mappings of computer commands to physical affordances of everyday objects (e.g., tap object to play/pause, open/close, and bookmark; drag or rotate object to show previous/next, zoom-in/out, and undo/redo).

Similarly, in our research, we designed interactions with our prototypes to leverage people's natural understanding of metaphors for peripheral interaction through smart furniture (Probst et al. 2014b). To identify meaningful gestures for our interactive chair interface (Fig. 9.10), we performed a guessability-style study where participants were asked to demonstrate movements on a flexible office chair that they would associate spontaneously with common Web browser commands (Probst et al. 2013, 2014a). Corresponding to the physical affordances of the flexible office chair, the proposed chair gestures included tilting, rotating, and bouncing movements in various combinations. Building primarily on their understanding of their bodies and the physical environment, participants suggested metaphors like simple tilting/rotating of the chair to navigate between Web sites and tabs (e.g., *progress is right;* tilt right to navigate to the next Web site, tilt left to navigate to the previous Web site), or bouncing for single-command operations (e.g., *sitting down is like coming home*, bounce to navigate to the home screen; *bouncing is like affixing a stamp*, bounce to bookmark).

Studying the defined chair gestures in action, the mapping of gestures to commands was found to provide understandable metaphors that were easy to learn and remember. Interestingly, when experiencing the gestures in practical use,

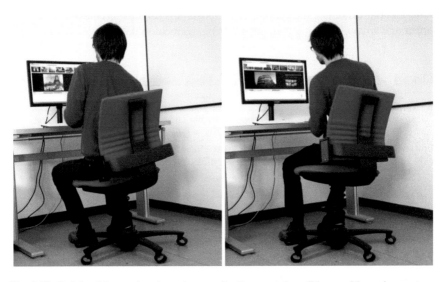

Fig. 9.10 Peripheral interaction through smart furniture: rotating, tilting, and bouncing gestures on an interactive flexible office chair

participants generally preferred subtle gestures over vigorous ones, as to minimize physical effort and maximize social acceptability. Designers of bodily gestures for peripheral interaction may thus carefully consider the trade-off between sensitivity and robustness of gesture recognition (e.g., by providing appropriate feedback on command invocations, supporting user-friendly mechanisms to enable/disable recognition on demand, avoiding the invocation of commands that may cause unrecoverable results, or providing methods to easily undo falsely activated actions).

To evaluate our smart furniture modules for under-the-desk kick, roll, and touch interactions (Fig. 9.11), we bundled a variety of secondary task interactions (i.e., music control, status updates, notification handling, task switching, window handling) into a configuration tool, and we let users define custom mappings of basic hand and foot gestures (e.g., tapping, swiping, nudging) to corresponding input commands. Although simple and intrinsically limited due to their physical nature, observations showed that the gestures still covered many common usage scenarios across varying degrees of freedom. Kicking was, for example, applied to single-command operations (e.g., *kicking is pushing away*, kick to decline a notification). Rolling was used for binary state toggles (e.g., *up is active*; roll up for IM status online, roll down for IM status away) or foot-based scrolling. Touching was associated with directional swiping for finite state transitions, or tapping for rapid command invocation (e.g., briefly mute sound to talk to a coworker).

Fig. 9.11 Peripheral interaction through smart furniture, under-the-desk foot, and hand gestures

Overall, the imprecise nature of the gestures seemed to support the habituation process, as participants would increasingly perform interactions in the periphery of attention. Interestingly, we observed participants applying a wide range of different metaphors when defining useful gesture mappings according to their regular working tasks, working styles, and individual preference. Designers of bodily gestures for peripheral interaction may thus take into account the highly personal nature of appropriate input commands and corresponding physical metaphors (e.g., by providing mechanisms to customize gesture-to-command mappings).

9.3   Conclusion

In this chapter, we discussed new peripheral interaction paradigms for human–computer interaction, specific to the domain of desktop computing. After providing a general review on current desktop computing paradigms, and reflecting on the evolutionary development of the traditional mouse-and-keyboard interface, we pointed out two interaction gaps of existing digital interfaces, i.e., the "digital versus physical" and "focused versus peripheral" divides between simplistic, parallel actions in the physical and complex world, and sequential actions in the digital world.

Reflecting upon existing peripheral interaction prototypes and our research on embodied peripheral interaction through smart furniture, we presented two themes that illustrate the huge potential of peripheral interaction to naturally complement the existing desktop interface, i.e., "from the screen to the world" discussing how to increasingly acknowledge our capabilities for diverse bodily interactions in the physical world and "from the world to the mind" discussing how to increasingly utilize real-world metaphors to improve our understanding of interactions with human–computer interfaces. Throughout these themes, we provided examples of peripheral interaction prototypes that engage multiple of our senses and support interactions to smoothly transition between the focus and periphery of attention. Traditional desktop interfaces have been shown to benefit from such peripheral interaction styles in terms of *reduced number of interaction steps* by providing direct access to frequently used application functions, *reduced physical effort* by supporting simple bodily actions on the physical environment, and *reduced mental effort* by translating abstract commands into meaningful metaphors.

We shared the many lessons we learned from the iterative design and evaluation of our prototypes for peripheral interaction through smart furniture. We hope that they can act as a starting point for researchers and interaction designers to come up with more alternative input modalities that increasingly take into account user's sensorimotor skills and real-world knowledge in order to bring us one step further beyond traditional mouse-and-keyboard interaction.

References

Bakker, S., Antle, A., & van den Hoven, E. (2011). Embodied metaphors in tangible interaction design. *Personal Ubiquitous Computer, 16*, 433–449.

Bardram, J. (2009). Activity-based computing for medical work in hospitals. *ACM Transactions on Computer-Human Interaction, 16*, 10.

Barr, P., Biddle, R., & Noble, J. (2002). A taxonomy of user-interface metaphors. In *Proceedings of the SIGCHI-NZ Symposium on Computer-Human Interaction (SIGCHI-NZ '02)* (pp. 25–30). New York, NY, USA: ACM.

Buxton, W., & Myers, B. (1986). A study in two-handed input. In *Proceedings of the SIGCHI Conference on Human Factors in Computing Systems (CHI '86)* (pp. 321–326). New York, NY, USA: ACM.

Cheng, K. Y., Liang, R. H., Chen, B. Y., et al. (2010). iCon: Utilizing everyday objects as additional, auxiliary and instant tabletop controllers. In *Proceedings of the SIGCHI Conference on Human Factors in Computing Systems (CHI '10)* (pp. 1155–1164). New York, NY, USA: ACM.

Chewar, C. M., McCrickard, D. S., Ndiwalana, A., et al. (2002). Secondary task display attributes—Optimizing visualizations for cognitive task suitability and interference avoidance. In *Symposium on Data Visualization (VISSYM '02)* (pp. 165–171). Aire-la-Ville, Switzerland: Eurographics Association.

Czerwinski, M., Horvitz, E., & Wilhite, S. (2004). A diary study of task switching and interruptions. In *Proceedings of the SIGCHI Conference on Human Factors in Computing Systems (CHI '04)* (pp. 175–182). New York, NY, USA: ACM.

Djajadiningrat, T., Matthews, B., & Stienstra, M. (2007). Easy doesn't do it: Skill and expression in tangible aesthetics. *Personal Ubiquitous Computer, 11*, 657–676.

Dourish, P. (2001). Where the action is: The foundations of embodied interaction. Cambridge: MIT Press.

Edge, D. (2008). Tangible user interfaces for peripheral interaction. Cambridge: University of Cambridge.

Edge, D., & Blackwell, A. (2009). Peripheral tangible interaction by analytic design. In *Proceedings of the 3rd International Conference on Tangible and Embedded Interaction (TEI '09)* (pp. 69–76). New York, NY, USA: ACM.

Finstad, K., Bink, M., McDaniel, M., & Einstein, G. (2006). Breaks and task switches in prospective memory. *Applied Cognitive Psychology, 20*, 705–712.

Fishkin, K. (2004). A taxonomy for and analysis of tangible interfaces. *Personal Ubiquitous Computer, 8*, 347–358.

González, V., & Mark, G. (2004). Constant, constant, multi-tasking craziness: Managing multiple working spheres. In *Proceedings of the SIGCHI Conference on Human Factors in Computing Systems (CHI '04)* (pp. 113–120). New York, NY, USA: ACM.

Hausen, D., Boring, S., & Greenberg, S. (2013a). The unadorned desk: Exploiting the physical space around a display as an input canvas. In *Proceedings of the 14th IFIP TC13 Conference on Human-Computer Interaction (INTERACT '13)* (pp. 140–158). Berlin, Germany: Springer.

Hausen, D., Boring, S., Lueling, C., et al. (2012). StaTube: Facilitating state management in instant messaging systems. In *TEI 2012* (pp. 283–290).

Hausen, D., & Butz, A. (2011). Extending interaction to the periphery. In *Embodied Interaction: Theory and Practice in HCI, Workshop at CHI 2011*.

Hausen, D., Richter, H., Hemme, A., & Butz, A. (2013b). Comparing input modalities for peripheral interaction: A case study on peripheral music control. In *Proceedings of the 14th IFIP TC13 Conference on Human-Computer Interaction (INTERACT '13)* (pp. 162–179).

Hausen, D., Tabard, A., Von Thermann, A. et al. (2014). Evaluating peripheral interaction. In *Proceedings of the 8th International Conference on Tangible, Embedded and Embodied Interaction (TEI '14)* (pp. 21–28). New York, NY, USA: ACM.

Hausen, D., Wagner, C., Boring, S., & Butz, A. (2013c). Comparing modalities and feedback for peripheral interaction. In *Extended Abstracts on Human Factors in Computing Systems (CHI EA '13)* (pp. 1263–1268).

Huynh, K., Stepp, C. E., White, L. W. et al. (2010). Finding a feature on a 3D object through single-digit haptic exploration. In: *IEEE Haptics Symposium.* IEEE, pp. 83–89.

Iqbal, S., & Horvitz, E. (2007). Disruption and recovery of computing tasks: Field study, analysis, and directions. In *Proceedings of the SIGCHI Conference on Human Factors in Computing Systems (CHI '07)* (pp. 677–686). New York, NY, USA: ACM.

Jin, J., & Dabbish, L. (2009). Self-interruption on the computer: A typology of discretionary task interleaving. In *Proceedings of the SIGCHI Conference on Human Factors in Computing Systems (CHI '09)* (pp. 1799–1808). New York, NY, USA: ACM.

Karam, M., Schraefel, M. C. (2005a). A study on the use of semaphoric gestures to support secondary task interactions. In *Extended Abstracts on Human Factors in Computing Systems (CHI EA '05)* (pp. 1961–1964). New York, NY, USA: ACM.

Karam, M., & Schraefel, M. C. (2005b). A taxonomy of gestures in human computer interaction.

Klemmer, S. R., Hartmann, B., & Takayama, L. (2006). How bodies matter: Five themes for interaction design. In *Proceedings of the 6th Conference on Designing Interactive Systems (DIS '06)* (pp. 140–149). New York, NY, USA: ACM.

Lakoff, G., & Johnson, M. (1980). *Metaphors we live by.* Chicago: University of Chicago Press.

Lederman, S. (1987). Hand movements: A window into haptic object recognition. *Cognitive Psychology, 19,* 342–368.

Lee, J. (2010). In search of a natural gesture. *XRDS Crossroads, 16,* 9.

Levine, J. (2002). Non-exercise activity thermogenesis (NEAT). *Best Practice & Research Clinical Endocrinology & Metabolism, 16,* 679–702.

MacIntyre, B., Mynatt, E., Voida, S., et al. (2001). Support for multitasking and background awareness using interactive peripheral displays. In *Proceedings of the 14th Annual ACM Symposium on User Interface Software and Technology (UIST '01)* (pp. 41–50). New York, NY, USA: ACM.

McCrady, S., & Levine, J. (2009). Sedentariness at work: How much do we really sit? *Obesity (Silver Spring), 17,* 2103–2105.

Newell, A., & Rosenbloom, P. (1981). Mechanisms of skill acquisition and the law of practice. In *Cognitive Skills and Their Acquisition.* USA: Lawrence Erlbaum Associates.

Norman, D. A. (2002). *The design of everyday things.* New York: Basic Books.

O'Sullivan, D., & Igoe, T. (2004). *Physical computing: Sensing and controlling the physical world with computers.* Thomson.

Olivera, F., García-Herranz, M., Haya, P., & Llinás, P. (2011). Do not disturb: Physical interfaces for parallel peripheral interactions. In *Proceedings of the 13th IFIP TC 13 International Conference on Human-Computer Interaction (INTERACT '11)* pp. 479–486.

Owen, N., Bauman, A., & Brown, W. (2009). Too much sitting: A novel and important predictor of chronic disease risk? *British Journal of Sports Medicine, 43,* 80–81.

Probst, K., Lindlbauer, D., Greindl, P., et al. (2013). Rotating, tilting, bouncing: Using an interactive chair to promote activity in office environments. In *Extended Abstracts on Human Factors in Computing Systems (CHI EA '13)* (pp. 79–84). New York, NY, USA: ACM.

Probst, K., Lindlbauer, D., Haller, M., et al. (2014a). A chair as ubiquitous input device: Exploring semaphoric chair gestures for focused and peripheral interaction. In *Proceedings of the SIGCHI Conference on Human Factors in Computing Systems (CHI '14)* (pp. 4097–4106). New York, NY, USA: ACM.

Probst, K., Lindlbauer, D., Haller, M., et al. (2014b). Exploring the potential of peripheral interaction through smart furniture. In *Peripheral Interaction: Shaping the Research and Design Space, Workshop at CHI 2014.*

Scarr, J., Cockburn, A., & Gutwin, C. (2012). Supporting and exploiting spatial memory in user interfaces. In *Foundations and Trends in Human–Computer Interaction* (pp. 1–84).

Scott, S. (2004). Optimal feedback control and the neural basis of volitional motor control. *Nature Reviews Neuroscience, 5,* 532–546.

Shneiderman, B. (1998). Designing the user interface: Strategies for effective human-computer-interaction.

Silva, M., & Bowman, D. (2009). Body-based interaction for desktop games. In *Extended Abstracts on Human Factors in Computing Systems (CHI EA '09)* (pp. 4249–4254).

Smith, D., Irby, C., Kimball, R., et al. (1982). Designing the star user interface. *Byte, 7*, 242–282.

Ullmer, B., & Ishii, H. (2000). Emerging frameworks for tangible user interfaces. *IBM System Journal, 39*, 915–931.

Weiser, M. (1996). *Designing calm technology*. Powergrid J.

Weiss, P., & Jeannerod, M. (1998). Getting a grasp on coordination. *News in Physiological Sciences, 13*, 70–75.

Wickens, C., & McCarley, J. (2007). Applied attention theory. Boca Raton: CRC Press.

Williams, L., Huang, J., & Bargh, J. (2009). The scaffolded mind: Higher mental processes are grounded in early experience of the physical world. *European Journal of Social Psychology, 39*, 1257–1267.

Wozny, L. (1989). The application of metaphor, analgoy, and conceptual models in computer systems. *Interacting with Computers, 1*, 273–283.

Chapter 10
Peripheral Interaction with Light

**Dzmitry Aliakseyeu, Bernt Meerbeek, Jon Mason,
Remco Magielse and Susanne Seitinger**

Abstract Light has a profound impact on the human body. Visually, light determines what aspects of our surroundings we can perceive and interpret.
Non-visually, light contributes to regulating our physiology and psychology. Light
is thus an unusual medium that can work both in and out of our conscious attention,
and with new lighting technology this aspect is falling within our control. Computer
controllable solid-state lighting has advanced such that they are now a commonplace technology in the world around us. While many of the characteristics of
light-emitting diode (LED) lighting must fulfill the same requirements as lighting in
the past, the ability to readily integrate LED technology into digital control systems
presents exciting new opportunities that were not possible with other artificial light
sources; for example, the potential to integrate the small form factor of an LED into
the very fabric of a material or control them remotely over the Internet are aspects
that set this technology apart from what has gone before. This unprecedented
flexibility presents the opportunity for new functionality and novel interactive
solutions for and with light. In this chapter, we present three categories of interactive lighting with many concrete examples: interacting with light at the center of
our attention, interacting with light outside our attentional field, and interacting with

D. Aliakseyeu (✉) · B. Meerbeek · J. Mason · R. Magielse
Philips Lighting Research, High Tech Campus 7, Eindhoven 5656 AE, The Netherlands
e-mail: dzmitry.aliakseyeu@philips.com

B. Meerbeek
e-mail: bernt.meerbeek@philips.com

J. Mason
e-mail: jon.mason@philips.com

R. Magielse
e-mail: remco.magielse@philips.com

S. Seitinger
Philips Lighting, 3 Burlington Woods Drive, Burlington, MA 01803, USA
e-mail: Susanne.seitinger@philips.com

© Springer International Publishing Switzerland 2016
S. Bakker et al. (eds.), *Peripheral Interaction*,
Human–Computer Interaction Series, DOI 10.1007/978-3-319-29523-7_10

light in the periphery of our attention. We conclude by considering the factors that make lighting a special medium for peripheral interaction and the role peripheral interaction can play in exposing the many new degrees of freedom ubiquitous digital lighting presents.

Keywords User interaction · Interaction techniques · Connected lighting · Lighting systems · Ambient display

10.1 Introduction

Long before the invention of the electric light bulb, light played an integral role in how we experience the world. The Sun, our main source of light, interacts with us on a physiological and psychological level regulating almost all aspects of our lives. Light influences our internal circadian clock, the production of vitamin D, our levels of alertness, and impacts our ability to navigate the world. Light also regulates social interaction in both work and leisure environments. However, the manner in which the light–dark cycle affects us has inevitably changed with our ability to harness artificial light. Originally, sources such as fire provided humans with light after dark. Later, gas lighting and electricity allowed us to fine-tune how we control our night-time environments. Our conscious interaction with artificial light has increased with our ability to direct light to our preferred activities. Nevertheless, like other infrastructures or devices, light is a means to an end; without light, we struggle to fulfill activities such as working, reading a book, or cooking food. Thus, lighting is often used unconsciously and it may only enter the conscious mind when we notice that something is not right. When we strain to read a menu in a restaurant, we naturally move it to a brighter point on the table. Also, sudden glare from direct sunlight causes us to shield our eyes and pull down a blind to decrease the amount of light to comfortable level.

The drive to produce artificial lighting has brought forth different light sources over the years; however, people's expectations of light have remained unchanged, that is until the relatively recent widespread adoption of the light-emitting diode (LED) for general illumination. Unlike traditional light sources, digitally controllable LEDs provide more degrees of freedom such as dynamic spectral control, instant on/off toggling, and seamless connectivity to other digital devices. Therefore, lighting has become a digital medium and it is playing an important role in the transformation to a world of smart and connected products that constitute the Internet of Things (Porter and Heppelmann 2014).

These digital forms of lighting open up opportunities for designing new ways people can interact with light that can shift between our conscious and unconscious awareness so to support a diverse range of needs. From now on our lighting need not provide only functional illumination of spaces, as it can also be used to transfer information, either as a direct carrier (such as Morse code) or in an ambient way using color codes. A lighting system can be tailored to suit different activities, for example to enhance a movie, to complement a romantic dinner, or to help reduce stress. This demonstrates that as customizable and interactive lighting devices become generally available, users can define the role their light could play in their lives in more detail than merely on or off. For reasons such as these, the popularity of integral and connected lighting systems as part of an ecosystem of digital products is increasing rapidly. Now is the time for exploring and applying how people will manage and understand these ecosystems of products as they grow to include more devices.

The pervasiveness of light and its infrastructure in most buildings lends itself well to this task of supporting people and their ecosystems, especially when using light's advantageous property of functioning seamlessly inside or outside of our attentional fields. In this respect, digital lighting fitted in well with technology visions of Ubiquitous Computing and Ambient Intelligence (Aarts and Marzano 2003; Weiser and Brown 1997). These visions described technology that would be: embedded in our environments; aware of people and situational context; personalized to individuals' needs; and adaptive in response to people. It would even be able to anticipate people's desires without their conscious mediation. Aspects of these visions have already become a reality as we are surrounded by smart and sensing technologies. We live in a digital era and are overloaded with stimuli that are designed to grab our attention; for instance, on a typical day more than 500 million tweets and more than 200 billion e-mails are sent (www.internetlivestats.com, 2015). For generations Y and Z, it is common to receive several hundred messages per day via social media such as WhatsApp, Instagram, Facebook, and Pinterest. The "Internet of Things" is expected to expand rapidly in the next few years and consequently, not only humans but also billions of devices will try to fight for people's attention as well. There is an increase in awareness that this cognitive overload is potentially problematic and that future technologies should become "calm," "ambient," and "peripheral" (Bakker et al. 2015; McCullough 2013).

We believe that digital lighting could support such calm or peripheral technology as a medium for providing feedback and notifying users in an unobtrusive way. Thus, light could not only be a natural medium for being controlled via peripheral interaction, but also be a suitable medium for providing feedback in this highly connected world. In this chapter, we explore both of these directions.

This chapter begins with an overview of how the human visual system works, touching on light perception and the non-visual effects of light on regulating our body. We then dive into the realm of how we interact with light both explicitly and implicitly before highlighting the role of the peripheral interaction. Finally, we discuss the different frameworks that have been developed to describe interaction with light and we surmise what role peripheral interaction can play in future lighting systems.

10.2 How Light Affects People

The human body has developed an advanced sensor system to collect and process light into meaningful information on conscious and unconscious levels. Our eye is our primary visual sensor that consists of a field of photoreceptors on the retina at the back of the eye: rods and cones (Fig. 10.1). Light[1] stimulates these receptors which then transmit electrical signals via the optic nerve to the visual cortex in the brain. The brain processes the information enabling us to perceive and appraise the world around us.

The rods and cones are not evenly distributed across the retina, enabling better responsiveness to the different types of visual experiences we encounter at the center and on the periphery. The cones are most concentrated at the center of the retina (the fovea) and this is where our visual perception is the most acute. The rods are distributed throughout the retina, but are found most densely on the outer edges and they provide us with our peripheral vision. Due to the optical system of the eye, light falling on the retina is not uniformly in focus. Our eyes are able to view a cone of vision that is approximately $110°$ wide with the fovea at the center. The portion of in-focus (central) vision is as small as $5°$ and thereafter the remaining cone is divided into near, mid-, and far peripheral vision.

Even though the visual system devotes most of its resources to the central part of our vision which provides us with color and detailed visual information, the rod cells enable us to respond quickly to motion on the periphery. The electrical signals that the rods and cones produce are also processed slightly differently. The rods used for the peripheral vision can detect and process fast movements very quickly, so to alert us of an impending danger that is outside of our main area of attention, such as a predator stalking us. Furthermore, the rods' sensitivity at low-light levels keeps this system functioning during night-time. During the day, our peripheral vision is mainly devoted to identifying things that need to be investigated in more detail by the central vision, requiring a turn of the head.

Visual stimuli are processed further in the brain enabling us to perceive, appraise, and add meaning. The psychological effects of light are related to attractiveness, atmosphere, and ambiance of an environment. Atmospheric conditions, of which light is a key contributing element, have been found to influence our perception of an environment, our mood, and well-being (Flynn 1977; Knez 1995). This complex relationship partly explains why we feel energized on a sunny day yet have the opposite feeling when it is dark and rainy outside (Vogels 2008).

Light can also impact behavior, in particular human attention, orientation, and movement in space. For example, people tend to move toward brighter areas (Antonakaki 2006) or take a path that is more brightly illuminated (Taylor and Socov 1974). Retail store designers take advantage of this effect and direct customers' attention to a particular part of the store or influence how they move

---

[1]Light as we perceive, it is the part of the electromagnetic spectrum in the region of 380–780 nm (Boyce 2014).

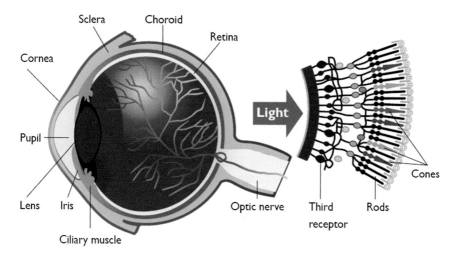

Sclera   Choroid

Retina

Cornea

Light

Pupil

Cones

Lens   Iris   Optic nerve   Third   Rods
                                               receptor

Ciliary muscle

Fig. 10.1 Schematic representation of the human eye [*source* Phillips Lighting (2014)]

through it. The light conditions also affect social behavior, for example, being in the dark (150 lx) compared to a well-illuminated (1500 lx) environment, increase cooperation, and reduce social distance (Werth et al. 2012). Findings from different laboratory studies have shown that the eye has a third type of cell (photosensitive Retinal Ganglion Cells) that is also responsive to light (Berson 2002). This third photoreceptor plays a central role in regulating the body's circadian rhythm via the release of the hormone melatonin which is affected by the receptors' exposure to blue light frequencies.

Understanding how the eye works can help to determine the types of peripheral interaction or peripheral perception that are possible when designing new user interactions and information systems. One example of this is how dynamic light may be more effective than a colored signal at catching our attention via our peripheral vision as this is what the rods are more adept at sensing.

10.3 Interacting with Light

In this section, we postulate how peripheral interaction is a suitable mode of interaction for lighting. It can be an important linking pin between centrally focused light control, such as light switches and mobile applications, and the use of light for influencing us outside of our attention, such as the use of light to influence our behavior or feelings. Peripheral interaction will act as a linking pin since we already have a peripheral relationship with light, where light acts as a signal or means of catching our attention. In this section, we first describe the two extremes of inter- action with light from the explicit to the implicit, before looking into detail of how peripheral interaction will help to connect these two extremes by providing a seamless spectrum of interaction for uses of artificial light. At the end of the section, we discuss the role of light as a medium to support and provide feedback in peripheral interactions with other systems.

10.3.1 Functions of Artificial Light

The use of light today has gone beyond its basic function of enabling us to see when there is insufficient daylight. Artificial lighting encompasses different types of light for different uses. General lighting, such as diffused ceiling lighting or up-lighting, allows us to orient ourselves in a space and complete a broad range of tasks. Dedicated task lighting is used for those moments when we must focus on small details. This is often a high-intensity, focused beam of white light that is positioned closer to the subject matter resulting in glare- and shadow-free illumination. Desk lights, hobby lights, and bedside reading lights can all provide task light when needed.

Ambient lighting is used to create an ambiance or promote a feeling in the environment. Lighting candles and using dimming controls provide this type of lighting in the home and are used to make spaces feel more cozy, romantic, or relaxing. This type of lighting is used extensively in retail to help reinforce the brand image. In theaters and at concerts ambient lighting is used to emphasize what is happening on stage. In the past, colored ambient lighting was limited to the amber glow of candles or to the professionals who had access to special filters to cover lamps and stage lights. The LED has since opened up the use of colored ambient lighting to non-professionals and colored lighting effects can now be found in many more contexts from the domestic to the public.

Decorative lighting refers to products and art installations, where the use of light is to enhance the appearance or experience without necessarily providing general, task, or ambient lighting. A common, everyday example are LED strip lights as these can be used to decorate areas of the home and highlight certain architectural features of a room (see Fig. 10.2).

Fig. 10.2 Under furniture decorative lighting (*source* Philips)

Indicator and warning lights provide the onlooker with precise meaning, feedback, and instructional information. These applications are commonplace throughout our world, from the slow pulsing light on a laptop informing the user that their device is now sleeping, to traffic lights for guiding motorists, to port and starboard lights on ships. With more people having connected lighting installed in their homes, the use of light to inform also increases in the domestic setting. For example connected lighting can be coupled to weather information, whereby—depending on the forecast—the lamp changes color informing the user if it is likely to rain that day.

Finally, with greater scientific understanding of the physiological and psychological effects of light (as outlined in the previous section) the number of health and well-being related uses of light is also increasing. Examples include ultra-bright white light sources that help reduce the onset or effects of seasonal affective disorder and special blue light sources that have been designed to help energize the user and overcome jetlag.

10.3.2 Interacting with Light at the Center of Our Attention

In many situations, our interaction with our lighting systems is one that is focused and intentional, such as wanting to turn on the lights or setting up an ambient light scene for an occasion. At the extreme end of this scale is the control panel for a light designer in a theater, where full attention is given to controlling precisely each light source or use of illumination. These light control panels allow a designer to change the position, color, and intensity of the lights as well as beam angle or apply gobo filters to focus the audience's attention or provide atmospheric effects. Domestic lighting rarely required light controls more sophisticated than a dimmer switch; however, with the popularity of versatile lighting devices increasing, new lighting situations have arisen for which existing controls are not suitable. This has resulted in new types of lighting control appearing in the home. Below are a few examples of dedicated control interfaces to illustrate how we might interact with these new connected home lighting systems.

Currently, the most common way of controlling connected lighting is via a smartphone or similar portable device. Notable examples include Lifx (www.lifx.com), Yeelight (www.yeelight.com), and Philips Hue (www.meethue.com), where most of the features are only accessible via a smartphone application (an app) (Fig. 10.3 shows screenshots of these three applications). These apps typically offer two levels of control: one that allows the control of each light individually and another that controls a group of lights. A common interaction mechanism for controlling a large group of lights is by using scenes or themes (see Fig. 10.4). A scene would include multiple light sources and their respective settings and are typically identified via an image or icon. These images or icons usually illustrate what the scene would look like, such as sunset or forest. Lucero et al. present a light control for

Fig. 10.3 Examples of light app control: Yeelight, Lifx, Hue

Fig. 10.4 Lifx themes and
hue scenes

controlling atmospheric lighting in a bathroom that uses the weather to illustrate the
light effects. They use a device with a small touch screen that can replace a conventional light switch (Lucero et al. 2006).

Offermans et al. (2013) introduced a set of diverse light controls, including
tangible light controls and smartphone-based apps that allow a user to control
lighting in the breakout area of an office. The application allows users to select
lighting scenes based on the activity or manually produce a specific light scene (see
Fig. 10.5). In another publication, Magielse and Offermans (2013) demonstrated a

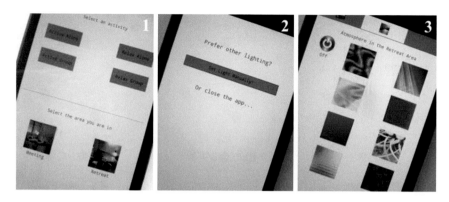

Fig. 10.5 *1* Initial screen to choose activity type and usage area, *2* screen displayed when activity and area were chosen, and when lighting is activated, *3* if the user wishes to adapt the lighting; he/she can manually select from the eight presets (Offermans et al. 2013)

light control application that extends the function of office lighting beyond the on/off presence detection we know today (see Fig. 10.6).

There are also a few examples of tangible light controls. Ross and Keyson (2007) introduced a tangible object, carousel, to set an atmosphere in a living room. In another publication, Mason and Engelen (2010) have described a tangible user interface for controlling light in a hotel room (see Fig. 10.7). Magielse et al. (2013) developed a personal light controller that allows users to control the size of the illuminated area, light intensity, color, and color temperature for of all the light sources (see Fig. 10.8).

These few examples demonstrate how lighting control systems are becoming more diverse and application-specific. The variety is a consequence of many factors such as the different capabilities of the lighting systems, the varying context of use, and the different uses of light, e.g., functional light, task lighting, ambient light, or a combination. To assist designers and developers with the task of creating new light controls, creation tools and prototyping kits are being developed as this area gains

Fig. 10.6 *Left* defining illuminated area; *right* controlling the color and brightness (Magielse and Offermans 2013)

Fig. 10.7 Globe UI (Mason and Engelen 2010)

Fig. 10.8 Personal light control (Magielse et al. 2013)

in popularity. ThorDMX is an example of a toolkit that enables rapid prototyping of lighting controllers. It supports the design of new user interfaces in multiple software languages and platforms (Bartindale and Olivier 2013). It also allows development of touch-based, tangible, and sensor-based light controls.

10.3.3 Interacting with Light Outside Our Attentional Field

In contrast with the previous section, we also interact with light unconsciously and for these situations we consider the light to be outside of our attentional field of view. Consequently, there is no direct user control of the applications and solutions described in this section. Enabled by advances in sensing technologies, software, lighting technologies, and intelligent systems, light can now be controlled (semi)-automatically. For instance, lighting can be activated based on people's presence or the time of day. For these types of interaction solutions, good models of the context are crucial. Perera et al. (2014) summarize four contextual elements: location, identity, time, and activity. These elements are used to trigger or modify a scene with new information, executing scripts, or tagging a scenario. With the advancement of technology, more people are beginning to expect such systems to operate around them requiring minimal input on their part.

A well-known example of automated light control is switching on or off lights using presence sensors. In some systems, the artificial light output is also linked to daylight sensors so to maintain the ideal light conditions while also saving energy (Galasiu and Veitch 2006). Another example is the gradual control of light intensity and color temperature throughout the day or season so people subconsciously associate the artificial light with natural daylight. Several researchers are looking into the psychological effect of lighting and they have developed electric lighting solutions that mimic the feeling of daylight by recreating the pleasant feeling of a blue-sky view and sunshine indoors (Marks 2014; Meerbeek and Seuntiens 2014). For this type of lighting system that has a direct association with natural light, it is logical to control the lights automatically based on the time and location, which is outside of the attentional field of users (Fig. 10.9). In an application of such a virtual skylight, in hospital patient rooms, the lights are controlled automatically based on the patients' daily schedule, taking into account their circadian rhythms and the functional lighting needs of different stakeholders and the patients' recovery status (Daemen et al. 2014).

Pihlajaniemi et al. (2014) investigated implicit interaction with a lighting system in a retail environment. They tested an adaptive lighting system that controls networked luminaries based on the movement of shoppers on the street and the shop floor. The shoppers' movement was translated into various dynamic light patterns intended to attract customers into the store, to focus their attention on specific products, and to try and keep them in the store for longer. The study revealed that most of the participants did not notice the lights changing or that they were a causal factor. A similar observation was made by Poulsen in a field study with an

Fig. 10.9 Daylight
mimicking luminaire (*source*
Philips)

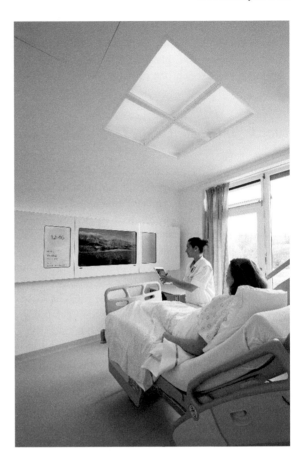

interactive urban lighting installation (Poulsen et al. 2012). The illumination of a
town square was controlled by the location, trajectory, and velocity of the people on
the square. Responsive lighting was tested and, in general, the people did not notice
the light change according to their actions. Interestingly, the observers located on
the edge of the square did notice the interaction and enjoyed the effects. In both of
these cases, the main goal of controlling the light was not necessarily in line with
the objectives of the users who were implicitly controlling the lights.

Particularly in the urban context, municipalities aim to maximize energy savings
in addition to providing safety. Adaptive dimming technology enables infrastructure providers to offer energy saving solutions. Authorities and technical bodies
such as the Illuminating Engineering Society, or CIE (International Commission on
Illumination), establish different lighting requirements based on the assessment of
a street's activity levels. It is essential though to ensure consistent and safe
behavior throughout the network to avoid unsafe conditions or erratic behavior
(Gibson 1978).

The field of interacting with light in a smarter and more automated manner is still in its infancy and the examples given are found in contexts that are rather stable and not exceedingly complex with regard to rapidly changing input or output sources. Until algorithms are able to judge the context and desires of the users more accurately, these systems may still require some form of conscious input to operate optimally. Note that complexity is not always related to the number of light sources being controlled, since street lighting with hundreds of light sources is an example of automatically controlled lighting that is proving to be quite reliable.

10.3.4 Peripheral Interaction with Light

In many situations, people would rather interact with lighting systems in a more casual, subconscious way since—as previously described—light is often a means to an end for achieving other goals. When entering a dark room, a typical person would not want to spend several minutes setting the light parameters of each light source. This is one reason why lighting is particularly suited to peripheral interaction.

The light switch is a universally understood user interface that is often conveniently positioned next to the entrance of a space or next to the light fixture. When entering a room, flicking the light switch is a daily routine that is done almost automatically by most people. In the introduction chapter, the editors of this volume classify interaction with a light switch as an example of peripheral interaction. We do, however, foresee a time when the light switch will not be a sufficient control means for providing the user with the choice of lighting outputs that LED lighting systems can provide. The question therefore is how can more advanced control options be provided to users while maintaining the advantages of the peripheral interaction of the current light switch? Can we manage and balance the increase in functionality that LED lighting systems can offer with intuitive user control that can be understood or operated within the periphery of our attention? This is the point on the spectrum of light control between full attentional control (and commissioning) and implicit automatic control. This midway point on the spectrum is not devoid of interaction examples, some of which utilize the concept of peripheral interaction and these are described below.

m!QBE is an example of a light controller that supports peripheral interaction through the use of physical objects. The user can assign different light behaviors to different sides of the cube and thus when the cube is turned over the light scene in the environment changes (m-q.be). Offermans et al. (2014) developed similar light controls for the office environment, where six different scenes where associated with different sides of the cube controller (Fig. 10.10). Turning the cube to activate a desired light scene can be as effortless as hitting a light switch, except the cube offers four more possibilities than a two-state traditional light switch.

Fig. 10.10 *Top* m!QBE (C. Herbold, m-q.be), *left* LightCube for atmosphere selection in the office environment (Offermans et al. 2014), *right* office lighting light control (Magielse and Offermans 2013)

Magielse et al. (2013) explored the use of a touch sensitive pad as a light controller for the office environment. The intention is that the controller can be used in an expressive way. Stroking the pad will move the light in the direction of the stroke. Applying pressure to the pad will increase the light intensity. Hitting the pad would place the user in a bright spotlight (Magielse et al. 2013). This form of interaction requires low cognitive effort and low levels of attention.

Offermans and Magielse use the same approach for a touch sensitive light switch for an office that activates different light scenes based on how the users touched it. A gentle touch activated relaxing and informal light settings while a firm press activated a bright formal lighting scene (Magielse and Offermans 2013) (Fig. 10.11). While this switch can be activated in the same way as a traditional one, it adds an additional (expressive) level of control, such that when activated the resulting light scene might reflect current mood of the user.

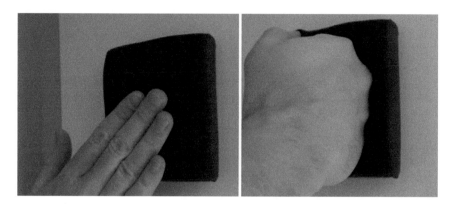

Fig. 10.11 Touch-sensitive light switch (Magielse and Offermans 2013)

The Fonckel lamp is an example of a luminaire that offers intuitive touch-based control of task lighting (Ross 2008). Using touch gestures on the top surface of the lamp, the user can control direction, beam size, and intensity of the light. This interaction can be quickly learnt, enabling the user to achieve precise light settings with minimal effort.

Andersen and Sørensen (2014) developed a set of in-air gestures for light control, some of which require very little effort and attention; for example, they developed a brightness control gesture based on the simple motion of moving one's hand up and down (Fig. 10.12). Curtis (2014) demonstrated gesture-based light control using the Pebble smartwatch. By rotating the arm to the left or right, the user could switch the neighboring light on or off. This is an example of where the simplicity of controlling light is supported by a position-tracking system that determines the location of the user (Curtis 2014).

Although the interaction via speech is one of the most natural modalities for human beings (Nass and Brave 2005), it has been rather infamous for many years in

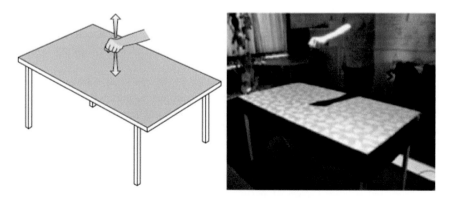

Fig. 10.12 Controlling brightness by moving hand up or down (Andersen and Sørensen 2014)

the Human–Computer Interaction field due to the technical limitations and inaccuracies in speech recognition technology. Recent technical developments, for example Apple's Siri and Google's Android speech recognition in mobile phones, have brought speech recognition to a level that is acceptable for most consumers. Several apps have been developed to incorporate speech control of the lights, including HueRemote (http://www.hue-remote.com/) and Speech Hue (Android app store). Also, dedicated products have been developed to enable the speech control of lights. Vocca is one example of speech-controlled lighting that consists of an adapter with a microphone that can be screwed into a light socket to switch standard light bulbs on and off with voice commands (http://voccalight.com/). Another example is Amazon's Echo, a voice-controlled connected speaker, which can also be used for controlling connected lights (http://www.amazon.com/oc/echo/).

The Responsive Environments group at the MIT Media Laboratory experimented with perception-based lighting controls that hid the individual degrees of freedom, which might have traditionally been represented by sliders on the wall (Aldrich et al. 2013). Instead, the users could move a slider across two dimensions in a single motion. One axis represented light distribution, such as focal light in the center of the room or indirect lighting on the walls, and the other axis was color temperature. The users were asked to create scenes that were described in everyday language rather than technical language: "turn on the three spotlights" versus "create a restorative light scene." In all of the cases, the users were able to produce their preferred final scene faster with this interface than with a typical slider-based system. Approaches such as these permit a more fluid and peripheral interaction with artificial lighting. These interfaces also enable users to explore the potential of a complex-lighting system available to them in a simple and enjoyable manner.

The aforementioned examples show how a variety of interaction technologies from tangible to speech can be used to support peripheral interaction. The concept of peripheral interaction can be used to inspire new ways of thinking for how users might customize the behaviors of their devices. If natural language interfaces or gesture interfaces enable a more intuitive connection with the lighting infrastructure, then users are still lacking the necessary rules of thumb to access all of their lighting system's capabilities. These more contextually based systems are linked with a desire to create technological experiences that are "enchanted" (Rose 2014). Enchanted objects enable users to navigate the boundaries between center and periphery in a more intuitive and satisfying way than traditional lighting control technologies.

An extreme illustration of this can be found in the realm of robotic and augmented objects. A robotic lamp created by robotics researcher Hoffman was designed to respond to gesture and sound interactions in everyday scenarios and in a theatrical manner (Hoffman et al. 2008). It is through the reorientation of a conversation or the generation of a focal point that the communication or action of the play is moved forward. Unlike other ubiquitous technologies, light can powerfully shift people's attention and behavior.

Illuminated robotic theatrical performances are of course unlikely to become widespread, everyday experiences in the short term; however, the ability to present

information and draw attention to a particular area of a large, complex data visualization can easily be driven by shifts in brightness. Though this moth-to-flame
effect or perceptual tropism has not been conclusively shown by perception
researchers, technologists have explored its role in interface design. Pioneering
work by Heun et al. (2012) explored our sensitivity to motion at the periphery of
our perceptual field and findings that directly contribute to this interaction domain.
As we enter into an era of increasingly rich and complex data, these types of
peripheral interactions will only increase in importance.

10.3.5 Light as Feedback in Peripheral Interaction

Light can also be a useful medium for providing feedback on the state of systems
that surround us. Light can be tuned to provide subtle feedback as well as
attention-grabbing effects, making it a suitable medium for providing peripheral
information.

A particular field of research in the domains of Ubiquitous Computing and
Ambient intelligence is the area of Ambient Information Systems. These are defined
as systems that (1) display information which is important but not critical, (2) can
move between the periphery and the focus of attention, (3) have tangible representations in the environment, (4) provide subtle changes, and (5) are aesthetically
pleasing (Pousman and Stasko 2006).

Many implementations of ambient information systems have been developed
using displays, sounds, mobile devices, everyday objects, or art pieces to inform the
user (Pousman and Stasko 2006; Tomitsch et al. 2007). Pintus (2010) describes a
single-pixel device language that we have grown accustomed to in all our electronic
devices. Compared to audio, which is typically omnidirectional, light is a medium
that can be directed and moved inside or outside people's field of view. Therefore, it
can easily move from the center of our attention to the periphery and back again.
A single color-changing light bulb can provide very abstract information, but more
advanced and multi-pixel LED lighting systems such as Large Luminous Surfaces
(www.largeluminoussurfaces.com) can provide more detailed information in an
aesthetically pleasing way (Offenhuber and Seitinger 2014). Moreover, lighting can
be used to present concrete information based on the existing associations that
people have (e.g., blue is cold and red is warm, or red is stop and green is go). Light
also has an abstract quality where its meaning can be highly personal; it can be used
to present personal information in public spaces better than explicit information
displays with text, numbers or images.

Research into the use of light as peripheral sources of information is slowly
increasing and current examples show potential for this type of information.
Gustafsson and Gyllenswärd (2005) designed the Power-Aware Cord. This cord
visualizes the electricity used by the product via glowing pulses. The light feedback
uses meaningful colors that are "glanceable" because it is situated at the location
where the energy is consumed.

Müller et al. (2012) developed the AmbiPower concept. This uses an ambient light display that visualizes power consumption using pulsating light and color: The faster the pulses, the greater the power consumption and the color represents the status of the daily power quota. They found that the brightness of the light was not effective in communicating information, due to the influence of daylight and ambient lighting, while color changes and pulsating effects were effective but had the potential to be irritating.

Maan et al. (2011) conducted a study comparing numerical feedback with ambient light feedback for monitoring energy consumption. Ambient lighting was found to be more persuasive than numerical feedback for encouraging energy saving. The ambient light feedback was also easier to process than the numerical due to the lower cognitive load. Kuznetsov et al. (2011) explored the presentation of air quality information publicly via color-changing balloons over public spaces such as city parks.

Locken et al. (2014) embraced the idea that light can be used in peripheral displays to address information overload in stressful situations. They designed a peripheral light display for cars to inform drivers about the position of other cars to assist during overtaking situations (see Fig. 10.13).

Freeman et al. (2014) also used light as an unobtrusive feedback means for household thermostats. The color around the thermostat would indicate the state of the heating and the light provided the user with feedback when controlling the thermostat via gesture commands (Freeman et al. 2014).

Using light in our periphery as an information source is not as futuristic as we may think as several ambient light information products are already available on the market. Ambient Devices offers the Energy Orb, a light-emitting ball that provides

Fig. 10.13 Peripheral light display in vehicles to inform drivers (Locken et al. 2014)

real-time data about energy consumption (Rose 2014). The Orb glows green if the demand for energy and pricing is low, while it glows red to indicate that demand and pricing is high.

In combination with the Web service IFTTT (ifttt.com), connected lighting systems, i.e., Lifx, Philips Hue, Lutron Caseta (www.lutron.com), Belkin Wemo (www.belkin.com), can be set up to change their light output based on information from the Internet. Some of the most popular links are changing the lamps' color to indicate the weather forecast, blinking the lights if a new e-mail message is received, and making a light flash if a favorite sports team scores. For those who are deaf or hard of hearing, an app has been developed that provides users with light cues when they get an incoming phone call or message, which they may ordinarily miss (Convo lights app).

While products are entering the marketplace that includes forms of peripheral interaction, there are still many unanswered research questions that need to be addressed. More knowledge is needed on how lighting affects our cognition and understanding of products, environments and ecosystems. What type of information and how much can be meaningfully communicated? A key research question for peripheral interaction is almost paradoxical in nature, as how can lighting be used to unobtrusively catch our attention? A study carried out by Arroyo and Selker (2003), for example, showed that light as an interruption modality results in a lower decrease in performance when compared to heat.

10.4 Discussion

There is no doubt that the environments around us, such as our homes, our offices, and our cities are becoming more interactive and responsive to our needs, desires and actions. Despite this increase in smart technologies, designed to make our lives more efficient, simpler, or exciting, they compete for our attention all the time. Since our attention is a limited resource, with our ability to make sensible decisions suffering fatigue over the course of a typical day, the benefits of these technologies may not be fully realized when operating in the real-world alongside each other. The connected lighting systems were some of the first smart home and home automation systems available; while they may have contributed to this modern issue of fighting for our attention, they may also be a key part of the solution due to the advantageous properties of light. Peripheral interaction using light as its medium could be adopted in multiple locations to provide users with relevant and meaningful information that can blend between the obtrusive and the unobtrusive as necessary. The guidelines for designing for peripheral interaction can also inspire designers, by showing that complex systems can be controlled using simple interactions that require less than our full attention to operate. In this discussion section, we explore frameworks for how peripheral interaction can support lighting interaction followed by design guidelines for its application.

10.4.1   Frameworks for (Peripheral) Interaction with Light

To provide some perspective on how digital lighting might evolve toward peripheral interaction, we review three frameworks that have been proposed in the literature. van Essen et al. (2012) describe a form of hybrid interaction for lighting systems. They argue that due to the increased interaction complexity, neither fully manual nor fully automatic control is desirable. If we take the example of the light switch, a hybrid interaction system would divide the manual and automatic aspects. The user would still be able to switch the light on by pressing the light switch; however, the automated system would define what light scene would be activated as a result of this user action. The automated system may determine the light scene based on the user's preferences which it has learned (van Essen et al. 2012).

Offermans et al. (2014) present an initial model for interaction with light, but at the time of writing this model has not been validated and is based on their preliminary findings from a single study. Nevertheless, one of the main findings of the study is worth noting, which is that while people consider lighting to be important it is not often translated into action to adjust the current light condition. This means that a typical user's threshold to make the effort to adjust the lighting and make it more optimal for their current activity is higher than we may first assume. Participants noted that it often happens due to the light condition being acceptable, and even if the light condition might be improved, it is perceived as requiring too much effort for too little gain. Another factor is awareness, with one participant commenting that they would not even notice that the light condition had changed or would not know that the lighting could be improved. The model highlights how different factors, such as context or knowledge of the light controls, may influence the motivation of a user to interact with lights in an environment (Interaction Motivation) (Offermans et al. 2014) (Fig. 10.14).

Andersen and Sorensen (2014) proposed a framework to describe in-air gestural interaction with light. This framework consists of: acceptable interaction effort;

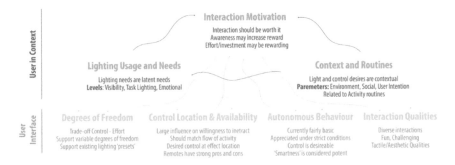

Fig. 10.14 Initial model to describe interaction with light (Offermans et al. 2014)

contextual lighting needs; details of control; mapping schemes; required interaction effort (see Fig. 10.15).

In this framework, peripheral interaction can be classified as interactions that require low effort. For example, one of the gestures they describe is for controlling the brightness by moving the hand up or down (Sørensen et al. 2015). Akin to the conventional dimmer switch, this action in some situations can be classified as peripheral interaction. All other interaction techniques proposed by the authors, even when classified in the framework as requiring little effort, are examples of conscious and intentional control.

The existing literature and thinking in this area of controlling smart lighting systems is still very much work in progress. There are no clear guidelines or rules on which type of interaction to apply for any given situation, since most installations tend to be unique. When a lighting system is installed the type, location and fixtures of the light sources are likely to vary from one location to the other. Even in small domestic environments, with only a few connected light points, people will set up their lighting in many different ways. Another factor is commissioning the lighting system so that it responds as the end users would want. This may include designing light scenes, such as cozy or energizing, setting any automatic inputs such as presence sensors or defining what each switch or control point will activate. An upcoming installation stage is that of applying rules to a lighting system, such as using IFTTT to set the lights based on the weather forecast. At each stage of this

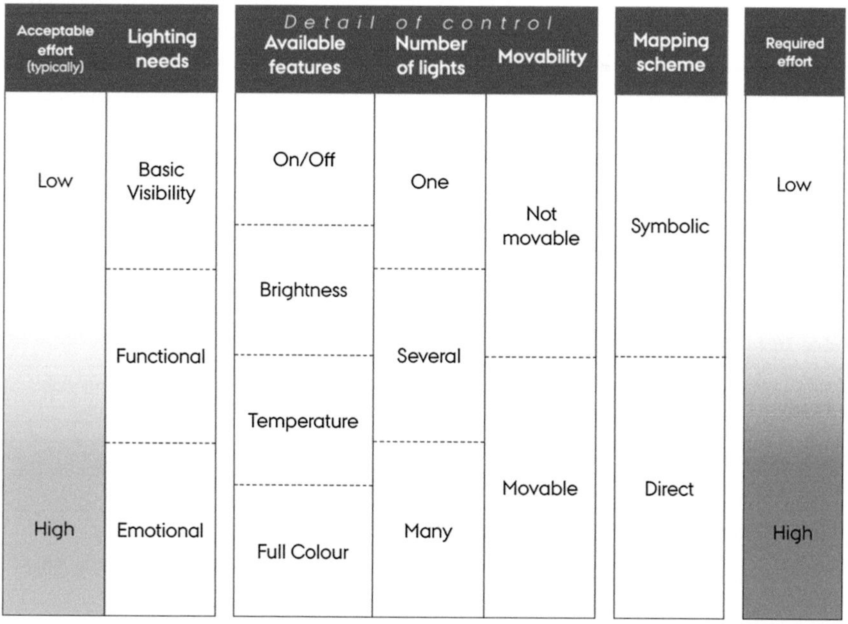

Acceptable effort (typically)	Lighting needs	Detail of control			Mapping scheme	Required effort
		Available features	Number of lights	Movability		
Low	Basic Visibility	On/Off	One		Symbolic	Low
				Not movable		
	Functional	Brightness	Several			
		Temperature				
High	Emotional	Full Colour	Many	Movable	Direct	High

Fig. 10.15 Framework for in-air gestural interaction with home control (Andersen and Sørensen 2014)

installation process, factors may arise that may support or detract from the potential to use peripheral interaction as a control means. However, one aspect is becoming apparent and that is its ability to bridge the gap between full and zero attentional interaction. This means that for any installation there is likely to be a sweet spot where peripheral interaction would work most optimally. Frameworks or guidelines may be most applicable with assisting designers in defining where this sweet spot may reside for their particular installation.

Analyzing the key characteristics of the installed lighting system can help to determine the suitability of employing peripheral interaction over other interaction modes that requires zero interaction (implicit automatic) or full attentional interaction (explicit user control). We found seven key aspects of a lighting system that could be used to question the suitability of different UI modes. We do not claim this to be a comprehensive list, but it is a starting point for exploration and discussion in this emerging domain. One reason for this lack of clarity is that modern lighting systems are evolving rapidly in smartness and intelligence which allows for new interaction options that are currently unprecedented. As smart algorithm development matures, it will enable us to interact with our lighting system in a more fluid or less precise manner and yet still obtain desired outcomes. Below are our seven aspects of lighting systems that could be used to assess the suitablity of a UI:

- **Context**, in what context is the interaction with light happening, e.g., environment, social settings, activity. Table 10.1 summarizes different aspects of the context [adapted from (Magielse 2014)].
- **Temporality**, interaction with a system can change over time, e.g., from commissioning to daily control.
- **Consequence of action**, this refers to the objective/subjective seriousness of the outcome of the interaction, e.g., the control of city lighting would affect millions of people.
- **Function**, what is the function of light in a specific situation, e.g., general lighting, ambiance, task lighting, info lighting, and decorative/artistic.
- **Scale**, related to the context but describes the complexity of the lighting system, e.g., number and density of light points.

Table 10.1 Factors that influence context when interacting with lighting systems

Environmental factors	Physical environment	What type of environment is this (e.g., personal, public), size and scale, temperature and noise
	Setup of the lighting system	What type of lighting is used, what is the directionality and location of the lights, what are the degrees of freedom
Human factors	User's activity	General viewing, focused activity, relaxing
	Emotion and mood	How does the user feel? Is she tired, stressed, happy, angry?
Social factors	Presence and relationship to others	Are there other people? Is the user familiar with them? What are the others doing?

– **Degree of control**, how much control does the user have over the lighting system, e.g., a user might have control over a single-task light in the open office, but the other light sources are out of his control, contrary to a user that has full control of all light points in his or her home.
– **Granularity of control**, what parameters of the lighting system can be controlled: ranging from single light sources to a group of light sources that can be controlled. What parameters of each light source can be controlled: on/off, dimming, color, scene, dynamic effects, etc.

To show how the above factors may be applied, we can use the traditional light switch as an example interaction case:

• **The context** is the home environment and this would determine the number and perhaps type of users who may interact with the light switch and lighting.
• **Temporality** of a traditional switch would imply that the electrician is the commissioner as they would have wired the switch to the light point. The main controllers of the light would be the household members.
• The **consequence of action** of interacting with the light switch is perhaps low, increasing slightly if its location was near a stairway or in a room with tools and equipment.
• The **function** of the light may be general illumination.
• The **scale** of the lighting system may be a single light point.
• **Degree of control** may be 100 %, as the user can turn the whole system on or off using the switch.
• **Granularity of control** may increase if a dimmer switch is also part of the switches mechanism.

These seven factors help to break down the lighting system and reveals aspects that may support or hinder the application of peripheral interaction. In this case, if the light point was for a stairway, peripheral interaction may not be as optimal as a fully automatic control which would ensure the light is on when it is needed. Whereas if it were located in a study room, peripheral interaction may be ideal, as the user can adjust the light without disturbing their study.

The applicability and the need of supporting peripheral interaction can be defined by these factors. Designers may use these seven factors to help guide their thinking with regard to what type of UI may be best suited for any given installation.

To illustrate this, let us use the factor *scale* as an example. The scale of a lighting system infers its complexity as each light point (or group of light points) in a system requires some degree of control. With an increase in the number of light points, there is a subsequent increase in the time and effort required to control them individually and this eventually becomes inefficient and undesirable. Figure 10.16 shows an approximation of the current distribution of existing lighting controls based on the scale of a lighting system. It demonstrates that larger, and thus potentially more complex, systems (such as those on a city scale) are often controlled using automated systems, whereas the majority of in-home lighting systems

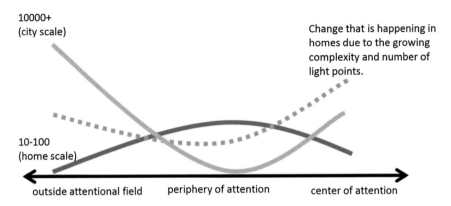

Fig. 10.16 Scale and interaction continuum (see Chap. 1 of this book). Approximate distribution of current city and home lighting systems based on scale and type of interaction supported

are controlled using direct or peripheral interactions. Scale is one of the factors that we believe describes a modern lighting system, but these factors should not be considered in isolation as systems are rarely that simplistic.

Note that even on the large-scale lighting systems, there may still be a role for peripheral interactions, but these are located toward the lower attentional part of the spectrum and so may take the form of peripheral information to inform the controllers that the lighting system is working or that the lights have switched on as intended under the automatic control. However, as more intelligence is applied to lighting systems, we may surmise that the dip in the middle of the graph may move upward as new types of (peripheral) interaction may become applicable. As the number of light points decreases, the option for other types of peripheral interaction may present itself. The figure also highlights one of the recent changes that is happening in the home domain: since the introduction of connected lighting, the complexity of lighting systems as well as number of light points has started to increase, leading to more systems being either controlled automatically (e.g., after being commissioned by the user) or shifting much more toward the center of attention. In a similar fashion to the more complex systems, as the home systems become more intelligent, we might see the return of peripheral interaction where the complexity of the system will become more hidden and so could be handled by the system itself.

The presented guidelines provide a first step toward a more systematic approach for investigating and designing interaction techniques for future lighting systems. Future lighting systems might become more versatile, where one lighting system may be used in a variety of contexts for multiple functions, or in small-scale or large-scale systems. Users may also have preferences with respect to the degree of control and decide on how they want to interact with their home systems themselves. The question is, will there be one superior interaction paradigm or seamless transitions between different interaction paradigms, with each catering for a particular context, function, scale, degree of control, and granularity of control?

One future approach is the provision of detailed control when the user requires it; otherwise, the system blends into the background of the environment and offers peripheral interaction for the day-to-day interactions and information provision. The Nest thermostat is currently experimenting with this kind of alternating approach.

10.4.2 Toward Design Guidelines for Peripheral Interaction with Light

Peripheral interaction appears to have the potential to bridge the gap between fully automated systems on one side and direct user control interface solutions on the other side of the attention spectrum. Based on our experience from researching and developing lighting control solutions, we have outlined a preliminary set of guidelines for designing peripheral interaction with lighting systems. These guidelines are not complete or validated by research, but are a starting point for future work on this topic. In the future, we will also consider that peripheral interaction solutions for lighting systems may also need to include the following points:

- support a hybrid (mix of automatic and user) control solution providing increasing amount of functionality without increasing complexity for the user (Aliakseyeu et al. 2014);
- use artificial intelligence techniques to learn user preferences for specific contexts and activities;
- support interactions on the go, such as passing by a light switch;
- have fast and accurate feedback mechanisms that enable users to control the light in a split second and return attention to the task at hand;
- use tactile, haptic, and audible feedback to support the visual feedback from the light system;
- be effective in guiding users' attention from periphery to focused;
- provide a degree of pleasure while using them.

Some of the key challenges for developing validated guidelines will be around striking the right balance between automation and user control: the sweet spot. The optimal balance is likely to differ between individuals, contexts, and activities, hence our recommendation for using the seven factors to guide thinking in this area. Another important challenge is to design peripheral interactions for multiuser situations. Optimal solutions will be needed to accommodate users that are in the same physical environment but have different interaction needs and levels of attention. A third challenge is to understand better the semantics of light relating to color, intensity, or dynamic patterns (like Harrison et al. (2012) who discusses the need for more emphasis on content development). This will particularly be relevant when light is used as a feedback modality in peripheral interactions with connected devices.

10.4.3 Future Challenges

Since light plays such a key role in modulating our attentional field, peripheral interaction with light is at the core of switching between tasks during everyday interactions. With numerous degrees of freedom, digital lighting and its associated embedded computing power could help to bridge the future gap between increasingly complex user interfaces. It is both a medium for peripheral interaction and a tool users can fine-tune in new ways that should not be burdensome. It can be a key element in sculpting and curating the seams between different types of context-aware systems that are still emerging, for example, the need to determine or redirect the behavior of different home automation tools that may or may not be responding as required by the user. The visceral and intuitive nature of light can be a playful and effective element in these interactions. Importantly, light can play a role in shaping what our vision for future smart environments should be. Will they perform entirely autonomously or are we just in a transitional phase? Alternatively, will smart environments evolve with a more variegated and layered set of practices and performances that will always require interaction with light? With a growing number of smart devices, we can offer people so much more from their environments. However, these tools may prove to be a burden. Electric light especially has always been easy to control—it was not advanced but it still served the purpose. Now we can use it as a much more diverse tool but with the added burden of configuration and commissioning. The right level of interaction (and peripheral interaction is central here) will play a significant role. The lighting industry is only just beginning to scratch the surface of what may be possible.

10.5 Conclusion and Outlook

Light is a remarkable medium that facilitates most of our interactions with the world. Due to the unique nature of our visual-cognitive system, most light signals provide an intuitive and fluid method for interaction. In the meantime, our artificial lighting systems have increased in complexity such that simple tangible interactions— like moving a task light closer to an activity—is no longer enough to access all the capabilities of an intelligent lighting system. Some of the intelligence resides in the system's ability to provide feedback, respond to behavior, or even react to biological cues. We need new paradigms for attention shifting between center and periphery much like tangible media researchers and ubiquitous computing experts predicted (Dourish 2001). With light's ability to bridge media and contexts, more interdisciplinary engineering and design approaches will challenge the status quo for lighting controls and create a more fluid spectrum of engagement through and with light.

Acknowledgments The authors would like to thank all their colleagues in Philips Research and Philips Lighting who contributed to this paper. Specifically, we would like to thank Debora Almeida and Stephanie Cohn.

References

Aarts, E. H. L., & Marzano, S. (2003). *The new everyday: Views on ambient intelligence.* 010 Publishers.

Aldrich, M., Badshah, A., Mayton, B., Nan Zhao, & Paradiso, J. A. (2013). Random walk and lighting control. In *Sensors, 2013 IEEE* (pp. 1–4).

Aliakseyeu, D., Meerbeek, B., Mason, J., Lucero, A., Ozcelebi, T., & Pihlajaniemi, H. (2014). Beyond the switch: Explicit and implicit interaction with light. In *Proceedings of the 8th Nordic Conference on Human-Computer Interaction: Fun, Fast, Foundational* (pp. 785–788). New York, NY, USA: ACM.

Andersen, O. D., & Sørensen, T. (2014). *Exploring in-air gestural interaction with home lighting* (Master thesis). Aarhus University.

Antonakaki, T. (2006). Lighting within the social dimension of space: A case study at the royal festival hall. In *Proceedings of the Space Syntax and Spatial Cognition Workshop.* Bremen.

Arroyo, E., & Selker, T. (2003). Self-adaptive Multimodal-interruption Interfaces. In *Proceedings of the 8th International Conference on Intelligent User Interfaces* (pp. 6–11). New York, NY, USA: ACM.

Bakker, S., Hoven, E., & Eggen, B. (2015). Peripheral interaction: Characteristics and considerations. *Personal and Ubiquitous Computing, 19*(1), 239–254.

Bartindale, T., & Olivier, P. (2013). ThorDMX: A prototyping toolkit for interactive stage lighting control. *CHI '13 extended abstracts on human factors in computing systems* (pp. 3019–3022). New York, NY, USA: ACM.

Berson, D. M. D. F. A. T. M. (2002). Phototransduction by retinal ganglion cells that set the circadian clock. *Science, 295*(5557), 1070–1073.

Boyce, P. R. (2014). *Human factors in lighting* (3rd Edn). CRC Press/Taylor and Francis: Boca Raton.

Curtis, S. (2014). Gesture controlled lighting using Pebble. Retrieved from https://www.youtube.com/watch?v=fy94V3iBSiQ

Daemen, E., Flinsenberg, I., Van Loenen, E., Cuppen, R., & Rajae-Joordens, R. (2014). Adaptable healing patient room for stroke patients. *Methods of Information in Medicine, 53*(5), 406–415. others.

Dourish, P. (2001). *Where the action is: The foundations of embodied interaction.* Cambridge: MIT Press.

Flynn, J. E. (1977). A study of subjective responses to low energy and nonuniform lighting systems. *Lighting Design and Application, 7*(2), 167–179.

Freeman, E., Brewster, S., & Lantz, V. (2014). Illuminating gesture interfaces with interactive light feedback. In *Proceedings of NordiCHI'14 Workshop—Beyond the Switch: Explicit and Implicit Interaction with Light.*

Galasiu, A. D., & Veitch, J. A. (2006). Occupant preferences and satisfaction with the luminous environment and control systems in daylit offices: A literature review. *Energy and Buildings, 38*(7), 728–742.

Gibson, J. J. (1978). The ecological approach to the visual perception of pictures. *Leonardo, 11*(3), 227–235.

Gustafsson, A., & Gyllenswärd, M. (2005). The power-aware cord: Energy awareness through ambient information display. In *CHI'05 Extended Abstracts on Human Factors in Computing Systems* (pp. 1423–1426). ACM.

Harrison, C., Horstman, J., Hsieh, G., & Hudson, S. (2012). Unlocking the expressivity of point lights. In *Proceedings of the SIGCHI Conference on Human Factors in Computing Systems* (pp. 1683–1692). New York, NY, USA: ACM.

Heun, V., von Kapri, A., & Maes, P. (2012). Perifoveal display: Combining foveal and peripheral vision in one visualization. In *Proceedings of the 2012 ACM Conference on Ubiquitous Computing* (pp. 1150–1155). New York, NY, USA: ACM.

Hoffman, G., Kubat, R., & Breazeal, C. (2008). A hybrid control system for puppeteering a live robotic stage actor. In *Proceedings of the 17th IEEE International Symposium on Robot and Human Interactive Communication*.

Knez, I. (1995). Effects of indoor lighting on mood and cognition. *Journal of Environmental Psychology, 15*(1), 39–51.

Kuznetsov, S., Davis, G. N., Paulos, E., Gross, M. D., & Cheung, J. C. (2011). Red balloon, green balloon, sensors in the sky. In *Proceedings of the 13th International Conference on Ubiquitous Computing* (pp. 237–246). New York, NY, USA: ACM.

Locken, A., Müller, H., Heuten, W., & Boll, S. (2014). Using light for interactions in a car. In *Proceedings of NordiCHI'14 Workshop—Beyond the Switch: Explicit and Implicit Interaction with Light*.

Lucero, A., Lashina, T., & Terken, J. (2006). Reducing complexity of interaction with advanced bathroom lighting at home. *I-Com, Zeithschrift Für Interaktive Und Kooperative Medien, 5*(1), 34–40.

Maan, S., Merkus, B., Ham, J., & Midden, C. (2011). Making it not too obvious: The effect of ambient light feedback on space heating energy consumption. *Energy Efficiency, 4*(2), 175–183.

Magielse, R. (2014). *Designing for adaptive lighting environments*. Eindhoven: TU/e.

Magielse, R., Hengeveld, B. J., & Frens, J. (2013). Designing a light controller for a multi-user lighting environment. In *Proceedings of the 5th International Congress of the International Association of Societies of Design Research* (Vol. 5, pp. 1–12).

Magielse, R., & Offermans, S. (2013). Future lighting systems. In *Ext. Abstracts CHI 2013* (pp. 2853–2854). ACM Press.

Marks, P. (2014). Blue skies on tap, whenever you need them. *New Scientist, 222*(2965), 21.

Mason, J., & Engelen, D. (2010). Beyond the switch: Can lighting control provide more than illumination? In *Proceedings of Design & Emotion*.

McCullough, M. (2013). *Ambient commons : attention in the age of embodied information*. Cambridge, Massachusetts : The MIT Press.

Meerbeek, B., & Seuntiens, P. (2014). Evaluating the experience of daylight through a virtual skylight. In *Experiencing Light 2014*.

Müller, H., Fortmann, J., Pielot, M., Hesselmann, T., Poppinga, B., Heuten, W., et al. (2012). Ambix: Designing ambient light information displays. In *Proceedings of Designing Interactive Lighting workshop at DIS*.

Nass, C., & Brave, S. (2005). *Wired for speech: How voice activates and advances the human-computer relationship*. Cambridge: MIT Press.

Offenhuber, D., & Seitinger, S. (2014). Over the rainbow: Information design for low-resolution urban displays. In *Proceedings of the 2Nd Media Architecture Biennale Conference: World Cities* (pp. 40–47). New York, NY, USA: ACM.

Offermans, S., van Essen, H., & Eggen, B. (2013). Exploring a hybrid control approach for enhanced user experience of interactive lighting. In *Proceedings of the 27th International BCS Human Computer Interaction* (pp. 1–9).

Offermans, S., van Essen, H., & Eggen, B. (2014). User interaction with everyday lighting systems. *Personal and Ubiquitous Computing, 18*(8), 2035–2055.

Perera, C., Zaslavsky, A., Christen, P., & Georgakopoulos, D. (2014). Context aware computing for the internet of things: A survey. *Communications Surveys Tutorials, IEEE, 16*(1), 414–454.

Phillips Lighting. (2014). *HealWell—White paper* (White paper). Eindhoven: Phillips Lighting.

Pihlajaniemi, H., Luusua, A., Markkanen, P., Herneoja, A., & Pentikäinen, V. (2014). Experiencing adaptive retail lighting in a real-world pilot. In *Experiencing Light 2014*. Eindhoven.

Pintus, A. V. (2010). Tangible lightscapes. In *Proceedings of the Fourth International Conference on Tangible, Embedded, and Embodied Interaction* (pp. 379–380). New York, NY, USA: ACM.

Porter, M. E., & Heppelmann, J. E. (2014). How smart, connected products are transforming competition. *Harvard Business Review, 92*, 11–64.

Poulsen, E. S., Andersen, H. J., Jensen, O. B., Gade, R., Thyrrestrup, T., & Moeslund, T. B. (2012). Controlling urban lighting by human motion patterns results from a full scale experiment. In *Proceedings of the 20th ACM International Conference on Multimedia* (pp. 339–348). ACM.

Pousman, Z., & Stasko, J. (2006). A taxonomy of ambient information systems: four patterns of design. In A. Celentano (Ed.), *AVI '06* (pp. 67–74). ACM Press.

Rose, D. (2014). *Enchanted objects: Design, human desire, and the Internet of things*. New York, NY: Scribner.

Ross, P. (2008). *Ethics and aesthetics in intelligent product and system design*. Eindhoven: TU/e.

Ross, P., & Keyson, D. (2007). The case of sculpting atmospheres: towards design principles for expressive tangible interaction in control of ambient systems. *Personal and Ubiquitous Computing, 11*(2), 69–79.

Sørensen, T., Andersen, O. D., & Merritt, T. (2015). "Tangible lights": In-air gestural control of home lighting. In *Proceedings of the Ninth International Conference on Tangible, Embedded, and Embodied Interaction* (pp. 727–732). New York, NY, USA: ACM.

Taylor, L. H., & Socov, E. W. (1974). Movement of people towards light. *Journal of the Illuminating Engineering Society, 3*, 237–241.

Tomitsch, M., Kappel, K., Lehner, A., & Grechenig, T. (2007). Towards a taxonomy for ambient information systems. *In Pervasive 2007 Workshop on the Issues of Designing and Evaluating G Ambient Information Systems* (pp. 42–47).

van Essen, H., Offermans, S., & Eggen, B. (2012). Exploring the role of autonomous system behavior in lighting control. In *Proceedings of DIS'12 Workshop—Designing Interactive Lighting*.

Vogels, I. (2008). Atmosphere metrics. *Probing Experience; Philips Research, 8*, 25–41.

Weiser, M., & Brown, J. S. (1997). The coming age of calm technology. In P. J. Denning & R. M. Metcalfe (Eds.), *Beyond calculation* (pp. 75–85). New York, NY, USA: Copernicus.

Werth, L., Steidle, A., & Hanke, E. (2012). Getting close in the dark: Darkness increases cooperation. *Proceedings of Experiencing Light*.

Part IV
Visions on the Future of Peripheral Interaction

Chapter 11
Interactive Soundscapes of the Future Everyday Life

Berry Eggen

Abstract This chapter reviews the inherent qualities of the human hearing system to focus on sounds that are relevant and ignore sounds that are irrelevant and do not require immediate action. Currently, auditory interaction styles that have been proposed and studied in human–computer interaction fail to leverage these human auditory perception capabilities to their full potential. This chapter envisions interactive soundscapes that, based on the capabilities of the human hearing system, offer direct but imprecise interaction control and provide people with explicit means to subconsciously yet intentionally control the shifting of activities back and forth to the periphery of their attention. Technological challenges in the area of advanced audio technology as well as social and ethical dilemmas that relate to interactive soundscapes becoming part of people's natural habitats are discussed. Interactive soundscapes can be considered one of the promising future design research areas where true peripheral interaction can be realized.

Keywords Human hearing · Psychoacoustics · Ecological perception · Sound design · Interactive sound · Soundscapes · Audio technology · Background–foreground shifts of activities · Peripheral interaction

11.1 Introduction

It is not easy to not hear the world around you. Closing your eyes or looking away will not help. Without any tools, the best thing you can do is covering both ears with your hands and if this is not sufficient, you may add some screaming and shouting. This looks and sounds like an awkward solution. As an alternative, you better can try to just ignore the sound. This last, much more elegant, strategy, actually, is the path human evolution has taken to deal with the auditory world we

B. Eggen (✉)
Industrial Design Department, Eindhoven University of Technology,
Eindhoven, The Netherlands
e-mail: j.h.eggen@tue.nl

© Springer International Publishing Switzerland 2016   239
S. Bakker et al. (eds.), *Peripheral Interaction*,
Human–Computer Interaction Series, DOI 10.1007/978-3-319-29523-7_11

live in: we tend to only hear and act upon sounds that are relevant to us and we easily ignore sounds that are irrelevant and do not require immediate action. I believe, this inherent quality of the human auditory system makes the auditory modality a prime candidate for designing peripheral interaction that enables people to interact with their everyday environment in a natural and elegant way.

But how does the human auditory system decide whether sounds are relevant or irrelevant? Currently, we know that the human auditory perceptual system is highly advanced, able to pick up the slightest differences and filter all incoming auditory streams for relevance below the level of conscious awareness (Bregman 1990). In this chapter, I briefly review what is known about human hearing and relevant for the design of peripheral interaction. However, the way audio is commonly used in human–computer interaction (HCI) fails to leverage these human capabilities. This chapter envisions interactive soundscapes of the future, which rely on the principles of peripheral interaction in order to optimally make use of human everyday auditory perception skills.

In this chapter, I will review the qualities of the human hearing system both from a psychoacoustics and ecological perception point of view. Next, the relevance of sound for peripheral interaction is addressed using the peripheral interaction model introduced in chapter of this book. I will look at the center of attention, outside the attentional field, and the periphery of attention, respectively. The next section on interactive soundscapes starts with a possible future peripheral interaction scenario, which implies a number of technological challenges as well as some social and ethical dilemmas. The chapter concludes with a summary of the findings.

11.2   Human Hearing

Any sound we hear in the world originates from a source. This sound source creates disturbances in the air pressure, which travel through the air as waves to finally hit the eardrum, the auditory doorstep to the brain. Sound waves can travel directly from the source to the ear, or they can be blocked or reflected, once or many times, by obstacles in the environment, before they reach their human destination. The fact that the sounds that we hear consist of a mix of direct and reflected sounds has two big advantages. Firstly, we do not have to direct our ears toward the source of the sound, because the reflected sounds are all around (Rossing et al. 2002). Secondly, the mix of direct and reflected sounds informs us about the characteristics of the environment itself (Rossing et al. 2002). This illustrates that the physical sound signal that reaches the ear is a fairly complex signal that contains rich information about the sources of the sound and their context. However, it is only after entering the human auditory system that this complex signal is transformed, filtered, and analyzed to finally be perceived by us as being relevant or to be ignored after all.

Before zooming in on the relevance of sound for peripheral interaction, we briefly review what is scientifically known about the capabilities of the human hearing system. Next, we address people's ability to listen to the sources of sound from an ecological perspective by following Gaver (1993) in asking the important question: 'What in the world do we hear?' This chapter does not address the integration of the hearing system with the general human attention management system, which also incorporates action and includes other sensorial, bodily and cognitive processes (for a review of the human attention system see, e.g., Bakker et al. 2012, or Chap. 3 of this book by Jim Juola).

11.2.1 Human Hearing from a Psychoacoustics Perspective

Although a detailed account of the truly mind-boggling perceptual versatility and prowess of the human auditory system is outside the scope of this chapter, some qualities need to be mentioned to fully appreciate how people deal with sound in their everyday life. For a long time, psychoacousticians have studied the functional relationships between objective parameters that can be measured in the physical world and subjective parameters that are perceived by the human brain (for an overview, see Moore 1989). At the lower levels of auditory perception, they have, for example, uncovered in fine detail the relationship between the physical frequencies that make up a sound and its perceived pitch (Moore 1989). Likewise, similarly complex relationships between perceptual constructs such as loudness, duration, timbre, masking, or localization and their physical correlates that describe the sound waves just before they hit the eardrum have been studied and are known today in great detail (Moore 1989). Current topics of research within psychoacoustics focus on understanding higher-level cognitive phenomena such as auditory stream segregation and auditory object formation (Denham and Winkler 2015). Starting from the physical sound signal arriving at the outer ear, it is currently still not completely understood how, on the one hand, the brain is able to 'dissect,' for example, the total incoming sound of an orchestra into the sound streams of the individual instruments; an auditory capability that allows us to follow the different instruments of the orchestra (Bregman 1990). On the other hand, the brain can only do this because it is able to 'fuse' selected spectrotemporal regularities in the sound signal into coherent auditory objects that together form the auditory scene that surrounds us (Yost and Fay 2012; Bizley and Cohen 2013). Patterson et al. (1992) have shown that three types of sound: transients (high amplitude, short-duration sounds), periodic sounds (sounds that contain a pattern that repeats itself over time), and noise (aperiodic, long-duration sounds) can be separated by the auditory system and therefore play an important role in auditory event perception. The psychoacoustic knowledge presented in this section is indispensible for sound designers to effectively map information parameters to acoustical characteristics in order to create auditory interfaces that indeed leverage the capabilities of people to only extract relevant information from the soundscapes that surround them and otherwise perceive the designed sounds as part of the usual background sounds of everyday life.

11.2.2   Human Hearing from an Ecological Psychology Perspective

Ecological psychologists approach the auditory world we live in and the phenomenal listening capabilities of humans in a different way than the psychoacousticians. According to Gibson (1966), the founder of ecological perception, people directly perceive their options for action when they encounter information sources in their environment. Gaver (1993) used this approach to investigate what people hear when they listen to their environment. As a true 'Gibsonian,' he argued that people listen to auditory events rather than the physical qualities of the sound itself; people listen to the sources that cause the sound in their environment. People are able to describe these sources in terms of their material and interaction properties. People can hear basic-level sound events that involve a single interaction and a single sound-producing event, but they can also hear more complex events that consist of structured combinations of basic-level events. These higher-level events are described in terms of the timing of successive events, or the mutual constraints put on the objects that participate in the related events (Gaver 1993). In addition to the perception of the auditory events, the location, i.e., the position, distance, and overall characteristics of the environment are also directly perceived. Whereas psychoacoustics provides sound designers the means to optimally fine-tune the perceptual qualities of the acoustical mapping of information to sound, the ecological perspective offers designers a language they can use more broadly in their sound design process. For ordinary people, as well as for untrained designers, the language of 'everyday listening' enables them to get actively involved in the generation of ideas and concepts for interactive soundscapes and in the evaluation of their utility, usability, and experiential qualities (Eggen et al. 2014).

11.3   Relevance of Sound for Peripheral Interaction

After quickly going past the capabilities of the human auditory system and the way we listen to our everyday environment, I now zoom in on the relevance of sound for peripheral interaction. Sound has been used in human factors from the early days on. But at the end of the 1980s and the early 1990s, it were people like Buxton, Gaver, and Bly (Buxton 1989) who advocated and presented their pioneering work on the use of non-speech sounds at the interface of human–computer systems. From the 1990s until today, a large community of interaction design researchers has come into existence that actively pursues this line of research [for overviews, see, e.g., Kramer (1994), and Brewster (2008)]. Much of the work has focused on the 'center of attention,' but, inspired by the new possibilities of ubiquitous computing and the emergence of intelligent environments, applications of auditory displays for informing people in an unobtrusive way about what is going on in their surroundings have also been explored. Below, I briefly review the lessons learned that we should take away to inspire future work on peripheral interaction. In doing so, I make use of the three types of interaction with computing devices (as defined in Chap. 1), which can take place in the center of attention, the periphery of attention, or outside the attentional field.

11.3.1   Center of Attention

When interaction takes place in the center of attention, the conscious interaction of a user with a system is focusing on a set of main tasks to fulfill a certain intention. To successfully perform these tasks, the user needs direct and precise control. As a consequence, the system has to provide feedforward to the user to initiate the interaction and give feedback to inform the user about system actions. The human senses and actuators enable people to engage in an effective user–system dialogue aimed to complete the tasks necessary to fulfill their intentions. Auditory interfaces that support interaction in the center of attention use sounds to warn or alert users to initiate action or provide auditory feedback to support the interaction dialogue. Warning sounds, ringtones, and auditory notifications represent clear examples of sounds explicitly designed to attract people's attention. The design of perceived urgency into the warning sound is one of the challenges for this class of sounds (see, e.g., Stanton and Edworthy 1999).

   In the 1980s, Gaver developed the 'SonicFinder,' which added sound to the graphical user interface of the Apple Macintosh (Gaver 1989). While performing an action, e.g., clicking on a graphical icon representing a file, an auditory icon was played that informed the computer user about the sources that caused the sound. The mouse click itself triggered an impact sound (dragging the icon would have resulted in a scraping sound) and the fact that this clearly was the sound of hitting a wooden object revealed that a file was hit (clicking an application would have sounded metal like). The pitch of the wooden impact sound also informed the user about the size of the file; a big file had a lower pitch than a small file. Since its publication in 1989, the SonicFinder has truly become an 'iconic' application that inspired many sound applications that came afterward and still represents a successful approach that is currently taken in, for example, the design of product sounds (Özcan and Egmond 2012). As an alternative to the auditory icon, or ecological, approach to sound design, others, like Bly (1982) and Blattner et al. (1989), focused on the capabilities people have or can learn to extract information from musical sounds. Blattner's so-called earcons mapped characteristics of objects or events to the parameters of little musical motifs. Whereas auditory icons leverage the everyday listening skills of people, earcons focus on musical listening. The mapping of information to the attributes of a musical motif can be arbitrary, whereas the design of an auditory icon calls for a metaphorical approach. This difference favors the learning of auditory icons over earcons, but, on the other hand, makes it more difficult for auditory icons to design sounds that can be easily manipulated to change their information content as the human–system interaction dialogue unfolds [for a more detailed comparison and discussion of auditory icons and earcons see, e.g., Brewster (2008)].

11.3.2 Outside Attentional Field

Sound or soundscapes, in principle, are designed to be perceived at some moment in time and by, at least, one person. When that moment happens, that person might become consciously or subconsciously aware of the information in the environment. In the first case, a person can consciously decide to intentionally act in the center of attention. In the second case, interaction in the periphery of attention might take place; this case will be further discussed in the next subsection.

As we have seen, it is possible to design sound in such a way that it can fade away into the periphery of our attention, but unless the sound is below the threshold of hearing or masked by another sound, it never can be completely outside the attentional field of people that are present in the space where the sound is generated. As a consequence, implicit interaction, i.e., interaction outside the attentional field, is not possible when audio is used as interaction modality.

But what does this mean for the general applicability of auditory interfaces in environments where more than one person is present? In these situations, it is likely that there will be people who consciously hear sound that they cannot ignore because they cannot attach meaning to it; in this case, sound is perceived as noise and easily can become obtrusive and annoying. One of the few strategies that can be used to address this unwanted situation is to design sounds or soundscapes in such a way that they fit the ecology of sounds that define an existing environment. One solution could be to mimic the sounds of existing objects or events, or, in case of man-made environments, one could shape the sound or soundscape in such a way that it will be perceived as a beautiful, or at least, interesting decoration to the environment (Eggen et al. 2008; Eggen and van Mensvoort 2009).

11.3.3 Periphery of Attention

When interaction takes place in the periphery of attention, the user is subconsciously aware that actions are going on to fulfill his or her intentions. These peripheral interactions, however, are not related to the main activity. Nevertheless, they still do require direct, but not necessarily precise control. The work of Gaver (1989) on auditory icons and that of Blattner et al. (1989) on earcons originally focused on HCI taking place in the center of attention. The sound design focused on the mapping of system information to carefully selected perceptual dimensions of everyday sounds and musical sounds, respectively. Both researchers, as well as their followers, however, also noticed and explicitly mentioned additional advantages that come for free with the use of sound as an interaction modality. Most notably, they observed that once initiated, ongoing processes that produce sound no longer need to be monitored in the center of our attention. The visual system is freed to engage in other activities in the center of attention, while the ongoing process shifts to the periphery of attention where it is subconsciously monitored by the auditory system. In a complementary fashion, changes in the sound, e.g., transient sounds, might trigger a shift back to the center of attention. It is the high sensitivity of the auditory system to fast changes in sound in particular that triggers and enables these shifts in attention. The fact that sound exists over space and there is no actual need to face the source of the sound, automatically and naturally leads to forms of multitasking where peripheral interaction is enabled by the auditory modality. Improved collaboration in work settings is another 'natural' phenomenon that arises from the use of sound at the human–machine interface. Intentionally or unintentionally, people listen to what their colleagues are doing and can anticipate on upcoming situation that might call for help or action [see, e.g., Gaver (1991) and Cohen (1994)]. The examples discussed in this subsection, so far, all demonstrate the natural and inherent way auditory information can support the moving back and forth of activities between the periphery of attention to the center of attention. This insight makes sound a prime candidate for interfaces that aim to support peripheral interaction.

When it comes to subconsciously monitoring activities in the periphery of attention, various applications have been proposed that use sound in the environment to unobtrusively inform people about the state of a system. Within computer games, Grimshaw et al. (2013) found that experienced game players do indeed extract meaningful information by integrating auditory and visual cues. In general, awareness systems use sound to create an auditory display but do not offer direct means to interact with the environmental display. Early examples include the EAR and OutToLunch applications by Gaver (1991) and Cohen (1994), respectively. Both aim to support casual awareness indicate informal communication opportunities and recreate an atmosphere of 'group awareness' for colleagues working at different locations. Also within the home context, such awareness systems were explored. Eggen et al. (2003), for example, developed the HomeRadio concept, which allows family members to 'stay in touch' with each other and their home anytime, anywhere. For all these systems, the auditory awareness information that is displayed in the environment has an impact on behavior: people subconsciously hear when to move for a social coffee break, or people sense when to leave for home and arrive just in time for dinner to be served. Despite the fact that the soundscapes generated by these auditory awareness systems do cause intentional human behavior, they often do not yet support direct interaction. Direct but imprecise control would enable people to actively explore and/or change the soundscapes in order to support peripheral interaction. More precisely, the direct but imprecise control would provide people with explicit means to subconsciously yet intentionally control the shifting of activities back and forth to their periphery of attention. But then, what would such audio-based peripheral interaction look like? This question will be addressed in the next section, where I will introduce the concept of interactive soundscapes, which facilitate peripheral interaction through sound at the interface.

11.4 Interactive Soundscapes of the Future

The future use of sound for peripheral interaction can be approached from different directions. One way is to review and extrapolate the work that has been done so far. We did that in the previous sections. Another option is to explore future audio technologies from the perspective of peripheral interaction. A third approach would be to envision a future world in which peripheral interaction has fully matured and is valued by people and accepted by interaction designers as the number one way of interaction with their environment. I pursue this last possibility in the following scenario, an envisioned story that captures an interactive soundscape that seamlessly integrates man-made sounds with the sounds of nature:

> Olivier and Yvonne relax in their lovely flower garden. Today, Yvonne is working at home and is reading. The song of the little dunnock that is hidden in the nearby foliage is so beautiful that it only just keeps Olivier from snoozing away. For the third time, Yvonne is waving away a mosquito buzzing around her head, when the, until now unnoticed, motif of the buzzing sound makes her interrupt her reading. She calmly closes her eyes and listens attentively to the garden's soundscape. There is a lot to hear in the immersive soundscape, but nothing worrisome to take immediate action, although the sound of that little dunnock might deserve some further inspection. With a subtle microgesture toward the foliage Yvonne summons the bird to reveal its song in more detail, but, then again, nothing is heard to worry about; she already has decided her colleagues at work can do without her. She opens her eyes and continues reading, while Olivier has fallen asleep in his 'jardin du sommeil d'amour.'[1]

This scenario puts forward a number of technological challenges. From a technological point of view, knowledge, methods, tools and techniques need to

---

[1]Olivier Messiaen, Jardin du sommeil d'amour, Jean-Paul Riopelle [Video file]. Retreived from https://www.youtube.com/watch?v=bAUcW6vn_xE.

become available for sound designers to create man-made sounds that seamlessly merge with existing sound ecologies. In this particular scenario, the synthesized sounds of insects and birds, including the added digital information that is encoded in them, should mimic the original sounds sufficiently to match the natural sound scene. On the other hand, people should be able to immediately perceive the affordances that are encoded in the sounds. Another challenge concerns the action aspects of the scenario. In this scenario, microgestures (Wolf et al. 2011) are suggested that mimic natural hand gestures subconsciously made in everyday life, such as waving away an annoying insect, or gesturing somebody to come closer. Next to a deep understanding of the auditory ecology in which the interactive sound application needs to be embedded, the combination of highly advanced audio technology and radically new styles to interact with auditory objects in the environment are needed to support future scenarios like the one above. In my opinion, these challenges make interactive soundscapes one of the most interesting areas where true peripheral interaction can be realized. In the remainder of this section, I will explore future audio technologies from the perspective of peripheral interaction and conclude this section by addressing some social and ethical dilemmas that are raised by the scenario.

11.4.1 Future Audio Technology

So far, very few peripheral interaction styles for interactive soundscapes have been proposed. One of the most innovative ones is a system proposed by Cohen (1993) to manipulate the loudness and the 3-D positioning of the voices of multiple participants in an audio conference. Explicit hand gestures can be detected through a data glove and trigger dedicated audio filtering operations that are applied to a particular voice selected. This enables the participants to rearrange the auditory scene to match their personal preference or to adopt it to the momentarily needs of the meeting; important people that need to be heard at any moment in time, could, for example, be positioned closer to one of the ears, unimportant people, however, could be positioned farther away in the 3-D audio space. Although this interaction style originally was meant for interaction in the center of attention, modifications or further developments could possibly make it suitable to be used as a peripheral interaction style. In particular, the gestural part might need to become more implicit. Recent work of Wolf et al. (2011) opens up opportunities to introduce microgestures in this context to enable true peripheral interaction.

Whatever technology will be developed, in the end, the information we want to communicate to people needs to be present and encoded in the sound signal when it arrives at the human eardrums. Consider the most natural, but also most challenging situation in which multiple persons are present in the same environment. We can distinguish two situations: (1) a situation where the information is targeted at an individual person, and the other persons should likewise be addressed by their own personal sound streams, or not be disturbed at all, and (2) a situation where the information, in principle, is relevant and should be available to all persons present.

For the first situation, individually tailored information should be delivered at the ears of the targeted person. This could be achieved by creating air pressure disturbances, or sound waves in the physical space by means of advanced speaker systems [e.g., the Audio Spotlight system by Pompei (1998)], or by sending an inaudible electrical signal to the targeted person. In the last case, the targeted person needs to wear a hearing device that transforms the electrical signal into an acoustic signal at the ears. For both cases, the audio system needs to know the exact location and head orientation of the targeted person. But also, head-related transfer functions of the persons need to be known to compensate for physical differences between the heads of different people. Currently, the second case in which electronic signals are made audible through advanced software and in-ear headphones is available, but has not become mainstream yet (Blauert 1996). The first case is not truly feasible yet, but can be simulated with expensive systems installed in dedicated spaces. Recently, various so-called 4D audio systems have been proposed and implemented that allow people to hear auditory objects and effects that can be precisely placed and moved in three-dimensional space. Examples include the recent Dolby Atmos system for cinemas (Dolby Inc. 2014) and the 4dsound.net system (4dsound 2015) that can also track persons or objects within the space and enables sound to respond to the movement behavior of listeners in the space. Future developments of these early 4D systems could bring their complexity and costs down to a level where, in principle, they could become part of the regular infrastructure of every indoor space.

For the second situation, addressing all persons in a space with the same soundscape, the individual sound requirements could be relaxed, but also in this case, multiple persons means individual preferences that need to be matched with personalized listening conditions, or preferences that can be enabled by interaction means. In this respect, recent developments in interactive and smart hearing devices might bring this personalization to public address systems.

11.4.2 Social and Ethical Dilemmas

The technological challenges, however, coin only one side of the medal. The other side concerns the social and ethical issues that are raised by this scenario. What about a universal 'right for silence' when it concerns man-made sounds in selected public areas? Or what about privacy, if we cannot easily 'hear' away? But even more pressing are ethical issues. Do we really want some of our most precious and beloved soundscapes, like the garden in this scenario, to be affected by peripheral interaction technology? In the past, technology-inspired visions have often promised to improve the quality of life, but have, equally often, not made these promises come true. Think about the smart technologies that currently seem to have such a big impact on all kinds of personal and social aspects of our everyday life.

So far, interaction with smart systems has claimed the center of our attention, but at closer inspection, almost exclusively making use of the human visual sensory system. Would the situation have been different if interaction designers had focused on the auditory modality, instead? Probably yes, but this does not seem the most interesting question within the context of this chapter. The question should be about the long-term impact of auditory-based peripheral interaction on the quality of our future everyday life.

11.5 Concluding Remarks

In this chapter, I have discussed the human auditory capabilities in the context of our interaction with the world we live in. From this overview, and from the insights gathered in application-oriented design research, it seems that humans are perfectly fit to deal with complex auditory soundscapes. The human auditory system has evolved in an audio-always-on-environment called nature. If interaction designers, therefore, base their future designs on knowledge of the human auditory system as well as on the understanding of acoustic characteristics of existing sound ecologies that are valued by people, we can only conclude that throughout human history people have been prepared for auditory-based peripheral interaction: People tend to only hear and act upon sounds that are relevant to them and they easily ignore sounds that are irrelevant and do not require immediate action. Throughout this chapter, I have argued, it is this inherent quality of the human auditory system that makes the auditory modality a prime candidate for designing peripheral interaction that enables people to interact with their everyday environment in a natural and elegant way. In this chapter, I have introduced interactive soundscapes as one of the most interesting future design research areas where true peripheral interaction can be realized.

References

4DSOUND (2015). Retrieved 2015-10-04.

Bakker, S., van den Hoven, E., & Eggen, B. (2012). Knowing by ear: Leveraging human attention abilities in interaction design. *Journal of Multimodal User Interfaces, 5*, 197–209.

Bizley, J. K., & Cohen, Y. E. (2013). The what, where and how of auditory-object perception. *Nature Reviews Neuroscience, 14*, 693–707.

Blattner, M., Sumikawa, D., & Greenberg, R. (1989). Earcons and icons: Their structure and common design principles. *Human Computer Interaction, 4*(1), 11–44.

Blauert, J. (1996). *Spatial hearing: The psychophysics of human sound localization.* Cambridge, MA: MIT Press.

Bregman, A. S. (1990). *Auditory scene analysis.* Cambridge, MA: MIT Press.

Brewster, S. A. (2008). Chapter 13: Nonspeech auditory output. In A. Sears & J. Jacko (Eds.), *The human computer interaction handbook* (2nd ed., pp. 247–264). USA: Lawrence Erlbaum Associates.

Bly, S. (1982) Presenting information in sound. In *Proceedings of the 1982 Conference on Human Factors in Computing Systems (CHI '82)* (pp. 371–375). ACM: New York, NY, USA.

Buxton, W. (1989). Introduction to this special issue on nonspeech audio. *Human Computer Interaction, 4*(1), 1–9.

Cohen, M. (1993). Throwing, pitching and catching sound: Audio windowing models and modes. *International Journal of Man-Machine Studies, 39*, 269–304.

Cohen, J. (1994). Out to lunch: Further adventures monitoring background Activity. In G. Kramer (Ed.), *Auditory display: Sonification, audification, and auditory interfaces* (pp. 15–20). Reading, MA: Addison-Wesley.

Denham, S. L., & Winkler, I. (2015). Auditory perceptual organization. In J. Wagemans (Ed.), *Oxford handbook of perceptual organization*. Oxford, U.K.: Oxford University Press.

Dolby Inc. (2014). *Dolby Atmos for home theaters: FAQ. Dolby Laboratories Inc*. Retrieved 2015-10-04. http://blog.dolby.com/2014/06/dolby-atmos-home-theaters-questions-answered/.

Eggen, J. H., Rozendaal, M., & Schimmel, O. (2003). Home radio—extending the home experience beyond the boundaries of the physical house. In *HOIT 2003 (Home Oriented Informatics and Telematics) International Conference on "The Networked Home and the Home of the Future"*. University of California, Irvine, April 6–8, 2003.

Eggen, B., van Mensvoort, K. , Menting, D., Vegt, E., Widdershoven, W., & Zimmermann, R. (2008). Soundscapes at workspace zero—design explorations into the use of sound in a shared environment. In *Position paper for workshop on Pervasive Visual, Auditory and Alternative Modality Information Display, organized at the 6th International Conference on Pervasive Computing*, May 19–22, 2008, Sydney, Australia. http://www.pervasive2008.org/Papers/Workshop/w8-03.pdf.

Eggen, B., & van Mensvoort, K. (2009). Making sense of what is going on 'around': Designing environmental awareness information displays. In P. Markopoulos, B. de Ruyter, & W. Mackay (Eds.), *Awareness systems: Advances in theory, methodology and design* (pp. 99–124). London: Springer.

Eggen, B., van den Hoven, E., & Terken, J. (2014). Human centered design and smart homes: how to study and design for the home experience? In J. van Hoof, G. Demiris, & E. J. M. Wouters (Eds.), *Handbook of smart homes, health and well-being* (pp. 1–9). London: Springer.

Gaver, W. W. (1989). The SonicFinder: An interface that uses auditory icons. *Human Computer Interaction, 4*(1), 67–94.

Gaver, W. W. (1991). Sound support for collaboration. In L. Bannon, M. Robinson & K. Schmidt (Eds.), *Proceedings of the second conference on European Conference on Computer-Supported Cooperative Work (ECSCW'91)* (pp. 293–308). Kluwer Academic Publishers, Norwell, MA, USA.

Gaver, W. W. (1993). What in the world do we hear? An ecological approach to auditory event perception. *Ecological Psychology, 5*(1), 1–29.

Gaver, W. W., Smith, R. B., & O'Shea, T. (1991). Effective sounds in complex systems: The ARKOLA simulation. In S. P. Robertson, G. M. Olson, & J. S. Olson (Eds.), *Proceedings of the SIGCHI Conference on Human Factors in Computing Systems (CHI '91)* (pp. 85–90). ACM, New York, NY, USA.

Gibson, J. J. (1966). *The senses considered as perceptual systems*. Boston: Hughton Mifflin.

Grimshaw, M., Tan, S. L., & Lipscomb, S. D. (2013). Playing with sounds: The role of sound and music in video games. In S. L. Tan, A. J. Cohen, S. D. Lipscomb, & R. A. Kendall (Eds.), *The psychology of music in multimedia*. Oxford: Oxford University Press.

Kramer, G. (1994). An introduction to auditory display. In G. Kramer (Ed.), *Auditory display* (pp. 1–77). Reading, MA: Addison-Wesley.

Moore, B. C. J. (1989). *An introduction to the psychology of hearing*. London: Academic Press.

Özcan, Elif, & van Egmond, René. (2012). Basic semantics of product sounds. *International Journal of Design, 6*(2), 41–54.

Patterson, R. D., Robinson, K., Holdsworth, J., McKeown, D., Zhang, C., & Allerhand, M. (1992). Complex sounds and auditory images. In Y. Cazals, L. Demany, & K. Horner (Eds.), *Auditory physiology and perception* (pp. 429–446). Oxford: Pergamon.

Pompei, J. P. (1998). The use of airborne ultrasonics for generating audible sound beams. In: *105th AES Convention Preprint 4853*, San Francisco, USA.

Rossing, T. D., Wheeler, P., & Moore, F. R. (2002). *The science of sound*. San Francisco: Addison Wesley.

Stanton, N. A., & Edworthy, J. (Eds.). (1999). *Human factors in auditory warnings*. GB, Ashgat: Aldershot.

Wolf, K., Naumann, A., Rohs, M., & Müller, J. (2011). Taxonomy of microinteractions: defining microgestures based on ergonomic and scenario-dependent requirements. In P. Campos, N. Nunes, N. Graham, J. Jorge & P. Palanque (Eds.), *Proceedings of the 13th IFIP TC 13 international Conference on Human-Computer Interaction—Volume Part I (INTERACT'11)*, (Vol. Part I, pp. 559–575). Springer-Verlag, Berlin, Heidelberg.

Yost, W. A., & Fay, R. R. (Eds.). (2012). *Human psychophysics* (Vol. 3). Springer Science & Business Media, Berlin.

Chapter 12
Weaving Peripheral Interaction Within Habitable Architectures

Brygg Ullmer, Alexandre Siqueira, Chris Branton
and Miriam K. Konkel

Abstract As researchers and practitioners seek to operationalize peripheral interaction, many key questions remain unresolved. Where might such technologically mediated interventions best be deployed? What might they look like? How might such deployments age and evolve through time? Toward engaging these questions, one path is to consider related exemplars from centuries past and use these to inform forward-looking prototypes and envisionments. With an eye toward the future of peripheral interaction and as description of our particular trajectory, we begin by reflecting on early "tangible bits" peripheral interaction experiences. We follow these with ancient examples from the walls of Lascaux, Ur, and Babylon. Drawing from these inspirations, we illustrate and discuss three grounding envisionments upon the halls and walls of habitable spaces.

Keywords Peripheral interaction · Tangible interfaces · Architectural interfaces · Entangled interfaces · Cartouche

12.1 Introduction

The walls of our human habitats, viewed through cyberphysical glasses, today stand largely naked, without sight, expression, or voice. Many walls are decorated with photographs, paintings, and other visual forms, but these are seldom functionally interlinked with cyberspace. Similarly, our walls are increasingly inscribed with screens large and small, but these are predominantly mediated with transient content, without enduring relation to their surrounding physical contexts.

We see this state of affairs as a lost opportunity on several fronts. Today, many businesses, researchers, and citizens are fixated on the interaction prospects of smartphones the size of playing cards, and tablets only slightly larger. In particular in such a time, the walls and portals of architectural real estate, interwoven with

B. Ullmer (✉) · A. Siqueira · C. Branton · M.K. Konkel
Louisiana State University, Baton Rouge, USA
e-mail: ullmer@lsu.edu

© Springer International Publishing Switzerland 2016
S. Bakker et al. (eds.), *Peripheral Interaction*,
Human–Computer Interaction Series, DOI 10.1007/978-3-319-29523-7_12

many of the most compelling spaces of our lives, cry out for awakening with new
life and vitality. Many have long wondered of the prospects, if walls could speak
(Sawkins 1799),[1] but seldom has this been operationalized.

In this chapter, we discuss and contextualize our twenty-year trajectory toward
these ends, in resonance with and pursuit of peripheral interaction. We begin with
motivational context from the ambientROOM, a prototype developed to support
early discussion of ambient displays (Ishii and Ullmer 1997; Wisneski et al. 1998).
These efforts lead to our awareness of diverse historical precedents. We consider a
guiding heuristic we abbreviate as LAVA (for legible, actionable, veritable, aspirational). We illustrate our ideas with three prototypes and envisionments for
"entangled" halls and walls.

12.2 A Point of Departure: Tangible Bits

Our perspective and trajectory toward awakening architectural space with cyberphysical intent began with "Tangible Bits" (Ishii and Ullmer 1997) (conducted at
the MIT Media Lab). This paper, which helped articulate the ideas of tangible
interfaces and ambient displays, was grounded both in prior work by many others,
as well as three new supporting prototypes: the metaDESK, ambientROOM, and
transBOARD. The most relevant of these to peripheral interaction (Bakker 2013;
Edge and Blackwell 2009; Hausen 2013), the ambientROOM, was birthed in part
through an aspiration voiced by a furniture salesman.

Steelcase Corp. was then (and presently remains) a sponsor of the MIT Media
Lab. In spring 1996, the company offered early support to the Tangible Media
Group, in a partnership enabling our prototyping with Steelcase's Personal Harbor
product (Benedetti 1995). In encouraging our engagement with the Harbor (an
innovative prefabricated cubicle-like unit), a Boston salesperson described Harbor
life as prospectively like "living inside a computer."

We found this aspiration insightful and provocative. Inspired also by
Jeremijenko's Dangling String (Weiser and Brown 1995), Raby and Dunne's Fields
and Thresholds/Benches (Dunne and Raby 1994), and Weiser and Seeley-Brown's
Calm Computing (Weiser and Brown 1995), and co-temporal with the blossoming
of the Web, the prospect of weaving flows of cyberspace into architectural space
strongly complemented our Tangible Bits vision (Negroponte et al. 1997).

As framed in Ishii and Ullmer (1997) and Wisneski et al. (1998), we explicitly
coupled graspable interfaces within the ambientROOM—bottles, phicons, and an
inverse clock—with ambient displays (e.g., diversely mediated projections onto the
Harbor's ceiling and walls). These demonstrations were driven by simulated
information sources.

---

[1]Google search: "if walls could speak". May 2015: 39,000 results. http://goo.gl/d5Idd2.

(a)   **(b)**   **(c)**

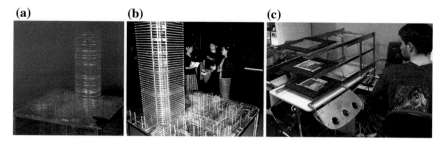

Fig. 12.1 a, b Strata/ICC: illuminated, with people (Ullmer et al. 2001); **c** Strata/ML (Ullmer 2002; Ullmer et al. 2000)

Our first attempts to couple graspable and ambient forms with actual information sources and (arguably) application contexts were Strata/ICC (Ullmer et al. 2001) and Strata/ML (Ullmer 2002; Ullmer et al. 2000) (Fig. 12.1). These systems interactively represented processes within physical buildings (an office tower and academic building, respectively), as kinds of tangible visualizations (Ullmer 2006) or physical visualizations (Jansen and Dragicevic 2013; Swaminathan et al. 2014). Both systems combined general purpose and special purpose tangibles—specifically, parameter tokens and building models—representing processes evolving over timescales ranging from seconds to years.

Strata highlighted the challenges of attempting to simultaneously innovate and realize usable systems on both special and general purpose fronts, and engaging new content and plotforms. In an effort to initially simplify the design space, for roughly a decade, we focused on more general purpose tangibles within diverse real-world application domains (especially visualization and genomics), without explicitly engaging ambient display modalities.

12.3   Evocative Historical Artifacts

During this intervening decade, our awareness of related exemplars from previous centuries grew. While Tangible Bits (Ishii and Ullmer 1997) began with the discussion of historic scientific instruments, we subsequently learned of many additional historical precedents for tangible, graspable, ambient, and peripheral modalities of interaction. We briefly summarize several specifically relevant to peripheral interaction.

12.3.1   *Lascaux*

The $\sim$17,000-year-old paintings in the cave of Lascaux, with some 2000 illustrations of animals, human figures, and abstract signs, are reknowned exemplars of

(a)   (b)   (c)

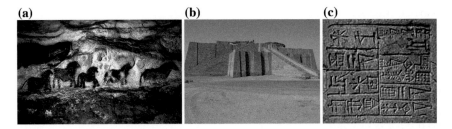

Fig. 12.2 **a** Lascaux cave paintings; **b** Ziggurat at Ur; **c** Ur-nammu embossed brick (**a**, **c**: public domain images as assessed by Wikimedia Foundation https://goo.gl/dt56Gn; **b**: public domain image per https://goo.gl/z18Ud9)

Paleolithic art (Leroi-Gourhan 1982) (Fig. 12.2).[2] Many have speculated how these images might best be interpreted: as accounts of hunting or predation by animals, in mystical and/or astronomical contexts, etc. (Leroi-Gourhan 1982; Whitehouse 2000; see Footnote 2).

Toward prospects for actionable representation within architectural space, in a perhaps peculiar exercise of anachronism, were one to integrate modern powers of computation, sensing, and mediation, while retaining Lascaux's artistic medium and living contexts, how might the walls of Lascaux have been brought to life?

Anachronistically assuming video surveillance and recognition (Aguzzi et al. 2009; Haering et al. 2008), might the paintings of animals—whether predator or prey—illuminate when these animals were detected in the area? In resonance with modern social media, if some of Lascaux's figures represented friendly or hostile bands of humans (Boehm 1999) (tribes did not develop for a few thousand years), might these glow when movement or activity were detected? Anachronisms aside, our intent is to illustrate that even the paintings of Lascaux might have considerable potential for cyberphysical mediation.

12.3.2 Ur and Babylon

Ur, home of the biblical Abraham, is regarded by archaeologists as among the first human cities (Bairoch 1988; Glancey 2006). There, the Ziggurat of Ur-nammu is regarded as one of humanity's most significant early architectural monuments (Glancey 2006). Each of the Ziggurat's bricks is stamped with the name of Ur-nammu,[3] the Sumerian king responsible for its construction (Glancey 2006).

This model of inscribed bricks has endured through the centuries. In constructing Babylon's Ishtar Gate,[4] each brick was inscribed "Nebuchadnezzar, King of

---

[2]Wikipedia. Lascaux, 2015. http://en.wikipedia.org/w/index.php?title=Lascaux.

[3]Wikipedia. Ur-nammu, 2015. http://en.wikipedia.org/w/index.php?title=Ur-Nammu.

[4]Wikipedia. Ishtar gate, 2015. http://en.wikipedia.org/w/index.php?title=Ishtar_Gate&oldid=664783320.

Babylon from far sea to far sea" (Makiya 1991; Vale 1999). In reconstructing the Ishtar Gate, Saddam Hussein repeated the brickwork in similar self-referential fashion (Makiya 1991; Vale 1999).

The bricks of Ur-nammu, Nebuchadnezzar, Hussein, and others can be regarded as embodied hyperlinks (Ishii and Ullmer 1997; Grønbæk 2003). For us, these bricks expand on the prospective styles of mediation explored for Lascaux's paintings. Reaching to the present, many institutions have brick-paved areas, where each brick is inscribed with the name of a donor.[5]

All of these semantically laden bricks can be seen as prospective loci for entangled mediation (Ullmer 2012). Visual, audible, and haptic responsiveness may be yielded by color-changing or illuminescent materials and enamels, internal or projective illumination, augmented glasses, or countless variants. Sensing—perhaps through integrated capacitives, embedded piezoelectric microphones, proximal Kinect or Leap variants, or symbioses with external smartphones and their varied descendants. The technological particulars are less critical, perhaps requiring periodic refreshes like the 1300-year bi-decade rebuild cycle of Ise[6] (Adams 1998; Ullmer 2012) or the reglazing of windows.[7] More relevant here is the evocative, representational, and actionable prospect for cyberphysical association embodied by these bricks and their descendents.

12.4 Reengagement with Peripheral Interaction

In Ishii and Ullmer (1997), tangible interfaces are described as incorporating both graspable and ambient media, noting "the smooth transition of users' focus of attention between background and foreground using ambient media and graspable objects is a key challenge." Since then, there has been much attention to graspables and ambient media separately but as noted in Bakker (2013), Edge and Blackwell (2009), and Hausen (2013), relatively little to their interplay with each other until emergence of the peripheral interaction concept.

Consistent with the peripheral interaction discussions of Bakker (2013), Edge and Blackwell (2009), Hausen (2013), and this book's introduction, we see strong interdependence between graspable and ambient media. In a future world rich with tangibles, we see it as both lost opportunity and diminished value proposition if tangibles do not support ambient awareness when not actively engaged. Equally important, if ambient displays do not provide paths for explicit interactive engagement—resources for peripheral interaction—they lose much of their actionable potential.

---

[5]Mike the tiger: donate a brick. http://www.mikethetiger.com/bricks.php.
[6]Wikipedia. Ise grand shrine, 2015. http://en.wikipedia.org/w/index.php?title=Ise_Grand_Shrine.
[7]Wikipedia. Architectural glass: Canterbury example. https://goo.gl/X19Gi5.

Our path toward reengagement with peripheral interaction has been shaped by a perception of three themes:

1. a symbiotic tension between visual and physical modes of representation;
2. pragmatic and conceptual tools supporting tangible and peripheral interfaces; and
3. opportunities for tangible and peripheral engagement with architectural space.

We elaborate upon these below.

12.4.1   Visual and Physical Modes of Representation

The Tangible Bits article begins with the text "We live between two realms: our physical environment and cyberspace" (Ishii and Ullmer 1997). Here, "cyberspace" can be interpreted in different ways. One might be a general equivalence with "digital information." A variant is the broad realm of digital and computational information, resources, activities, inhabitants, and services.

A third interpretation concerns relationships between the world of physical things and the (then nascently blossoming) Internet. In our present conception, we do not limit ourselves to digital information per se, but rather think in terms of "cyberphysical associations." For example, in peripheral interfaces that engage social media (Kaplan and Haenlein 2010), one might use a physical object to represent a person or group of people, as mediated by teleconferencing or social media tools such as Skype (Hausen et al. 2012), Facebook, and Twitter. Here, while a person is *describable* with digital information, an associated tangible might most naturally represent *her*, not her data. In this spirit, we consider cyberphysical associations as referencing not only Web and cloud content, but also computationally mediated people, places, and things.

We see this third interpretation, which we have embraced, as having a number of implications. If we seriously consider associating billions of physical-world artifacts and spaces with billions of cyberphysical associations, the question of representation—the ascertainment of what a given *specific* object represents—looms large.

A number of approaches are possible. These include handles, like Fitzmaurice et al.'s Bricks (Fitzmaurice et al. 1995), and containers, like Bishop's Marbles (Bishop 1992). In both cases, often generic objects are coupled with prospectively arbitrary cyberphysical associations. Alternately, evocative objects like Ishii et al.'s Bottles (Ishii et al. 2001) might poetically conjure cyberphysical couplings.

In our view, these three approaches are sufficient and appropriate for some tangible and peripheral context—but not all. Specifically, we see a balance and symbiosis between visual and physical representations as central for tangible and peripheral interfaces to seriously engage the challenges and opportunities of Internet-scale cyberphysical associations.

This tangible interplay of physical and visual representations extends back at least four decades. Early examples include the action, variable, and number cards of Perlman et al.'s 1976 Slot Machine (Perlman 1976; McNerney 2004); and the paper storyboards of Mackay's 1994 Video Mosaic (Mackay and Pagani 1994). Both of these divided paper or card tangibles into regular, visually labeled partitions with human legibility and computational semantics. Other such examples are found within Blackwell et al. (2004), Buur and Soendergaard (2000), Ishii and Ullmer (1997), Nelson et al. (1999), Sokoler et al. (2002), and Ullmer et al. (1998, 2008).

Amidst these many examples, spanning many decades, implicitly reside questions regarding interoperability and composition. These have led us to investigate relationships and complementarities between physical and visual (e.g., text + graphics) design languages, and manifestations and extrapolations of cartouches (Ullmer et al. 2010, 2011).

12.4.2 Cartouches

For thousands of years, in contexts as diverse as Egyptian hieroglyphs (Wilkinson 1992), rifle butts (Ball 2006), map embellishments (Harley 1989), and fine art signatures (Edeline 2006), cartouches (per the French term) have entailed a class of visual signifiers. Their characteristics include a visually bounded, humanly legible referent to a particular meaning. Examples from the last sentence include the names of Egyptian pharaohs, rifle manufacturer and batch, geosocial vignette, and artist name, respectively.

While long serving as signifiers of meaning purely within the mind of the viewer, when viewed through the lens of the Slot Machine (Perlman 1976), Video Mosaic (Mackay and Pagani 1994), or our HyperCards (Ishii and Ullmer 1997) [borrowing from Snow Crash (Stephenson 2003)], we came to believe cartouches had strong relevance to tangible and peripheral interfaces. Specifically, cartouches suggested the prospect of signifying cyberphysical associations in fashions that might scale, disambiguate, and generalize across diverse systems.

In 2002, we began operationalizing these ideas in a class co-taught by Ullmer and Konkel at Hong Kong Polytechnic University (cf. Konkel et al. 2004). Both there and toward a proposed follow-on course, we developed an RFID reader array that was shared among a number of student projects, a supporting software development environment, and a GUI simulator. Two challenge/opportunities stood out. First, how might we aid students to rapidly reassociate the shared hardware with their diverse project behaviors? Second, in the context of student poster presentations, might they compellingly integrate RFID reader/tags and other interactors into the posters themselves, in a kind of "tangible interactive poster?"

These motivations lead to several long-running project themes. First, we evolved many iterations of employing RFID-tagged cards as signifiers for diverse cyberphysical associations. From the perspective of tagged cards (whether RFID or otherwise) triggering mediated computational responses, as earlier cited, many related systems have been developed; our focus concerned iteration toward systemic visual representations and functional associations.

Our variations began as textually and graphically labeled ISO-format RFID cards (Ullmer et al. 2003); changed into playing card form factors (Ullmer 2006, 2008); and then evolved into a constellation of regularized sizes (Ullmer et al. 2010, 2011). Conceptually, we first associated each card with a single datum or computation. To increase scalability, these evolved into structured lists of associations that we called tangible menus (Ullmer et al. 2008). Inspired by the Egyptian pharaoh-cartouches, we generalized our idea with the cartouche concept (Ullmer et al. 2010, 2011). Initially, we associated cartouches with specific visual, physical, functional, and conceptual proposals. As we learned about the term's longer, broader history, we have come to understand cartouches as a crosscutting concept, of which both we and others have realized complementary instantiations.

12.4.3 Tangible Interactive Posters

As briefly alluded, a second major theme in our efforts to engage peripheral interaction has been the pursuit of tangible interactive posters. For roughly a decade, these and our cartouche efforts remained somewhat distinct. Initially, our thought was to enable students in their tangible design projects. Here, students would realize paper-based posters that also integrated interactive sensing, display/actuation, and computational mediation.

In attempting to operationalize this, we progressed into a long series of iterations, encountering what David Merrill has identified as a tension between content versus platform development (Merrill 2014). As a paraphrase, Merrill asserts that simultaneously attempting to newly create product-grade content and platforms (which we will abbreviate as C+P) is, in general, very hard (Merrill 2014).

Figure 12.3 illustrates a small subset of our tangible interactive poster efforts. Figure 12.3a illustrates a 2005 undergraduate summer project research poster. There, a mocked-up poster combines regions of "traditional" textual and graphical poster content with interspersed tiles indicating mocked-up interactive content

Fig. 12.3 Tangible interactive kiosk iterations: **a** summer REU poster exploring tangible interactive posters, 2005; **b** SIGGRAPH'07 kiosk; **c** university open day kiosk, 2010; **d** regional kiosk, 2011; **e** summer student interactive poster, 2014

(Rekimoto et al. 2001) and our cartouche + viz tangibles efforts (Ullmer et al. 2010, 2011).

This first effort began to communicate to us the challenges—in the context of existing technologies—for individual undergraduate students to swiftly develop interactive posters combining both novel content (the subject of their work) with novel platforms (underlying implementations prospectively interweaving purpose-built hardware and software). Toward this, in our next iterations, we interspersed arrays of LCD screens with passive printed contents and complemented these with proximal interaction tangibles (Fig. 12.3b).

Partly as we had not yet learned of Merrill's heuristic, these poster iterations again were marked by the challenge of attempting parallel content and platform development. We realized three further successive generations:

1. Figure 12.3c: tiled $\sim 15''$ displays, controlled by tablets with slotted-widget passive haptic constraints we called casiers (Ullmer et al. 2011);
2. Figure 12.3d: single or dual 40+" 16:9 aspect-ratio screens, again controlled by tablets backed by slotted-widget casiers; and
3. Figure 12.3e: single or dual 40+": screens, controlled by tablets or smartphones absent slotted-widget casiers.

The above examples were each realized by summer students or associated staff. In addition, we have progressed through 10 years of class projects engaging similar technologies. These have yielded similar lessons; details remain beyond the scope of this chapter.

Several trends were evident in these efforts. In iterations toward more tractable environments for joint content+platform development, we iterated toward progressively greater uses of and roles for dynamic screens. Second, even amidst this abstraction, the challenges of mixed content+platform development remained steep. On one hand, our evolving team was able to realize more than a dozen such functional iterations. On the other, with each of these, both the content and the platform were impacted, per the challenges of rapid, few-implementor efforts toward parallel C+P innovations (Merrill 2014).

12.4.4 LAVA: Legible, Actionable, Veritable, Aspirational

In these iterative developments of cartouches and tangible interactive posters, another broader challenge stood out: What makes for good design? On the one hand, this is a question that does not lend itself to simple, generalizable answers (e.g., as argued by Hummels 2000). Nonetheless, toward (e.g.) assisting novice students with creating their own cartouches and tangible interactive posters, at a time when exemplar content is not plentiful, establishing some form of guiding heuristics seems important.

Toward this, we have evolved a set of heuristics we abbreviate as *LAVA*[8]: legible, actionable, veritable, and aspirational. These concern different aspects of the role of representation within user interfaces, especially tangible and peripheral interfaces.

- *legible*: Are tangibles expressed in physical and visual representational forms that allow users to "read" them (Lynch 1960)?
- *actionable*: Do tangibles provide paths to access and/or manipulate aspects of their cyberphysical associations?
- *veritable*: Do tangibles and their mediations provide means to ascertain the accuracy of represented content, and their readings thereof?
- *aspirational*: Do tangibles provide aesthetic motivation to engage and suggest paths toward creating like forms?

12.4.5   Tangibles and Peripherals in Architectural Space

Before turning to specific peripheral interaction prototypes and envisionments, we consider a final motivation and guide. Adding to the Steelcase furniture salesman ambientROOM anecdote introduced earlier, we consider a perhaps unlikely companion: a 1727 anecdote by Swift (1727).

As we (Ullmer 2002) and others have noted, arguably one of the most insightful passages on tangible interface design was expressed 300 years ago by Jonathan Swift. In "Gulliver's Travels" (Swift 1727), recounting the "Sages of Lagado," Swift wrote:

> The other project was, a scheme for entirely abolishing all words whatsoever. An expedient was therefore offered, "that since words are only names for things, it would be more convenient for all men to carry about them such things as were necessary to express a particular business they are to discourse on." However, many of the most learned and wise adhere to the new scheme of expressing themselves by things; which has only this inconvenience attending it, that if a man's business be very great, and of various kinds, he must be obliged, in proportion, to carry a greater bundle of things upon his back, unless he can afford one or two strong servants to attend him. I have often beheld two of those sages almost sinking under the weight of their packs, like pedlars among us, who, when they met in the street, would lay down their loads, open their sacks, and hold conversation for an hour together; then put up their implements, help each other to resume their burdens, and take their leave.
>
> But for short conversations, a man may carry implements in his pockets, and under his arms, enough to supply him; and in his house, he cannot be at a loss. **Therefore the room**

---

[8]In Ullmer (2012), we suggested the terms "legible, actionable, inspirational, aspirational" (LAIA). We see a distinction between "inspirational" and "aspirational" but are unsure whether it is sufficiently large or clear for widespread use. The "veritable" term was not mentioned in Ullmer (2012). When "inspirational" was retained, we considered both LAIVA (Finnish for "ship," among other meanings) and AVAIL (an anagram trading off memorability for an alternate ordering of the key terms) as prospective acronyms, before tentatively settling upon LAVA.

**where company meet who practise this art, is full of all things, ready at hand, requisite
to furnish matter for this kind of artificial converse**. (Swift 1727) (emphases are ours)

We find a great deal in these (and surrounding) passages worthy of careful
consideration in tangible contexts. It is important to keep in mind that the text was
of satirical intent, possibly relating to then contemporary topics in philosophical
circles. But if, at some jeopardy, we project the above text upon tangible interfaces,
imagine replacing each app on a smartphone with tangibles. If each app was
associated with 10 unique tangibles, each tangible averaged 40 g (comparable to a
weighted chess piece), and 100 apps were present, the entire 1000-piece ensemble
might weigh 40 kg (89 pounds), excluding packaging.

Relative to the mass of a contemporary smartphone, or the portable effects an
average pedestrian might carry (Strickland et al. 1998), this is rather weighty. But
relative to the cumulative artifacts in some "average" living room, gaming room, or
library reading room, this number or mass is not so large. We see this as closely
resonant with the Swift's contrast between "sinking under the weight of their packs,
like pedlars among us" versus "the room where company meet who practise this art,
is full of all things, ready at hand." While not forgetting the satirical intents or 1727
publication date, we have long considered these passages as charge to "practitioners
of tangible arts" to contemplate their most promising architectural locales; and
proceed to "stack the decks," "furnish[ing appropriate] matter" within such spaces.

12.5 Grounding Envisionments

Influenced by the historical exemplars of Lascaux, Ur, and Japan; contemplations of
visual/physical representations and LAVA design heuristics; the Steelcase and
Lagado inspirations; and our early work and tangible interactive poster/kiosk iterations, we contemplated paths toward increased resonance between tangible and
peripheral interaction and engagement with architectural space. We sought to
integrate passive and dynamic visual representations with physical and virtual
interactors. These aspirations have led us to three grounding envisionments. We
refer to these partly through their associated LSU building names: Johnston, Coates,
and Frey. While these names are not intrinsically meaningful to those beyond our
campus, they compactly differentiate and label evolving use, audience, and physical
contexts.

12.5.1 Johnston: Entangled Hallway

Our first recent peripheral interaction prototype began with considering cyberphysical entanglements for the 63-year-old building then hosting our research
center (Ullmer 2012). The building was constructed as a university dormitory and

used for a half-century toward these ends. We have recently considered the term "aspirational." This building was not intrinsically such an exemplar. In this respect, our building offered a relatively generic canvas, raising prospects for generalizing and applying our approach within diverse legacy spaces. We sought to aspirationally transform aspects of our space—not only in a decorative fashion, but also in a legible, actionable, and veritable form, deeply interwoven both with cyberspace and other physical spaces. The "entangled" term refers to the conceptual and technical weaving of interlinkages between physical and online networked spaces, per our earlier discussion of the cyberphysical term; this is elaborated in Ullmer (2012).

Our efforts were directly motivated and shaped by several opportunities. First, we were given the opportunity to write an invited article envisioning future prospects for human–computer interaction, with a deadline in several months (Ullmer 2012). Partly in the spirit of Djajadiningrat et al. (2002), we did not wish to leave our discussion in the abstract; we sought to offer a grounding instance worthy of discussion. We focused on prospective intersections between cyberspace and interior architectural space. This exercise was also influenced by in-progress construction of a new building, as joint home for our academic center and a major company. We anticipated another such opportunity might not arrive for many years. The dominant internal and external material of our new building was to be glass— not known as the most forgiving or easily evolved architectural material (Brand 1995). If major interventions in our new building were required to host our envisioned entangled hallways (Ullmer 2012), we would need to quickly offer a compelling case.

Figure 12.4 shows a view of our entangled hallway prototype. We engaged hallways as an actively trafficked mixed public/private space. Specifically, we reskinned a ~ 10-m hallway span, adjacent the offices and laboratories of several of the authors. As an interior basement hallway, the space generally did not receive natural illumination. In part inspired by Aliakseyeu et al. (2011), Gross and Green (2012), and Yeh et al. (2006), we sought to transform the hall to a space illuminated by the information-bearing light of remote people, places, and processes.

Figure 12.4c illustrates our resulting prototype. A previously passive wall was reworked to include several vertical tiers of interactively illuminated cartouches. As described in the Fig. 12.4 legend, the upper-right cartouche (Ullmer et al. 2010) array (adjacent the ceiling) represents people on our research team. Each 5×7 inch (DH7) cartouche was illuminated from beneath by an LED lamp and flanked above and below with an LED-illuminated colorbar legend.

For people cartouches, the upper colorbar indicates spatial activity—in which of four primary physical buildings the individual is located (as inferred by CalDAV/Google Calendar entries). The lower colorbar represents online status per several cybermediums (Skype, iChat, Facebook, and SVN). The left Tier 1 cartouches represent different subsets of our team's SVN information repository (analogous to DropBox and other cloud-based information repositories). Examples include tech content (largely software and electronics), grant proposals + reports, and talks. The upper illuminated colorbar represents the level of activity (number of

(a)   (b)   (c)

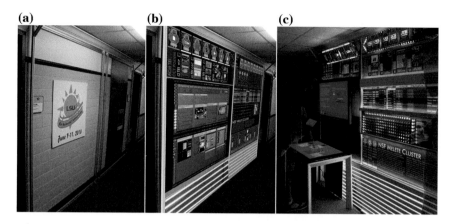

Fig. 12.4 Entangled hallway prototype: **a** view of basement hallway after installation of 80–20 skeletons, before reskinning; **b** envisioned view of planned augmentations; **c** photograph of illuminated augmentations (Ullmer 2012). Edge between wall and ceiling entangled with selected SVN subspaces of nearby groups research repository, and physical and virtual locality of several group members. Tier 2 (*second from top*) includes key supporting grants, major projects, and recent events. Tier 3 includes LCD and panels highlighting evolutions of local supercomputing assets. Tier 4 includes interactive matrix providing upper half of the NSF Melete cluster's "face node," aspirationally allowing a variety of per-node usage data to be observed and queried as a function of time and type. Tier 5, the lower half of Melete's face node, provides other complementary information on the cluster. The wall proximal to the floor is illuminated with down-facing LEDs for floor illumination

repository commits/updates), while the lower colorbar represents recency (last commit this day, week, month, or semester).

As shown in Fig. 12.4, the upper-left cartouches are canted at a 45° angle, while the upper-right cartouches are flushed with the wall. We found the left approach somewhat more visible and legible to hallway occupants. Also, Fig. 12.4 shows the experimentation relating to the colorbar legends (middle section). We see these as one of the most critical sections of our prototype, as they are central to ascertaining the meaning of different color illuminations. Their visual and physical form remains a work in progress.

Below the SVN and people cartouches, three kinds of cartouches are visible. On the left are four cartouches representing grants providing core funding to the group (some active, others pending, rejected, or complete). We envisioned linking these with the SVN repositories and people but have yet to realize this in practice.

These are followed by cartouches representing major group projects. To the right are four letter-sized [FH7 (Ullmer et al. 2010)] cartouches representing major events or performances. In our first-round implementation, cartouches were uniformly illuminated with a channel of white LEDs but not actively mediated. Our intention was to sense absolute or relative deictic (pointing) interaction with these cartouches through an array of Microsoft Kinect, Leap Motion, or other trackers (e.g., similar to Maimone and Fuchs 2012).

12.5.2 Coates: Entangled Teaching Laboratory

We created our Johnston entangled hallway prototype shortly before our center vacated the building. After exiting Johnston, we considered how best to develop this research thread. With the Johnston hallway content centering upon activities of our own research group, we were uncertain about the cleanest prospects for evaluation. Also at the time, we were newly aware of Merrill's C+P heuristic (Merrill 2014). In response, we decided to explore a possible pivot toward a new platform around a base of content, and community of content creators, that largely already existed, within a physical space over which we had some control.

Specifically, we decided to target past and present student projects from Digital Media courses at our university. We did this in the context of a room in a 90-year-old university building that was slated as an undergraduate computer science teaching laboratory. Before commencing actual platform development (e.g., the LED and capacitive sensing hardware deployed in Johnston), we decided to illustrate a mock-up and elicit feedback from our envisioned primary users and content creators: the students of these classes.

Our first envisionment is illustrated in Fig. 12.5. Figure 12.5a illustrates the space prior to our activities. The view is dominated by a large, empty wall. Figure 12.5b illustrates our envisioned intervention. As shown in the Fig. 12.5

(a) **(b)**

Fig. 12.5 Coates entangled wall envisionment: **a** photograph of undergraduate research/teaching laboratory before augmentation. To our knowledge, the rear wall had remained in a similar state for roughly 90 years (since the building's construction in 1924). **b** Envisionment of augmented wall within laboratory. Two 42″ 16:9 LCD screens were planned for installation mid-wall. The remaining wall real estate was envisioned as printed on poster printers (perhaps with semiannual reprintings) and illuminated (for dynamic interactive highlighting) either via projection or proximal addressable LED strips

caption, our concept was for ∼80 % of the wall's surface to be covered by passive printed surfaces, which could be computationally spot-illuminated both by direct interaction, and as triggered by related activities via peripheral interaction. The remaining ∼20 % of the wall would be populated by dynamic displays that could provide navigation of metadata and details on demand.

Wall contents were chosen to be "common denominators" relating to the university's digital media curricula: courses, students, faculties, project properties, and students' eventual employers. A row/column grid, loosely inspired by the periodic table of the elements' representational style, was employed. This was seen as having both pragmatic, conceptual, perceptual, and aesthetic advantages.

The wall is illustrated as occupied by six regions. The left peripheral ∼40 % represents a 10-year span of courses relating to digital media. Each row represents a different course. The background color of each cell indicates the faculty responsible for that year's section. Beyond the course name, number, and faculty initials, each course cell includes the name of each participating student.

In the middle of the wall, two 42″ 16:9 screens were envisioned as mounted. Our intension was to display metadata from selected tiles (at larger scale, to promote visibility and allow precise selection), as well as images from or actual interactive course projects on these displays. These would be selected from interaction with other regions of the wall.

Next, a column of project properties is displayed. The cells here represent programming languages, platforms, input and output modalities, degrees, and majors. Each of these cells is labeled with rows of associated parameter values: Java, Python, C; Desktop, Raspberry Pi, Arduino, etc. In our envisionment, upon selection of a cell, its contents would be displayed upon the top 42″ display. Specific properties (e.g., projects coded using Python) could be selected there.

The fourth section represented faculty responsible for the digital media courses. As described earlier, these were color coded along a gradient, matched to the backgrounds of their courses. The fifth section listed employers of alumnal students. The intention here was motivational, showcasing the diversity of employers —local, regional, national, and international—to which students ultimately progressed. Finally, the sixth section was populated with text describing the intent and use of the wall.

Critical to this envisionment was the idea of "entanglement." Specifically, each cell and subcell from the first five wall regions was interrelated with cells and subcells in the other four regions. Our intension was to make these relationships interactively actionable. For example, if a visitor were to select "Python" under the properties/languages cell, all wall elements were associated with the specified property—all students writing class projects in Python; all faculty teaching those students; all platforms and I/O modalities; and all alumnal employers would be projectively illuminated in response.

12.5.3 Frey: Entangled Teaching Laboratory

Based upon the heavy utilization by our and other students of another combined classroom, visualization laboratory, and teaching laboratory in LSU's Frey building, we decided to make our next (and present) design iteration within this third space. This design was informed by feedback from a number of students, among the intended target user population of the Coates design, that we leave for description elsewhere. Our present design concept is illustrated in Fig. 12.6.

The Frey lab has different constraints from the Coates space. First, three tiled displays along the rear wall were in use by classes prior to our envisionment exercise. As a resource actively used by our students, these seemed likely to stay. Second, the Frey target wall is narrower and shorter than the Coates wall—further impacted by the relative height of the tiled displays. As evident in Fig. 12.6, this left the available horizontal Frey wall real estate at roughly 30 % that of our Coates space.

That said, the Frey envisionment of Fig. 12.6 endeavored to improve on Fig. 12.5 Coates design in a number of ways. In our feedback from prospective users of the Coates envisionment, among the most common and perhaps difficult question was roughly "how to begin." In the Frey design, we attempted to engage this explicitly and prominently in the center bottom of the wall. Additionally, a QR code is displayed upon the wall's top right, providing a handhold for engagement via occupants' smartphones and tablets. Toward our tangible interface interests, an economical 27″ multitouch screen (bottom left) was envisioned for use with several capacitive parameter tokens. For legibility both by users and others in the space, the

Fig. 12.6 Frey visualization laboratory wall envisionment: Three tiled displays (in 2 × 2, 3 × 2, and 1 × 2 configurations) have long been installed for researcher and classroom use. Building on responses to the Coates hall envisionment, some aspects are envisioned as retained. The 3 × 2 and 1 × 2 tiled displays present student projects. These are illustrated as selected via tangible interaction with a 27″ multitouch monitor on the *bottom left*, the contents of which are mirrored on the 2 × 2 tiled display

room's existing 2 × 2 tiled display mirrors the multitouch at larger scale, in vertical orientation, and proximal to other wall resources.

The presence of multiple tiled displays facilitates comparison of multiple student projects engaging similar themes (e.g., in Fig. 12.6, Louisiana's movie industry). While these displays were already deployed and active via traditional keyboard/mouse control, our tangible and smartphone controls provided paths for more readily coordinating across the multiple display resources. Finally, Fig. 12.6 illustrates a floor locus under consideration for prospective deictic gestural control.

12.6 Discussion

The work of this chapter is a study in contrasts. While targeting future opportunities for research and practical deployment of peripheral interfaces, we have also sought actionable roots among some of mankind's earliest architectural efforts. Our research engaging peripheral interaction spans twenty years; yet the two examples most illustrative of our current approach are unimplemented envisionments each less than a year old (relative to completion of this chapter).

Central to our present approach are several themes, altogether consistent across our final three envisionments:

1. a balance between physical and visual modes of representation;
2. symbioses between static and dynamic forms of mediation;
3. prominence of visual and physical structures, often in matrix-like forms, that identify and mediate important common-denominator facets of their host spaces' activities and missions (e.g., courses, students, and time); and
4. anchoring in specific physical spaces, with content specifically matched to the roles and goals of these spaces (per Swift's implicit admonition).

Our core interest and ambitions center on prospects, opportunities, and roles for physical representational modes. At the same time, our latest examples err more toward the visual, as part of our still-unfolding effort toward realizing legible, actionable, and veritable modes of interactive communication; and respecting the content+platform (C+P) heuristics of Merrill (2014) that we have discussed, and many times over relived. And while we have indicated that peripheral interaction modalities are central to our intentions for our last three prototypes, their present actuality—both of the prototypes themselves, and peripheral interaction within them—is in some respects latent and implicit.

We imagine such contrasts and flux are consistent with the relative youth and diversity of peripheral interaction, as a research perspective articulated within the last decade (Bakker 2013; Edge and Blackwell 2009; Hausen 2013). As sister interaction themes such as hypertext, virtual reality, augmented reality, and tangible interfaces have illustrated, we believe it is common for many decades to pass from first instances to mass-market adoption. Arguably for hypertext, VR, and AR, their passages to successful mass deployments spanned roughly a half-century, and for VR and AR remain, from mass market perspectives, still within early childhood.

Examples of peripheral interfaces have perhaps presently traversed 25–30 years (Dourish and Bly 1992; Dunne and Raby 1994; Krueger et al. 1985).

To contribute toward and accelerate this realization, we have progressively endeavored to leverage and cultivate ecologies among mass-market technologies (e.g., tablets and large displays) and to iterate toward specific use contexts that seem particularly promising for progressive realization. In synergy with our companion chapters, we hope this ensemble of trajectories illustrates new potentials for legible, actionable, veritable, and aspirational interior architectural embodiments of peripheral interaction.

Acknowledgements This research has been supported in part by NSF (CNS-0521559, CNS-1126739, IIS-0856065, and EPSCoR), NIST CDI, LSU CCT, and the Louisiana Board of Regents. Narendra Setty, Landon Rogge, and Bob Kooima co-lead the implementation of the Johnston Hall prototype. Ben Guitreau co-lead the implementation of an interim illuminated system not discussed within this manuscript, but influential to the later envisionments. Kevin James, Rajesh Sankaran, Srikanth Jandbyala, and Kristen Barrett lead the implementations of Fig. 12.3. Sarah Baldwin and Kristen Barrett contributed substantially to the ideas and visuals of the final two envisionments. Nadine Couture and Guillaume Riviere have collaborated actively on the cartouches research described within. Bernt Meerbeek and Dzmitry Aliakseyeu inspired and extended our concepts of lighting in architectural spaces. Many individuals contributed to the Johnston Hall entangled hallway prototype, listed individually within Ullmer (2012). IBM, Mitsubishi Electric Research Laboratories, AT&T, and the Things That Think consortium supported the research described at the MIT Media Laboratory, under the direction of Hiroshi Ishii. Special thanks to the editors for substantial improvements to the chapter.

References

Adams, C. (1998). Japan's Ise shrine and its thirteen-hundred-year-old reconstruction tradition. *Journal of Architectural Education, 52*(1), 49–60.

Aguzzi, J., Costa, C., Fujiwara, Y., Iwase, R., Ramirez-Llorda, E., & Menesatti, P. (2009). A novel morphometry-based protocol of automated video-image analysis for species recognition and activity rhythms monitoring in deep-sea fauna. *Sensors, 9*(11), 8438–8455.

Aliakseyeu, D., Mason, J., Meerbeek, B., van Essen, H., & Offermans, S. (2011). The role of ambient intelligence in future lighting systems. In *Ambient Intelligence. Lecture Notes in Computer Science* (Vol. 7040, pp. 362–363). Berlin: Springer.

Bairoch, P.(1988). *Cities and economic development: from the dawn of history to the present.* Chicago: University of Chicago Press.

Bakker, S. (2013). *Design for peripheral interaction* (Ph.D. thesis). TU/Eindhoven.

Ball, R. (2006). *Mauser Military Rifles of the World.* Gun Digest Books.

Benedetti, M. (1995, June 4). Keep in touch, and keep your space. *Bloomberg Business.*

Bishop, D. (1992). *Marble answering machine.* http://tangint.org/v/1992/bishop-rca-mam/

Blackwell, A., Stringer, M., Toye, E., & Rode, J. (2004). Tangible interface for collaborative information retrieval. In *Proceedings of CHI'04* (pp. 1473–1476).

Boehm, C. (1999). *Hierarchy in the forest: The evolution of egalitarian behavior.* Cambridge, MA: Harvard University Press.

Brand, S. (1995). *How buildings learn: What happens after they're built.* New York: Penguin.com.

Buur, J., & Soendergaard, A. (2000). Video card game: An augmented environment for user centred design discussions. In *Proceedings of DARE'00* (pp. 63–69).

Djajadiningrat, T., Overbeeke, K., & Wensveen, S. (2002). But how, Donald, tell us how? On the creation of meaning in interaction design through feedforward and inherent feedback. In *Proceedings of DIS'02* (pp. 285–291).

Dourish, P., & Bly, S. (1992). Portholes: Supporting awareness in a distributed work group. In *Proceedings of CHI'92* (pp. 541–547). ACM.

Dunne, A., & Raby, F. (1994). Fields and thresholds. In *Proceedings of the Doors of Perception-2*.

Edeline, F. (2006). Le monogramme - un genre intersémiotique. In *L'hétérogénéité du visuel: Les syncrétismes* (Vols. 2–3).

Edge, D., & Blackwell, A. F. (2009). Peripheral tangible interaction by analytic design. In *Proceedings of TEI'09* (pp. 69–76).

Fitzmaurice, G., Ishii, H., & Buxton, W. (1995). Bricks: Laying the foundations for graspable user interfaces. In *Proceedings of CHI'95* (pp. 442–449).

Glancey, J. (2006). *Architecture*. Metro Books.

Grønbæk, K., Kristensen, J. F., Ørbæk P., & Eriksen, M. A. (2003). Physical hypermedia: Organising collections of mixed physical and digitalmaterial. In *Proceedings of Hypertext and Hypermedia 2003* (pp. 10–19). ACM.

Gross, M. D., & Green, K. E. (2012). Architectural robotics, inevitably. *Interactions, 19*(1), 28–33.

Haering, N., Venetianer, P. L., & Lipton, A. (2008). The evolution of video surveillance: An overview. *Machine Vision and Applications, 19*(5–6), 279–290.

Harley, J. B. (1989). Deconstructing the map. *Cartographica: The International Journal for Geographic Information and Geovisualization, 26*(2), 1–20.

Hausen, D. (2013). *Peripheral interaction: exploring the design space* (Ph.D. thesis). Ludwig-Maximilians-Universität München.

Hausen, D., Boring, S., Lueling, C., Rodestock, S., & Butz, A. (2012). StaTube: Facilitating state management in instant messaging systems. In *Proceedings of TEI'12* (pp. 283–290). ACM.

Hummels, C. C. M. (2000). *Gestural design tools: Prototypes, experiments and scenarios* (Ph.D. thesis). TU Delft, Delft University of Technology.

Ishii, H., Mazalek, A., & Lee, J. (2001). Bottles as a minimal interface to access digital information. In *CHI'01 Extended Abstracts* (pp. 187–188). ACM.

Ishii, H., & Ullmer, B. (1997). Tangible Bits: Towards seamless interfaces between people, bits and atoms. In *Proceedings of CHI'97* (pp. 234–241).

Jansen, Y., & Dragicevic, P. (2013). An interaction model for visualizations beyond the desktop. *IEEE Transactions on Visualization and Computer Graphics, 19*(12), 2396–2405.

Kaplan, A. M., & Haenlein, M. (2010). Users of the world, unite! The challenges and opportunities of social media. *Business Horizons, 53*(1), 59–68.

Konkel, M., Leung, V., Ullmer, B., & Hu, C. (2004). Tagaboo: A collaborative children's game based upon wearable RFID technology. *Personal and Ubiquitous Computing, 8*(5), 382–384.

Krueger, M. W., Gionfriddo, T., & Hinrichsen, K. (1985). Videoplace—an artificial reality. In *ACM SIGCHI Bulletin* (Vol. 16, pp. 35–40). ACM.

Leroi-Gourhan, A. (1982). The archaeology of Lascaux cave. *Scientific American, 246*(6), 104–112.

Lynch, K. (1960). *The image of the city* (Vol. 11). Cambridge, MA: MIT Press.

Mackay, W., & Pagani, D. (1994). Video Mosaic: Laying out time in a physical space. In *Proceedings of Multimedia'94* (pp. 165–172).

Maimone, A., & Fuchs, H. (2012). Reducing interference between multiple structured light depth sensors using motion. In *Virtual Reality Workshops (VR), 2012 IEEE* (pp. 51–54). IEEE.

Makiya, K. (1991). *The monument: Art, vulgarity, and responsibility in Iraq*. Oakland, CA: University of California Press.

McNerney T. (2004). From turtles to tangible programming bricks: explorations in physical language design. *Personal and Ubiquitous Computing, 8*(5):326–337.

Merrill, D. (2014). Personal communications: content+platform heuristic, 2014.

Negroponte, N., Ishii, H., & Ullmer, B. (1997). Tangible Bits. *WIRED*, 1997.

Nelson, L., Ichimura, S., Pedersen, E., & Adams, L. (1999). Palette: A paper interface for giving presentations. In *Proceedings of CHI'99* (pp. 354–361).

Perlman, R. (1976). Using computer technology to provide a creative learning environment for preschool children. *MIT Lego Memo*, #24.

Rekimoto, J., Ullmer, B., & Oba, H. (2001). DataTiles: A modular platform for mixed physical and graphical interactions. In *Proceedings of CHI'01* (pp 269–276).

Sawkins. C. (1799). A Sermon preached before the University at St. Mary's. http://goo.gl/zW2aal, February 27, 1799.

Sokoler, T., Edeholt, H., & Johansson, M. (2002). VideoTable: A tangible interface for collaborative exploration of video material during design sessions. In *Proceedings of CHI'02* (pp. 656–657).

Stephenson, N. (2003). *Snow crash*. Spectra, 2003.

Strickland, R., Burns, C., Cohen, J., & Back, M. (1998). A museum exhibit for capturing visitors' insights about nomadic design practice. http://www.portablefx.com/synopsis/PFXTR1998-003.html

Swaminathan, S., Shi, C., Jansen, Y., Dragicevic, P., Oehlberg, L. A., & Fekete, J.-D. (2014). Supporting the design and fabrication of physical visualizations. In *Proceedings of CHI'14* (pp. 3845–3854). ACM.

Swift, J. (1727). *Gulliver's travels: Lemuel Gulliver's travels into several remote nations of the world*, Part III, Chapter V. London: Methuen.

Ullmer, B. (1997). Models and mechanisms for tangible user interfaces (Master's thesis). MIT, 1997.

Ullmer, B. (2002). *Tangible interfaces for manipulating aggregates of digital information* (Ph.D. thesis). Massachusetts Institute of Technology, 2002.

Ullmer, B. (2006). Core tangibles and tangible visualizations: Prospects for tangible convergence and divergence. In *CHI'06 Workshop on "What is the Next Generation of Human-Computer Interaction?"*, 2006.

Ullmer, B. (2012). Entangling space, form, light, time, computational steam, and cultural artifacts. *Interactions, 19*(4), 32–39.

Ullmer, B., Dell, C., Gil, C., et al. (2011). Casier: Structures for composing tangibles and complementary interactors for use across diverse systems. In *Proceedings of TEI'11* (pp. 229–236).

Ullmer, B., Dever, Z., Sankaran, R., et al. (2010). Cartouche: Conventions for tangibles bridging diverse interactive systems. In *Proceedings of TEI'10* (pp. 93–100).

Ullmer, B., Hutanu, A., Benger, W., & Hege, H.-C. (2003). Emerging tangible interfaces for facilitating collaborative immersive visualizations. In *NSF Lake Tahoe Workshop for Collaborative Virtual Reality and Visualization*, 2003.

Ullmer, B., Ishii, H., & Glas, D. (1998). MediaBlocks: Physical containers, transports, and controls for online media. In *Proceedings of SIGGRAPH'98* (pp. 379–386).

Ullmer, B., Kim, E., Kilian, A., Gray, S., & Ishii, H. (2001). Strata/ICC: Physical models as computational interfaces. In *CHI '01 Extended Abstracts on Human Factors in Computing Systems, CHI EA'01*, New York, NY, USA (pp. 373–374). ACM.

Ullmer, B., Patten, J., Ishii, H. (2000). Strata: Physical representations for layered information structures. Submitted to *Proceedings of SIGGRAPH'00*. http://tangviz.cct.lsu.edu/papers/ullmer-siggraph00sub-strata.pdf

Ullmer, B., Sankaran, R., Jandhyala, S., Tregre, B., Toole, C., Kallakuri, K., Laan, C., Hess, M., Harhad, F., & Wiggins, U. (2008). Tangible menus and interaction trays: Core tangibles for common physical/digital activities. In *Proceedings of TEI'08* (pp. 209–212).

Vale, L. J. (1999). Mediated monuments and national identity. *The Journal of Architecture, 4*(4), 391–408.

Weiser, M., & Brown, J. S. (1995). *The coming age of calm computing*. http://www.ubiq.com/weiser/calmtech/calmtech.htm

Whitehouse, D. (2000). *Ice age star map discovered*, 9 August 2000. http://news.bbc.co.uk/2/hi/science/nature/871930.stm

Wilkinson, R. H. (1992). *Reading Egyptian art: A hieroglyphic guide to ancient Egyptian painting and sculpture*. London, UK: Thames and Hudson.

Wisneski, C., Ishii, H., Dahley, A., et al. (1998). Ambient displays: Turning architectural space into an interface between people and digital information. In *Proceedings of CoBuild'98* (pp. 22–32).

Yeh, R., Brandt, J., Klemmer, S., Boli, J., Su, E., & Paepcke, A. (2006). Interactive gigapixel prints: Large paper interfaces for visual context, mobility, and collaboration. Technical report, Stanford University, 2006.